The Environmentalism of the Poor

A Study of Ecological Conflicts and Valuation

Joan Martinez-Alier

*Department of Economics and Economic History,
Universitat Autonoma de Barcelona*

Edward Elgar
Cheltenham, UK • Northampton, MA, USA

Published by
Edward Elgar Publishing Limited
The Lypiatts
15 Lansdown Road
Cheltenham
Glos GL50 2JA
UK

Edward Elgar Publishing, Inc.
William Pratt House
9 Dewey Court
Northampton
Massachusetts 01060
USA

This book has been printed on demand to keep the title in print.

A catalogue record for this book
is available from the British Library

Library of Congress Cataloguing in Publication Data
Martinez-Alier, Joan.
    The environmentalism of the poor: a study of ecological
conflicts and valuation/Joan Martinez-Alier.
        p. cm.
    Includes bibliographical references and index.
    1. Environmental economics. 2. Environmental policy.
    3. Economic development—Environmental aspects. I. Title.
HC79.E5 M35865 2002
333.7—dc21

                                                    2002023626

ISBN 978 1 84064 909 3 (cased)
        978 1 84376 486 1 (paperback)

Contents

Preface

There is a new tide in global environmentalism. It arises from social conflicts on environmental entitlements, on the burdens of pollution, on the sharing of uncertain environmental risks and on the loss of access to natural resources and environmental services. There is a boom in mining and oil extraction in tropical countries. Is compensation paid for reversible and irreversible damage? Is restitution possible? Mangrove forests are sacrificed for commercial shrimp farming. Who has title to the mangroves, who wins and who loses by their destruction? Many ecological conflicts, whether they take place inside or outside markets, whether they are local or global, come about because economic growth means an increased use of the environment. Environmental impacts will be felt by future generations of humans, and they are abundantly felt already by other species. Some impacts fall now disproportionately on some human groups. They would be felt even without economic growth, since many resources and sinks are already exhausted at the present level of use. For instance, the carbon sinks and reservoirs are already overflowing, so to speak. The question is, who is entitled to use them, and in which proportion?

Ecological distribution conflicts are studied by political ecology, a field created by geographers, anthropologists and environmental sociologists. The unrelenting clash between economy and environment, with its ups and downs, its new frontiers, its urgencies and uncertainties, is analysed by ecological economics, another new field of study created mainly by ecologists and economists who endeavour to 'take Nature into account', not only in money terms but also in physical and social terms. Ecological economics puts incommensurability of values at the centre of its analysis. Thus the book has the explicit intention of helping to establish two new fields of study, political ecology and ecological economics, investigating the relations between them.

The outline of the book is as follows. Chapter 1 delineates the main currents of environmentalism with emphasis on the environmentalism of the poor. Today, the environmental movement worldwide continues to be dominated by two main currents, the cult of wilderness and (increasingly) the gospel of eco-efficiency. However, a third current, called 'environmental justice', 'popular environmentalism', or 'environmentalism of the poor', is growing, and it is increasingly aware of itself. Chapters 2 and 3 consider the origins and scope of ecological economics, tackling issues such as the attribution of money values to negative externalities and to positive environmental services, the links between economic growth and the use of energy and materials, the management of uncertain hazards by 'extended peer review', the debate on the 'dematerialization' of consumption, the physical indicators of unsustainability, the acceleration in the use of time and the rate of discount, the balance between population and resources, and the debates on human carrying capacity and feminist neo-Malthusianism over the last hundred years.

After explaining some historical and present-day conflicts in copper mining as examples of the pervasive ecological conflicts caused by economic growth, Chapter 4 goes on to consider in its final sections the birth of the field of political ecology and its development since the 1980s, and also the relations between forms of property and resource management with emphasis on the misleading notion of the 'tragedy of the commons'. Chapters 5 and 6 constitute the empirical heart of the book. They contain detailed case studies of the environmentalism of the poor in different countries. I do not argue that poor people are always and everywhere environmentalists, since this is patent nonsense. I argue that, in ecological distribution conflicts, the poor are often on the side of resource conservation and a clean environment, even when they themselves do not claim to be environmentalists. In these chapters, both structural and cultural elements are considered. Poor people have a better chance of defending their interests in a non-economic terrain. They sometimes use the language of economic compensation but sometimes appeal instead to non-economic values. I emphasize that ecological conflicts are fought out in many languages, and that the economic valuation of damages is only one of such languages. What is the interplay between non-material values such as sacredness, and livelihood interests? *Who has the power to impose particular languages of valuation?*

Chapter 7 deals with conflicts over urban planning, and over urban pollution and traffic. Do cities produce anything of commensurable or comparable value in return for the energy and materials they import, and for the residues they excrete? Do they contribute in a way which is sustainable to the increasing complexity of the system of which they are a part? Are cities to be seen as 'parasites', or rather (to use another metaphor) as 'brains' that, with their higher metabolism, dominate and organize the whole system? Are indicators of urban unsustainability simultaneously indicators of social conflicts? On which geographical scales should urban unsustainability be assessed?

South Africa and the United States are two contrasting countries with some elements in common. Chapter 8 considers the organized 'environmental justice' movements which fight against 'environmental racism' in both countries (including the disputes in the USA on the siting of waste dumps and urban incinerators, and the disputes about nuclear waste disposal in Native American territories). The environmental justice movement was impressively successful in getting President Clinton to enact an Executive Order (11 February 1994) by which all federal agencies must identify and address disproportionately high and adverse health or environmental effects of their policies and activities. The explicit use of 'environmental justice' also by activists in South Africa is an exciting harbinger of a wider international movement. Chapter 9 looks at the roles of the state and other actors (corporations, NGOs, international networks). I try to disentangle the different roles played by different state organs in different conflicts. Which resources are mobilized, which alliances are formed, which leaderships evolve? Why are environmental conflicts described in the languages of human rights and of indigenous territorial rights? Some small-scale sustainable alternatives have grown out of resistance movements, sometimes with state help, sometimes without. This chapter also considers the feminist approaches to ecological distribution conflicts, overcoming the opposition between essentialist eco-feminism and social eco-feminism.

Chapter 10 deals with international trade, also with 'greenhouse politics', and with recent conflicts over the export of genetically modified crops. Instead of looking at so-called 'green protectionism' (northern environmental standards as non-tariff barriers), I emphasize the opposite case, explaining the theory of ecologically unequal exchange. This chapter develops the notion of the ecological debt which the North owes the South because of resource plundering and the disproportionate occupation of environmental space, and it also brings in the language of environmental security. Chapter 11 summarizes the relations between ecological distribution conflicts, sustainability and valuation. It gives our list of ecological distribution conflicts, and it explains why the failures of economic valuation open up a large social space for environmental movements. Prices depend on the outcomes of local or global ecological distribution conflicts, we cannot know *a priori* what the 'ecologically correct' prices would be. Thus the purpose of the present book is to explain how *the unavoidable clash between economy and environment (which is studied by ecological economics) gives rise to the 'environmentalism of the poor' (which is studied by political ecology)*. This is potentially the most powerful current of environmentalism, and *it is becoming a strong force for sustainability* ('sustainability' is a concept discussed in Chapters 2 and 3). *Which are the languages of the environmentalism of the poor? Who has the procedural power to determine the bottom line in an environmental discussion? Who has the capacity to simplify complexity, ruling some points of view out of order?*

The geographical reach of this book is wider than anything I have written until now, unearthing historical and present-day conflicts from Japan to Nigeria, from Spain to South Africa, from Thailand and Papua New Guinea to Ecuador and Peru, from India to the United States and Brazil. There are here drillbits, nuggets and tailings from conflicts in the South and in the North, rural and urban, in highlands and wetlands, such as preservation of mangroves against shrimp farming, resistance to dams and disputes over underground water, movements against oil or gas extraction in tropical areas, struggles against the import of toxic waste, conflicts over appropriation of genetic resources, conservation of fisheries against external use, complaints against tree plantations (whether oil palms or eucalyptus), labour conflicts over health and safety in mines, factories or plantations, and also urban environmental conflicts over land use, water availability, transport systems, refuse disposal and air pollution. The issue of corporate liability appears often in this book, whether in Superfund cases or in the case of Union Carbide or other international court cases under the Alien Torts Claims Act (ATCA).

There should be no confusion about the central theme: the resistance (local and global) expressed in many idioms to the abuse of natural environments and the loss of livelihoods. Therefore I am trying to bring into the open the contested social perceptions of environmental damage, but this book could not even be conceived without the solid ground provided by the environmental sciences – the reader is assumed to have a working knowledge of concepts invented by humans in the course of history, such as 'joules and calories', 'heavy metals', 'greenhouse effect', 'second law of thermodynamics', 'genetic distance', and 'sulphur dioxide', which are not easy objects of deconstruction in seminars on cultural theory.

In my book of 1987 (with Klaus Schlüpmann) on the history of the ecological critiques against economics, I showed the contradictions between economic accounting and energy accounting, and I introduced the question of incommensurability of values which has been the focus of later work with Giuseppe Munda and John O'Neill. My research on the links between ecological distribution conflicts and value system contests has built upon ideas first clearly put forward by Martin O'Connor, shared and developed by a coherent group of ecological economists including Silvio Funtowicz and Jerry Ravetz, the theorists of postnormal science. My work also owes much to Ramachandra Guha, who has written several books and essays on environmental movements of the North and the South, and at whose home and library in Bangalore this book was finished in August 2001. I am also indebted to other friends, among them Bina Agarwal, Maite Cabeza, Arturo Escobar, Miren Etxezarreta, Enrique Leff, James O'Connor, Ariel Salleh and Victor Toledo. The first draft of this book was written in 1999–2000, while I was enjoying a year's fellowship at the Program in Agrarian Studies at Yale University under Jim Scott's guidance, where I profited from the company of Enrique Mayer, Richard Grove, Rohan D'Souza, Arun Agrawal and other colleagues. I also remember several well-travelled doctoral students from the Yale School of Forestry and Environmental Studies. I am grateful to the Spanish Dirección General de Ciencia y Tecnologia (DGCYT) (project PB98–0868) and the Social Ecology group in Vienna (project on South-East Asia) for research funds.

I have been one of the midwives at the protracted births over the last 20 years of ecological economics and political ecology. I have a vested interest in their rapid consolidation, equipped with journals, chairs, doctoral programmes, institutes, research grants and even textbooks. Beyond university territorial disputes, which are important, looking now towards a more distant and optimistic future, I am interested in reflective activism and participatory research in ecological conflicts, whether this helps academic advancement or not, whether it fits into any academic discipline or not. We are witnessing the growth of a worldwide movement for environmental justice which might become a powerful factor in forcing the economy into ecological adjustment and social justice. I am glad to be part of this movement. This book is dedicated to the members of Acción Ecológica (Ecuador).

1. Currents of environmentalism

This is a book about the growth of the environmental movement, an explosion of activism that recalls the beginning of the socialist movement and the First International, almost a century and a half ago. This time, in the networks society (as Manuel Castells calls it), there is no executive committee.

The environmental movement grows in reaction to economic growth. Not all environmentalists are against economic growth. Some might even be favourable to it because of the technological promises it carries. Indeed, not all environmentalists think and act alike. I separate here three main intertwined clusters in the environmental movement: the 'cult of wilderness', the 'gospel of eco-efficiency' and the 'environmentalism of the poor', which are as channels of a single river, branches of a big tree, or varieties of the same crop (Guha and Martinez-Alier, 1999, 2000). They have a lot in common, and all three are opposed by anti-environmentalists or despised or neglected by them. An explanation of the main clusters of environmentalism is now provided, which will stress the differences among them. One distinctive trait of each of them, emphasized here, is its relation to different environmental sciences. Their relations to feminism, or to state power, or religion, or business interests, or other social movements, are not less important as defining features.

THE CULT OF WILDERNESS

Chronologically, and also in terms of self-awareness and organization, the first current is the defence of immaculate Nature, the love of old-growth forests and wild rivers, the 'cult of wilderness' represented already a hundred years ago by John Muir and the Sierra Club in the United States. Some 50 years ago, Aldo Leopold's *Land Ethic* appealed not only to the beauty of the environment but also to the science of ecology. Leopold was trained as a forest manager. Later, he used both biogeography and systems ecology, together with his literary gifts and keen observation of wildlife, in order to present economic use and wilderness (wood production but also wildlife) as joint products of the forest (Leopold, 1970).

The 'cult of wilderness' does not attack economic growth as such, it concedes defeat in most of the industrial world, but it fights a 'rearguard action' (Leopold's phrase) in order to preserve the remnants of pristine natural spaces outside the market.[1] It arises from the love of beautiful landscapes and from deeply held values, not from material interests. Conservation biology, as it has developed since the 1960s, provides scientific support for this first current of environmentalism. Among its achievements are the Biodiversity Convention in Rio de Janeiro in 1992 (sadly, not yet ratified by the USA) and the remarkable Endangered Species Act in the USA, whose rhetoric appeals to utilitarian values but which sets a clear priority for preservation over market use. We need not answer or even ask here how the step from descriptive biology to normative conservation is taken, or in other words, whether it would not be consistent for biologists to let evolution run its course towards a sixth great extinction of biodiversity (Daly, 1999). In any case, conservation biologists have concepts and theories of biodiversity (hot spots, keystone species) which show that the loss of biodiversity proceeds by leaps and bounds. Indicators of human pressure on the environment such as HANPP (human appropriation of net primary production of biomass – see Chapter 3) show that less and less biomass is available for species other than humans and those associated with humans. In some European countries (Haberl, 1997) forest areas are increasing, but this is because of the substitution of fossil fuels for biomass, and also increasing imports of feedstuffs. Europe is small and poor in biodiversity. What matters is whether the increasing HANPP in Brazil, Peru, Mexico and Colombia, in Madagascar, Papua New Guinea, Indonesia, Philippines and India, to name some of the countries of 'megadiversity', will lead to the disappearance of wildlife.

If not scientific reasons, there are other motives to preserve Nature, aesthetic and religious, even utilitarian (future edible species, future medicines) and one may also bring into play the presumed instinct of human 'biophilia' (Kellert and Wilson, 1993; Kellert, 1997). Moreover, some argue that other species have a right to exist: we have no right to annihilate them. This current of environmentalism sometimes appeals to religion as so often happens in the political culture of the United States. It may appeal to pantheism or to oriental religions less anthropocentric than Christianity and Judaism, or choose appropriate events in the Old Testament such as Noah's Ark, a remarkable instance of *ex situ* conservation. There is also in the Christian tradition the exceptional St Francis of Assisi concerned both about poor people and about some animals (Boff, 1998). More plausibly in a North or South American context, appeal is made to the sacredness of Nature in the indigenous beliefs which survived the European conquest, and there is always the possibility of inventing new religions.

The sacredness of Nature (or parts of Nature) will be taken in earnest in the present book because of its reality in some cultures and because it helps to clarify one central issue for ecological economics, namely, *the incommensurability of values*. Not only sacredness, also other values are incommensurable with economic values, but when sacredness intrudes in market society, then conflict is inevitable, as when, in the opposite direction, merchants invaded the temple or indulgences were sold in the church. Over the last 30 years the 'cult of wilderness' has been represented at the activist level by the 'deep ecology' movement (Devall and Sessions, 1985) which favours a 'biocentric' attitude to Nature in opposition to an anthropocentric 'shallow' attitude.[2] Deep ecologists dislike agriculture, whether traditional or modern, because agriculture has historically grown at the expense of wildlife. The main policy proposal coming out of this first current of environmentalism consists in keeping nature reserves, called 'national parks' or something similar, free from human interference. There is a gradation in the amount of human presence that protected territories tolerate, from total exclusion to comanagement with local peoples. Comanagement is seen by wilderness fundamentalists as making a virtue out of impotence. The HANPP index could become policy-relevant, once there is a critical mass of research and a consensus on calculation methods, and also its more exact relation to loss of biodiversity is elucidated. Then a country could decide to decrease its HANPP, say from 50 to 30 per cent over a period of time, and also world objectives could be established, very much as limits and quotas are now established or discussed on chlorofluorocarbon (CFC) or sulphur dioxide or carbon dioxide emissions, or on fishing of some species.

Biologists and environmental philosophers are active inside this first current of environmentalism, which irradiates its powerful doctrines from northern capitals such as Washington and Geneva towards Africa, Asia and Latin America through well-organized bodies such as the International Union for the Conservation of Nature (IUCN), the Worldwide Fund for Nature (WWF) and Nature Conservancy. Today, wilderness in the USA is not only preserved, it is also restored through the decommissioning of some dams, the restoration of the Florida Everglades and the reintroduction of wolves in Yellowstone Park. Whether wilderness will be tamed and reshaped into thematic parks (perhaps virtual wilderness thematic parks), nobody yet knows.

Since the late 1970s, the growth of wilderness environmentalism has been interpreted by political scientist Ronald Inglehart (1977, 1990, 1995) in terms of 'post-materialism', that is, a culture shift towards new social values implying, inter alia, an increased appreciation of Nature as material needs diminish in urgency because they are mostly satisfied. Thus the top US environmental sociology journal, *Society and Natural Resources*, evolved out of a group doing leisure studies, as if the environment were a Sunday luxury and not an everyday necessity. The membership of the Sierra Club, the Audubon society, the WFF and similar organizations increased considerably in the 1970s, so there was perhaps a culture shift towards Nature appreciation among a part of the population of the USA. Nevertheless, 'post-materialism' is a terrible misnomer (Martinez-Alier and Hershberg, 1992; Guha and Martinez-Alier, 1997) in societies such as the USA, the European Union (EU), or Japan, whose economic prosperity depends on their use per capita of a very large amount of energy and materials, and on the availability of free sinks and reservoirs for their carbon dioxide.

In opinion polls, people in the Netherlands score at the top in the so-called 'post-materialist' scale of social values (Inglehart, 1995) but the Netherlands is an economy with a large throughput per capita of energy and materials (World Resources Inst. *et al.*, 1997). Against Inglehart, I argue that western environmentalism grew in the 1970s not because the western economies had reached a 'post-material' stage but, precisely the contrary, because of material concerns about increasing chemical pollution and nuclear risks. This materialistic, conflictual view of environmentalism has been proposed since the 1970s by American environmental sociologists such as Fred Buttel and Allan Schnaiberg.

Friends of the Earth was born around 1969 because the director of the Sierra Club, David Brower, disagreed with his organization on several issues, one of them being the Sierra Club's lack of opposition to nuclear energy (Wapner, 1996: 121). Friends of the Earth took its name from a quotation from John Muir: 'the earth can do all right without friends, but men, if they are to survive, must learn to be friends of the earth'. Resistance to hydroelectricity in the North American west, such as the Sierra Club was offering, went easily hand-in-hand with the defence of beautiful scenery and wild spaces in celebrated struggles at the Snake River or the Columbia and Colorado rivers. Resistance to nuclear energy was to be based on the dangers of radiation, worry about nuclear waste, and the links between the civil and military use of nuclear power. Today, the problem of nuclear waste deposits (Kuletz, 1998) is looming larger and larger in the USA. Now more than 30 years of age, Friends of the Earth is a confederation of diverse groups from many countries. Some have a wilderness orientation, some are concerned with industrial ecology, some are involved above all in environmental and human rights conflicts caused by transnational corporations in the Third World.

Friends of the Earth – Netherlands became well known in the early 1990s because of its calculations of 'environmental space', showing that the country was using environmental resources and services much beyond its own territory (Hille, 1997) and indeed a concept such as the 'ecological debt' (see Chapter 10) was incorporated in the late 1990s into the international programmes and campaigns of Friends of the Earth.

THE GOSPEL OF ECO-EFFICIENCY

The currents of environmentalism are indeed intermingled, but the first current, the 'cult of wilderness', has long been challenged by a second current, worried about the effects of economic growth not only on pristine areas but also on the industrial, agricultural and urban economy, a current here baptized as the 'gospel of eco-efficiency', which focuses on the environmental and health impacts of industrial activities and urbanization, and also of modern agriculture. This second current of the environmental movement is concerned about the whole economy. It often defends economic growth, though not at any cost. It believes in 'sustainable development', in 'ecological modernization', in the 'wise use' of resources. It is concerned with the impacts of the production of commodities, and with the sustainable management of natural resources, and not so much with the loss of natural amenities or the loss of the intrinsic values of nature. Representatives of this second current scarcely use the word 'Nature'; rather, they use 'natural resources' or even 'natural capital' or 'environmental services'. Disappearing birds, frogs or butterflies 'bioindicate' that something is amiss, as did canaries in coalminers' hats, but they have not by themselves a self-evident right to exist. This current is here called the 'gospel of eco-efficiency' in homage to Hays' description of the 'Progressive Conservation Movement' in the USA between 1890 and 1920 as the 'gospel of efficiency' (Hays, 1959). It is today a gospel of engineers and economists, a religion of utility and technical efficiency without a notion of the sacred. Its main temple in Europe in the 1990s has been the Wuppertal Institute, set in the midst of an ugly industrial landscape. Its best-known figure in the USA a century ago was Gifford Pinchot, trained in European scientific forestry management, but this current has roots also outside forestry in the many studies in Europe since the mid-19th century on the efficient use of energy and on agricultural chemistry (cycles of nutrients), as when Liebig in 1840 sounded the alarm on dependence on imported guano, or when Jevons in 1865 wrote his book on coal, pointing out that the increased efficiency of steam engines could paradoxically lead to an increasing use of coal by making it cheaper relative to output. Other roots of this current are to be found in the many 19th-century debates by engineers and public health experts on industrial and urban pollution.

Today, in the USA and even more in overpopulated Europe, where there

is little pristine nature left, the 'gospel of eco-efficiency' is socially and politically in command in the environmental debate. Key concepts are 'Kuznets
environmental curves' (increasing incomes first increase environmental
impacts but eventually they lead to decreased impacts), 'sustainable development' interpreted as sustainable economic growth, the search for
'win–win' solutions, and 'ecological modernization' (an expression coined
perhaps by Martin Jaenicke, 1993, and by Arthur Mol, who did research
on the Dutch chemical industry: Mol, 1995, Mol and Sonnenfeld, 2000,
Mol and Spaargaren, 2000). Ecological modernization walks on two legs:
one economic, eco-taxes and markets in emission permits; two, technological, support for materials- and energy-saving changes. This current rests,
scientifically, on environmental economics (whose message is condensed
into 'getting the prices right' by 'internalizing the externalities') and on the
new discipline of industrial ecology, which studies 'industrial metabolism',
as developed both in Europe (Ayres and Ayres, 1996, 2001) and in the USA
(the Yale University School of Forestry and Environmental Studies,
founded under Gifford Pinchot's auspices, edits the excellent *Journal of
Industrial Ecology*: a double first).

Ecology thus becomes a managerial science mopping up the ecological
degradation after industrialization (Visvanathan, 1997: 37). Chemical engineers are especially active in this current. Biotechnologists tried to jump
into it with promises of engineered seeds which will dispense with pesticides
and will perhaps synthetize atmospheric nitrogen, though they have
encountered public alarm at genetically modified organisms (GMOs).
Indicators and indices such as material input per unit service (MIPS), and
direct and total material requirement (DMR/TMR) (see below, Chapter 3)
measure progress towards 'dematerialization' relative to gross national
product (GNP) or even in absolute terms. Improvements in eco-efficiency
at firm level are assessed by life cycle analysis of products and processes,
and by environmental auditing. Indeed, 'eco-efficiency' has been described
as 'the business link to sustainable development'. Beyond its 'greenwashing' properties, 'eco-efficiency' describes a research programme of
worldwide relevance on the energy and material throughput in the
economy, and on the possibilites of 'delinking' economic growth from its
material base. Such research has a long history (Fischer-Kowalski, 1998;
Haberl, 2001). There is an optimistic side and a pessimistic side (Cleveland
and Ruth, 1998) to the 'great dematerialization debate' which is now starting.

Classifications of the streams of a movement, as attempted in this
chapter, are apt to annoy people who try to swim in their whirlpools.
Nevertheless, a recent competent account of today's American
Environmentalism (Shabecoff, 2000) starts like this:

About a century ago, in the middle of a thunderstorm high in the Sierra Nevada, a gaunt, bearded man climbed to the top of a wildly swaying evergreen tree, in order, he later explained, to enjoy riding the wind. A few years later, the first head of the USDA Forest Service, a patrician, European-trained forester, was riding his horse through Rock Creek park in Washington D.C., when he had a sudden flash of insight. The health and vitality of the nation, he realized, depended on the health and vitality of the country's natural resources. (Shabecoff, 2000: 1)

Easy to guess, the two characters described were John Muir and Gifford Pinchot, and the usual difference is traced between them: transcendental reverence towards Nature in one case, scientific management of natural resources for permanent use in the second case. More controversial, a third character is reported by Shabecoff to have presided over the birth of the modern environmental movement in the USA as Pinchot's supporter: President Theodore Roosevelt, not an 'eco-pacifist' by a long shot. To this short list of three, other great precursors (G.P. Marsh) and great successors (Aldo Leopold, Rachel Carson, Barry Commoner) are added. As much as I would complain about the non-inclusion of Lewis Mumford, as much as I would like to emphasize other traditions of environmentalism, including the towering figure in the Americas of Alexander von Humboldt two centuries ago, the genealogy of US environmentalism is too well established to be modified. I accept it, as I also accept US intellectual hegemony over the environmental movements as a whole, at least since the 1970s. There have been, then, two main currents of environmentalism: the 'cult of wilderness' (John Muir) and the 'gospel of eco-efficiency' (Gifford Pinchot).

The history of environmental concern is more complicated than in my account so far. Around 1900, the American nation, like all western society, was committed to the notion of Progress; it was utilitarian. American civilization was just emerging from its frontier mentality, where it seemed natural to shoot anything you could. For example, the ornithologist Frank Chapman instituted the Christmas Bird Count in 1905 to awaken public opinion to the irrationality of the New Year's shoots that were still common, just as the annual rattlesnake kills have remained a local sport in the southwest. Then there was also a reaction characterized by the sports fishermen's complaints against stream pollution and dams, also against deforestation and the extirpation of the bison. The Audubon movement was born (1896), more influential at the time than the Sierra Club.[3] So the 'John Muir versus Gifford Pinchot' simplification of environmental currents in the USA leaves aside part of the story. In Europe and in America there were also many ecological critics of economics from the mid-19th century onwards, to whom I devoted a whole book 15 years ago. Why not quote again, for instance, from amongst the American authors, Henry Adams' 'Letter to the American Teachers of History', with his (second-hand) discussion on entropy and the economy? Why not the 'energy imperative' of Henry Adams' mentor, Wilhelm Ostwald: 'do not waste any energy, use it profitably' (Martinez-Alier with Schlüpmann, 1987)?

In the colonial European context, Richard Grove explained the achievements and the limits of the early French and British attempts to preserve forests as long ago as in the late 18th century, at least in some small islands such as Mauritius, where the recipe seems to have been nine spoonfuls of sugar plantation for each spoonful of forest preservation – a better record than the Spaniards in colonial western Cuba or than the North Americans in post-colonial eastern Cuba in the early 20th century. Thus, as Richard Grove tells the story, a belief in the French 'desiccation' theory on deforestation as the cause of rainfall decline led to legislation as early as 1791 in the Caribbean island of St Vincent, where some forests were strictly protected 'in order to attract rain'.[4] This environmental policy, also practised in other islands such as St Helena under the doctrines of Pierre Poivre and other colonial observers, was implemented 120 years before Gifford Pinchot went up to Yale. In Brazil, Jose Augusto Padua (2000) has emphasized the explicit awareness which has existed since the early 19th century of the links between slavery, mining and plantation agriculture, and the ruin of the Atlantic forest. However, despite all such precedents, despite the very many environmental authors and writings from outside Euro-America, despite the complexities of environmental concern inside the USA itself, for the purposes of this book I reiterate the view that the two currents of environmentalism which command not only the USA but also the world scene are the 'cult of wilderness' and the 'gospel of eco-efficiency' (the latter with much European input in the last two decades). The German Greens, who used to be internationalists, have now joined the European eco-efficiency movement. The head of the European Environment Agency, Domingo Jiménez Beltran, gave a speech at the Wuppertal Institute in 1998 with the title, 'Eco-efficiency, the European response to the challenge of sustainability'. I wrote back to him, saying I would write a book on 'Eco-Justice, the Third World response to the challenge of sustainability'.

According to Cronon, 'the idea of wilderness has for decades been a fundamental tenet – indeed, a passion – of the environmental movement, especially in the United States' (Cronon, 1996: 69). There seems to be an affinity between 'wilderness' and the 'American mind' (Nash, 1982). We know, however, that there is much that is not 'natural' in wilderness. Thus, as Cronon makes clear (also Mallarach, 1995), the 'national parks' were established after the displacement or elimination of native peoples who lived in these territories. Yellowstone had no immaculate conception. Nevertheless, the relation between society and nature has been predominantly seen in the United States not in terms of changing socioecological history but in terms of a deeply held permanent reverence for 'wilderness'. I rather believe in the Trevelyan thesis, that the appreciation of Nature grew proportionately to the destruction of landscapes wrought by economic growth (Guha and Martinez-Alier, 1997: xii).

It has also been argued that, in the USA, contrary to received opinion, the second current, concerned with the efficient conservation and use of natural resources, precedes the first current, concerned with the preservation of (parts of) Nature, a chronology which is plausible because of the rapid industrialization of the USA in the late 19th century. Thus Beinart and Coates (1995: 46), in their short comparative environmental history of the USA and South Africa, considered the preservation of wilderness as being of more recent origin than the eco-efficiency current: 'while the utilitarian ethos [of Pinchot] held sway, this preservationist tributary, only a trickle at the time, deserves attention because it would swell into the main channel of modern environmentalism'. Samuel Hays, an expert on the history of health and urban issues in the USA, concurs (Hays, 1998: 336–7).

Whichever was first, nowadays the two currents of environmentalism (the 'cult of wilderness' and the 'gospel of eco-efficiency') are simultaneously alive, sometimes crosscutting. Thus the utilitarian search for efficiency in forest management might clash with animal rights. Or, in the opposite direction, real or fictitious markets for genetic resources or for natural amenities may come to be seen as efficient instruments for their preservation. The idea of bioprospecting contracts was pioneered in Costa Rica by a conservation biologist, Daniel Janzen, who evolved into a utilitarian resource economist. The Biodiversity Convention of 1992 emphasized mercantile access to genetic resources as the main instrument for conservation (see Chapter 6). Nevertheless, the merchandising of biodiversity is a dangerous instrument of conservation. The pharmaceutical companies have short time horizons (of 40 or 50 years at most), while conservation and coevolution of biodiversity is for tens of thousands of years. If the monetary returns of conservation are low in the short run, and if the logic of conservation becomes purely an economic logic, conservation will be even more threatened than before. Indeed, other American conservation biologists (Michael Soulé, for instance) complain that the preservation of Nature is losing its deontological foundation because economists with their utilitarian philosophy are taking over the environmental movement. In other words, a lamentable recent change has occurred in the environmental movement; the idea of sustainable development has overcome the idea of wilderness. This chronology of ideas is plausible, if sustainable development is taken at face value, but it is more doubtful if we see sustainable development, a twin brother of ecological modernization, as a reincarnation of Pinchot's eco-efficiency.

Sometimes, those whose interest in the environment is exclusively in terms of preservation of wilderness exaggerate the ease with which the economy can dematerialize, and become opportunistic believers in the gospel of eco-efficiency. Why should this be so? By asserting that technical change will make the production of commodities compatible with ecological sustainability, they emphasize the preservation of that part of Nature which is still outside the economy. So the 'cult of wilderness' and the 'gospel of eco-efficiency' sometimes become bedfellows. Hence, for instance, the WWF and Shell partnership for the plantation of eucalyptus in several places in the world, the argument being that this will diminish pressure on the natural forests and will presumably also increase carbon uptake. The preface to a popular edition of Aldo Leopold's *A Sand County Almanac* (1949) by his son Luna Leopold (1970) contains a strong plea, written in 1966, against hydroelectric power in Alaska and the west which would flood a large portion of the breeding areas of migratory waterfowl. Economics should not be the deciding factor, wrote Luna Leopold 35 years ago, and in any case the economic accounts were flawed because 'alternative and feasible sources of electric power can be found'. Here we find the preservation of wilderness and a pro-nuclear position side by side. Not all American environmentalists would agree. Years earlier, in 1956, Lewis Mumford, more concerned with industrial pollution and urban sprawl than wilderness preservation, had already sounded the alarm against peacetime uses of nuclear power: 'we have scarcely yet begun to cope with the problems of ordinary industrial pollution. Yet, without even a prudent look over their shoulders, our governmental and industrial leaders are now proposing to manufacture atomic energy on a vast scale, before they have the slightest notion of how to dispose of the fissioned waste products' (Mumford, in Thomas *et al.*, 1956: 1147).

ENVIRONMENTAL JUSTICE AND THE ENVIRONMENTALISM OF THE POOR

As seen throughout this book, both the first and second currents of environmentalism are nowadays challenged by a third current, variously called the environmentalism of the poor, popular environmentalism and the environmental justice movement. It has also been appropriately called livelihood ecology (Garí, 2000), even liberation ecology (Peet and Watts, 1996). This third current of environmentalism points out that economic growth unfortunately means increased environmental impacts, and it emphasizes geographical displacement of sources and sinks. Thus the industrial countries are dependent on imports from the south for a growing part of their growing requirements of raw materials or consumption goods, so that the oil and gas frontier, the aluminium frontier, the copper frontier, the euca-lyptus and palm oil frontiers, the shrimp frontier, the gold frontier, the transgenic soybeans frontier . . . are advancing into new territories. This creates impacts which, before there is time to redress them through eco-nomic policy or changes in technology, have already been felt dispropor-tionately by some social groups that often complain and resist (even though such groups do not necessarily describe themselves as environmentalists). Some threatened groups appeal to indigenous territorial rights, and also to the sacredness of Nature in order to defend and secure their livelihood. Indeed, there are long traditions in some countries (documented in India by Madhav Gadgil) of leaving stretches of habitat alone as sacred groves or forests. However, the main thrust of this third current is not a sacred rev-erence for Nature but a material interest in the environment as a source and a requirement for livelihood; not so much a concern with the rights of other species and of future generations of humans as a concern for today's poor humans. It has not the same ethical (and aesthetic) foundations of the cult of wilderness. Its ethics derive from a demand for contemporary social justice among humans. I see this both as a strength and a weakness.

This third current points out that indigenous and peasant groups have often coevolved sustainably with Nature. They have ensured the conserva-tion of biodiversity. Organizations representing peasant groups exhibit an increasing agroecological pride in their complex farming systems and varie-ties of crops. This is not only retrospective pride, there are also today many unacknowledged inventors and innovators, as the Honey Bee network proves in India (Gupta, 1996). The debate started by the Food and Agriculture Organization (FAO) on so-called 'farmers' rights' helps this trend, pushed by global non-governmental organizations (NGOs) such as RAFI (Rural Advancement Foundation International) and GRAIN (Genetic Rources Action International). Chemical and seed companies require payments for improved seeds and pesticides and they demand respect for their intellectual property rights through trade agreements, while traditional knowledge on seeds, pesticides and medicinal herbs has been exploited gratis without any recognition. This is 'biopiracy'. (See Chapter 6 for a detailed discussion.)

The environmental justice movement in the United States is an organized social movement against local instances of 'environmental racism' (see Chapter 8). It has strong links to the civil rights movement of the 1960s. One could say that, even more than the cult of wilderness, this movement for environmental justice is a product of the American mind so obsessed with racism and anti-racism. 'Grass-roots projects in inner cities and indus-trial areas around the country have drawn attention to urban air pollution, lead paint, transfer stations for municipal garbage and hazardous waste, and other environmental dangers that cluster in poor and minority neighborhoods' (Purdy, 2000: 6). So far, environmental justice as an organized movement has been almost confined to its country of origin, while popular environmentalism or livelihood ecology or the environmentalism of the poor are names given to the myriad of movements in the Third World that struggle against environmental impacts that threaten poor people who are in many countries a majority of the population. These include movements of peasants whose crops or pasture land have been destroyed by mines or quarries, movements of artisanal fishermen against modern high-tech trawlers or other forms of industrial fishing (Kurien, 1992; McGrath *et al.*, 1993) that destroy their livelihood even as they deplete the fish stocks, and movements against mines or factories by communities damaged by air pollution or living downstream. This third current receives academic support from agroecology, ethnoecology, political ecology and, to some extent, from urban ecology and ecological economics. It has also been supported by some environmental sociologists.

This third current is growing worldwide, emphasizing inevitable ecological distribution conflicts. As the scale of the economy increases, more waste is produced, natural systems are damaged, the rights of future generations are undermined, knowledge of plant genetic resources is lost, some groups of the present generation are deprived of access to environmental resources and services, and they endure a disproportionate amount of pollution. New technologies may decrease the energy and material intensity of the economy, but only after much damage has already been done, and moreover they may unleash the Jevons effect. Besides, new technologies often imply uncertain 'surprises' (analysed in the next chapter under the rubric of 'postnormal science'). Thus new technologies are not necessarily a way out for the conflict between the economy and the environment. On the contrary, the uncertain hazards from new technologies often increase environmental justice conflicts: for instance, over the siting of dioxin-producing incinerators, over the siting of nuclear waste disposal sites or over the use of transgenic seeds. The environmental justice movement has produced instances of participatory science, under the name of 'popular epidemiology'. In the Third World, the blending of formal and informal science, the idea not so much of 'science for the people' as of 'science with the people', characterizes the defence of the traditional agroecological peasantry and of indigenous groups, from whom there is much to learn.

The environmental justice movement in the United States became aware of itself in the early 1980s. Its 'official history' dates its first appearance from 1982, the first academic writings from the early 1990s. The notion of an environmentalism of the poor also has a 20-year history. Ramachandra Guha identified the two main early currents of environmentalism as 'wilderness

thinking' (which we now call the 'cult of wilderness') and 'scientific industrialism', which we now call the 'gospel of eco-efficiency', 'ecological modernization', 'sustainable development' or 'managerial ecology'. The third
current was identified from 1985 onwards as environmental 'agrarianism'
(Guha and Martinez-Alier, 1997: ch. 4), similar to 'ecological narodnism'
(Martinez-Alier with Schlüpmann, 1987), implying a link between peasant
resistance movements and the ecological critique of both agricultural modernization and 'scientific' forestry (cf. Guha's history of the Chipko movement: Guha, 1989, rev. ed. 2000).

In 1988, the Peruvian historian Alberto Flores Galindo, who was himself
deeply interested in the old Narodniki from Eastern Europe and Russia,
complained that the expression 'eco-narodnism' demanded historical
knowledge not widely available, and suggested that 'environmentalism of
the poor' should be used instead. The journal *Cambio* from Lima in
January 1989 published a long interview with the present author under the
title *El ecologismo de los pobres* ('The environmentalism of the poor').[5]
Under the auspices of the Social Sciences Research Council (New York),
three international meetings were convened by Ramachandra Guha and
myself in the early 1990s on varieties of environmentalism and the environmentalism of the poor (Martinez-Alier and Hershberg, 1992). As explained
in Chapter 4, much research on political ecology was devoted in the 1990s
to this current of environmentalism.

The convergence between the rural Third World notion of the environmentalism of the poor, and the urban notion of environmental justice as
used in the USA, was suggested by Guha and Martinez-Alier (1997: chs 1
and 2). One of the tasks of the present book is precisely to compare the
environmental justice movement in the USA and the more diffuse environmentalism of the poor worldwide, in order to show that they can be understood as one single current. In the USA, a book on the environmental
justice movement could well carry the title or subtitle 'The environmentalism of the poor and the minorities', because this movement fights for
minority groups and against environmental racism in the USA, but the
present book is concerned with the *majority* of humankind, those who
occupy relatively little environmental space, who have managed sustainable agroforestal and agricultural systems, who make prudent use of
carbon sinks and reservoirs, whose livelihoods are threatened by mines, oil
wells, dams, deforestation and tree plantations to feed the increasing
throughput of energy and materials of the economy within or outside their
own countries. How to do research on the thousands of local ecological
distribution conflicts, which sometimes are not even reported in the
regional newspapers, and which have not yet or never were picked up by
local environmental groups and the international environmental networks?

In which archives will historians find the materials for reconstructing the grassroots history of the environmentalism of the poor?

What minorities and majorities are depends on context. The USA has a growing population which represents less than 5 per cent of the world's population. Of the population of the USA, 'minorities' comprise about one-third. In the world at large, the majority of countries, which together are the majority of humankind, have populations which in the US context would be classified as belonging to minorities. The Chipko movement, or the Chico Mendes struggle in the 1970s and 1980s, were environmental justice conflicts, but it is not necessary or useful to interpret them in terms of environmental racism. The environmental justice movement is potentially of great importance, provided it learns to speak not only for the minorities inside the USA but also for the majorities outside the USA (which locally are not always defined racially) and provided it gets involved in issues such as biopiracy and biosafety, or climate change, beyond local instances of pollution. The civil rights heritage of the environmental justice movement of the USA is also useful worldwide because of its contributions to non-violent Gandhian forms of struggle.

Thus, in summary, three clusters of environmental concern and activism are recognized:

- the 'cult of wilderness', concerned with the preservation of wild Nature but without anything to say on industry and urbanization, indifferent or opposed to economic growth, most worried by population growth, backed up scientifically by conservation biology;
- the 'gospel of eco-efficiency', concerned with the sustainable management or 'wise use' of natural resources and with the control of pollution not only in industrial contexts but also in agriculture, fisheries and forestry, resting on a belief in new technologies and the 'internalization of externalities' as instruments for ecological modernization, backed up by industrial ecology and environmental economics;
- the environmental justice movement, popular environmentalism, the environmentalism of the poor, livelihood ecology, and liberation ecology, grown out of local, regional, national and global ecological distribution conflicts caused by economic growth and social inequalities. Examples are conflicts over water use, over access to forests, over the burdens of pollution and over ecologically unequal exchange, which are studied by political ecology. Actors in such conflicts have often not used an environmental idiom, and this is one reason why this old third current of environmentalism was not identified until the 1980s and 1990s. This book analyses environmental injustices of a century ago, and also of only a few months ago.

There are points of contact and points of disagreement among these varieties of environmentalism. We notice that one single environmental organization may belong to more than one variety. Even the Sierra Club has been known to publish books on environmental justice, although it has been devoted to wilderness above all. Greenpeace started some 30 years ago as an organization concerned with military nuclear testing, and also with the preservation of some endangered species of whales. It has moved towards environmental justice. It was instrumental in getting under way the Basel Convention banning exports of toxic waste to Africa and elsewhere. It has sided with, and instructed, poor urban communities in their fight against the risk of dioxins from incinerators. It has given support to mangrove communities in their fight against the shrimp export industry. Greenpeace has also gone sometimes, at least in Europe, into an eco-efficiency mode, for instance by endorsing a practical and economical eco-fridge in Germany which not only does not use CFC, but is also energy-efficient. One thing brings all environmentalists together. There is a powerful anti-environmental lobby, even more vocal in the south than in the north. In the south, environmentalists are often attacked by business and government (and the remains of the old left) as being motivated by foreigners wishing to stop economic development. In India, anti-nuclear activists are seen as anti-nationalists. In Argentina, anti-transgenic activists are seen as traitors by the agricultural export lobby.

NOTES

1. Or, rather, outside the industrializing economy, one should say, because nature protection in the form of a network of scientific nature reserves, *zapovedniki*, existed also in Russia under the Soviet regime (Weiner, 1988, 1999).
2. Cf. Callicott and Nelson (1998) on 'the great Wilderness debate' in the United States, started by Ramachandra Guha's (1989) 'Third World critique' against 'deep ecologists' and conservation biologists.
3. For the previous lines, I am indebted to written comments made by Roland C. Clements, 28 January 2000.
4. Lecture at the School of Forestry and Environmental Sciences, Yale University, 4 February 2000, also Grove (1994).
5. 'Environmentalism of the poor' was used in Gadgil and Guha (1995: ch. 4) and Guha and Martinez-Alier (1997: ch. 1). Probably, it first appeared in English (the academic equivalent of a work permit for a *sans papiers*) in Martinez-Alier (1991).

2. Ecological economics: 'taking Nature into account'

In modern industrialized and industrializing societies there has been a strongly argued view that enlarging the economic pie (GNP growth) represents the best way of alleviating economic distribution conflicts between social groups. The environment came in, if at all, as an afterthought, as a preoccupation arising out of deeply held values on the sacredness of Nature, or as a luxury (environmental 'amenities' rather than necessities). The poor were 'too poor to be green'. They must 'develop' to get out of poverty and, as a by-product, they could then acquire the taste and the means to improve the environment. 'You claim [wrote after Seattle the executive director of Greenpeace, Thilo Bode, to *The Economist*, 11 December 1999] that greater prosperity is the best way to improve the environment. On what economy's performance in what millennium do you base this conclusion? . . . To claim that a massive increase in global production and consumption will be good for the environment is preposterous. The audacity to make such a claim with a straight face accounts for much of the heated opposition to the World Trade Organisation.'

Economic growth can go together with increasing international or national inequality, a topic which the original 'Kuznets curve' explored. In the debate on the purported 'trickle-down' effects of economic growth, it is generally accepted that the rising tide of economic prosperity may indeed raise all boats, but maintaining their hierarchical positions. In other words, economic growth is good for the poor but only in proportion (statistically speaking) to their initial position. If the lower 25 per cent of the population received only 5 per cent of income, after a period of economic growth it will still receive 5 per cent but of a larger total income. Disparities in absolute terms will have increased but the poorest's level of income will also have increased. This much is accepted generally. Some optimists believe that distribution becomes more equal with economic growth. Others, on the contrary, insist that disparities have also increased, and anyway monetary income does not imply greater economic security because it hides environmental degradation and some other social effects. An increased share of marketed goods (buying water instead of getting it freely, eating more often outside the home, increased travel to work, compensating environmental nuisances) which is part and parcel of the trend toward urbanization, means that increased incomes do not represent increased welfare. The UN Index of Human Development takes into consideration a number of social issues, but not environmental effects.

Granting (for the purposes of this book) that *economic* distribution conflicts are eventually pacified by economic growth, the question remains whether *ecological* distribution conflicts are likely to improve with economic growth or, on the contrary, whether economic growth leads to a deterioration in the environment. Certainly, health and environmental damage from sulphur dioxide, or lead poisoning, have decreased in rich countries – not only because of income growth but also because of social activism and public policies. There is research showing the scope in rich countries for a decrease in material intensity by 'factor 4' or even 'factor 10' without a decrease in welfare (Schmidt-Bleek, 1994; Lovins and Weizsaecker, 1996). However, such optimistic beliefs (the 'gospel of eco-efficiency') cannot overcome the perceived realities of increased exploitation of resources in environmentally fragile territories, increased south–north physical flows of materials and energy (Bunker, 1996; Naredo and Valero, 1999; Muradian and Martinez-Alier, 2001b), the increased greenhouse effect, the awareness of past and recent 'robbery' of genetic resources, the disappearance of traditional agroecology and *in situ* agricultural biodiversity, the pressures on surface or underground water often at the expense of human livelihoods and of ecosystems, and the unexpected 'surprises' which have come or might still come from new technologies (nuclear energy, genetic engineering, synergies among chemical residues) which cannot be managed in terms of insurance against probabilistic risks. Instead of win–win opportunities, sometimes lose–lose fiascos occur. Accepting the argument that rich economies have the financial means to correct reversible environmental damage, and the ability to introduce new production technologies favourable to the environment, it might be that such turning points in negative environmental trends arrive when much damage has already accumulated or when thresholds have been surpassed. Technological and social 'lock-in' (consumption habits, patterns of urban settlement) makes it difficult to delink economic growth from growth in material and energy flows.

Production may become less intensive in terms of energy and materials, but the environmental load of the economy is determined by consumption. John Ruskin, who criticized the industrial economy both from aesthetic and ecological points of view, believed that the material necessities of human livelihood were easy to cover, and therefore production, even when hideous, was potentially 'for art'. It could become artistically valuable if beautifully designed. While in the 1960s and 1970s there were trends described as the 'dematerialization of the art object', this does not apply to the increased mass consumption of private cars, air travel, paper and built-up suburbia – this is 'artistic' consumption in Ruskin's sense of not being for strict livelihood but, beautiful or not, it is certainly not 'dematerialized'. Rich citizens may choose to satisfy their needs or wants by new patterns of consumption which are themselves highly resource-intensive, such as the fashion for eating shrimps imported from tropical countries at the expense of mangrove destruction, or the use of gold (Princen, 1999).

THE ORIGINS AND SCOPE OF ECOLOGICAL ECONOMICS

A systemic view of the relations between economy and environment is provided by ecological economics. The study of environmental conflicts is then not only a collection of entertaining anecdotes, it is closely connected to the systemic, evolving conflicts between economy and environment The economy (a 'full-world' economy, to use Herman Daly's image) is embedded in social institutions, and in the social perception of physical flows and environmental impacts. The relation between Nature and society is historical in two senses. First, human history is played out against a background of natural circumstances, but also human history modifies Nature. Second, the perception of the relations between humans and Nature changes with time. For instance, the laws of thermodynamics were not understood before 1840–50. The theory of evolution was not available until the 1850s. The link between thermodynamics and evolution was not made until the 1880s. Ecological economics must be aware of these historical aspects despite its reluctance, which I share, to see Nature as 'socially constructed'.

Ecological economics is sometimes misconceived as the attempt at giving money values to environmental resources and services. This is only part of a larger enterprise which is crucial to one main theme of this book: *the relations between environmental conflicts and the languages of valuation*. To give an example of valuation in a non-environmental context: German corporations and government agreed in 1999 to compensate remaining survivors of Nazi labour camps (after 55 years) by paying US$5·2 billion. An event can be judged according to several criteria or scales of value. It was wrong to use slave labour, and moreover the price-tag is too cheap. But, one may say, no 'real' compensation is possible, although US$5·2 billion is reasonable on the monetary scale of value (and given that most stakeholders are dead). In no case does this mean that corporations and states may use slave labour by paying compensation later, when found out. One may say that the human sacrifice which took place cannot be assessed only in money terms.

Ecological economics is a recently developed field, which sees the economy as a subsystem of a larger finite global ecosystem. Ecological economists question the sustainability of the economy because of its environmental impacts and its material and energy requirements, and also because of the growth of population. Attempts at assigning money values to environmental services and losses, and attempts at correcting macroeconomic accounting, are part of ecological economics, but its main thrust is rather in developing physical indicators and indexes of (un)sustainability, looking at the economy in terms of 'social metabolism'. Ecological economists also work on the relations between property rights and resource management; they model the interactions between the economy and the environment; they use management tools such as integrated environmental assessment and multi-criteria decision aids; and they propose new instruments of environmental policy.

The book that came out of the first world conference of ecological economists in Washington, DC in 1990 (Costanza, 1991) defined the field as 'the science and management of sustainability'. In the late 19th and early 20th centuries the biologist and urban planner Patrick Geddes, the 'narodnik' revolutionary and physician Sergei Podolinsky, the engineer and social reformer Josef Popper-Lynkeus had unsuccessfully tried to promote a biophysical view of the economy as a subsystem embedded in a larger system subject to the laws of thermodynamics (Martinez-Alier with Schlüpmann, 1987). By 1850 or 1860, the carbon cycle and the cycles of plant nutrients had been discovered, while the first and second laws of thermodynamics (conservation and transformation of energy, but also dissipation of energy and increase in entropy) had been established. The contrived conflict between the 'optimistic' theory of evolution which explained the diversity of life, and the 'pessimistic' second law of thermodynamics, was a staple of the cultural diet of the early 1900s. Therefore the main ingredients for an ecological view of the economy were present much before the birth of self-conscious ecological economics, delayed by the strict disciplinary boundaries between the natural and the social sciences.

The biologist and systems ecologist Alfred Lotka, born in 1880, introduced in the 1910s and early 1920s the fundamental distinction between the endosomatic use and the exosomatic use of energy by humans, or in other words, between 'biometabolism' and 'technometabolism'. The Nobel prize winner in chemistry, Frederick Soddy, born in 1877, who wrote also on energy and the economy, compared 'real wealth' which grows at the rhythm of nature and which, if turned into manufactured capital, is worn down, with 'virtual wealth' in the form of debts which apparently could grow exponentially for ever at compound interest. Later, four well-known economists, who did not yet form a school, are seen in retrospect as ecological economists: Kenneth Boulding, born in 1910, worked mainly on general systems analysis, K.W. Kapp, also born in 1910, and S. von Ciriacy-Wantrup, born in 1906, were both institutionalist economists; Nicholas Georgescu-Roegen, born in 1906, was the author of *The Entropy Law and the Economic Process* (1971). The systems ecologist H.T. Odum, born in 1924, studied the use of energy in the economy: some of his former students were among the founders of the International Society for Ecological Economics. Other sources of ecological economics are in environmental and resource economics (that is, microeconomics applied to environmental pollution and the depletion of natural resources), in human ecology, ecological anthropology, agroecology and urban ecology, and also in the study of 'industrial metabolism' as developed by Robert Ayres, now known as industrial ecology.

After an influential meeting in Sweden in 1982 on the integration of economics and ecology organized by the ecologist AnnMari Jansson (Jansson, 1984), the decision to launch the journal *Ecological Economics* and to found the International Society for Ecological Economics (ISEE) was taken at a workshop in Barcelona in 1987, the same year as the Brundtland Report on 'sustainable development' was published. Herman Daly (a former student of Georgescu-Roegen, and today's best known ecological economist) proposed that the word 'development' should mean changes in the economic and social structure, while 'growth' means an increase in the scale of the economy which probably cannot be ecologically sustained. 'Sustainable development' is thus acceptable to most ecological economists while 'sustainable growth' is not (Daly and Cobb, 1994). In my own view, 'development' is a word which has too strong a connotation of economic growth and uniform modernization to remain useful. It is preferable to drop it, and talk only of 'sustainability'.

The first issue of the successful academic journal *Ecological Economics* came out in 1989, edited since then by the ecologist Robert Costanza, who was also the first president of ISEE. The ISEE has affiliated societies in Argentina and Uruguay, Australia and New Zealand, Brazil, Canada, the European Union, India and Russia.

Outside the United States and Europe, the Japanese 'entropy school' of economic analysis (Tamanoi *et al.*, 1984) studied the environmental services provided by the water cycle, and also the urban ecosystem of Edo, the ancient name for the capital of Japan. In India, there was much work since the 1970s by economists but also by biologists (Madhav Gadgil) on the links between forest or water management and common property rights (Jodha, 1986, 2001), nowadays one main focus of interest both in ecological economics and in political ecology (Berkes and Folke, 1998). Other early ecological economists (whose major works were not in English) were, in

France, René Passet (1979, 1996) and Ignacy Sachs, who proposed in the early 1970s the notion of 'eco-development'; Roefie Hueting (1980) in the Netherlands, Christian Leipert (1989) in Germany; Jose-Manuel Naredo in Spain. (For general introductions to the field: Costanza *et al.* (eds), 1997; Costanza *et al.,* 1997; Common, 1995).

In ecological economics the economy is seen as embedded in the ecosystem (or, more accurately, in the historically changing social perception of the ecosystem). The economy is also embedded in a structure of property rights on environmental resources and services, in a social distribution of power and income, in social structures of gender, social class or caste, and this links ecological economics to political economy and to political ecology (Figure 2.1). Let me give an example. Growth of an economy based on fossil fuels may (or may not) encounter a first limit in the structure of property rights on the carbon sinks and reservoirs. It may encounter a second limit in the absorption capacity of the biosphere to recycle carbon dioxide, in a given time, without a change in climate. Excessive carbon emissions might be curtailed by a change in property rights on carbon sinks and reservoirs, and/or by changes in the price structure (through eco-taxes or emission permits). Climate policy requires an integration of the analysis of the three levels. Instead, in conventional economics the economy is seen as a self-sufficient system where prices for consumer goods and services, and prices for the services of production factors, are formed. This pre-analytic stand is reflected in the category of 'externalities'. Ecological economists sympathize with attempts at 'internalizing' externalities into the price system, they readily concur with proposals to correct prices by taxes (such as 'natural capital depletion taxes' or taxes on pollution) but they deny that there exists a set of 'ecologically correct prices'.

In summary, ecological economics is a new transdisciplinary field which develops or introduces topics and methods such as the following:

- new indicators and indices of (un)sustainability of the economy;
- the application of ecological notions of carrying capacity and resilience to human ecosystems;
- the valuation of environmental services in money terms, but also the discussion on incommensurability of values, and the application of multi-criteria evaluation methods;
- risk assessment, uncertainty, complexity and 'postnormal' science;
- integrated environmental assessment, including building of scenarios, dynamic modelling and participatory methods of decision making;
- ecological macroeconomics, the measurement of 'natural capital', the debate between 'weak' and 'strong' notions of sustainability;

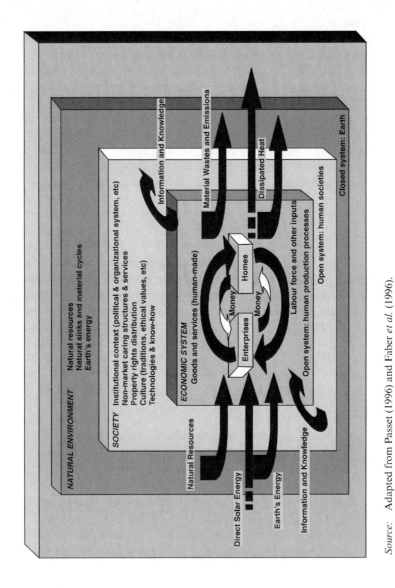

Source: Adapted from Passet (1996) and Faber *et al.* (1996).

Figure 2.1 The economy embedded in the social system and in the ecosystems

22

- relations between ecological and feminist economics;
- ecological distribution conflicts;
- relations between the allocation of property rights and resource management, old and new communal institutions for environmental management;
- international trade and the environment, the 'ecological debt';
- environmental causes and consequences of technological change or technological 'lock-in', relations between ecological economics and evolutionary economics;
- theories of consumption (needs, satisfactors), as they relate to environmental impacts;
- the 'dematerialization' debate, relations with industrial ecology, applications in business administration;
- instruments of environmental policy, often centred on the 'precautionary principle' (or on 'safe minimum standards', as developed by Ciriacy-Wantrup).

Only some of the previous points particularly relevant to the main topic of the present book, namely the relation between ecological distribution conflicts, sustainability and valuation, will be developed in the present chapter, and in Chapter 3.

NO PRODUCTION WITHOUT DISTRIBUTION

Although, in neoclassical economic theory, the study of the allocation of resources to production is seen as analytically separated from distribution of the produce among different categories of people, in ecological economics both aspects must be dealt with together. Moreover, 'distribution' means in ecological economics not only economic distribution but also ecological distribution. Therefore, in the present book, 'equity considerations' are not introduced as a charitable afterthought but, rather, distributional issues become central to valuation and allocation.

In classical economics, before the neoclassical revolution of the 1870s, economic production and distribution were not analytically separated. Ricardo's theory of land rent is a theory on the distribution of production and also a theory of capitalist dynamics. Let us assume an agricultural structure composed of big landlords, capitalist farmers who rent the land from the landlords, and wage labourers. As agriculture advances into less fertile territories, or as more inputs are used in the existing fields, a phase of decreasing returns will be reached. Assuming wages to be stable at subsistence level, the decreasing returns, coupled with competition between capitalist farmers to get the best land, will drive rents up. If we assume that the landlords squander the rents in consumption (instead of investing them, or instead of getting their daughters and sons married into thrifty capitalist farmers' families), then the lower share of production going to capitalist profits and the larger share going to landlords' rent will lead to economic stagnation.

Objections to Ricardo's predictions are well known. First, landlords' and capitalists' families intermarried in Britain. Second, the new territories, not in Britain but overseas, were more fertile, not less fertile. The analytical point, however, is that economic production and distribution were brought into a single framework. Environmental distribution was not considered. Similar considerations apply to Marxist economics. Increased production, coupled with a deficiency of buying power among the exploited proletariat (and among the exploited suppliers of raw materials and labour in colonial territories, as Rosa Luxemburg was to add), was an inescapable contradiction of capitalism, which would lead to periodic crises. Socially and politically, the proletariat would become more and more organized, and crises would lead to revolution. Henry Ford's insight that the workers should be able to buy the cars they produced (something which did not make sense at the level of one single factory or firm) gave its name (via Gramsci's analysis) to the 'Fordist' or 'regulation' school of political economy, while Keynesian economics was similarly based on the idea that effective demand could, in capitalist economies, be less than potential supply at full capacity utilization and full employment level, and therefore policies should be devised to increase effective demand. Here again, economic distribution and production were brought together. However, these economic schools did not include environmental deterioriation in their analyses.

Unless distribution arrangements have been made beforehand, no production decisions will be made. A landowner who uses sharecroppers will not start producing unless an agreement has been reached or a customary arrangement exists on the share of the crop that will be his. For instance, at 40 per cent for the sharecroppers, he will use the land for cotton; if the sharecroppers demand 70 per cent he will have to change the use of land to another much more labour-intensive crop or throw them out and use the land for pastures. Distribution precedes production decisions. This is an obvious point to make also for other relations of production, such as slavery or wage labour. Thus full employment in the 1960s led in Europe to a strong bargaining position for workers, and to a 'profit squeeze' solved later by the economic downturn of the mid-1970s and by the new neoliberal policies.

Moving now from economic distribution to ecological distribution, one can say again that no production decisions will be taken unless there is an agreement or a customary arrangement on how to get the natural resources and what to do with the waste. For instance, a decision to produce nuclear energy requires a decision on the distribution of the radioactive waste. Will it be kept in the nuclear power stations, will it be shipped to a final disposal site (such as Yucca Mountain in the USA)? The siting of the nuclear power stations themselves requires a decision on the geographical and social distribution of the uncertain risks of nuclear radiation. A decision to produce electrical energy from coal instead requires a previous decision on the disposition of mining waste, sulphur dioxide, nitrogen oxides and carbon dioxide to sinks or reservoirs on different geographical scales. Who has property rights on them? In economic terms, if externalities may be kept as such, as external to the firm's accounts, the decisions will be different than if externalities must be factored into the accounts (at some economic value). Indeed, should car manufacturers be required not to produce externalities or to include in the price of the car all the unavoidable externalities along its 'life'-cycle, from cradle to grave and then again from grave to cradle as all materials are recycled, including the externalities produced by carbon dioxide, then production decisions in our industrial economy would be quite different, to an extent which would depend on the price assigned to such externalities. Being able to dispose of (*to distribute*) cars in junkyards and to dispose of (*to distribute*) pollutants into the air at low or no cost makes a difference to production decisions. Are there social groups that complain about cars?

For instance, if a cellulose factory in Brazil may plant eucalyptus without compensating for the loss of fertility, and may dispose of the effluents by exercising de facto property rights on the river or the sea, its production decisions will be different than if it would have to pay for such externalities. Since production cannot take place without drawing on natural resources and without producing waste, the idea of a 'second contradiction' of capitalism was fruitfully proposed by James O'Connor in 1988. It might be that the cotton sharecroppers, ill-paid in economic terms, also suffer the health effects of malathion together with their own families and their neighbours who do not work in the plantations. Here the distributional aspects do not necessarily fall on the producers. It might be that a fight against cellulose effluents is led by a group of naturalists, or by a group of local women, or (in Brazil) by a residual group of Indians, all of them demanding compensation, that is demanding in the language of economists the 'internalization of externalities'. If they are successful, costs will be different for the firms concerned; production decisions will also be different. The agents of ecological distribution conflicts are not so well identified as the agents of Ricardian or Marxian economic conflicts – landlords and capitalist farmers, in one case, industrial capitalists and proletarians, in the second case.

DISPUTES ON VALUE STANDARDS

The Greek distinction (as in Aristotle's *Politica*) between 'oikonomia' (the art of material provisioning of the household) and 'chrematistics' (the study of the formation of market prices, in order to make money) seems irrelevant today because material provisioning *appears* to be mostly achieved through market exchanges, and there is a fusion of chrematistics with oikonomia. Thus, apart from picking some berries and mushrooms in the countryside, and collecting wood for their secondary residences, most citizens of the rich urbanized world get their provisions from the shops. Hence the proverbial response of urban children to the question of where does the milk or do the eggs come from – the supermarket. However, many caring activities in families and in society, and many services of Nature remain outside the market. In ecological economics the word 'economics' is used in a sense closer to 'oikonomia' than to 'chrematistics'. Ecological economics is not committed to a unique type of value expressed in a single numeraire. Ecological economics encompasses money valuation, and also physical appraisals of the contribution from Nature and the environmental impacts of the human economy measured in their own physical 'numeraires'. Ecological economists 'take Nature into account' not so much in chrematistic terms as in terms of physical and social indicators.

In macroeconomics, assessing performance exclusively in terms of gross national product (GNP) makes invisible the unpaid care in the families and in society, and it also makes invisible the uncompensated environmental and social damage, a symmetry first pointed out by the eco-feminist Marilyn Waring (1988). Some feminist and environmental economists have challenged and tried to improve the procedures for calculating GNP, other groups might wish to substitute other indicators or indexes for GNP so as to make visible their own contributions and concerns. Similarly, in concrete ecological distribution conflicts, some social groups will insist on the logic of extending economic valuation to environmental services and losses, while other groups will throw into the ring other non-economic values. Indeed, stakeholders sometimes appeal simultaneously to different standards of valuation. Thus the refusal of economic valuation may allow alliances to be established between the interests (and the values) of poor people and the disinterested 'wilderness' values of 'deep ecologists'.

Nature provides resources for the production of commodities and it also provides environmental amenities. As shown by Gretchen Daily, Rudolf de Groot and other authors, Nature, more importantly, gives gratis essential life-support services such as the cycling of nutrients, the water cycle, soil formation, climate regulation, conservation and evolution of biodiversity, concentration of minerals, dispersal or assimilation of pollutants and diverse forms of useful energy. Attempts have been made to assign money values to the annual flows of some environmental services, to compare them to GNP in monetary units of account. For instance, the cycling of nutrients (nitrogen, phosphorous) in some natural systems may be given a plausible money value by comparison with the costs of alternative human-made technologies. Could this same methodology (that is, the cost of alter-native technology) be applied consistently to the valuation of biodiversity in a kind of Jurassic Park framework? For biodiversity, money valuation has taken a completely different tack, namely the small sums exchanged in some bioprospecting contracts, or fictitious subjective money values in terms of willingness to pay for conservation projects; that is, the so-called 'contingent valuation' method favoured by environmental economists (though not by most ecological economists). Moreover, how do we count (in terms of the costs of alternative technology) the service with which Nature has provided us by concentrating minerals which we disperse? ('Exergy' costs have been calculated by industrial ecologists, but the tech-nology for creating mineral deposits does not exist). Therefore, the figures obtained for the money values of environmental services provided free by Nature are methodologically incongruous (Costanza *et al.*, 1998). They are useful, however, in stimulating the debate on how 'to take Nature into account'.

Ecological economics studies different modes of decision-making pro-cesses in the presence of distributional conflicts, incommensurable values and unresolvable uncertainties. Here I shall explain the meaning of 'weak comparability of values' (O'Neill, 1993), leaving uncertainty for a later section. One example of decision making under weak comparability of values would be the following one. Let us assume that a new large garbage dump must be built near a city, and that there are three possible locations, A, B and C, one of which will be sacrificed. In our example, the three different locations are compared under three different types of value: value as habitat, value as landscape and economic value. Location A is a most valuable publicly owned wetland (valuable as habitat or ecosystem because of its richness of species) but a monotonous and boring landscape, much visited by bird-watchers and schools (and, as such, of some economic value according to the 'travel cost method'). Location C produces much rent as industrial and urban land, and therefore ranks first in economic value, but ranks only third as an ecosystem or habitat, and comes second as landscape (because of its historical qualities). Location B is an old agricultural area of beautiful derelict orchards and ancient abandoned manor houses, which ranks first as landscape, but ranks only third as rent-producing, and second as ecosystem or habitat. Which location should be sacrificed? How to decide? Should and could all values be reduced to a super-value, so as to achieve strong comparability, and even strong commensurability (cardinal measurement)? In the example, the economic values (in actual or fictitious markets) of all three locations have been taken into account, but there is no supreme value (economic, or otherwise, such as net energy production by which the wetland would presumably come out on top).

	Value as habitat	Value as landscape	Economic value
Location A	First	Third	Second
Location B	Second	First	Third
Location C	Third	Second	First

Economic value will be given in dollars per hectare, on a cardinal scale, and value as habitat, if defined as richness in species, could also possibly be assessed by a cardinal measure (strong commensurability). In the example, for simplicity, and probably by necessity in the case of landscape value, all three types of value are measured on an ordinal scale (weak commensurability inside each type of value).

Certainly, the present rankings could be reconsidered. Thus the landscape value of A could be upgraded, and its economic value (as also that of B) could be increased by contingent valuation based on willingness-to-pay in a fictitious market. Also, giving more weight to some criteria than to others, or 'veto thresholds' for some criteria such as the 'endangered species' provision in American legislation or the international Ramsar convention which protects some wetlands, or the introduction of 'sacredness' as a trumping criterion (say, an old church and graveyard at one location), would help us to escape from the present deadlock. Location A could be notified as a 'bird *sanctuary*', for instance. Some groups in society could challenge the methods of valuation in each of the scales, or they could suggest new criteria or new alternatives, according to their own interests or their own outlooks on what is important in life. The point of the exercise is merely to show the meaning of 'weak' comparability of values (O'Neill, 1993) and to introduce the reader briefly to the large field of multi-criteria decision aids (Munda, 1995). The decision-making process need not be irrational (by lottery, for instance). On the contrary, a decision could be reached through appropriate deliberations. Or, perhaps, the political authority might instead impose a reductionist cost–benefit analysis in money terms supplemented by a cosmetic environmental impacts assessment.

The distinction between 'strong' and 'weak' comparability of values is useful in order to classify the methods of ecological economics. In project evaluation, there is strong comparability of values, and even strong commensurability, in cost–benefit analysis where the projects to be evaluated are all valued in the same numeraire (present value in money terms of costs and benefits, including of course monetarized externalities and environmental amenities). In contrast, in some forms of multi-criteria evaluation, there is irreducibility among the different types of value, and we are in a weak comparability situation. In microeconomics, there is strong comparability of values, and indeed strong commensurability, when externalities are internalized into the price system, as in the definition of a Pigovian tax as the economic value of the externality at optimum pollution level. In macroeconomics, El Serafy's practical proposals to 'green' the GNP (in Costanza, 1991) – the results of which will depend on the chosen rate of interest – do not go beyond strong commensurability in money terms. According to El Serafy, not all receipts from the sale of exhaustible resources ('natural capital') should be included in GNP; only one part should be included, 'true' income, and the rest should be counted as 'decapitalization' or the 'user cost' of such 'natural capital' which should be invested at compound interest over the period until the resource is exhausted, so as to allow the country to live at the same standard of living even when running out of the resources. This proposal, based on the definition of 'income' by Hicks, and related to Hotelling's rule in resource microeconomics, is based on a notion of 'weak' sustainability only. 'Weak' sustainability allows the substitution of manufactured capital for so-called 'natural capital' – implying, therefore, a common unit of measurement – while 'strong' sustainability refers to the maintenance of physical natural resources and services (Pearce and Turner, 1990) which should be assessed through a battery of physical indicators and indexes. Therefore, in ecological macroeconomics,

- weak sustainability implies strong comparability of values,
- strong sustainability implies weak comparability of values, as in project evaluation,
- cost–benefit analysis implies strong comparability of values,
- multi-criteria evaluation implies weak comparability of values.

The discussion on value standards (O'Connor and Spash, 1999) may be phrased also in the framework of the 'environmental Kuznets curve', an inverted U-curve which relates income to some environmental impacts (Selden and Song, 1994; Arrow *et al*, 1995; de Bruyn and Opschoor, 1997). In urban situations, as incomes grow, sulphur dioxide emissions first increase and then decrease, while carbon dioxide emissions increase with incomes. If something improves and something deteriorates, one reaction from the conventional economist might be to put weights or to put prices on such effects, in the pursuit of commensurability of values. However, the uncertainty and complexity of such situations (sulphur dioxide may counteract the greenhouse effect, for instance), and the fact that the price of externalities would depend on social power relations, imply that the economist's accounts would be convincing only for the believers of the same school.

When the pattern of use of environmental resources and sinks is shown to depend on changing social power and income distribution, we enter the field of political ecology which originates in geography and anthropology, and which is defined as the study of ecological distribution conflicts. Economic growth leads to increased environmental impacts, and to increased conflicts (often outside the market sphere). Examples abound of the failure of the price system to indicate environmental impacts, or (to use K.W. Kapp's idea) examples abound of cost-shifting successes. Anyone is owner, except slaves, of her or his own body and health; however, poor people sell their health cheaply when working for a wage in mines or plantations. The poor sell cheap, not out of choice but out of lack of power. Free use of sinks has been modelled in a neo-Ricardian framework by Charles Perrings, Martin O'Connor and other authors, showing how the pattern of prices in the economy would be different assuming different outcomes for ecological distribution conflicts. As Martin O'Connor has often written, a zero price for extracting resources or dumping waste may signal not non-scarcity but rather a historical relation of power.

LUDWIG VON MISES' PRICELESS WATERFALL AND OTTO NEURATH'S NATURALRECHNUNG

In ecological economics, in human ecology and in the new field of industrial ecology, much work has been done in the last 20 years on 'social metabolism', that is, counting the energy and material input into the economy, and counting also the waste products. Work on 'social metabolism' attempts to create a typology of societies characterized by different patterns of material and energy flows. In ecological economics, this work on 'social metabolism' is related to current debates on the 'dematerialization' of the economy. The field was started (in my view) by Josef Popper-Lynkeus' work of 1912 (written in Vienna) on material and energy analysis.

As we have seen, ecological economics differs from orthodox economics in its focus on the incompatibility between economic growth and the maintenance of ecological resources and services over the long term. Ecological economists address the issue of translating environmental services and damages into monetary values, but they get beyond the chrematistic outlook by looking for physical and social indicators on unsustainability. We are confronted by incommensurability of values in a context of unavoidable uncertainties. Rather than seeking to internalize externalities or value environmental services through actual or surrogate markets, ecological economists recognize the 'fetishism of commodities', even the 'fetishism of fictitious commodities', as in contingent valuation methods. This is a possible link between Marxism and ecological economics.

Marxists, while emphasizing class conflict, neglected environmental issues. This was a mistake. Engels rejected Podolinsky's attempt in 1880 to introduce the study of energy flow into Marxist economics. Although Marx adopted the notion of 'metabolism' (*Stoffwechsel*) to describe human relations with Nature (Martinez-Alier with Schlüpmann, 1987), Marxists did not take up the study of human ecology in terms of energy and material flows. Kautsky could have discussed the use of energy in agriculture, but he did not. Rosa Luxemburg, who had a view of the relations between the industrial world and the Third World somewhat similar to that of the present book, did not focus on material and energy flow analysis. They were economists, albeit Marxist economists. Moreover, as Marxists, perhaps they feared that the introduction of ecology would mean the 'naturalizing' of human history, and indeed there have been attempts to do this, ranging from Malthusianism to sociobiology. However, introducing human ecology into history does not so much naturalize history as historicize ecology. The exosomatic use of energy and materials by humans is socially driven, depending on economics, politics and culture. Also demography is related to changing social structures, and it is a reflective system, while human migration patterns depend on economics, politics and law rather than on natural imperatives.

Popper-Lynkeus' work on energy and material flows of 1912 was, then, not in the Marxist tradition. Many schemes have been proposed in order to guarantee economic security in the form of minimum incomes, or a minimum allocation of subsistence goods. One of the first such schemes was that proposed by Popper-Lynkeus' remarkable work on material and energy analysis, which was also a critique of conventional economics, within a neo-Malthusian perspective, leading to 'practical utopian' proposals for an economic system which would be divided into two sectors: the subsistence sector, outside the market economy, and a market sector, with transactions in money and based on a free labour market. The scale of the market sector would be subject to a restriction of ecological

sustainability (to use today's words). For example, Popper-Lynkeus discussed the perspectives for the substitution of biomass energy for coal,
and he took a pessimistic view. In the subsistence sector, the essentials of
livelihood in food, clothing and built living space would be provided in
kind to everybody (men and women, independently), by means of the
work performed by some (carefully calculated) years of universal con-
scription in a citizen 'army' of unpaid workers. Both a notion of economic
security for all and an environmental approach were the building blocks
of Popper-Lynkeus' work. In contemporary debates on sustainability in
southern countries, the idea of a 'dignity floor' for all (as the NGO Red
de Ecologia Social (Redes) from Uruguay and Instituto de Ecologia
Politica from Chile have put it) often reappears. Today's proposals for universal basic incomes for all citizens (Van Parijs, 1995) remove the compulsory labour-service (for the subsistence sector) which Popper-Lynkeus
favoured, together with other practical–utopian writers of a hundred
years ago. This is a good thing. They also often forget to include environmental considerations, and in that sense they are less relevant than
Popper-Lynkeus who, for instance, appraised Kropotkin's figures for
potato yields in greenhouses in Guernsey and Jersey, and criticized
Kropotkin's optimism because he had forgotten to take into account the
energy inputs for heating the greenhouses.

It is well known among analytical philosophers that Popper-Lynkeus
influenced the Vienna Circle and particularly Otto Neurath on different
issues. First, Popper-Lynkeus, who was an engineer, wrote some pieces on
the history of thermodynamics where he insisted on the strict separation of
scientific propositions and metaphysical propositions, complaining about
Lord Kelvin's religious tirades based on the Second Law and on a (doubtful) theory on the source of energy in the sun. Second, Popper-Lynkeus
(together with Ballod-Atlanticus) influenced Neurath's positive view of
practical utopias. The writing of plausible 'histories of the future' required
that findings from the different sciences be put together, and that contradictions among such findings be removed. Finally, Popper-Lynkeus developed a strong attack on conventional economics because it praised the
market and forgot about the needs of the poor and also about energy and
material flows.

Otto Neurath's contribution to the debate on the relations between the
environment and the economy, the connection between Neurath's economic writings and Popper-Lynkeus' work of 1912, and the link between
Neurath's position in the socialist calculation debate of the 1920s and the
debate on incommensurability of values in ecological economics, have been
carefully explored only in the last 15 years or so (Martinez-Alier with
Schlüpmann, 1987; O'Neill, 1993). In fact, they should have been better

known because Neurath's influence was explicitly acknowledged in some footnotes in K.W. Kapp's work. Also Neurath's ideas were summarized in several pages of Max Weber's *Economy and Society*. Moreover, Hayek's well-known disparaging remarks (Hayek, 1952) about scientistic 'social engineers' lumped together Patrick Geddes, Lewis Mumford, Otto Neurath and other authors who shared a view of the economy as 'social metabolism', while Hayek's pro-market position in the socialist calculation debate was well-known since the 1930s. As John O'Neill has put it, the current debate on environment and the economy may be seen as a very large and delayed footnote to the socialist calculation debate of the 1920s.

The arguments about economic commensurability and its place in environmental decision making are not new to the economic debate. The socialist calculation debate took place in central Europe (Hayek, 1935) in the aftermath of the First World War, when it seemed practically relevant because of the wave of revolutions in central and eastern Europe. Neurath himself, a philosopher and social theorist (who would be a leader of the positivist Vienna Circle) explained the essence of economic commensurability by means of the following example. Let us consider two capitalist factories, achieving the same level of production of the same type of product, one with 200 workers and 100 tons of coal, the second one with 300 workers and only 40 tons of coal. Both would compete in the market, and the one using a more 'economic' process would achieve an advantage. However, in a socialist economy (where the means of production are socialized), in order to compare two economic plans, achieving the same result but with different labour and fossil fuel intensities, a present value should be given to future needs for coal (and, we would now add, a present value should be given also to the future uncertain impact of carbon dioxide emissions). We must not only decide, therefore, a rate of discount and a time horizon, but also guess the changes in technology: use of solar energy, use of water power, use of nuclear power. The answer to whether coal-intensive or labour-intensive methods should be used could not be given by the market, not only because the coal market did no longer exist in a socialist economy and there was no price for coal, not only because there was no longer (perhaps) a price for labour (these were the objections that von Mises knew how to answer, and Lange and Taylor were later also to answer), but because of the moral dilemmas and technical uncertainties involved in such choices. In Neurath's own words (1928 (Neurath, 1973: 263), the answer 'depends for example on whether one thinks that hydraulic power may be sufficiently developed or that solar energy might come to be better used. If however one is afraid that when one generation uses too much coal thousands will freeze to death in the future, one might use more human power and save coal. Such and many other non-technical matters determine the choice of a technically calculable plan . . . we can see no possibility of reducing the production plan to some kind of unit and then to compare the various plans in terms of such units'. Elements in the economy were not commensurable.

Neurath's positions in the socialist calculation debate were answered by Ludwig von Mises. For him, the principle of subjective use value was what mattered. Not only the values of consumer goods but also, indirectly, of inputs into production could only be based on subjective values expressed in prices. In practice, we must rely on exchange values determined in actual markets. As von Mises' faithful disciples put it:

> He explained that economic calculation would not be possible in a purely socialist society. Prices arise in the market as private owners bid and compete with one another for goods and services. These prices indicate in summary form the relative scarcities of the productive inputs. Under full-fledged socialism, therefore, where all property would be publicly owned, there could be no market prices. Thus, the central planners would have no prices to guide them, no clues to help them decide what goods and services to produce, and how to produce; they would be unable to calculate.[1]

However, under full-fledged capitalism, markets fail to value some goods (and some 'bads'). Hence, in his discussion of alternative sources of energy which was so much a part of the opening salvos in the socialist calculation debate, von Mises remarked: 'If, for example, we are considering whether a hydraulic power-works would be profitable we cannot include in the computation the damage which will be done to the beauty of the waterfalls unless the fall in values due to a fall in tourist traffic is taken into account. Yet we must certainly take such considerations into account when deciding whether the undertaking shall be carried out' (von Mises, 1922 (1951: 116)).[2] So, in order to give a price to the beauty of the waterfall, economists could introduce a method of money valuation nowadays called the 'travel cost method'.

According to von Mises, without prices as a common denominator, there could not be a rational economy. However, von Mises' position is in retrospect too narrow, in the light of today's discussions on the pervasiveness of externalities, and on the merits of 'procedural' rationality (and compromise or satisficing solutions) over the rationality of the objective or the outcome (with 'optimum' solutions).

> The issue is not whether it is only the market place that can determine [economic] value, for economists have long debated other means of valuation; our concern is with the assumption that in any dialogue [or conflict], all valuations or 'numeraires' should be reducible to a single one-dimension standard. (Funtowicz and Ravetz, 1994: 198)

EMERGENT COMPLEXITY AND POSTNORMAL SCIENCE

Ecological economics, based on methodological pluralism (Norgaard, 1989), must not follow the reductionist road, rather, it should adopt Otto Neurath's image of the 'orchestration of the sciences' proposed 60 years ago, acknowledging and trying to reconcile the contradictions arising between the different disciplines which deal with issues of ecological sustainability. The need to consider simultaneously the different types of knowledge appropriate for different levels of analysis is shown not only by the birth of ecological economics, but also by the frequent demands for integrated assessment, or a holistic framework, or consilience (without reductionism), or systems research, or the 'orchestration of the sciences', which fit well with the ideas of 'coevolution' and of 'emergent complexity' implying the study of the human dimensions of ecological change and therefore the study of human environmental perceptions. This means introducing self-conscious human agency and reflective human interpretation in ecology. While 'emergent complexity' looks more to the unexpected future, 'coevolution' looks towards history. Complexity arises from the non-linear behaviour of systems under study, and from the relevance of findings from different disciplines for predicting what will happen. For instance, the policy on the greenhouse effect must consider not only complex physical and chemical relations but also human demography, environmental sociology, economics and politics. Hence the call for an 'integrated assessment' which acknowledges the legitimacy of different points of view on the same issue. When there are environmental conflicts, information from the alleged finding of the environmental sciences is used to swing the argument in one or other direction. Thus, genetically modified organisms (GMOs) are 'safe', but nuclear power is risky, while dioxin presents no real threat although we are threatened by endocrine disruptors. Often the unavoidable uncertainties of ecological information, which arise not only from insufficiencies of research but also from system complexity, are themselves brought to bear on the discussion. 'Governance', then, requires this integrated approach, but how is integration to be achieved?

So, how could a history of the industrialized agricultural economy be written today, taking into account the viewpoint both of conventional agricultural economics and of agroecology? In some scientific languages, modern agriculture is characterized by lower energy efficiency, genetic and soil erosion, ground and water pollution, uncertain environmental and health risks. In other scientific languages, modern agriculture achieves increased productivity. Another non-equivalent description of agricultural reality will emphasize the loss of indigenous cultures and knowledge. There is a clash of perspectives. Over the last 30 years, pioneers of the environmental logic of traditional sedentary agriculture such as Howard (1940) and of shifting cultivation such as Conklin (1957) have been joined by enthnoecologists and agroecologists (Paul Richards, Victor Toledo, Miguel Altieri, Anil Gupta) praising ancient farming systems, and *in situ* coevolution of agricultural seeds and techniques. Not only for agriculture, but also for artisanal fishing and for forest use and management, the virtues of traditional knowledge have been extolled. As Shiv Visvanathan has put it, every person is not only a consumer and a citizen, she is also a carrier of knowledge threatened by modernization.

In rural resource conflicts the knowledge traffic goes perhaps in the opposite direction to that in industrial pollution conflicts. In the first, the scientists research and translate local practical knowledge into universal terms (for instance, everyday keeping and experimenting with potato seeds becomes '*in situ*' biodiversity conservation). In the latter, local interpreters translate scientific knowledge (and scientific ignorance) into a language which is locally useful. Traditional knowledge cannot be invoked in urban ecological conflicts, or for global problems such as the greenhouse effect, or for coping with new technological risks. Here the notion of 'postnormal science' connects the old and the new, the rural and the urban, the local and the global. True, no traditional knowledge existed on nuclear risks, on the effects of DDT, DBCP or malathion, on the relations between urban pollution and infantile asthma, on the effects of lead and asbestos, or on the hazards of transgenic crops. In the same way as copper miners and miners' families became experts on sulphur dioxide pollution, local stakeholders learn the vocabularies they need.

This is what a whole generation of anti-nuclear activists did in the 1970s. My first encounter with an environmental conflict was in the lower Ebro valley in Spain in the 1960s and early 1970s, because of a proposed hydroelectric dam at Xerta (not built) and because of two new nuclear power stations at the village of Ascò (of 1000MW each) which were built. The local fight in Ascò was led by a tailor, Carranza, and by a priest, Redorat. The priest did pass around a few publications in English on nuclear risks, and tried to convince the villagers (still under the Franco regime) that they should oppose the nuclear power stations. He himself liked to say in private that, since the villagers knew he could speak some Latin, they believed he could also read English texts on radioactivity. In any case, popular environmentalism is not hampered by lack of knowledge, it either relies on old traditional knowledge on resource management or it relies on the uncertainty or ignorance which scientific knowledge cannot dispel about the risks of new technologies. Industry spokesmen get frantic when science can no longer (in such situations of uncertainty) be used in the service of power. Thus activists are described as 'master manipulators' who rely on 'junk science' or on 'tabloid science', who demand 'zero-risks', who 'substitute politics for sound policy', making it impossible for regulators to base their decisions on 'sound science'.[3]

Ecological economics as an 'orchestration of the sciences' takes into account the contradictions between the disciplines; it also takes into account changing historical perceptions of the relations between humans and the environment, and it highlights the limits of the authoritative judgments of any particular expert in a particular discipline. As explained by Funtowicz, Ravetz and other students of environmental risks, in many current problems of importance and urgency, where values are in dispute and uncertainties (not reducible to probabilistic risk) are high, we observe that 'certified' experts are often challenged by citizens from environmental groups. A given problem of environmental management may stay for a while in the peaceful realm of 'normal' science, where there is time to go to the lab and do the tests. Then challenges arise. In postnormal science, in contrast to normal science, outsiders cannot be excluded, because the insiders are manifestly incapable of providing conclusive answers to the problems they confront. Ulrich Beck's 'risk society' (Beck, 1992) contains a similar analysis, though 'risk' is technically not the right word to use because it implies known probability distributions, while uncertainty does not. In complex situations, or when confronted by new technologies, uncertainty predominates. Dangers and hazards rather than risks must be managed, and this is not easy. Hence, for instance, the inconclusive statistics of the environmental justice popular epidemiology movement in the USA, continuing debates on nuclear hazards, today's debates on the hazards of new biotechnological foods, or proud and plausible arguments developed by ethnoecologists based on the practical knowledge of indigenous and peasant populations in favour of keeping traditional agriculture alive in India, China, Africa and Latin America, dismantling the divide between scientific and indigenous knowledge. Environmental activism often becomes a great source of knowledge. This is 'postnormal science' based on 'extended peer review', leading towards participatory methods of conflict resolution and towards 'deliberative democracy', notions which are dear to ecological economists.

Based on this background of ecological economics and postnormal science, in Chapter 3 the physical indices which have been proposed to judge whether societies are moving towards sustainability will be discussed, along with carrying capacity and human demography, before we proceed in Chapter 4, to the study of concrete instances of ecological distribution conflicts.

NOTES

1. See the website of the Foundation for Economic Education (www.fee.org/about/misesbio).
2. John O'Neill has repeatedly drawn attention to this argument by von Mises.
3. Advertisement in *New York Times*, 26 November 1999, placed by Daniel J. Popeo, Chairman, Washington Legal Foundation, referring to exaggerated claims on the dangers of dioxin. Such spokesmen for industry ought to take a course in postnormal science.

3. Indices of (un)sustainability, and neo-Malthusianism

Because of the shortcomings of money valuation, ecological economists favour physical indicators and indices in order to judge the overall impact of the human economy on the environment. Therefore, we leave here aside monetary corrections to GNP, such as El Serafy's (see above), or Hueting's, which computes the economic costs of adjusting the economy to norms or standards of pollution and resource extraction. Where do the norms and standards come from? Are they themselves subject to social and political negotiations? We also leave aside Cobb's and Daly's ambitious Index of Sustainable Economic Welfare (ISEW), first calculated for the United States, which has inspired work in many countries, and whose end-result is a figure in money terms commensurable with GNP, though often showing quite a different trend (Daly and Cobb, 1989, 1994). The main physical indices of (un)sustainability discussed at present are as considered below.

HANPP, ECO-SPACE, EROI, MIPS AND DMR

HANPP

HANPP (human appropriation of net primary production) is proposed by Vitousek *et al.* (1986). The NPP is the amount of energy that the primary producers, the plants, make available to the rest of living species, the hetero-trophs. It is measured in tons of dry biomass, in tons of carbon or in energy units. Of this NPP, humankind 'coopts' around 40 per cent in terrestrial ecosystems. The higher the HANPP, the less biomass is available for 'wild' biodiversity. The proportion of NPP appropriated by humans is increasing because of population growth, and also because of increasing demands on land per person for urbanization, for growing feedstuffs, for growing timber ('plantations are not forests' is a slogan of environmental activists in the Tropics). Humans should decide whether they want HANPP to go on increasing, crowding out other non-domesticated species, or whether they want to reduce HANPP to 30 or 20 per cent in terrestrial ecosystems. International agencies could calculate and include this index in their publications. Leaving it out of public debate, making of it a non-political issue, also implies a decision by default.

HANPP is an index which comes from systems ecology. Whether it is a good indicator of loss of biodiversity is not so certain, because the relations between energy flow, growth of biomass and biodiversity are not simple. A desert can have little biomass because of hydric stress, and nevertheless have a few most interesting endemic species. Moreover, the measurement of HANPP is not so easy. There are technical questions: should primary production underground also be included? There are also conceptual questions (Vitousek *et al.*, 1986; Haberl, 1997). The idea is that human appropriation does not consist only in harvesting but also in diminishing the production of biomass (parking lots, for instance). In changes from forest or natural vegetation to non-irrigated agriculture, it is the case that the NPP of potential vegetation will be above the NPP of the actually prevailing vegetation which will be largely agricultural product. Thus, if NPP of potential vegetation is 100, and NPP of the actually prevailing vegetation is 60 and, of this, half is harvested for human use, HANPP is not 50 per cent but 70 per cent. However, in changes from dry habitats to irrigated agriculture, and perhaps in tree plantations, NNP of the actually prevailing vegetation might be above the NPP of naturally occurring potential vegetation. In general, does agriculture increase or decrease NPP? And what types of agriculture are more or less compatible with biodiversity?

Finally, who are the social agents in conflicts on HANPP? One would have to study the interests of different social groups in different types of land use. For instance, when converting a wildlife delta or wetland (the Wash, near Cambridge, UK, in the 18th century) into a privately owned agricultural area, or when converting a mangrove forest into shrimp farms, which uses of NPP are privileged, which are sacrificed, which categories of people benefit, which suffer most? Perhaps some countries are importing other countries' NPP. At which prices? Beyond internal human conflict, which social values come into play when discussing the rights of other species which will be secured by assuring them of a proper share of NPP?

Eco-Space and Ecological Footprint

What is the environmental load of the economy, in terms of space? H.T. Odum posed the question, and later authors (Opschoor, Rees) developed some answers. Rather than asking what maximum population a particular region or country can support sustainably, the question becomes: how large an area of productive land is needed (as source and sink) in order to sustain a given population indefinitely, at its current standard of living and with current technologies? Computations, not only for cities or metropolitan regions (whose 'ecological footprint' is hundreds of times larger than their own territories) but for whole countries, show that some densely populated European countries (assuming per capita eco-footprints of 3ha) or Japan or Korea (with per capita eco-footprints of 2ha) occupy eco-spaces ten or 15 times larger than their own territories. This is 'appropriated carrying capacity', from which an 'ecological debt' arises. (For details, see Wackernagel and Rees, 1995; for a critique and historical application, see Haberl *et al.*, 2001).

EROI

EROI, which stands for 'energy return on (energy) input', also originates in H.T. Odum's work. Is there a trend towards an increasing energy-cost of obtaining energy (see Hall *et al.*, 1986)? The idea of looking at the basic economics of human society as a flow of energy is well known to ecological anthropologists (through Roy Rappaport's *Pigs for the Ancestors*, and similar work). It goes back to Podolinsky in 1880. For an economy to be sustainable, the energy productivity of human work (that is, how much energy is made available per day, by one day of human work) must be higher (or equal, if everybody is working) than the efficiency of the transformation of the energy intake into human work. This is Podolinsky's principle. The energy productivity of a coalminer (wrote Podolinsky) was much larger than that a primitive agriculturalist could obtain, but this energy surplus from fossil fuels was transitory, and moreover there was a theory which linked climatic changes to concentrations of carbon dioxide in the atmosphere, as Sterry Hunt had explained at a meeting of the British Society for the Advancement of Science in the autumn of 1878. This was a few years before Svante Arrhenius established the theory of the greenhouse effect.

In 1909, Max Weber still criticized Wilhelm Ostwald's interpretation of economic history in terms of (a) an increased use of energy and (b) an increased efficiency in the use of energy, because economic decisions on new industrial processes or new products were based on prices. Entrepreneurs did not pay attention to energy accounts *per se* (Weber, 1909). (No environmental auditing of firms was required in 1909, and it is not yet required in 2002). Max Weber (whose book review against Ostwald was much praised by Hayek in later years), did not yet question energy prices from the environmental point of view, as we would today.

In the early 1970s, there were a number of studies on energy flow in agriculture, of which the best known were those of David Pimentel showing a decrease in energy efficiency in maize cultivation in the USA, because of the large energy input from outside agriculture itself. A new field (historic and cross-sectional) was opened up by such studies on the efficiency in the use of energy in different sectors of the economy, including the energy sector itself (fuelwood, oil, gas and so on) (Peet, 1992), also taking into account the point that increased energy efficiency might, paradoxically, lead to increased energy use, by reducing its cost (the Jevons effect). Such energy analysis has nothing to do, in principle, with the adoption of an 'energy theory of value', or with the view that sources of energy are more problematic for sustainability than sinks for waste.

MIPS and DMR/TMR

The indicator called MIPS (material input per unit service) was developed at the Wuppertal Institute (by Schmidt-Bleek). It adds up the materials used for production directly and indirectly (the 'ecological rucksack') such as mineral ores, the energy carriers (coal, oil), all biomass (though not water, which is used in much larger amounts), including the whole 'life cycle' down to the disposal or recycling phases. This material input is measured in tons, and it is compared with the services provided, sector by sector and, in principle, for the whole economy. For instance, in order to provide the service of one passenger-km, or in order to provide the service of living space of so many square metres, which is the amount of materials involved, comparing different regions of the world, or historically? MIPS is useful as a measure of the material intensity of production, but not as a measure of toxicity of materials. The MIPS notion has been developed further in the statistics published by the World Resources Institute in 1997 on the direct material requirement and the total material requirement (that is, the aggregate tonnage of raw materials including in the TMR the 'ecological rucksacks') coming into the economies of some countries (USA, Germany, Netherlands, Japan) both from domestic sources and from imports, therefore testing the hypothesis of 'dematerialization' of production.

The DMR is the domestic extraction/production of natural resources in a country during a year, plus imports minus exports of such resources. This includes both non-renewable materials (fossil fuels, minerals) and renewable materials (wood, materials to be processed as food). Domestic production includes at least a part of the 'ecological rucksacks' but imports and exports in DMR refer to products (that is, paper pulp and not wood). When, as in Europe, imports are much larger in tonnage than exports, choosing DMR over TMR shows only one part of the displacement of environmental loads to other continents. One honest reason for the choice is the statistical difficulties in calculating the 'ecological rucksacks' of imports produced in distant places under different geographical and social conditions and technologies. Further work on material flows (yearly DMR, and accumulation of materials) was presented by the World Resources Institute and other research centres in 2000, comparing the performance of the same countries and also Austria on the 'dissipation' and the accumulation of material flows per capita (Matthews *et al.*, 2000).

All the indexes mentioned here are measured in different units. How should a situation be judged in which, for instance, a synthetic indicator or index such as DMR deteriorates while HANPP improves, EROI decreases and GNP grows? Commensurability would imply reducing such values to an encompassing super-value but this is not necessary in order to reach reasonable judgments by a sort of macroeconomic multi-criteria evaluation or integrated assessment (Faucheux and O'Connor, 1998).

THE 'DEMATERIALIZATION' OF CONSUMPTION?

In economic theories of production and consumption, compensation and substitution reign supreme. Not so in ecological economics, where diverse standards of value are deployed 'to take Nature into account'. In the ecological economics theory of consumption, some goods are more important and cannot be replaced by other goods (orthodox economists call this a 'lexicographic' order of preferences, and they believe it is a very extraordinary event). Thus no other good can substitute or compensate for the minimum amount of endosomatic energy necessary for human life. This does not imply a biological view of human needs; on the contrary, the human species exhibits enormous intraspecific socially caused differences in the use of exosomatic energy, that is, in its 'technometabolism'. To call either the endosomatic consumption of 1500 or 2000kcal or the exosomatic use of 100000 or 200000kcal per person/day a 'socially constructed need or want' would be to leave aside the ecological explanations and/or implications of such use of energy, while to call the daily endosomatic consumption of 1500 or 2000kcal a 'revealed preference' would be to betray the conventional economist's metaphysical viewpoint.

There is another approach which, as pointed out by John Gowdy, builds upon the 'principle of irreducibility' of needs (proclaimed by Georgescu-Roegen in the *Encyclopedia of the Social Sciences*, in the article on 'Utility'). According to Max-Neef (Ekins and Max-Neef, 1992) all humans have the same needs, described as 'subsistence', 'affection', 'protection', 'understanding', 'participation', 'leisure', 'creation', 'identity' and 'freedom', and there is no generalized principle of substitution among them. Such needs can be satisfied by a variety of 'satisfactors'. Instead of taking the economic services as given, as in MIPS (passenger-km, square metres of living space), we may ask why is there so much travel, why so much building of houses with new materials instead of restoration of old ones. There is now research on the following question: is there a trend to use 'satisfactors' increasingly intensive in energy and materials in order to satisfy predominantly non-material needs? (Jackson and Marks, 1999). Expectations that an economy which has less industry will be less resource-intensive are perhaps premature. Input–output analysis of household life-styles (by Faye Duchin and other authors) shows the high material and energy requirements of the consumption patterns of many of those employed in the 'post-industrial' sector.

TIME AND SPACE, AND THE DISCOUNT RATE

One accepted principle for all ecological economists is that the economy is an open system. In thermodynamics, systems are classified as 'open' to the entry and exit of energy and materials, 'closed' to the entry and exit of materials though open to the entry and exit of energy, such as the Earth, and 'isolated' systems (without entry or exit of energy and materials). The availability of free energy and the cycling of materials allows life forms to become ever more organized and complex, and the same applies to the economy. Dissipated energy and waste are produced in the process. At least part of the waste can be recycled or, when not, the economy takes in new resources. However, if the scale of the economy is too large and its speed is too rapid, then the natural cycles cannot produce the resources or absorb or assimilate the residues such as, for instance, heavy metals or sulphur dioxide or carbon dioxide.

As the economy grows, resources and sinks from new territories are brought into a fast-moving regime of exploitation. For example, new tree plantations are grown for paper pulp or carbon sinks, there is destruction of mangroves for shrimp exports at rates quicker than replanting, oil extraction takes place at rates quicker, not only than the geological forma-tion of oil, but also than the ability of the local ecosystems to assimilate the extraction water. In other words, local *resilience* becomes threatened by the new rhythm of exploitation, now driven by the rate of interest or by the rate of profit on capital. Resilience means the ability of a system to maintain itself despite a disturbance, without flipping over to a new state. It is also defined as the capacity of a system to return to the initial state.

The geographical displacement of environmental loads quickens the rhythm of use of Nature, as was pointed out by Elmar Altvater in his work on Northern Brazil's mining projects (Altvater, 1987). There are instances where local perceptions and values, local cultures and institutions have retarded local resource exploitation by establishing a different conception of the use of space (for instance, by claiming indigenous territorial rights), or by affirming non-economic values (such as 'sacredness'). There are other cases in which local resource exploitation and sink use do not exceed critical loads, nor do they endanger local resilience, because capacities have expanded successfully. There are, finally, many other cases where local resistance and cultures have been destroyed.

The economic system lacks a common standard of measurement for environmental externalities. Estimates of environmental values depend on the endowment of property rights, the distribution of income, the strength of environmental movements and the distribution of power. The issue is further complicated by the difficulty of weighing future costs and benefits. It must be accepted that the notion of *ecological distribution conflicts*, which is central to this book, refers to conflicts within the present generation of humans. It does not refer to injustices across generations, or towards other species, except insofar as they are taken into account by members of the present generation.

How do economists explain the use of a positive discount rate which gives less value to the future than to the present? Economists explain discounting of the future by subjective 'time preference', or because economic growth per capita caused by today's investments will make the marginal utility of consumption lower for our descendants than it is for us today. The justification for pure time preference is weak. The alternative argument that future generations will be better off, and therefore have a decreased marginal utility of consumption, is not wholly acceptable for ecological economics because a larger consumption today may well leave our descendants with a degraded environment, and therefore worse off. We must distinguish between genuinely productive investment and investment which is environmentally damaging. Only *sustainable* increases in productive capacity should count. But the economic assessment of what is sustainable involves a *distributional* issue. If natural capital has a low price, because it belongs to nobody or to poor and powerless people who must sell it cheaply, then the destruction of nature will be undervalued. Accepting that discounting arises from the productivity of capital, and taking into account that such 'productivity' is a mixture of true increases in production and a lot of environmental destruction, the discount factor should be the per capita rate of sustainable economic growth, subtracting therefore the destruction of environmental resources and services. Now, in order to determine the present economic value of such destruction caused by economic growth (loss of biodiversity, filling up of carbon sinks, production of radioactive waste and so on), we not only need to put money figures on it (as discussed throughout this book), we also need a discount rate. Which one? The *optimist's paradox* occupies the scene. The future is undervalued because of today's optimistic views on technical change and increasing eco-efficiency, and therefore more resources and sinks are used at present than there would otherwise be, thereby undermining the original view that the future will be more prosperous.

Ecological economists (Norgaard, 1990) dispute the view, expressed in the 1960s by Barnett, Krutilla and other resource economists, that since raw materials are cheap, they must be abundant. Markets are myopic, they discount the future, they cannot see future uncertain scarcities of sources or sinks. Sustainability must be assessed not in economic terms but through a battery of biophysical indicators. The distribution of property rights, income and power determines the economic value of so-called 'natural capital'. Thus, for instance, prices in the economy would be different without the free use of carbon sinks. Another example: should legislation require dispersed minerals to be concentrated again to their previous state and the dispersed overburden restored, this would indeed change the pattern of prices in the economy. One may easily imagine other restrictions upon the economy urged by some social groups: renunciation of nuclear energy, restriction of HANPP to 20 per cent, a ban on cars in cities, countries to have 'ecological footprints' not exceeding twice their territory, oil extraction and export only as it is replaced by renewable energies, a world programme for the long-run economic viability of most traditional farmers and conservation of the associated *in situ* agricultural biodiversity. Such changes in the economy would certainly change the pattern of prices.

Beyond economic values, choices on the use of natural capital involve decisions about which interests and forms of life will be sustained and which will be sacrificed or abandoned. A common language of valuation is not available for such decisions. When we say that someone or something is 'very valuable' or 'not very valuable', this is an elliptical statement which requires the further question, by which standard of valuation (O'Neill, 1993)? For policy, what is needed is a non-compensatory multi-criteria approach able to accommodate a plurality of incommensurable values (Munda, 1995; Martinez-Alier *et al.*, 1998, 1999).

Instead of accepting value incommensurability, there are those who for policy purposes prefer to resort to the authorities (to the environmental police, we could say) and choose a cost-efficiency approach. The targets, norms or limits to the economy are set from outside by so-called 'scientific experts' (for instance, increasing CO_2 concentration in the atmosphere to 550ppm becomes acceptable) and the discussion is then only on the cheapest methods of keeping within such limits, aiming when possible at 'win–win' outcomes. However, the targets, and indeed the indicators themselves, should be open to discussion insofar as they are contested by different stakeholders. Cost-efficiency cannot get us out of the valuation dilemma.

CARRYING CAPACITY

Many ecological economists have emphasized the pressure of population on resources. Has humankind exceeded 'carrying capacity'? This is defined in ecology as the maximum population of a given species, such as frogs in a lake, which can be supported sustainably in a given territory without spoiling its resource base. However, the large differences internal to the human species in the exosomatic use of energy and materials mean that the first question is, maximum population at which level of consumption? Second, human technologies change at a rapid pace. In 1965, Boserup's thesis of endogenous technical change, according to which *pre-industrial* agricultural systems had changed in response to increases in population density, had turned the tables on the Malthusian argument. Third, international trade (similar to horizontal transport in ecology, but which humans can regulate consciously) may increase carrying capacity when one territory lacks a very necessary item which is abundantly present in another territory. Liebig's law of the minimum would recommend exchange. Then the joint carrying capacity of all territories would be larger than the sum of the carrying capacities of all autarchic territories (Pfaundler, 1902). This could link up with NGO proposals for fair and ecological trade. On the other hand, one territory's carrying capacity will decrease when it is subject to ecologically unequal exchange (see Chapter 10). Fourth, the territories occupied by humans are not 'given': other species are pushed into corners or into oblivion (as the HANPP index implies) and, internal to the human species, territoriality is politically constructed through state migration policies.[1]

Because of the shortcomings of 'carrying capacity' as an index of (un)sustainability for humans, and because of Barry Commoner's arguments in the early 1970s against Paul Ehrlich's fixation on population growth, the formula $I = P.A.T$ was proposed by Paul Ehrlich from the mid-1970s, where I is environmental impact, P is population, A is affluence per capita, and T stands for the environmental effects of technology. Efforts are being made to operationalize $I = P.A.T$. Population then becomes only one variable in order to explain environmental load. Charges of 'neo-Malthusianism' against Ehrlich are now seen to be unfounded. True, population remains one important variable. True also, 'neo-Malthusian' policies inspired and legitimized by the image of the 'population bomb' have caused many forced sterilizations and large-scale female infanticide in some countries, and they threaten small surviving ethnic groups. However, a hundred years ago, *the* original neo-Malthusian movement in Europe and America opposed Malthus' view that poverty was due to overpopulation rather than social inequality, and fought successfully for limiting births by exercising women's reproductive rights (to use today's language), appealing also to ecological arguments of pressure of population on resources without forgetting the pressure of overconsumption on resources. The demographic transitions are not mere automatic responses to social changes, such as urbanization, and their timing does not depend only on social institutions, such as inheritance patterns and family forms. Human demography is self-conscious or reflective. Though it also follows Verhulst's curve, it is different from the ecology of a population of frogs in a lake.

FEMINIST NEO-MALTHUSIANISM

Many feminists still tend to dismiss the link between population growth and environmental deterioration (for example, Silliman and King, 1999) instead of putting it centre stage as the neo-Malthusians did a hundred years ago by their very choice of name. Today's feminists are seemingly unaware of the environmental debates in their own ancestry. They are irritated by the weight given to population in the $I = P.A.T$ equation (which will depend anyway on which coefficients are allocated to P, A and T), rightly irked by the racism of those insensitive to the plight of disappearing populations and minority cultures in the world, indignant at patriarchal and state arrogance in the choice of contraceptive methods forcibly introduced in the Third World. Of course, environmental problems are not only population problems. From the beginning of political ecology (Blaikie and Brookfield, 1987) a strong distinction has been made between population pressure on resources and production pressure on resources. Africa and Latin America are both poor and not overpopulated (on average) (Leach and Mearns, 1996). New illnesses are spreading, old illnesses coming back, and populations might decline in some African countries. All this is known, but it does not explain why the feminist movement, which supports women's right to safe birth control and abortion (still illegal in so many countries) as part of comprehensive health care, forgets its own historical role in the demographic transitions. Why not be proud instead of the strength shown by women against social and political structures and, often, male irresponsibility, in taking control of their own reproductive capacity, collectively achieving demographic transitions without which the world environment would eventually be ruined?

There is a connection between population density and environmental load. This connection (which is not straightforward) is shown by an index such as HANPP. It is also shown by the 'ecological footprint' which also emphasizes, and rightly so, consumption per capita. When feminists appeal to ecological footprint analysis (Patricia Hynes, in Silliman and King,

1999: 196–9), in order to emphasize wealth as the main threat to the environment, they cannot evade the importance of population density. The ecological footprint of rich metropolitan areas is hundreds of times their own territories, while that of rich densely populated countries such as the Netherlands, Germany or Japan is at most tens of times their own territories, precisely because of different population densities in metropolitan areas and in the country as a whole. Canada has an ecological footprint smaller than in its own very large territory.

Among feminists today, the very idea of neo-Malthusianism appears abhorrent. Today's neo-Malthusianism is linked to state population policies, as in China, or to pressure from international bullies such as the World Bank. In India there has been a high reliance on female sterilization, although Indira Gandhi also promoted mass male sterilization (with politically counterproductive effects). Research shows that a declining fertility rate because of female sterilization is linked in India (with the well-known exception of Kerala and other states) to greater female infanticide (because of the preference for male children). Moreover, sterilized women seem to be subject to greater physical abuse by insecure husbands. Women who will not have children get less food at home than otherwise (Krishnaraj *et al.*, 1998). Such consequences of birth control arise because of gender-biased cultural values and not because of birth control itself. However, there is no denying that state-imposed population policies are not at all inspired by the feminist movement, and that their consequences are terrible from a feminist perspective and from a general humanist perspective. On the contrary, it is well understood among scholars in India that 'engendering population policy involves moving beyond family planning to focus on changes in social structure that would allow women to make marital and fertility choices free of social or economic constraints' (Desai, 1998: 49). Notice here how lack of freedom in 'marital choices' goes together with lack of freedom in 'fertility choices'. Women are in a weak position in India, because of a cultural context which often still links caste membership to control over women's sexuality. Notice also that some regions of India have population densities as high or higher than the most densely populated European countries. How large will India's ecological footprint become, as its large population, we hope, achieves a higher standard of living?

European fertility came down *not because of* state policies, but *against* state policies. Democratic governments in Europe forbade neo-Malthusian activism as late as the 1920s, and Fascist governments even later. Between 1865 and 1945, the Prussian, and later the German, state wanted more soldiers to fight the French, and vice versa. The French state, which had done so much for the depopulation of France in 1914–18, patriotically banned the neo-Malthusian movement in 1920 (Ronsin, 1980: 83–4). In European history, the words 'state population policy' mean attempts to increase population by increasing the birth rate. In America, it meant increasing the immigration of populations of suitable origins. Recent interventions in China, India and elsewhere have changed the meaning of 'state population policies'. The science of demography was sponsored in France by populationist governments, still producing fervent anti-Malthusian scholars such as Alfred Sauvy after 1945 (Sauvy, 1960). Demographers have usually been silent on ecology ('this is not my department') and it fell to a biologist such as Ehrlich, innocent of social and historical knowledge, to raise stridently again, in 1968, the population/environment question with his book *The Population Bomb*, given the silence (in the best of cases) not only of demographers but also of economists (earlier economists, such as Wicksell, had been militant neo-Malthusians). Most communist governments allowed freedom of contraception and abortion, with exceptions such as Ceaucescu in Romania in the 1970s and 1980s, but they also emphasized Marx's political critique against Malthus' reactionism. Marx had also an economic argument against Malthus: there were no decreasing returns in agricultural production; rather, as the British experience was already showing in the 1850s and 1860s, yields increased and simultaneously the rural labour input diminished through migration to cities. Marx was not an ecological economist. Nowadays we dispute the economists' measurement of agricultural productivity for reasons which Marx never incorporated into his analysis (despite his side remarks on soil erosion and loss of nutrients). Ecological analysis moves the debate on agriculture much beyond the old economists' quarrels on 'decreasing returns'.

Related to eco-feminism, the link between women's 'reproductive rights', and the awareness of population pressure on the environment is a preoccupation which did not start at the UN Cairo Conference on Population and Development of 1994, but rather a hundred years earlier. Radical, feminist neo-Malthusianism in Europe and America, opposed by the Catholic Church and by the state, already claimed, in 1900, 'reproductive rights' by insisting on women's freedom to choose the number of children they wanted to have. Thus Emma Goldman (1869–1940), the American anarchist and feminist, was a participant at the first neo-Malthusian conference in Paris in 1900. The conference in fact became a small meeting hosted by the Catalan anarchist Francisco Ferrer Guardia. It was attended by Paul Robin, a pedagogue and freemason who believed in coeducation; he was also a former Bakuninist member of the International, and the moving force behind French neo-Malthusianism; Dr George Drysdale (1825–1904) who, in 1854, had published in England a famous neo-Malthusian book, *Elements of Social Science*; and Dr Rutgers from the Netherlands, the editor of *Het gelukkig huisgezin* (the happy family). There were earlier strands in neo-Malthusianism such as the booklets published in England in the 1820s by Francis Place and Robert Owen, and the famous court case against Annie Besant in London in 1877 when she openly published and sold the neo-Malthusian book by Dr Charles Knowlton of Boston, *Fruits of Philosophy* (first edition, 1833) (Ronsin, 1980; Masjuan, 2000).

But how could a radical feminist and anarchist such as Emma Goldman attend a neo-Malthusian conference? It certainly requires explanation, because Malthus was a true reactionary, against the French Revolution. For Malthus, improving the situation of the poor was a hopeless task because population increase would immediately absorb such gains. Population tended to increase in geometrical progesssion, only to be checked by lack of food supplies (themselves subject to decreasing returns) or, in the best of cases, by the moral restraint of chastity and late marriages. The neo-Malthusians of 1900 took from Malthus their interest in the relations between population growth and food supplies. They often discussed the carrying capacity of the Earth, as many other authors did at the time (Martinez-Alier with Schlüpmann, 1987, chapters on Pfaundler and Ballod-Atlanticus, and Cohen, 1995), framing the question as 'How large a world population could be fed?' The answers were not conclusive. They varied between 6000 million and 200 000 million. Thus Paul Robin's son-in-law, Gabriel Giroud, wrote a pessimistic book on *Population et Subsistances* published in Paris in 1904. Today the question must be asked in a different way: how large a human population can be fed, and live sustainably at an acceptable standard of living, provided that 20 per cent or 40 per cent (or 60 per cent or 80 per cent) of biomass production is not pre-empted for human use?

A hundred years ago, there were heated disagreements between neo-Malthusian anarchists (such as Sebastien Faure) and anti-Malthusian anarchists (such as Kropotkin or Reclus, who were technological optimists). Kropotkin believed that food supply could increase enormously through greenhouse agriculture. Kropotkin was no feminist, either, and Emma Goldman had a sisterly debate with him on women's rights. The neo-Malthusians of a century ago agreed with Malthus that poor people had too many children, but they did not believe in chastity and later marriages. They promoted more vigorous 'preventive checks' than Malthus had foreseen, exhorting the poor populations of Europe and America to use contraceptives, and to separate love making from child bearing and even from marriage. The movement was careful to insist that its adherents were not Malthusians but *neo*-Malthusians, devoted to 'sexual freedom and parental prudence' (Paul Robin, in 1896; cf. Ronsin, 1980: 70). Active feminists in French *neo*-Malthusianism around 1900 had been Marie Huot (who first used the words *la grève des ventres*) and Madaleine Pelletier, who proposed not only contraceptives but also the legalization of abortion. First in France, later in Spain, there were journals entitled *Generation Consciente* (conscientious procreation).

Whether Malthus would have claimed property rights on the proper use of the word 'Malthusianism', we do not know. Many clerics of 1900 found the neo-Malthusian ideas and practices sinful. Many statesmen found them subversive. Neo-Malthusians urged women's and men's agency to turn Malthus' exponential curve into a logistic curve, the true law of population. Human demography became in Europe and America socially self-reflective, perhaps more so than it had been in other societies (except for some small 'primitive' groups which closely controlled reproduction). Hence Emma Goldman's active presence at the neo-Malthusian conference in Paris in 1900, and her active role as a propagandist for this cause in later years. Goldman published *Mother Earth* between 1906 and 1917. Environmentalists of the 1960s and 1970s revived the title of her journal. She was active as a feminist neo-Malthusian before Margaret Sanger (1879–1966), who also belonged to the same radical Greenwich Village group in New York and who is rightly credited as the main force behind the social and legal acceptance of contraception in the USA. Contraceptives were forbidden in the USA under the Comstock Act of 1873. Sanger was an International Workers of the World (IWW) organizer, and therefore familiar with anarchist ideas. She learned about birth control techniques in France and, after her return to the USA in 1914, she began to publish the journal *The Woman Rebel*, which supported socialism, feminism and contraception. She was indicted for violating the Comstock Act. Sanger no longer used the term 'neo-Malthusianism', which (paradoxically) had become politically too radical, and used 'birth control' instead, with emphasis on the prevention of abortions, to be replaced later by even less controversial terms, 'family planning' or 'planned parenthood'. Margaret Sanger successfully pushed at a half-open door. Both in Europe and in the USA, only strong-willed radicals dared preach contraception in late 19th century and early 20th century. This was so also in Latin America. The main figure of neo-Malthusianism in Brazil was the feminist and anarchist Maria Lacerda de Moura who wrote several books in the 1920s and 1930s, one of them entitled '*Love one another, and do not multiply*' (Gordon, 1976; Ronsin, 1980; Morton, 1992; Masjuan, 2000). Fertility decline in Brazil in the 1970s and 1980s took place without state support – rather, against the state (Martine *et al.*, 1998).

Historians debate whether neo-Malthusian propaganda had an influence on the demographic transition, or whether the causality runs the other way, in the sense that a social practice of birth control made neo-Malthusianism acceptable despite court cases and brochure seizures. In France, fertility started to decline decades before the neo-Malthusian movement existed, though the rate of decline accelerated in the early 1900s. In other countries, the neo-Malthusian movement preceded the decline in fertility. This was (I believe) the case in the Netherlands, in Germany and in parts of Spain, an exception being Catalonia, where the organized neo-Malthusian movement became active in 1904 (led by Luis Bulffi, who had been at the conference in Paris in 1900) and where fertility was already declining. Many journals and leaflets were printed in Barcelona and disseminated to other Spanish regions, and also to some Latin American countries (Masjuan, 2000). Among the contraceptive methods recommended by the neo-Malthusian movement in Europe and America, some were geared to women, but condoms were popular. Vasectomies started to be endorsed in French anarchist circles in the early 1930s; the state's response was a court case (Ronsin, 1980: 202). However, by the 1920s and 1930s, despite state populationist policies, in Europe the debate on the freedom to choose the number of children was already settled in practice in favour of the neo-Malhusians. In conclusion, population pressure remains a factor of importance in the clash between economy and environment. Decreasing human fertility across the world means that the main factor is now over-consumption.

When America was 'discovered' in 1492, Europe and America had approximately equivalent populations. It is well known that the indigenous population of America plummeted in the following centuries, as would also happen in Australia and the Pacific Islands. European population increased considerably in the 19th century, sending overseas a considerable number of migrants. Fortunately for Europe and the world, our fertility rates later declined rapidly. The feminist neo-Malthusians of a hundred years ago deserve some credit. We cannot begin to imagine what Europe would be like today with a fourfold increase in population between 1900 and 2000, as the world in general has experienced. Why not combine again the issues of women's freedom, reproductive rights (including the choice of abortion when other methods have failed) and the pressure of human population on the environment? This link will soon become one of the explicit doctrines of eco-feminism.

NOTE

1. In 2001, one or two hundred Africans, mostly young people, will die attempting to cross in small boats the Straits of Gibraltar into Andalusia; there will be no exact official statistics, their names will not be recorded.

4.   Political ecology: the study of ecological distribution conflicts

The preliminaries of this book are now almost completed. The clash between economy and environment cannot be convincingly solved by pious invocations to 'internalize the externalities' into the price system, spreading the gospel of 'sustainable development', 'ecological modernization' and 'eco-efficiency'. Studies of social metabolism show that the economy is not 'dematerializing'. The environment is under threat because of population growth and overconsumption. Although we lack a synthetic index of overall environmental performance, we can assess this threat through physical indicators of (un)sustainability. This is one of the main tasks for the new ecological economics.

The unequal incidence of environmental harm gives birth to environmental movements of the poor. We enter now into the description of their actions and idioms. There is already a long list of martyrs of environmentalism. Martyrdom does not prove that their cause was right, but that they had a cause. This book argues that the cause itself is not new. In this chapter I consider some cases of environmentalism from the late 19th century and early 20th century related to copper mining, and then go on to explain the birth of political ecology in the 1980s as the study of ecological distribution conflicts.

I have chosen copper mining as a starting point, for two reasons. First, it provides historical examples, as could be found also in forest or water conflicts. By looking at historical cases of environmental conflict which were not yet represented in the language of environmentalism, we may then interpret, as environmental conflicts, instances of social conflict today where the actors are still reluctant to call themselves environmentalists (Guha, 1989). Second, by comparing such historical cases in copper mining with present-day conflicts also on copper mining, I make the point that copper has not become obsolete (despite aluminium and optic fibre). On the contrary, the frontier for the extraction of copper is reaching new territories pushed by economic growth, and this is a good point to make against the believers in 'dematerialization'. Copper is not scarce in an absolute sense. Neither are other metals. The Earth is full of metals, and it also abounds in energy sources. However, the frontiers of extraction advance into new territories as old sources become depleted or too expensive.

ENVIRONMENTALISM AVANT-LA-LETTRE: COPPER MINING IN JAPAN

Environmentalists in Japan remember Ashio as the infamous site of Japan's first major industrial pollution disaster. This was a large copper mine not far from Tokyo owned by the Fukurawa corporation, which witnessed a major workers' riot against working conditions in 1907. Japanese social historians have debated whether the riot was 'spontaneous' or organized by ancient brotherhoods. There were also already some 'direct action' socialists in Japan at the time. While, as we shall see, in Rio Tinto in Andalusia in 1888 there was a common front between miners and peasants against pollution, this does not seem to have been so at Ashio, where tens of thousands of peasants along the Watarase river fought for decades against pollution from heavy metals which damaged not only crops but also human health. They also fought against the building of a large sediment basin to store the polluted waters, which implied the destruction of the village of Yanaka, including its cemetery and sacred shrines, in 1907.

> The mine's refinery belched clouds containing sulfuric acid that withered the surrounding forests, and the waste water . . . ran off into the Watarase River, reducing rice yields of the farmers who irrigated fields with this water . . . Thousands of farming families . . . protested many times. They petitioned the national authorities and clashed with the police. Eventually their leader, Tanaka Shozo, created a great stir by directly petitioning the emperor for relief . . . As environmental destruction reemerged in the 1960s as a major social issue, and popular concern with the impact of pollution intensified, so Ashio's legacy as 'the birthplace of pollution in Japan' has endured . . . At that time copper played a major role in the Japanese economy, ranking second to silk among Japan's exports. (Nimura, 1997: 20–21, see also Strong, 1977)

Ashio was not unique in the world, and Fukurawa's public relations campaign remarked that Butte in Montana was a fearful place to live: 'The smelting process has utterly destroyed the beauty of the landscape, evil gaseous smoke has killed all plant-life for miles round about; the streams are putrid with effluent, and the town itself seems buried under monstrous heaps of slag' (Strong, 1977: 67). Such were then the realities of copper mining in America. Ashio in comparison was not that bad, except that, unlike Montana, there were thousands of unhappy peasants downstream.[1]

Fukurawa had bought the Ashio mines in 1877. In 1888, he made a deal for the supply to a French syndicate of 19000 tons of copper over two and a half years. The target was met in full. Three thousand miners were then working at Ashio and their number was to increase later to fifteen thousand. The contract with Fukurawa was signed on behalf of the French syndicate by the manager of Jardine Matheson, a firm founded by Sir James Matheson of the Lews, who was an uncle of Hugh Matheson, the founder of the Rio Tinto company (Strong, 1977: 67). Fukurawa procrastinated for decades on anti-pollution measures, profiting from the novelty and uncertainty of the chemical pollution in question, and from the closeness between government and business in Japan.

In cost–benefit language, it was argued: 'Suppose for the sake of the argument that copper effluent were responsible for the damage to farmlands on either side of the Watarase – the public benefits that accrue to the country from the Ashio mine far outweigh any losses suffered in the affected areas. The damage can in any case be adequately taken care of by compensation' (article in the *Tokio Nichi Nichi Shinbun* of 10 February 1892, in Strong, 1977: 74). In today's parlance, a Pareto improvement means, in the strict sense, that a change such as a new mining project improves somebody's situation, and does not worsen anybody's situation. In this sense, Ashio did not fulfil the criterion. However, in a wider sense a Pareto improvement allows for compensation under the so-called 'Kaldor–Hicks rule', so that those better off can (potentially) compensate those worse off, and still with a net gain achieved. This was Fukurawa's claim. Tanaka Shozo (1841–1913), the son of a peasant headman of a village in the polluted area, the leader of the anti-pollution struggles, could not yet have known welfare economics. He became in the 1890s a member of the Diet in Tokyo. Famous for his fervent speeches, he was a man with deep religious feelings, the retrospective father figure of Japanese environmentalism, born therefore more in a tradition of pro-peasant environmental justice (and also of care for the urban ecology and concern for forest protection and the water cycle: Tamanoi *et al.*, 1984) than of wilderness preservation, although within a national context of industrialism and militarism which put environmentalism on the defensive.

Today Japan is of course a big importer of copper through active transnational companies like Mitsubishi. Pollution from copper mining and smelting still plays a big role in the ecological economies of some exporting countries. If world copper extraction was in 1900 of the order of 400000 tons per year, a hundred years later it is of the order of 10 million tons, an increase by a factor of 25 (compared to a fourfold increase in the human population, from 1·5 to 6 billion people between 1900 and 2000). Over 60 per cent of copper production comes from such new mined ores, the rest from recycling, hence the relentless expansion of the copper frontier. The cheaper the cost of fresh extraction, the less recycling there is. When I started to write this book in 1999, I was aware of the world boom in aluminium production and its displacement to the south, but I thought that copper had become an obsolete raw material, and that my examples on environmental conflicts in copper mining would be only historical. However, extraction of copper was still increasing at about 1·5 per cent per year in the 1990s. If prices go down it is because of oversupply and not because of lack of demand.

Ashio was not the only case of Japanese early popular environmentalism. Thus, when

> the Nikko company built its copper refinery on the tip of the Saganoseki peninsula (in Oita Prefecture) in 1917, local farmers objected strenuously. They feared that the acrid smoke from the refinery would blight the mountains and ruin the mulberry trees, on which their silk industry depended. Ignoring them, the town officials agreed to the refinery. The farmers felt betrayed. The angry farmers swarmed into town and cut through the village leader's house pillars, a tactic (*uchikowashi*) drawn straight from the Tokugawa period . . . The police brutally suppressed this protest, beating and arresting 100 participants. Nikko built the mill, and it operates to this day. (Broadbent, 1998: 138)

Michael Adas' preface to Ramachandra Guha's *Environmentalism: a global history* (Guha, 2000) insists (wrongly in my view) on the 'fundamental differences that separate Euro-American environmental activists and theorists and those who argue from the perspective of post-colonial societies, where the great majority of humanity lives'. The notion of 'post-colonialism' is not used by Guha himself. The Japanese environmentalism of the poor when Japan was neither a colonial territory nor (yet) a colonial power has much in common with other cases worldwide. Indeed, the environmentalism of the poor is a movement inside and across countries with different histories and cultures.

ONE HUNDRED YEARS OF POLLUTION IN PERU

Work by several authors in the Central Sierra of Peru 20 years ago explained the defence of the communities against expanding haciendas (Mallon, 1983). Indian shepherds and peasants successfully resisted the modernization of the haciendas. Modern hacienda owners wanted to throw them out, along with their *wakcha* non-pedigree sheep (Martinez-Alier, 1977). The communities also had to struggle on another related front, against mining companies, and they still do. The Cerro de Pasco Copper Corporation polluted pasture lands in the 1920s and 1930s. Mines were not new to the Peruvian highlands. Huancavelica had supplied mercury to Potosi as early as the 16th century. Silver had been mined in colonial and post-colonial times.

Towards 1900, there was a world boom in copper, lead and zinc mining because of the proliferation of electrical instruments, tools, machines, armaments and railroads. Domestic capitalist miners (such as Fernandini in the Central Highlands of Peru) were making small fortunes. In 1901, the Peruvian government changed the mining code allowing private ownership of mining deposits (instead of state ownership and a regime of administrative concessions) (Dore, 2000: 13–15). The Cerro de Pasco Corporation from New York bought many of the deposits and started a large scale underground mining operation. It could rely on the railroad opened to the coast, an engineering feat carried out by Henry Meiggs, the Yankee Pizarro. The Cerro de Pasco company built roads, railroads, dams, hydroelectric plants and mining camps, at 4000m above sea level. It first built several small smelters, and then in 1922 a big smelter and refinery at La Oroya, the effects of which became a *cause célèbre* (Mallon, 1983: 226–9, 350–51). 'The new smelter polluted the region's air, soil and rivers with arsenic, sulphuric acid and iron-zinc residues' (Dore, 2000: 14). The pastures withered, people became ill.

A legal case was brought against the company by peasant communities, and by old and new hacienda owners up to 120km away. The mining company was forced by the court to buy the lands it had polluted, as a form of indemnity. When in later years the mining operations and La Oroya smelter became less polluting (at least with respect to the air, because of the scrubbers, if not with respect to the rivers), the property of all this land became a valuable asset for the company, which then started a large sheep-raising business, getting into border conflicts with surrounding communities. In the early 1900s, the Cerro de Pasco Corporation initially had difficulties in recruiting skilled labour. It resorted to the *enganche*, a form of debt peonage. As Elizabeth Dore points out (Dore, 2000: 15), the large-scale pollution caused by the La Oroya smelter contributed to solving the labour shortage, because agricultural yields decreased in the small plots where agriculture is practised at such altitude, and animals died. Peasant labour became available. This was another blessing in disguise.

Many years later, in 1970, the enormous ranch (of about 300 000 ha) was expropriated by the Land Reform, but it still exists as the SAIS Tupac Amaru, owned by surrounding communities, one of the few large sheep ranches in Peru which has not been taken over and split up into individual peasant communities.

Mining in Peru was long dominated by the Cerro de Pasco Copper Corporation, but in the 1950s and 1960s, and increasingly until today, the main extraction of copper moved southward, towards Cuajone and Toquepala. These are large open-pit mines near Ilo, an extension of the rich deposits of Chuquicamata and other mines in northern Chile. Underground mining, as in Cerro de Pasco, has been replaced around the world by open-pit mining.[2] Copper ores are now obtained by open-cast mining in Southern Peru (and in Chile), with enormous amounts of overburden and tailings, and damage to water availability (in regions where it rains little). Moreover, there is the familiar problem of sulphur dioxide from the smelters. The Southern Peru Copper Corporation owned by Asarco and Newmont Gold subjected the city of Ilo in southern Peru, of 60000 inhabitants in the late 1990s, to water and air pollution for 30 years. The smelter was built in 1969, 15km north of Ilo, and spewed out daily almost two thousand tons of sulphur dioxide, while tailings and slag were discharged without treatment onto land, and also into the ocean where, it was claimed, 'several kilometres of coastline are totally black'.[3] The Southern Peru Copper Corporation is among the ten top copper producers in the world, Peru's major single exporter. The conflict is more urban than it was in the central Sierra; local NGOs have intervened, as have European environmentalists. Two international appeals to courts have been made. The local authorities presented a successful complaint in 1992 to the (unofficial) International Water Tribunal in the Netherlands obtaining its moral support. A class-action suit was initiated at the District Court for the Southern District of Texas, Corpus Christi Division, in 1995 (*New York Times*, 12 December 1995) but is was dismissed after the Peruvian state typically asked for the case to be brought back to Peru. The plaintiffs, on behalf of people from Ilo, most of them children with respiratory illnesses, complained that the pollution from sulphur dioxide had not appreciably decreased in recent years, despite the construction of a sulphuric acid plant (which recuperates sulphur dioxide). The federal court judge decided on 22 January 1996 against admitting the case into the US judicial system on grounds of *forum non conveniens.*

THE STORY OF RIO TINTO AND OTHER STORIES

The romantics reacted against the social and aesthetic horrors of industrialization. There is at least one good reason to romanticize the past: the romantics had a nose for dark, smoky mills and smelters, for environmental chemistry and industrial pollution. It was in Huelva, in the sunny southern Spanish region of Andalusia in the 1880s, years before the words 'environment' and 'ecology' became common social coinage, that the first big environmental conflict associated with the name of Rio Tinto took place (Avery, 1974; Ferrero Blanco, 1994; Pérez Cebada, 2001). The old royal mines of Rio Tinto were bought in 1873 by British and German interests, under Hugh Matheson, first chairman of the Rio Tinto Company. A new railway to the harbour of Huelva was built immediately, which was kindly made available also to local passengers on weekdays (not on local holidays or Queen Victoria's birthday). A very large open-pit mining operation was launched. Eighty years later, in 1954, the mines were sold back to new Spanish owners, the original Rio Tinto company keeping one-third interest.

This British company, Rio Tinto (renamed Rio Tinto Zinc) went on to become a worldwide mining and polluting giant (Moody, 1992). Its name, its business origins, its archive in Britain, all point to Andalusia, where a massacre by the army on 4 February 1888 of local farmers and peasants, and syndicalist miners, was the culmination of years of protests against sulphur dioxide pollution. The Spanish state was not very good at statistics, and historians still debate the number of deaths caused when the Pavia Regiment opened fire on a large demonstration in the plaza of the village of Rio Tinto: 'The company could not find out, and in any case soon decided it was better to play down the seriousness of the whole affair and gave up its attempts to discover the number of casualties, though Rio Tinto tradition puts the total number of dead at between one and two hundred' (Avery, 1974: 207, also Ferrero Blanco, 1994: 83 ff).

Historians also debate whether the miners complained only about the fact that excessive pollution prevented them from working on some days (days of *manta*: blanket) and therefore from earning full wages on those days, or whether they complained about pollution *per se* because of damage to their own and their families' health. The company, employing some ten thousand miners, was taking out a large quantity of copper pyrites. The idea was to sell the copper for export, and also as a by-product the sulphur in the pyrites (used for manufacturing fertilizers). The amount of ore extracted was so large that, in order to obtain the copper quickly, a lot of the sulphur was not recuperated but was discharged into the air as sulphur dioxide when roasting the ore in *teleras* in a process of open-air calcination, previous to smelting the concentrate. 'The sulphurous fumes from the calcining grounds were a major cause of discontent. They produced an environment that everyone resented, for the pall of smoke which frequently hung over the area destroyed much of the vegetation and produced constant gloom and dirt' (Avery, 1974: 192). Though the company was paying monetary compensation to them, large and small farmers managed to convince some of the councils from small surrounding villages to forbid open-air calcination in their own municipal territories. The company successfully intrigued (through members of the Spanish Parliament in its pay) to segregate Rio

Tinto as a municipal territory of its own (being until then a part of the territory of Zalamea, a larger town), on the reasonable argument that population in the mining area had increased considerably. The company was keen to have local municipal officers favourable to it.

On 4 February 1888, the immediate causes for the strike had been the complaint against the non-payment of full wages on *manta* days, the demand for the abolition of piecework, and for the end of the deduction of one *peseta* weekly from the wage bill to cover expenses of the medical fund. Maximiliano Tornet, the miners' syndicalist leader, an anarchist who had been deported from Cuba back to Spain some years earlier, had managed to make an alliance with the peasants and farmers (and some landowners and local politicians) who had constituted the Huelva Anti-Smoke League. When the army arrived in the plaza full of striking miners and peasants and peasant families from the region damaged by sulphur dioxide, an argument was going on inside the Rio Tinto town hall over whether open-air *teleras* should be prohibited by municipal decree not only in surrounding villages but also in Rio Tinto itself. In terms of today's language, the local stakeholders (syndicalists, local politicians, peasants and farmers) did not achieve successful conflict resolution, let alone problem resolution. Had the municipality publicly announced a decree against open-air calcination, the tension in the plaza would have diminished, the strike would have been called off. Other stakeholders, that is, the Rio Tinto company and the civil governor in the capital of the province, were in the meantime mobilizing other resources, namely arranging for troops to be brought into action. It is not known for sure who first shouted 'fire', perhaps a civilian from a window (Avery, 1974: 205), but the soldiers understood the shout as an order to start shooting into the crowd.[4]

The interpretation of this episode in terms of *environmentalism* became unexpectedly relevant a century later, as the village of Nerva, in precisely this region, struggled in the 1990s against the regional authorities over the siting of a large hazardous waste dump (precisely in a disused mine), local environmentalists and village officials explicitly appealing to the living memory of that 'year of shots' of 1888 (Garcia Rey, 1996), 50 years before the civil war of 1936–9, when miners of Rio Tinto were massacred again, this time for non-ecological reasons. Meanwhile, sceptics on the thesis of popular environmentalism point out that, in 1888, the workers were more worried about wages than about pollution, and that the peasants and farmers were manipulated by local politicians who wanted to make money from the Rio Tinto company or who had their own disagreements with other politicians at the national level on the treatment given to the British company – so conspicuously British that it sported an Anglican church and a cricket team.[5]

'Retrospective' environmentalism related to mining and air pollution is becoming a staple of social history in many countries. Not only air pollution, but also water pollution (as in the Watarase river in Japan, and in Ilo, Peru) is important. It is present in other types of mining, for instance pollution by mercury, the *azogue* which the Spaniards employed in Potosi and also in Mexico to amalgamate with silver, and which today is used in Amazonian rivers to amalgamate with gold. Mercury was the origin of famous cases of disease in Japan from the 1950s onwards (through the consumption of fish).

*   *   *

Being still few, environmentalists must often go on the defensive. They would love to be proactive but they are reactive, rushing from one threat to the next. In the late 1990s, in the region of Intag (Cotocachi, province of Imbabura) in northern Ecuador, Mitsubishi was defeated by a local non-governmental organization, Decoin, with help from Ecuadorian and international groups, in its plans to start mining for copper. I know this case first-hand, because of my relation with Acción Ecológica (Quito) which helped Decoin. The idea was to relocate a hundred families to make way for open-cast mining, bringing in thousands of miners in order to extract a large reserve of copper. This is a beautiful and fragile area of cloud forest and agriculture, with a mestizo population. Rio Tinto had already shown interest, but its previous incursions in Ecuador (at Salinas in Bolivar, at Molleturo in Azuay) ended in retreats. A Mitsubishi subsidiary, Bishi Metals, started in the early 1990s some preliminary work in Intag. After many meetings with the authorities, on 12 May 1997, a large gathering of members of affected communities resorted to direct action. Most of the company's goods were inventoried and removed from the area (and later given back to the company) and the remaining equipment was burnt with no damage to individuals.

The government of Ecuador reacted by bringing a court case for terrorism (a rare event in Ecuador) against two community leaders and the leader of Decoin, but the case was dismissed by the courts one year later. Attempts at the time to bring in Codelco (the Chilean national copper company) to mine were also defeated, when Acción Ecológica from Quito sent one activist, Ivonne Ramos, to downtown Santiago to demonstrate with support from Chilean environmentalists on the occasion of a state visit of the president of Ecuador, and she was arrested. The publicity convinced Codelco to withdraw. Acción Ecológica also organized a visit by women belonging to the Intag communities, to copper mining areas in Peru, such as Cerro de Pasco, La Oroya and Ilo. The women did their own interviews in those areas, and came back to Intag with their own impressions, carrying sad miners' music and lyrics that became immediate hits in Intag. These triumphant local women still deny to this day that they are environmentalists or, God forbid, eco-feminists.[6] Today there are several initiatives for alternative forms of development in Intag, one of them being the export of 'organic' coffee to Japan arranged through environmental networks first contacted in the fight against Mitsubishi. But the copper ore is still there, underground, and the world demand for copper keeps increasing.

There has long been an awareness that mining implies *Raubwirtschaft* on two grounds: the uncompensated pollution and the exhaustion of the resource without sufficient alternative investment in the colonial or post-colonial territory. Debates on mining royalties are of course much older than the discussion on 'weak' sustainability. Thus the British South Africa Company (BSAC) drew up in 1911 a mining code for Northern Rhodesia (today's Zambia, with its rich copperbelt) which was submitted to the Colonial Office for approval. The Colonial Office attempted to secure some return from mining activities to the local chiefs, for local investment or expenditure. BSAC claimed to have obtained mining concessions from these chiefs. One of the suggestions from London entailed the payment of 1 per cent royalty to the local chiefs. The BSAC strongly objected, and it wrote to the Colonial Office that there was no point in a mining law which would in any way curtail its rights and profits. In the end the British government accepted the 1911 draft which became the Mining Ordinance for a long time (Ndulo, 1987: 123, quoted in Draisma, 1998). Years later, at the end of the 1960s, Kaunda not only nationalized the mines, he also tried to set up CIPEC, a cartel of copper exporting countries (together with Chile, Peru and Congo), but this soon collapsed.

If prices of raw materials go down it is because of oversupply, though some countries (such as Zambia, with copper) have managed both to produce less and to sell at a lower price. The south to north current of raw materials (including energy carriers) is not decreasing in weight terms. Japan is, together with Europe and the USA, one of the main importers. Broadbent (1998: 223–5) tells of a case from Japan, where local activists were successful in the 1970s in keeping the company Showa Denko from building an aluminium smelter in what was called Landfill 8 in Oita Prefecture. (A landfill means in this context the enclosure of a portion of the coastal sea, filling it up with rocks, gravel and earth.) The activists' success led to a decision to build the aluminium smelter elsewhere. Since Showa Denko's image was worsening domestically, the company went to Venezuela to build the smelter, using energy from the very large Guri dam. This hydroelectric energy is much cheaper than it would be in Japan. So displacement occurs because of both push and pull factors.

BOUGAINVILLE AND WEST PAPUA

In the island of Bougainville, the Rio Tinto Zinc company got into trouble because of local opposition despite the agreement the company had made with the government of Papua New Guinea, which has sovereignty over Bougainville, in order to exploit the site of what was described as the most profitable copper and gold mine in the world. The conflict on the island of Bougainville had perhaps really started two centuries years earlier, when the island was visited by the traveller Bougainville, who gave his name both to the island and to the plant now so common in sunny garden walls. Diderot, in his *Supplement to Bougainville's Voyage* (written in 1772), pointed out how the Europeans taught Christianity to the Pacific islanders but also plotted how to enslave them. European arrivals were regularly followed by demographic collapse in many of the Pacific islands. Europeans punish islanders for stealing trinkets – wrote Diderot – and meanwhile they themselves steal a whole country.[7] Two hundred years later, in 1974, it was reported that 'the natives of Bougainville have stopped throwing geologists into the sea ever since the company [Rio Tinto Zinc] declared itself willing to compensate them for the land it had taken with cash and other material services'. However, it was also reported that monetary compensation was not enough:

> The village communities affected gave the highest importance to land as the source of their material standard of life. Land was also the basis of their feelings of security, and the focus of most of their religious attention. Despite continuing compensation payments and rental fees, local resentment over the taking of the land remains high, and there is strong opposition to any expansion of mining in Bougainville, whether by the existing company, the government, or anyone else. (Mezger, 1980: 195)

Finally, the tiny island of 160000 inhabitants erupted into a secessionist war at the end of the 1980s. We notice here the use of languages which are well known but were not actually deployed in Andalusia or Ecuador: the language of sacredness, and the language of national independence. We notice also that, in all cases considered, the language of monetary compensation was brought into play.

Not far from Bougainville, the copper extraction frontier reached Irian Jaya, that is, West Papua, under Indonesia's sovereignty, 30 years ago at a copper and gold mine called Grasberg owned by Freeport McMoRan from New Orleans, a company run by a colourful CEO, Jim Bob Moffet.[8] Rio Tinto has a participation in this mine. The plan was in 2000 to mine *daily* 300000 tons of ore, of which 98 per cent would be dumped into the rivers as tailings. The 'ecological rucksack' of this operation includes not only the discarded tailings but also the overburden, that is all the materials removed before reaching the ore. The total copper content to be finally recovered would be nearly 30 million tons, three years of world production, which would come into the market at a rate which would make Grasberg the supplier of nearly 10 per cent of world copper every year. This open-cast mine is at high altitude, next to a glacier. The deposit originally formed the core of a 4100m mountain, and the bottom of the open pit now lies at the 3100m level. The current expansion would mean an annual extraction of ore which would allow an annual output of 900000 tons of copper and of 2·75 million ounces of gold.[9] Water pollution in the Ajkwa river has been up to now the major environmental complaint, and acid drainage will be an increasing problem.

The ecology of the island is particularly sensitive, and the scale of operations is enormous. In 1977, in the initial stages of operation, some Amungme rebelled, and destroyed the slurry pipeline carrying copper concentrate to the coast. Reprisals by the Indonesian army were terrible. Many complaints against Freeport McMoRan led to an initially unsuccessful class-action suit in New Orleans in April 1996 by Tom Beanal and other members of the Amungme tribe. Tom Beanal declared (at a speech at Loyola University, New Orleans, 23 May 1996):

> These companies have taken over and occupied our land . . . Even the sacred mountains we think of as our mother have been arbitrarily torn up, and they have not felt the least bit guilty . . . Our environment has been ruined, and our forests and rivers polluted by waste . . . We have not been silent. We protest and are angry. But we have been arrested, beaten and put into containers: we have been tortured and even killed.

Tom Beanal was reported later to have received some money from the company for his own NGO, a classic procedure for conflict resolution, but the legal case made some progress in the Louisiana courts in March 1998 on the issue of whether US courts could have jurisdiction. The best-known representative of the Amungme is now Yosepha Alomang, subjected to detention in horrible conditions in 1994, and who was prevented from leaving the country in 1998 when she wanted to attend a Rio Tinto's shareholders' meeting in London.[10]

Some of Freeport's shareholders have been publicly concerned about the liabilities incurred by the company in Indonesia. Henry Kissinger is a director of Freeport. The company was deeply involved with the Suharto regime, giving shares in the company to relatives and associates of the ex-president. Freeport is also the biggest source of tax revenue for Indonesia. What line will the new Indonesian government take? How will the separatist movement in West Papua (Organisasi Papua Merdeka, OPM) see the plans by Freeport (and Rio Tinto) to expand the extraction of copper and gold ore? The OPM has staged ceremonies raising the Papuan flag over the last 30 years, answered violently by the Indonesia Army and by Freeport's security forces (one famous instance took place on Christmas Day of 1994 at Tembagapura, a locality near the Grasberg mine). Will claims for environmental liabilities to be paid by Freeport McMoRan be made, not through a private class-action suit brought by indigenous tribes but as a result of an Indonesian governmental action, an international replica of a Superfund case in the United States? Attempts to obtain indemnities for externalities caused by TNCs outside their legal country of residence are interesting ingredients in the calculation of the many environmental liabilities which the north owes to the south, the sum of which would amount to a large ecological debt (see Chapter 10).

Not only have vast quantities of tailings been dropped in the rivers of that region with major environmental damage, but also many human rights abuses have taken place, including forced displacement of people and many killings by the Indonesian military and police, in cooperation with Freeport's own security service. The Indonesian state had an authoritarian regime (or, less politely, was a capitalist dictatorship) from the mid-1960s until the end of the 1990s, and the circumstances in West Papua, with both a very rich mine and an independentist movement, provided reasons for a heavy military presence. It would be a cruel joke to say that a suitable environmental policy would have allowed externalities to be internalized into the price of exported copper and gold. Environmental economists forget to include the distribution of political power in their analysis. Some of them even believe, in their touching innocence, that environmental damages arise because of 'missing markets'. The language of indigenous territorial rights (whose official acceptance would be a novelty in Indonesia) and the stronger language of a separate national Papuan identity (which is historically relevant, since West Papua was annexed by Indonesia after the departure of the Dutch) may be used nowadays after the end of the dictatorship in order to fight the human and environmental disaster caused by the world's largest gold mine and the third-largest copper mine.

In another case, Broken Hill Proprietary, one of Australia's largest companies, settled a lawsuit brought by indigenous leaders from the area surrounding its Ok Tedi mine, 300 miles east of Freeport's operation in West Papua, inside Papua New Guinea territory. This is a smaller mine than Freeport's. A settlement of about US$400 million was agreed at Ok Tedi. The initial claim against Freeport because of Grasberg was for US$6000 million. Freeport McMoRan is building, with Mitsubishi, a large smelter at Gresik in Java, for export of copper to Japan. Freeport McMoRan also happens to own, in Huelva, Spain, the firm Atlantic Copper, which is the successor to the copper smelting and refining operation of the Spanish Rio Tinto company formed after 1954, and where copper concentrate from Grasberg is taken. It is all one big family.

POLLUTION MIRACLES, AND THE SOCIAL CONSTRUCTION OF NATURE

Sulphur dioxide is produced, not only by copper ore roasting and smelting, but also, and in many regions of the world in much larger quantities, by burning low-quality coal in electric power stations. Such sulphur dioxide emissions have given rise to local conflicts, and even to international conflicts, as in Europe over 'acid rain' in well-known cases of 'transboundary pollution' which also exist in other continents, for instance inside the USA, where acid rain reaches New England from western states. It is not so difficult to decrease emissions of sulphur dioxide by installing scrubbers, or by changing the fuel in power stations. *An intensification of the social conflict may lead to a solution to the problem.* The *teleras* disappeared in Huelva some ten years after the massacre, and nevertheless exports of Rio Tinto copper kept increasing. Broadbent (1998) shows how, following some well-known environmental conflicts in Japan at the end of the 1960s and the beginning of the 1970s, there was a minor 'pollution miracle' in Japan as relates to some pollutants such as sulphur dioxide, and as relates also to mercury contamination, so conspicuous because of the Minamata and Nigata cases (which started in the 1950s). Sulphur dioxide emissions started to decrease in absolute terms earlier in Japan than in Europe.

In Germany, in the mid-19th century, there was a so-called 'chimney war'. Complaints about pollution from sulphur dioxide led to the building of taller and taller chimneys of up to 140 metres even before 1890. The authorities ordered the tall chimneys to be built in order to pacify protests in the immediate surroundings. The factory owners complied willingly in order to disperse the pollution over a larger territory where, it was hoped, it would be mixed up with the pollution from other factories, thus evading responsibility in judicial cases which required cause-and-effect proof of the source of the damage. Discussions on the effects of sulphur dioxide, not on people's health but on the forests, are also over a hundred years old (Bruggemeier and Rommelspacher, 1987, 1992: 35). Momentarily, the chimneys resolved the conflict, if not the problem. Later, the problem of sulphur dioxide emissions itself was to be solved, even in the Ruhr.

In international political conflicts without real substance, such as a dispute between states over a strip of useless territory, by reaching a peace agreement and drawing a new frontier, both the conflict and the problem disappear. Sometimes, as in the last 20 years with the threat by CFC to the ozone layer, or with transboundary sulphur dioxide emissions in Europe, agreements are reached which lead to regimes which resolve both the conflict and the problem. In many other environmental cases, resolving the conflict is not equivalent to solving the problem. On the contrary, resolving the conflict may lead to perpetuating the problem. Both internal and international conflicts are solved by establishing pollution regimes (or regimes of access to natural resources, such as water or fisheries); that is, some sort of agreement is reached on environmental standards and on the rules of behaviour of actors. The standards are not necessarily sustainable. The regimes established may be such that they lead to global warming, to loss of biodiversity or to the exhaustion of an aquifer. For instance, an international conflict over fishing rights may be solved by increasing the fishing quotas, making overfishing ever more acute.

Many anti-nuclear conflicts have been resolved, or never arose (as in Japan or France), though the uncertainties about nuclear accidents remain, together with the doubts on how to control increasing amounts of nuclear waste safely for tens of thousands of years. The French and Japanese attitudes to nuclear power are socially and historically constructed in complicated ways. Both Britain and the USA long ago gave up the idea of building plutonium reactors for electricity production. Both France and Japan have had a love affair with the plutonium economy, recovering waste from nuclear power plants in the hope of using it again. Creys-Malville in France is now closed, a delayed environmental victory nailed down by the arrival of a Green minister in the government in 1998. In Britain, Sellafield, the plutonium-reprocessing plant, which certainly would prefer to stay out of the public limelight, was in 2000 featured in newspaper headlines because of cheating in technical specifications in its exports to Japan. In Japan itself, after the accident at Tokaimura in September 1999, the nuclear industry is on the defensive, and the more obvious objective for the anti-nuclear activists would be the plutonium reactor. In France, the pro-nuclear position of the powerful Communist Party into the 1970s and 1980s is part of the explanation for French attitudes. Japanese attitudes are attributed to lack of energy sources in the country itself, but Japan is a country with a surplus on current account and a very painful experience of nuclear radiation. Though the social conflict over nuclear energy has long been subdued in both countries, the problem of nuclear waste remains, and the possibility of nuclear accidents is also real, in fact enhanced because of the treatment given to nuclear waste through plutonium recovery and reprocessing. Conflict management does not necessarily imply problem resolution.

In order to advance towards problem resolution, what is needed is not conflict resolution, but *conflict exacerbation*. This is not the perspective of public policy experts, or of students of international relations, who professionally have no conception of what an ecological economy should be like, and who are interested in conflict-resolving regimes for their own sake. Conflict resolution experts do not study the indicators and thresholds of the depletion of fisheries, or the enhanced greenhouse effect, or the loss of terrestrial biodiversity, or the accumulation of nuclear waste. They study the regimes by which such issues are resolved, or are pushed under the carpet – it does not matter which.

Coincidentally, in the postmodern, discursive approach, 'Nature' is socially and culturally constructed, and so are, *a fortiori*, conflicts over the use of Nature, similar to disputes between states over a few square miles of useless territory, without real substance. This is not my approach. On the contrary, this is a materialist book. Certainly, conflicts are socially and politically moulded, and their specific forms require contextual analysis. For instance, increased carbon dioxide concentration in the atmosphere is real. Economic growth is still based on burning fossil fuels. The increased greenhouse effect was adequately described in the 1890s, but a hundred years later no (effective) action has yet been taken. No precautionary principle was applied. The delay is due to the joys of free-riding, and also to the distributional obstacles to an agreement on reduction of emissions of carbon dioxide. It is also due to the optimistic interpretation of the phenomenon by scientists for many decades, including Svante Arrhenius himself.

However, the issue-attention cycle of environmental activism cannot be explained only socially. The realities of environmental impacts, the possibilities of technical remediation and the uncertainty of the threats themselves, play an important role. As explained by Downs (1972), public mobilization against the environmental and health costs of pollution achieves media attention, which contributes to further mobilization. Downs believed that the downward part of the attention cycle comes either from technical solutions to the problem (the case of sulphur dioxide) or from the fact that the increasing marginal costs of pollution abatement are seen as too high. Mobilization and media attention are great when solving the issue is feasible and cheap. For instance, diminishing carbon dioxide emissions by commuting less by car and travelling less by plane is feasible, but it is seen as too expensive in the USA in terms of economic costs and in terms of changes in a lifestyle based on cheap oil. Thus, Downs' prediction is that attention to the greenhouse effect will increase and wane according to the price of remediation and consequent social mobilization and media attention. However, against a purely social explanation, the case is that climate events, such as hurricanes, insofar as there are arguments to link them to the trend of climate change, revive the greenhouse issue very much as nuclear incidents have kept the nuclear industry in the spotlight in a pattern of attention which cannot be explained solely by social dynamics.

When problems are real, applying the ostrich principle (instead of the precautionary principle) affords only temporary relief. A social-constructionist view is helpful, nonetheless, to account for the flows and ebbs of environmental protests, for the shifting of public interest from one issue to another, for Japanese dislike of sulphur dioxide and French suspicions over transgenic crops, and for the pro-nuclear atmosphere in both countries at least until the end of the 20th century. Nevertheless, the relentless clash between economy and environment cannot be permanently silenced by socially-constructed hopes of an angelical dematerialization. This clash goes together with the displacement of costs to weaker partners, with the exercise of de facto property rights on the environment, with the disproportionate burden of pollution which falls on some groups, with the dispossession of natural resources for other groups. All this gives rise to real grievances over real issues. Hence the birth of political ecology.

THE ORIGINS AND SCOPE OF POLITICAL ECOLOGY

Ecological distribution conflicts (that is, conflicts over traded or untraded environmental resources or services) are studied by political ecology, a new field born from local case studies of rural geography and anthropology which today extends to the national and international levels. Thus the first sections in this chapter could be titled 'The political ecology of copper mining'.

Anthropology and ecology have long been in contact, as ecological anthropology or cultural ecology. This field was characterized by adaptationist and functionalist approaches, as in Roy Rappaport's splendid book of 1967 on the Tsembaga-Maring, where social conflict was excluded, or in Netting's work on peasant families and sustainable agriculture (Netting, 1993). It was the functionalist method and not the realities of human ecology themselves which converted ecological anthropology into the study of localized adaptations to specific ecosystems. In fact, human ecology is characterized by social conflict, in the sense that humans have no biological instructions on the exosomatic use of energy and materials, and our territoriality is politically constructed. Humans are certainly not exceptional in the fact that they make use of energy and materials, they are in that respect very much like other animals. To understand human society we must study the physical, biological and social determinants of such patterns of 'societal metabolism' (Fischer-Kowalski, 1998; Fischer-Kowalski and Haberl, 1997; Haberl, 2001). What makes humans exceptional, in comparison to other animals, is not only our talking and laughing and our evolving cultures but our potential for enormous and historically increasing *intra–specific differences* in the exosomatic use of energy and materials, as Lotka put it almost 90 years ago. Before ecological anthropology became functionalist and adaptationist, the anthropologist Leslie White, influenced by European social energetics and also by Marxism, tried unsuccessfully to develop a theory of energy use linked to modes and relations of production (as Podolinsky had also tried to do in 1880) (Martinez-Alier with Schlüpmann, 1987).

The anthropologist Eric Wolf, in 1972, introduced the expression 'political ecology'. It had been used already by Bertrand de Jouvenel in 1957 (Rens, 1996). Geographers have been more active in the new field of political ecology than anthropologists. Also several journals started by activists carry or have carried the title 'Political Ecology', in Germany, Mexico, France, Austria, Italy and probably in other countries since the 1980s and early 1990s. Since 1991, I myself have edited the journal *Ecologia Politica*, a Hispanic sister to James O'Connor's journal, *Capitalism, Nature, Socialism*. The field of political ecology is growing. The electronic *Journal of Political Ecology*, based at the University of Arizona, gives a Netting Prize to the best article each year. Netting's work was done mostly at that university, and it was geographically wide-ranging, extremely scholarly and of great significance. His analysis emphasized adaptation over conflict. He praised the peasant economy as able to absorb population increases by changing cultivation systems, and to this argument by Boserup, supported by careful fieldwork in several countries, he added the argument that peasant agriculture was more energy-efficient than industrial agriculture. This is a good ecological argument (known since Pimentel's research of 1973), useful information when criticizing the prices in the economy. However, Netting's reasoning that the peasantry would survive as a consequence of increased energy prices is not convincing because modern agriculture, although intensive in fossil fuel energy, uses only a small share of all the energy inputs in the economy (not including in the accounts the sun energy for photosynthesis, which is a continuous and gratuitous flow). Keeping the world peasantry alive would not by itself save a lot of energy compared with the energy input for a large modern economy. However, the collateral effects of avoiding industrialization and urbanization in the western pattern in China, India, Indonesia and Africa while there is still time would be extremely significant.

Netting's pro-peasant position was certainly not popular in the 1960s and 1970s. He saw Soviet collectivization as a manifestation of the trend to concentration of farms, which also existed in the USA. This was a bad model for the majority of humankind. He regularly dismissed class conflict inside rural society. Sharecropping was interpreted by Netting, not as an exploitative system designed to increase labour input and intensity to the landowner's benefit, but as an adaptive system, the virtues of smallholding triumphing over the inequality of land ownership. Netting died before he could join the discussion on conservation of biodiversity, which would have strengthened his pro-peasant position against industrial agriculture. A political movement is growing (ecological neo-Narodnism, eco-agrarianism, eco-Zapatism), drawing on ecological economics, which will insist that increases in agricultural productivity as commonly measured do not take environmental impacts into account. Political struggle explains more than functionalist adaptation.

A more conflictual political ecology than that of Netting (who considered himself an ecological anthropologist or cultural ecologist, not a political ecologist) began in the 1980s in rural researches by geographers, such as those collected in Blaikie and Brookfield (1987), studying the changing relations between social (economic, political) structures and the use of the environment, taking into account not only class or caste divisions, not only differences in income and power, but also the gender division of property, labour and knowledge (Agarwal, 1992). For instance, there are different explanations for land erosion caused by peasants. Sometimes, peasants are forced to farm mountain slopes because the valley land is appropriated by large landholdings. As they themselves acknowledge, farming on the slopes is likely to cause erosion (Stonich, 1993). Or, in other cases, because of state policies, peasants are caught up in a 'scissors crisis' of low agricultural prices, which forces them to shorten fallow periods and intensify production in order to support their meagre incomes, and this implies increased soil erosion (Zimmerer, 1996). In other cases, the communal system of collectively fallowed lands break down (because of population growth or because of the pressure of production for the market) and land is degraded. In yet other cases, there might be overgrazing, perhaps connected to failures in the communal control of pasture land. Social structures and the use of the environment are linked in many ways. In India in the 1970s and 1980s, there was much work on the management of common property resources. Elsewhere there was also research on the birth of new communal institutions for resource management (McCay and Acheson, 1989; Berkes, 1989; Ostrom, 1990; Hanna and Munasinghe, 1995; Berkes and Folke, 1998). Much research has been done on the different ways by which communities have developed institutions in order to resist social and environmental 'tragedies of enclosures' (whether triggered by state takeover or by privatization). There is, then, an immense amount of research on rural political ecology produced by Third World activists themselves, either in English or, more often, in other languages.

The field of political ecology is now moving beyond local rural situations into the wider world. Political ecology studies ecological distribution conflicts. By ecological distribution is meant the social, spatial and inter-temporal patterns of access to the benefits obtainable from natural resources and from the environment as a life support system, including its 'cleaning up' properties. The determinants of ecological distribution are in some respects natural (climate, topography, rainfall patterns, minerals, soil quality and so on). They are clearly, in other respects, social, cultural, economic, political and technological.[11] In part, political ecology overlaps with political economy, which in the classical tradition is the study of economic distribution conflicts. For instance, there are urban people so poor and powerless that they cannot buy potable water (Swyngedouw, 1997). Rural poverty will intensify the collection of wood in arid lands, or the use of dung as fuel, with negative consequences on land fertility. In fact, urban poverty also intensifies even more absurdly the use of firewood, brought by the trainload into the large metropolises of India. A different income endowment might allow poor families to 'climb up' the cooking fuel ladder towards bottled liquefied petroleum gas (LPG), a real 'win-win' solution for once.

In many other conflicts, there is no market (use of carbon sinks and reservoirs, pollution from sulphur dioxide, tailings dumped on rivers, oustees from dams, 'biopiracy'). Ecological distribution conflicts therefore take place outside actual markets, or even outside fictitious markets (where compensations may be assessed or negotiated). The orthodox economists disguise ecological distribution conflicts under words such as 'externalities' or 'market failures', and the ecological economists retort that 'externalities' are 'cost-shifting successes'. Problems are displaced, costs are indeed shifted, but then, as pointed out in Chapter 2 and throughout this book, one fundamental question of ecological economics arises, namely, in which numeraires or in which qualitative scales, such shifted 'costs' will be valued. As Shiv Visvanathan (1997: 237) puts it in his application of Gandhian economics to the Narmada oustees: the accountant's ledger is not commensurable with a mourning ritual.

Many books[12] have collected a number of studies on different ecological conflicts on land degradation, agricultural seeds, biopiracy and bioprospecting, use of water, urban ecology, industrial pollution, defence of the forests and struggles over fisheries. In some books (Bryant and Bailey, 1997) the emphasis is not on issues but on actors: the state, business, NGOs, the grassroots. In a few political ecology books (for instance, Rocheleau *et al.*, 1996) the emphasis is on gender. A common theme of these books is the study of social conflicts over the access to, and the destruction of, environmental resources and services (whether such resources and services are traded or not). This defines the field of political ecology. Studies on political ecology in Canada have been collected by Keil *et al.* (1998), thus moving the field towards the north. 'Environmental justice' conflicts in the USA in the 1980s and 1990s (see below, Chapter 8) are still absent from most books on political ecology, perhaps owing to disciplinary demarcation disputes.

Anthropologists and geographers working on the rural Third World have acquired a proprietary interest in political ecology, while environmental justice in the USA is the turf of the civil rights activists, the sociologists and the experts on race relations. However, DiChiro's study of successful women-led struggles in South Central Los Angeles against an incinerator of 1600 tons of waste per day, LANCER (Los Angeles City Energy Recovery Project), was included in a book on political ecology (Goldman, 1998). Laura Pulido's pioneering research (1991, 1996) on urban struggles against pollution and on enclosure threats in the western USA against remaining communal land and water rights, belongs simultaneously to political ecology and to studies on environmental justice. This also applies to Devon Peña's work on Chicano environmental struggles (Peña, ed. 1998). Research on occupational health and safety, from the popular more than the engineering viewpoint, as also of conflicts over urban waste disposal, urban planning and the system of transport in cities, belongs to political ecology.

PROPERTY RIGHTS AND RESOURCE MANAGEMENT

The analysis of this topic would be easier if the terminology had not been thrown into a state of confusion for some years (at least in English) as a result of Garrett Hardin's article, 'The Tragedy of the Commons' (1968). Parking space in the streets of Santa Barbara, California, was still unregulated in the 1960s, and Hardin, who lived there, wrongly asserted that this situation of open access could be described as a 'commons'. There is no excuse for Hardin's mistake (soon pointed out by Aguilera Klink, Berkes, Bromley and other authors), for the word 'commons' is known among the population at large, including biologists. A commons is an area shared by a community according to some rules, as with for instance, the original Boston Commons.

In his article, Hardin discussed only two situations: (1) open access (which he falsely termed 'commons') and (2) private property. A better classification of forms of property would be: (1) open access, (2) community property, with rules of use for the members, and excluding non-members, (3) private property, and (4) state property. There are also other forms, such as municipal property, whose effects on the management of resources will differ greatly, depending on the size of the town and its economic activity.

Attacks on the commons on grounds of economic efficiency have been part of the capitalist diet for three centuries: the magic of private property would turn sand into gold, wrote Arthur Young. Hardin's new twist was to attack the (misnamed) commons on grounds of environmental mismanagement. Hardin called attention in his article to a phenomenon which actually exists in situations in which there is *open access* or *free access* to resources, as in the case of high seas whaling in the absence of international regulation. Thus, from an economic point of view, there would be no incentive to conserve whales, not just with a view to future generations but even for the present one. As long as the additional revenue obtained from fishing is greater than the additional cost (that is, if catching one more whale is cheap in comparison with the income obtained by turning it into meat or oil), that whale will be caught. It may happen that people have non-economic motivations, for instance, Captain Ahab's revengeful obsession with Moby Dick at whatever marginal cost, or on the contrary they may entertain a feeling that whales should be outside the market to prevent them from being killed. According to Hardin, the open-access situation was highly frequent, and the best cure was the privatization of resources (or strict state regulations). Privatization would allow whale-lovers to outbid whale-killers in the market.

To Hardin's way of thinking, when the population rose, open-access resources would be increasingly exploited. Individual gain would lead to collective wretchedness, not just in coming generations but even in the present one. One cannot but agree except that he mistakenly termed *commons* what are open-access resources and he emphasized population growth more than market pressures. Indeed, according to Hardin the very growth of population could be interpreted in terms of the (falsely named) 'tragedy of the commons', since the additional cost to ecosystems of one more child was scarcely noticeable for the family into which it was born. The only consideration for the family would be the private cost of supporting the child and this cost would, moreover, soon turn into profit in the case of poor families, when the child was sent out to work. The environment has no owner, and this is where the problem lies; we load it with burdens without paying anything out of our private economies in return. Hardin (in line with Kenneth Boulding) proposed a system of procreation quotas, whereby each couple (or each woman) would be entitled to have only two children and would have to pay a fee if they (or she) had more, on account of the environmental costs deriving from a growing population. A market in procreation permits could easily develop out of such a system.

As regards fishing, the threat to the existence of resources as a result of open access led some time ago to international agreements (the 200 miles exclusive zone) the purpose of which is to manage such resources as if they were in communal ownership, which implies exclusion of those not belonging to the communal group. Similarly, there are agreements whereby the atmosphere is not always treated as a free-access dump where anybody may get rid of his or her effluents. Thus emissions of CFC which destroy the ozone layer are regulated. Some agreements are scarcely binding, like the international treaty on climatic change signed in Rio de Janeiro in 1992 and its additional protocols. Nevertheless, their very existence provides an indication that it is known that open access leads to abuse.

A famous paragraph from Hardin's famous article begins as follows: 'Picture a pasture open to all. . .'. In such circumstances, as with open-sea whaling, anybody might well be interested in putting an extra cow or sheep on the land, because the environmental costs would be suffered by everybody in the form of the degradation of the pasture through overgrazing, whereas the revenue from fattening the extra cow or sheep, and the milk or the wool, would be appropriated by the owner. The question now is, where is that famous pasture open to all? There were conflicts on access under the Spanish Mesta, or in Great Britain after the enclosure of common lands, when 'sheep ate men'. There was open access in America after 1492. Elinor Melville explained how the number of sheep increased and the number of Otomi Indians decreased in the Mezquital Valley in Mexico, until the number of sheep also collapsed because of the effect of such an irruption of ungulates on the quality of the pastures. An agricultural irrigated valley became almost a desert (Melville, 1994). It remains the case that, in pasture lands, open access is the exception rather than the rule.

In community property, all the owners hold the right to use the natural resource (not always in equal shares), while non-owners are excluded from its use. It may happen that the resources are also abused in community property situations if the rules are not respected. It may be that the community becomes increasingly involved in commercial logic to the detriment of the logic of use value, and then the pressure of export production on resources surges, which is added to the rising demographic pressure. Forms of property coevolve according to social and environmental circumstances. In many cases, human communities have invented systems for community management of resources. Thus, as water in aquifers becomes scarce, perhaps it will cease to be of open access. According to the power of different groups, it might become private property or communal property. There exists also a powerful 'institutional lock-in' when, despite the obvious environmental disadvantages of a given situation, forms of property do not change.

As argued by Hardin, it is indeed true that private property causes the costs of excessive exploitation of resources to fall on the owner, who will compare them with his private revenue. However, if there is a temporal asymmetry between costs and revenue, as is usually the case, that is, if revenue is due now and costs are due in the future, as occurs for instance with costs of future non-availability when an exhaustible wood, fishing ground, pasture or mining resource is exploited, then community property is probably a better system. The individual owner will most likely have a shorter time horizon and a higher implicit rate of discount than those managing a community property. A community lasts longer than a company, than a private owner and even than a family. In practice, however, we would find many different situations. Lastly, with regard to state property, its influence on the management of natural resources will depend on the logic applied. If the state as owner leaves such resources in community hands that apply their own logic of use (as in mangrove swamps used sustainably by local groups), then the situation is different from that of a state which directly or indirectly (through administrative concessions to private enterprise) applies short-term commercial logic to the exploitation of such resources.

NOTES

1. Butte has been known as the 'richest hill on Earth' in Montana local lore and history, an honour which belongs rather to Potosi's Cerro Rico. Butte recently 'has earned the more dubious distinction of being the Environmental Protection Agency's geographically largest 'Superfund' cleanup site, a legacy of mining history' (Finn, 1998: 250, fn.8). Butte used to belong to the Anaconda company, which bought from Guggenheim the Chuquicamata mine in Chile, possibly the largest copper mine on earth. No superfund for Chuquicamata . . . or for Potosi.
2. In Bolivia, from the early 20th century, tin was extracted from Siglo XX and Catavi, underground mines in the altiplano. The development of open-cast mining in other countries contributed to the collapse of Bolivia's tin industry in the 1980s. In particular, open-cast mining in Brazil, and the substitution of other metals such as aluminium for tin undermined profitability in the Bolivian mines (Dore, 2000: 16).
3. Ivonne Yanez, in the ELAN website, 4 October 1996; also Diaz Palacios (1988), Balvin *et al.* (1995).
4. Ferrero Blanco, (1994: 214) lists the articles of the Criminal Code which, according to the politician Romero Robledo, were infringed.
5. Sceptics also point out correctly that in Aznalcollar, a village inside the polluted area of 1888, the miners of Bolliden clamoured in 1999 for 'their' mine to reopen, against middle-class environmentalists from Seville and Madrid. Bolliden is a Swedish–Canadian company whose tailings dike collapsed in 1998, contaminating with heavy metals ten thousand hectares of irrigated agriculture (where cultivation has been discontinued) and threatening the Doñana national park in the delta of the Guadalquivir. Bolliden has since abandoned the Aznalcollar mine.
6. Acción Ecológica (Quito) and Observatorio Latinoamericano de Conflictos Ambientales (Santiago de Chile), *A los mineros: ni un paso atras en Junin-Intag*, Quito, 1999.

7.   I am grateful to Aaron Sachs for reminding me of Diderot's writings on Bougainville.
8.   Documentation on this case comes from the files from the Permanent People's Tribunal on Global Corporations and Human Wrongs organized by the Lelio Basso Foundation at the School of Law, University of Warwick, Coventry, 22–5 March 2000. See also Eyal Press, 'Freeport-McMoRan at Home and Abroad', *The Nation*, 31 July–7 August, 1995, and Robert Bryce (from the newspaper *Austin Chronicle*), 'Spinning Gold', *Mother Jones*, September–October 1996.
9.   *Mining Journal* (London), 329 (8448), 26 September 1997.
10. Survival for Tribal Peoples (London), Media Briefing May 1998, 'Rio Tinto critic gagged'.
11. O'Connor (1993a, 1993b), Martinez-Alier and O'Connor (1996, 1999), Beckenbach (1996). For a pioneering collection of essays, see Schnaiberg *et al.* (1986).
12. Ghai and Vivian (1992), Friedman and Rangan (1993), Taylor (1995), Gadgil and Guha (1995), Gould, Schnaiberg and Weinberg (1996), Peet and Watts (1996), Guha and Martinez-Alier (1997), Goldman (1998). This is not an exhaustive list.

5.   Mangroves versus shrimps

As we have seen, the clash between economy and environment is studied by ecological economics. I have also explained the birth of political ecology as the study of ecological distribution conflicts. This chapter will now turn to empirical research on one current ecological distribution conflict. I shall describe instances of resistance to shrimp farming. First, some remarks on sources of information are in order. The bibliography to the present book lists publications mostly in English and of academic origin, but there is an explosion of research and communication by activists themselves which recalls the beginning of the international socialist movement, though this time with wider geographical reach, with many more women activists, and using not only printed journals and leaflets but also the Internet. I have doubts concerning the preservation of source materials in NGO archives, or briefly posted on the Internet. The present chapter is based on information from around the world, some of it gathered through participant observation, most of it from the archives of the environmental organization Acción Ecológica from Ecuador.

Shrimp are produced in two different ways. As for other commodities in world trade, by studying such *filières* or 'product-regimes' (as Konrad von Moltke calls them), we can identify and follow the interventions of different actors at different points in the chain, motivated by differents interests and values. Shrimps are fished in the sea (sometimes at the cost of destroying turtles) or they are 'farmed' in ponds in coastal areas. Such aquaculture is increasing as shrimp become a valuable item of world trade. Mangrove forests are sacrificed for commercial shrimp farming. This chapter considers the conflict between mangrove conservation and shrimp exports in different countries. Who has title to the mangroves, who wins and who loses in this tragedy of enclosures? Which languages of valuation are used by different actors in order to compare the increase in shrimp exports and the losses in livelihoods and in environmental services? The economic valuation of damages is only one of the possible languages of valuation which are relevant in practice. Who has the power to impose a particular language of valuation?

A TRAGEDY OF ENCLOSURES

In many coastal areas of the tropical world, in Ecuador, Honduras, Sri
Lanka, Thailand, Indonesia, India, Bangladesh, the Philippines and
Malaysia, there is social resistance to the introduction of shrimp farming
for export since this implies the uprooting of mangroves in order to build
the ponds. In such areas, poor people live sustainably in or near the mangrove forests, by collecting shellfish, by fishing, by making use of mangrove
wood for charcoal and building materials. The mangroves are usually
public land in all countries, being in the tidal zone, but governments give
private concessions for shrimp farming or the land is enclosed by shrimp
growers despite specific environmental laws and court decisions protecting
the mangroves as valuable ecosystems.

Shrimp or prawn production entails the loss of livelihood for people
living directly from, and also selling, mangrove products. Beyond direct
human livelihood, other functions of mangroves are also lost, perhaps
irreversibly, such as coastal defence against sea level rise, breeding
grounds for fish, carbon sinks, repositories of biodiversity (for example,
genetic resources resistant to salinity), together with aesthetic values.
Pollution from the shrimp ponds destroys the local fisheries. Also wild
shrimp disappear because of the loss of breeding grounds in mangroves
and because they are overharvested as seed for the ponds. As John Kurien
has put it:

> Large tracts of coastal lands and expanses of open seas, which were under the
> de jure control of the state and/or having some customary rights of access to
> local communities, are being handed over to industrial interests to raise shrimp
> or harvest fish. This has created the beginnings of a modern enclosure move-
> ment, pushing out from the coastal lands and offshore sea, persons who had tra-
> ditionally made a livelihood from these natural resources. (Kurien, 1997: 116).

The focus of this chapter is on shrimp aquaculture, strongly supported
by the World Bank until the mid-1990s and even later, as part of the drive
for non-traditional exports to repay the external debts and to enter the path
of export-led growth. The 'Blue Revolution' was going to produce 'pink
gold'. A new world industry of about US$10 billion exports per year has
indeed been created, at high cost. It is a non-sustainable industry, migrating from place to place, leaving behind a trail of barren landscapes and des-
titute people. What was traditionally, in some areas, small-scale use of
marine resources, or traditional aquaculture, became privately owned
single-purpose enterprises. Not only mangroves, but also some farming
areas have been destroyed, particularly in India and Bangladesh, where
small farmers, who once harvested rice and other crops near the sea in small

plots of land, have been dislodged by force, or by salinization from the encroaching shrimp ponds.

The opposition to shrimp industrial exploitation is led by poor people, who live from mangroves in a sustainable way. That is to say, mangrove destruction is not only an ecological threat to a valuable ecosystem but also a social threat for them. External debt pressure on exporting countries, neo-liberal doctrines and ecological blindness of northern importing consumers, together with a flagrant lack of local governmental action to protect the environment in most shrimp-producer countries, are the main driving forces of mangrove destruction. These cases are also examples of unequal trade because of environmental and social cost shifting to exporting areas. In political terms, the conflict between mangrove protection and the shrimp industry is an example of two, more general, competing political regimes, namely global free trade and environmental protection.

Although the conflicts analysed below have local scenarios, attention will be paid to the relationship between local actions (or omissions) and global environmental networks. Consumer daily decisions and local governmental permissive attitudes damage ecosystems and people's livelihoods. On the other side, local action to protect mangroves by poor people trying to preserve their way of life has beneficial consequences for their own survival. It also sets in motion international networks which have a role in global environmental governance. There are then different spatial and temporal scales at which social actors intervene, and there are also different languages of valuation deployed. In principle, local livelihoods are not a concern of international organizations devoted to the 'cult of wilderness'.

Official decision makers may decide that a proper cost–benefit analysis would help them in taking a decision on whether the shrimp industry should be stopped, and they may also demand environmental impact assessments. Other stakeholders, such as international environmental organizations or local environmental groups, or local groups of inhabitants who do not call themselves environmentalists, may use other languages of valuation, and try to implement different procedures of decision making. At each of the particular locations where the conflict of mangroves versus shrimp exists, we could ask, what is the value of shrimps compared to the value of lost livelihoods and the value of lost environments? In which metrics should such values be measured?

ECUADOR, HONDURAS AND COLOMBIA

In the fight against shrimp farming, people who make a living from the mangroves have resorted, when circumstances have allowed them, to destroying the shrimp ponds, replanting rhizofora seedlings as a symbolic gesture and perhaps with some real hope of reconstructing the vanished mangroves. Greenpeace participated in a joint action in July 1998 with Fundecol (a local grassroots group of about 300 people in Muisne, Ecuador), together with some other environmental groups and sympathetic observers (such as myself). This consisted in destroying at sunrise one crop of shrimps from an illegal pond by opening a hole in one wall, letting the water flow out, and replanting mangrove seedlings. The presence of the *Rainbow Warrior*'s motley crew gave the necessary moral strength to the local groups but both the destruction of that particular illegal pond, and the replanting, were ideas proposed earlier by Fundecol. Whether replanting the mangroves is a successful instance of restoration ecology, or whether it results in a much simplified ecosystem, is a controversial issue of importance for assessing the benefits and costs of mangrove destruction by shrimp farming.

People who make a living in the mangroves are learning to introduce the words 'environment' and 'ecology' into their vocabularies of protest. It is the intermediary NGOs which have given an explicit environmental meaning to their livelihood struggles, connecting them to wider networks such as the Mangrove Action Project or the International Shrimp Action Network (ISANet). In Ecuador there was a rumour in early 1999 that shrimp ponds built on destroyed mangroves in public lands over the five previous years were going to become legal private property, or at least that payment of a fee of US$1000 per hectare would convert 60 000ha of illegal ponds built after 1994 into legal 99-year leases (under art. 12 of a proposed Law for the Rationalization of Public Finances). Greenpeace, in its campaign against shrimp farming, sent a letter to Ecuador's president, arguing in terms of the livelihood of the local population, the ecological and economic value of the functions of mangroves, and citing also Odum's and Arding's 1991 analysis of the 'emergy' (embodied energy) of mangroves which is dilapidated when they are destroyed (Odum and Arding, 1991).

'We are aware of economic research of Ecuador's mangrove ecosystem,' wrote, on 18 March 1999, Michael Hagler, Greenpeace's ocean and fisheries campaigner, member of the steering committee of ISANet, 'that has valued the various goods and services provided by such ecosystems to the economy annually at US$13 000 per hectare . . . we fail to see the economic justification of sacrificing tens of billions of dollars of long term economic benefits to be gained over the proposed period of the 99 years leases in order to gain a one-off payment of 60 million dollars in the short term.' Greenpeace warned the president of other dangers, such as new diseases (as actually happened with the 'white spot', later in 1999) and the potential for a major eco-conscious consumer backlash against farmed shrimp. An alternative policy was urged on the president, based on coastal ecosystem restoration and preservation, and the bolstering of coastal communities' self-reliance and development. This was supported by the accounts of the enormous 'emergy' exports which the shrimp industry represented. Studies elsewhere in Latin America and in Asian shrimp-producing countries gave similar results. Hence the Supreme Court of India's order of December 1996 (see below) to close and ban all industrial shrimp aquaculture within the country's coastal regulation zone. The court had accepted evidence which clearly demonstrated that the costs of the harm done to coastal environment and coastal communities far outweighed the value of any benefits, including foreign exchange earnings, that could be attributed to the shrimp industry.

One week earlier, Fundecol had distributed a message to international environmental networks couched in a different language. It included (in Spanish) the following call from a woman against what would be described in the USA as 'environmental racism':

> We have always been ready to cope with everything, and now more than ever, but they want to humiliate us because we are black, because we are poor, but one does not choose the race into which one is born, nor does one choose not to have anything to eat, nor to be ill. But I am proud of my race and of being *conchera* because it is my race which gives me strength to do battle in defence of what my parents were, and my children will inherit; proud of being *conchera* because I have never stolen anything from anyone, I have never taken anybody's bread from his mouth to fill mine, because I have never crawled on my knees asking anybody for money, and I have always lived standing up. Now we are struggling for something which is ours, our ecosystem, but not because we are professional ecologists but because we must remain alive, because if the mangroves disappear, a whole people disappears, we all disappear, we shall no longer be part of the history of Muisne, we shall ourselves exist no longer . . . I do not know what will happen to us if the mangroves disappear, we shall eat garbage in the outskirts of the city of Esmeraldas or in Guayaquil, we shall become prostitutes, I do not know what will happen to us if the mangroves disappear . . . what I know is that I shall die for my mangroves, even if everything falls down my mangroves will remain, and my children will also stay with me, and I shall fight to give them a better life than I have had . . . We think, if the *camaroneros* who are not the rightful owners nevertheless now prevent us and the *carboneros* from getting through the lands they have taken, not allowing us to get across the *esteros*, shouting and shooting at us, what will happen next, when the government gives them the lands, will they put up big 'Private Property' signs, will they even kill us with the blessing of the President?[1]

Killing threats must be understood literally even in Ecuador, which has been an island of peace between Colombia and Peru. In Honduras (Stonich, 1991) the conservation of mangroves has exacted a price in human lives such as those of Israel Ortiz Avila and Marín Zeledonio

Alvarado killed on 4 October, 1997 in an area called 'La Iguana'. The movement in Honduras has been successful because of the effectiveness of Coddeffagolf (Comité para la Defensa y Desarrollo de la Flora y Fauna del Golfo de Fonseca) led by Jorge Varela, recipient of the Goldman Prize in 1999. An international meeting in Honduras in 1996 (with representatives from Latin America, the USA, India and Sweden) had issued the Declaration of Choluteca (16 October 1996) asking for a worldwide moratorium on shrimp farming. After the deaths of October 1997, Varela stated:

> Today, the artisanal fishermen cannot move freely across the swamps and mangroves where before they found their livelihood (*sustento*), for the camaroneros have appropriated not only the land concessions granted to them by the government but also the surrounding areas. With the complicity of our government, we have given away our people's patrimony to a few national and foreign individuals, and we have deprived thousands of persons of their livelihood. We have turned the blood of our people into an appetizer.[2]

Such statements from Honduras and Ecuador carry the implication that human life and human dignity have dimensions beyond money valuation. The appropriate languages are livelihood, food security, human rights, community territorial rights, and not 'the internalization of externalities' in the price system, or the 'polluter pays principle', or 'cost–benefit' analysis.

Mangroves are also under threat at various points in other central American countries, such as Guatemala. In San Blas, Nayarit, Mexico, local groups are fighting against gigantic projects for shrimp farming and for tourism involving the destruction of thousands of hectares of mangroves, particularly a project by Granjas Aquanova.[3] Even in eco-friendly Costa Rica there was the intention of changing in 1998 the legislation protecting mangroves so as to allow shrimp aquaculture, permitting the construction of channels through the mangroves to provide shrimp ponds with both access to sea water and convenient discharge points for pond effluent. Greenpeace and other members of ISANet urged Costa Rican legislators to oppose this change.[4]

On the Pacific Coast of Colombia pressure by the shrimp industry is increasing, though mangroves have been mostly preserved until now. Very near the border with Ecuador, in Tumaco, sustainable extraction of shells sold locally or to Ecuador is part of the everyday economy of a few thousand women. On both sides of the border, the defence of the mangroves is connected to the birth of an African–American movement in a vigorous process of 'ethnogenesis' (as shown by Grueso *et al.,* 1997).[5] In the case of Colombia, the demand for political autonomy gets more legal support from the Constitution than in Ecuador. There is much contact among family members across the Colombia–Ecuador border in this area. On both sides of the border, women are the main losers when mangroves are converted into shrimp farms, because they lose access to a communal source of food and cash income, in a pattern well known from other ecological distribution conflicts around the world related to access to water, fuelwood and pasture lands (Agarwal, 1992). In Tumaco, one or two local cooperatives have been successful in settting up small-scale shrimp farming, though industrial shrimp growers predominate, and they exercise increasing pressure to build large shrimp ponds. Pressure of exports on local resources is exercised also by oil palm plantations along the coast on both sides of the border and inland from the mangrove area. Local leaders are against such external pressures and they convey a doctrine of sustainable use of the mangroves. Thus an interview in Tumaco with José Joaquín Castro, leader of Asocarlet (the association of charcoal makers, who sell it for local consumption), elicited a description in the late 1990s of the burgeoning conflict in the following terms:

> The mangroves are part of our culture, as you can see. From the time the first slaves arrived here, what they found as an alternative for livelihood was the wide mangrove forest, and today, when we are moving out of the 20th century towards the 21st century, the mangroves still exist despite development. For us in the Pacific Coast, the priority are the mangroves as a means of subsistence, as a means of protection. From the mangroves we obtain our food, and the charcoal for cooking food, and also the wood to build our homes which are 80 per cent mangrove wood. The young mangroves are not cut down. We cut in one zone today, we come back in one year, and there is new material to be cut. If we keep the mangroves, then we have fish, we have shrimp, we have crabs. But the industrial camaroneros started to invade our lands, without asking us, the *Negro* people, not taking into account that this is the terrain of the charcoal maker, the wood collector, the concheras, the fishermen. They surveyed the area from the air, flying over it and making topographic measurements, then they asked for concessions from the State of one thousand or more hectares each, and they cut and uprooted all the mangroves, then the mangroves will not grow again. They did not take into account that behind this strip of mangroves there are many families who obtain their livelihood from them, and without any piety at all, they displaced the charcoal maker, and the fishermen . . . They put up notices of 'private property'.[6]

So, despite the fact that property rights on the mangrove forests are legally clearly established in favour of the state, and despite the fact that there has been a traditional usage by local communities, the shrimp growers attempt to *change* the property rights to their own benefit. This is locally perceived as a social and environmental 'tragedy of enclosures' not only in Ecuador, Honduras and Colombia but also in other places around the world where similar conflicts have arisen.

SHRIMP FARMING IN SOUTH AND SOUTH-EAST ASIA

While Ecuador was producing about 105 000 metric tons of shrimp in 1995 (of which about 95 per cent was farmed, and only 5 per cent fished), other giants of the industry were Thailand and Indonesia, the former with 330 000 tons (of which 67 per cent was farmed), the latter with 195 000 (of which 41 per cent was farmed). Vietnam is rapidly increasing its farmed shrimp production. India and Bangladesh are important producers, but opposition is strong in both countries. China is an important producer, and Taiwan's industry flourished in the 1970s, and then declined. The world total production of shrimp in 1995 was 2 607 000 tons, of which 712 000 tons were farmed and 1 895 000 fished. The trend is towards an increase in farmed shrimp, and a decrease in wild caught shrimp because of overexploitation of fisheries and because of turtle protection.[7]

In the Philippines, aquaculture activities were primarily responsible for the clearing of more than 338 000ha of mangrove forest since 1968, and seriously affected the coastal fisheries catch (Gopinath and Gabriel, 1997: 201). Broad and Cavanagh (1993: 114–15) reported:

> Eliodoro 'Ely' de la Rosa, a forty-three-year-old father of five, had been a fisherman and a leader of the fishers' group LAMBAT . . . Ely was deeply concerned that Manila Bay was dying, that there would be no fish for his children and grandchildren. He talked of his organization's efforts to halt the destruction of the coastal mangroves. He spoke eloquently of the dangers of prawn pond expansion, of the need to stand up to the prawn-pond owners and other mangrove destroyers, and of his plans to start a mangrove replanting program. For his visions and for his ability to inspire others to take action against the impediments to these visions, he was murdered [on 22 January 1990].

For the general context in the Philippines, see Primavera (1991).

In Thailand, despite the opposition of environmental groups such as Yadfon in Trang province, the destruction of mangroves has followed a familiar pattern. Ponds have an average lifespan of less than five years: 'shrimp farmers simply march down the coastline, leaving hundreds of miles of poisonous brown blotches in their wake. The ponds saturate the surrounding soil with salt and pollute the land and water with a chemical sludge made up of fertilizer and antibiotics as well as larvicides, shrimp feed and waste' (Mydans, 1996).

In Malaysia, where 20 per cent of the available mangroves have been slated for aquaculture development, there are artisanal fishermen's movements in some parts of the country trying to stop industrial fishing and also the destruction of mangroves. Thus, in Penang, an association led by Haji

Saidin Hussain resorted in the mid-1990s to replanting mangrove seedlings outside the large Penshrimp farm. The association takes a stand on many issues: overfishing by trawlers near the coast, shrimp aquaculture, mangrove destruction, toxic dumping and tourist development (Ahmed, 1997: 25–6). In some areas, the value of the mangrove forest products has played a role in averting the conversion of remaining mangroves into shrimp ponds, and to this is added an interesting sustainable alternative, the culture of clams in the mudflats as practised in the Matang mangrove reserve, with no infrastructure requirements, no feeds or chemicals. The clams feed on the detritus produced by the mangroves, and this alternative relies on naturally produced clam 'seeds' (Gopinath and Gabriel, 1997: 201–2).

In Bangladesh, the coastal shrimp farms are located in the Cox's Bazaar district in the east, and Satkhira, Khulna and Bagerhat districts in the west, where large landowners have appropriated the lands of small farmers and turned them into shrimp farms, with loss of trees and fodder, scarcity of potable water and salinization of fields. There are also movements by fishermen who complain about the loss of fisheries: 'They are creating alternatives. They want to fill all the ponds with soil and plant mangroves' (Ahmed, 1997: 19). In the Chakaria Sunderbans, in Cox's Bazaar, some 50000 acres of mangroves have been converted into shrimp ponds since the early 1980s, with initial support from the World Bank. Television reports of flooding and loss of life in Bangladesh are regularly seen in northern homes, but the connection with destroyed mangroves, abandoned shrimp farms and decreased coastal defence against cyclones is not often made. Deforestation has left the area highly vulnerable to sea water intrusion when cyclones strike. Thus the lack of food security because of the enclosure of the mangroves in order to produce a luxury export product such as shrimps is compounded by environmental insecurity.

There have been some deaths in shrimp conflicts in Bangladesh, the most famous that of Karunamoi Sardar on 7 November 1990, defending her village of Horinkhola, in Khulna. That village and some surrounding villages have declared themselves a 'shrimp-free' zone, and every 7 November thousands of peasants gather there in memory of Karumanoi Sardar and in solidarity with the resistance of her village to the shrimp industry (Ahmed, 1997: 15).

In Indonesia, there was still a plan in the year 2000, under the name Protekan 2003, to increase shrimp production at the expense of mangroves in the next three years, occupying an extra 320000ha, after a viral disease destroyed most of Indonesia's shrimp production in 1995. In comparison, shrimp ponds in Ecuador (the largest Latin American producer), whether active or already abandoned, occupy 210000ha. Land to be used for shrimp production in Indonesia is often taken away from mangrove forests or from villagers by force and physical violence. Clashes will undoubtedly take place in the new, more democratic, atmosphere.[8] The pressure for increasing shrimp farming comes from the demand in rich countries, and from the decline in the sea shrimp fishery. In Indonesia, most of the shrimp ponds were originally concentrated on the north coast of Java, where mangrove forest was destroyed between the mid-1970s and the mid-1990s. Nowadays, most of these ponds are abandoned because of low productivity and environmental degradation, and there is a search for new frontiers. The Protekan 2003 plan looks towards the south coast of Sulawesi, Kalimantan and Maluku. Some of the largest shrimp entrepreneurs in Indonesia are Thai firms, in a characteristic migrating pattern after destroying their own mangroves. These firms sometimes use a 'nucleus–satellite' contracting system, buying the farmed shrimp from local suppliers.

In India, commercial shrimp farming started with a US$425 million loan from the World Bank in the mid-1980s, to which government subsidies were added. As in Bangladesh and other countries, the shrimp farms invade not only mangroves but also agricultural areas near the sea in states such as Tamil Nadu and Andhra Pradesh. Former farms become salinized and without further agricultural use once the shrimp farms fall into disuse. At least 9000 hectares of paddy lands have been rendered useless in the coastal areas of Andhra Pradesh as a result of 'the aborted blue revolution of modern shrimp aquaculture' (Vivekanandan and Kurien, 1998: 31–2). Pumps and pipes to draw sea water into the ponds, and channels to discharge polluted water, interfere with the coastal fishermen's tasks. Groundwater is also polluted.

In India, 'responding to this destruction of their livelihoods, landless and impoverished coastal dwellers took their struggle for justice to the streets, the state-level bodies and finally to the courtroom' (Ahmed, 1997: 4). In December 1996, the Supreme Court of India delivered a remarkable verdict. The court comprised judge Kuldip Singh, the litigation was filed by the noted elderly Gandhian S. Jagannathan together with an NGO called Prepare, and it was argued by lawyer M.C. Mehta. The court ordered the closure of all commercial aquaculture operations within 500 metres of the high tide line, or within 1000 metres of the coast of Lake Chilika in Orissa, forbidding shrimp farms in converted agricultural areas also beyond such limits. The verdict directed that the prawn farms should treat their workers as 'retrenched', in the meaning of the Industrial Disputes Act. They should be paid a compensation equal to six years' wages, as ordered (also by judge Kuldip Singh) in the case of workers in polluting industries in Delhi which opted for closure instead of relocation (see p. 165–6).

The decision rested on a cost–benefit analysis commissioned by the court and carried out by NEERI (the National Environmental Engineering

Research Institute). The export earnings ('forex') were given a premium value in the cost–benefit analysis. NEERI calculated (in monetary terms) that India's prawn industry in 1994 generated four times as much environmental damage as the value of its export earnings, but of course the results of cost–benefit analyses will depend very much on the time horizon considered, on the discount rate applied and on the fictitious values chosen for extra-market costs and benefits. The court's decision was based not only on this cost–benefit analysis (whose results went against shrimp farming) but also on studies of environmental impact and other considerations. The decision helped the resistance movement against shrimp farming not only in India but around the world.[9]

The NGO Prepare, led by Jacob Raj from Chennai, organized a large gathering in Delhi in November 1998, the International People's Conference against Industrial Shrimp and Trade. Prepare has also tried to set up a south–south network. True, a small network based on the north (the Mangrove Action Project led by Alfredo Quarto) has carried out a long struggle defending local populations and promoting 'silvofisheries' (that is, supporting traditional fisheries while preserving mangrove forests), but a larger network, ISANet set in the mid-1990s was (from Jacob Raj's point of view) not radical enough. It was too far from the grassroots, too much inclined to negotiate with the shrimp industry at international meetings. Hence the attempt to create this south–south network, the initial stimulus coming from India.

The movement in India against industrial shrimp farming involves displaced peasants, as in Bangladesh, but it is also part of a large movement for the defence of artisanal fisheries active both on the west coast, in Kerala particularly, and also on the east coast. It comprises hundreds of thousands of fishworkers who complain about trawlers that fish in the deep sea and discard large quantities of fish caught in the trawl – a baglike net dragged by the vessel – and that export part of their catch. Trawlers are sometimes owned by joint venture firms, with foreign participation. On 4 February 1994 there was a strike organized by the national Fishworkers' Forum, a federation of small-scale, artisanal fishermen of all coastal states in India. There was no fishing or unloading of fish during the strike. The same movement denounced the tensions caused by the expansion of shrimp production in Chilika Lake in Orissa, where there are new developments after fishermen successfully forced Tata Industries to withdraw their plans for aquaculture in the early 1990s. On 11 June 1999, four fishworkers, including one woman, demonstrating against illegal prawn farms, were killed by the police.[10]

The aquaculture conflicts in India show other variations. Small farms in some regions have included extensive prawn cultivation in the paddy

rotation. Now, the short-term economic benefits from prawns lead sometimes to rice being given up altogether, endangering local food security and
to the annoyance of landless labourers, since prawn growing is far less
labour-intensive than paddy.

MANGROVES THREATENED IN EAST AFRICA

Outside South and South-East Asia and Latin America (where large mangrove forests in Colombia, Venezuela and Brazil are still intact), the shrimp
frontier also advances in East Africa. In Tanzania, a project by the African
Fishing Company for almost 10000ha of prawn farming in the Rufiji Delta
has given rise to much opposition. A previous project had been proposed
by NORAD, a Norwegian private company, and the Bagamoyo
Development Corporation in the early 1990s. It was not implemented. It
led to the dismissal for corruption of the Minister of Lands: 'the Minister
had attempted to insert himself into the venture by allocating the land
reserved for construction of the prawn farm to a business partner' (Gibbon,
1997: 81).

The Rufiji Delta contains some 20 islands and 31 villages with more than
40000 people, and is famed for supporting the largest continuous block of
mangrove forests (53000ha) in East Africa. 'The Rufiji Delta is one of the
most physically stunning areas in Africa. Over an area of perhaps 1500
square kilometres a web of rivers and channels intersect seemingly endless
mangrove stands, interrupted occasionally by rice fields' (Gibbon, 1997: 5).
In this area there is fishing of wild-caught prawns. Conflicts between artisanal fishermen and trawlers have been researched by Gibbon (1997). The
prawn farming project introduced a new type of conflict. It raised a storm
of protest from environmentalists and from some local communities which
would be displaced. This enormous project became an issue in national
politics, being strongly opposed by the Journalists' Environmental
Association. The promoter of the project, the African Fishing Company,
was said to be Reginald John Nolan, an Irish investor whose money came
from selling arms (Gibbon, 1997: 52).

Support from outside organizations such as Prepare from India, and the
Natural Resources Defense Council from the USA, was brought to bear on
the government of Tanzania. The WWF also intervened, proposing a
project for so-called 'improved prawn farming' in the Rufiji Delta to the
MacArthur Foundation (which sometimes promotes controversial 'eco-
efficiency projects' in the Third World), with a view 'to document when and
how constructive criticism can be best used to improve proposed projects'.
The WWF's conciliatory approach was opposed by the Mangrove Action

Project: 'What right does any one NGO have in experimenting with the shrimp farm project in the first place? It is the local inhabitants of Rufiji who will be subjected to such a grand test, which risks the future of both the environment and the local communities.'[11] This is a type of situation which is not uncommon. Organizations such as the WWF and the main American foundations are closer in cultural terms to large foreign investors than to the local people whose livelihood is threatened, and they do not yet always adopt an 'environmental justice' perspective.

As in Tanzania in the Rufiji Delta, also in Kenya in the Tana Delta there are plans for industrial shrimp farming. Hence the Mombasa Declaration of 6 February 1998 on mangrove conservation and industrial shrimp aquaculture drawn up at a workshop co-sponsored by the East African Wildlife Society, Prepare, the Mangrove Action Project and the Swedish Society for Nature Conservation, an interesting alliance among NGOs concerned with the defence of wilderness and with environmental justice and the environmentalism of the poor. The Mombasa Declaration emphasizes the 'concern over the increasing environmental destruction evident worldwide, and in particular the destruction of mangrove forests, estuaries, sea grass beds, coral reefs and lagoons, in general the conversion of coastal wetlands and areas to industrial shrimp units, an unsustainable activity which is growing in an uncontrolled manner throughout the tropics and subtropics'. It also emphasized the concern over imminent deprivation, displacement and marginalization of local communities that depend on coastal wetlands in the event of the establishment of industrial shrimp units in these areas.

THE TURTLE CONUNDRUM AND THE CALL FOR A CONSUMERS' BOYCOTT OF FARM-RAISED SHRIMP

It took a few years for northern environmentalists to become aware of the connection between shrimp exports and mangrove destruction. Initially, their main worry about shrimps was fishing in the high seas and the death of turtles. The Earth Island Institute, through Todd Steiner of the Sea Turtle Restoration Project, had successfully put the turtle issue on the US trade agenda in the early 1990s. In May 1996, the US government agreed that shrimps could not be imported into the USA from countries whose trawlers did not use Turtle Excluder Devices (TEDs). Three years later, at the anti-WTO demonstrations in Seattle in 1999, there were many people disguised as turtles. Is it more difficult to see the world from the perspective of a woman shellfish collector than from the perspective of an ensnared turtle? As reported from Bangkok back in 1993,

An unlikely-sounding creature is deforesting mangroves, despoiling coral reefs and leaving cropland barren across Thailand. The culprit is shrimp. This is bad news for many who think that cultivating the succulent black tiger shrimp in man-made ponds is somehow more ecologically sound than plucking them out of the sea, but Thailand is paying a high environmental price for its status as the world's largest producer of cultured shrimp.[12]

In response to the US turtle outcry of May 1996, India started 'to issue certificates to marine exporters declaring that trawlers catching fish and shrimp in the high seas have taken measures to use Turtle Excluder Devices . . . [moreover] certificates for 'turtle safe' shrimp were being issued to shrimp caught in inland waters or shrimp from aquaculture farms'.[13] Several southern governments took the USA to the GATT (later the WTO), complaining at the requirement to certify that shrimp were caught in turtle-safe nets. In 1998, the WTO unfortunately overruled the US decision that required wild shrimp imported into the USA to be caught in such a way that turtles were not killed.[14] Progress has been made in imposing the use of TEDs in many countries, though it is a fact that many thousands of turtles (such as the Olive Ridley turtles in eastern India) are killed every year by illegal trawling. Not only in the north, but also in the south, there are groups concerned about turtles, so it is not accurate to view attempts to stop the killing of turtles when fishing for shrimp (or the killing of dolphin when fishing for tuna) as the foisting of northern environmental values on southern peoples. Similarly, not only in the south, but also in the north, there are some NGOs and groups of people concerned about the destruction of mangroves, though the strongest protests come from the south, where a number of people have lost their lives directly (and many more have lost their livelihoods indirectly) while defending the mangroves against shrimp aquaculture.

In the meantime, diverse business interests in the USA (this being the country at the top of the league of shrimp consumers), and also in other countries, continue to mount efforts to promote aquaculture as an environmentally friendly alternative to catching shrimp in nets that ensnare sea turtles.[15] Notice, however, that shrimp farmers are usually local investors, or investors from neighbouring countries, not transnationals. Globalization here does not mean the presence of Exxon, Shell or Rio Tinto. It means rather the global ideology of export-led growth, and also the demand for an item of consumption which is not an input to any manufacturing process, and which is not consumed because of its protein content. There are signs of an alternative globalization in the resistance to shrimp farming, where the many local struggles eventually give rise to international networks, and to alternative proposals for replanting mangroves and for 'silvo-fisheries'.

Harm to sea turtles is only one problem of fishing for shrimp with trawlers. Another problem is that the nets scrape the sea bottom, seriously impairing benthic communities. In addition, industrial shrimp fishing has one of the highest rates of discarded bycatch of any fishery. However, as emphasized by Gurpreet Karir and Vandana Shiva in 1996, northern environmental groups were not yet aware, first, that some aquaculture farms were situated in former mangrove forests on which turtles and many other marine organisms depend for their survival, or, second, that the shrimp import ban in the USA did not consider the impact of commercial aquaculture on another threatened species, the poor people living in the coastal areas.

There was, then, a danger around 1995 which is today acknowledged by environmental groups, north and south, that the ban on wild-caught shrimp could lead to an undesirable expansion of the volume of farmed shrimp around the world. In Ecuador, where 95 per cent of shrimp exported are farm-raised, local environmental groups were baffled by the insistence of US groups on banning imports of wild-caught shrimp, while they themselves were proposing, at high local risk, a northern boycott of farmed shrimp imported from Ecuador and elsewhere. The call for a boycott became international news. Gina Chávez, a young lawyer and at the time an activist with Acción Ecológica, got a letter published in the *Financial Times* (24 July 1995) replying to a previous article published on 15 June, in which the Ecuadorian President of the Chamber of Aquaculture and the Minister of Industry, Trade and Fisheries were quoted as saying that the call for an external boycott of farm-raised shrimp was 'irresponsible, ridiculous and unpatriotic'. Gina Chávez factually replied that destruction of mangroves in the south of the country was nearly complete, and that the industry was recently relocating towards Esmeraldas, 'the site of the best-conserved mangrove stands in Ecuador'. More than half the mangrove forests of Ecuador had been destroyed by the shrimp-farming industry. Also in 1995, the movement in Orissa, India, of coastal fishermen and farmers that included the Chilika Bachao Andolan which had defeated Tata Industries in 1992 in their attempt to grow shrimp in Lake Chilika, held a convention. It called upon 'the affluent countries to boycott prawn imports for consumption of this luxury item, which is nothing but the blood, sweat and livelihood of the common people of the third world countries'. The convention further called upon 'the commercial prawn industry to immediately quit the coast and allow the common people to make their honourable and respectable living' (Consumers' Association of Penang *et al.*, 1997: 11).

The Shrimp Tribunal in New York in April 1996 was convened by the UN Commission for Sustainable Development. The Natural Resources

Defence Council of Washington DC invited NGOs, industry and government representatives to take part in the sessions, because

> the harvesting of wild shrimp accounts for about 35 per cent of the world 'by catch' – fish and other marine life caught, and generally thrown back to the sea as waste. Most recently, attention has focussed on the deaths of endangered sea turtles in shrimp nets each year. The boom in shrimp aquaculture had led to the ruin of millions of acres of biologically-rich mangrove forests and to severe contamination and pollution at shrimp farms.

Both wild-caught and cultivated shrimps were therefore to be considered. There was a clash at the Shrimp Tribunal in New York between Gina Chávez, from Acción Ecológica of Ecuador, and Juan Xavier Cordovez, the president of the National Chamber of Aquaculture, on the statistics of mangrove destruction. The unwillingness of the Ecuadorian government to produce official figures on mangrove forests is well known but the country is small enough for plausible statistics to exist. The official representative of the government of Ecuador, Franklin Ormaza, from the National Institute of Fisheries, helped Juan Xavier Cordovez to make his case against the unexpected environmental offensive at a UN-sponsored meeting, and he later suggested to the Minister of Industry, Trade and Fisheries that Gina Chávez be prosecuted for 'treason to the Fatherland'.[16]

In October 1997, the somewhat disappointing meeting that set up ISANet (held in Santa Barbara, California, not in a southern country) did not call for a moratorium on shrimp farming, as proposed in the Declaration of Choluteca in 1996, or for a boycott, as proposed from Ecuador since 1995. It called instead for a 'shrimp break' (whatever that meant) on farm-raised shrimp. Other northern proposals have been even more shy. Consider, for instance, the following statement:

> Working with exporting countries, industry and citizens' groups [importing countries] need to identify policy instruments that will build incentives for sustainability into the markets, through, for instance, labeling and certification. Ideally, the consumer should pay the full cost of production – including environmental costs which the producers inflict on others. Mechanisms for channeling back the revenues to restore and repair the ecosystems and species impacted should also be set up.[17]

Notice here how environmental destruction may be compensated and restored. Irreversible damages are not taken into account. The livelihoods of poor people are brought into a money valuation standard. The notion of 'full environmental costs' is uncritically accepted. Incommensurableness of values is put aside. Respect for human rights has no veto power. There is no appeal to the sacredness of nature.

An anthropologist working in coastal areas of Ecuador (Muisne and Olmedo, both in Esmeraldas) wrote in her thesis: 'Many of the people interviewed in this study expressed feelings of powerlessness towards the kind of society they live in. They underlined the fact that there are few opportunities for them to find work and to make a living' (Handberg, 1998). That is, externalities that fall on poor and powerless people are cheap, even when 'internalized'. If poor people want to defend ecosystems on which they depend for their livelihood, they had better appeal to other languages of valuation, which are culturally relevant.

COST–BENEFIT VERSUS VALUE PLURALISM

A team of economists performed in 1999 a cost–benefit analysis of shrimp aquaculture in Thailand, looking at Tha Po village, on the coast of Surat Thani province, where about 130 households depend almost entirely on fishing for their livelihood. The area around the village used to be covered by mangrove. In the past decade over half of the area has been cleared for commercial shrimp farming. Thailand's exports of frozen shrimp produce annually about US$1200 million in foreign exchange. In order to put a money value on the destroyed mangroves, Dr Suthawan Sathirathai and her colleagues gave money values to fuelwood and other products, and also translated into money values the mangroves' environmental services as nurseries for fish and as barriers to storms and soil erosion. In financial terms, taking into account marketable products only, the net present value per rai (6·25 rai = 1 ha) of a commercial shrimp farm was far higher than the NPV of a rai of mangrove forest: US$3734 against US$666. Now, however, taking into account the indirect benefits from mangroves, considering a time horizon of only five years for the shrimp farms (before profits start to decrease) and taking into account that replanting must then wait for 15 years, the NPV of mangroves per rai would increase to US$5771. Such figures depend very much on the chosen discount rate. The mangroves are less valuable, relative to the shrimp farms, the higher the discount rate. A slight increase in the rate of discount applied in such analysis, would condemn the mangroves.[18] However, as mangroves become more and more scarce, a case could be made (inside a neoclassical framework) for applying Krutilla's rule (Krutilla, 1967), favouring mangrove conservation. Nevertheless, previous to manipulations such as ad hoc discount rates and fancy monetary valuation of environmental services, another question arises. Do all the actors in the conflict wish to be ensnared in monetary cost–benefit valuation, or do they prefer (given their own interests and values) to move outside into a multi-criteria perspective? Not all actors would give the same answer. A cost–benefit analysis could be one of the relevant criteria, though not necessarily a decisive one. Who, then, has the 'procedural power' to choose the languages and techniques of valuation?

Several values and interests come into play in the conflict between mangrove conservation and shrimp farming. A decision on mangrove conservation could be reached by applying the reductionist logic of cost–benefit analysis, arguing that the stream of benefits from shrimp farming cannot compensate the losses from mangrove destruction, which would be monetarized and discounted (the discount rate being a distributional issue in itself) in order to obtain present values. Such losses would include the loss of landscapes (for ever, or until replanting takes place), the loss of the coastal defence function (perhaps counted at replacement cost, of building a wall), the loss of food security and subsistence (direct food intake and availability of wood, and also money income from sales of mangrove products), the loss of cultural values (measured perhaps by willingness to accept compensation), the loss of fisheries and so on. It would be no less reductionist to defend the mangroves only in terms of 'emergy' (embodied energy). Another way of trying to assess the ecological costs of shrimp farming in physical terms would be to calculate its 'ecological footprint' (Larsson *et al.*, 1994).

Such different dimensions could be incorporated into a multi-criteria analysis. In the application of multi-criteria methods, the relevant alternatives, and the relevant criteria, could arise from stakeholders' and experts' interaction, and each alternative would be valued in quantity or quality and ranked across all the criteria. One could, indeed, also include a financial analysis or even an extended cost–benefit analysis as one of the criteria, without double counting because the other criteria would still be valued on their own physical or social scales. 'Compromise' solutions would be suggested. More important is to see the matrix as a way of structuring and making explicit the social conflicts over interests and values (Martinez-Alier *et al.*, 1998). (A similar multi-criteria matrix, with more alternatives and more criteria – partly in money terms, partly in physical terms – may be seen in Gilbert and Janssen, 1998.)

In this chapter, the loss of human livelihoods as a consequence of the growth of the shrimp industry has been emphasized, but also purely environmental values have been taken into account. It is clear, however, that the defence of mangrove forests against the shrimp industry is not a manifestation of wilderness environmentalism, but rather one typical example of the 'environmentalism of the poor', with women often in leading roles.

The shrimp versus mangroves conflict adopts slightly different aspects in different places in the world according to cultural differences, but it has common structural roots. It is an ecological distribution conflict, that is a conflict on environmental entitlements, on the loss of access to natural

Shrimp farming vs. mangrove conservation – A multicriteria approach

Criteria *Alternatives*	Biomass production	Food security	Cultural values	Financial results	Coastal defence	Landscape value
1) Keep mangroves						
2) Grow shrimp						
3) Other alternatives (for example very small cooperative ponds)						

resources and environmental services, on the burdens of pollution and on the sharing of uncertain environmental hazards.

Despite judicial decisions such as that in India in 1996, the trend towards mangrove destruction continues worldwide, fuelled in part by shrimp consumption in rich countries, halted only by virus outbreaks in shrimp farms or by successful local environmental movements. Southern calls for northern consumer boycotts of farmed shrimp have gone unheeded, even inside environmental networks. The situation is not one of northern 'green protectionism' against imports produced with low environmental standards (as in the case of complaints against shrimp or tuna fish imports which imply the death of turtles or dolphins). On the contrary, the northern consumers profit from prices of imported farmed shrimp which do not include compensation for local externalities (a general rule that also applies to substantial items such as cheap oil, wood, copper or aluminium imports), and southern complaints have not yet successfully alerted northern consumers to the damage suffered in the exporting territories. Some northern groups are perhaps ready to believe the good intentions expressed in the new Thai Code of Conduct issued by the industry in 1999, or in Yolanda Kakabadse's sincere promises in Ecuador when she was Minister of the Environment for some months up to January 2000, or in the temporary injunction on the Rufiji project in Tanzania. Such northern groups push, not for a boycott, but for integrated coastal management and some form of 'eco-labelling' of shrimp. Alfredo Quarto, of the Mangrove Action Project, with seven years of experience behind him, asked his partners in ISANet on 26 May 1999: 'Have we won a victory, or are we merely now witnessing a short reprieve before the next storm? I myself urge us to prepare for the next storm wave, while making an honest attempt to undertake projects that offer positive alternatives [such as] the promotion of low-intensity, community-based silvo-fisheries.' Meanwhile, world demand for farmed shrimp keeps increasing, most consumers still blissfully unaware of the social and environmental havoc they cause.

The management and resolution of local or global ecological distribution conflicts would require cooperation between business, international organizations, NGO networks, local groups and governments. Can this cooperation be based on common values and on common languages? We argue that this is not always the case; that, whenever there are unresolved ecological conflicts, there is likely to be not only a discrepancy but incommensurability in valuation (Faucheux and O'Connor, 1998; Funtowicz and Ravetz, 1994; Martinez-Alier *et al.*, 1998, 1999; Martinez-Alier and O'Connor, 1996, 1999; O'Connor and Spash, 1999). The conflicts might arise because of the existence of different values but also because of different interests. Some people want to preserve the mangroves because they appreciate their ecological and aesthetic values. Other people want to preserve the mangroves because they live from them, and/or because they understand their practical role as coastal defence and as fish breeding grounds. Other people (or the same people, in other contexts) appeal to the sense of culture and place the mangroves provide for their traditional inhabitants. They might even argue that there are sacred mangroves. In all cases, environmental conflicts are expressed as conflicts over valuation, either inside one single standard of valuation, or across plural values. 'Semiotic resistance' (M. O'Connor, 1993b; Escobar, 1996: 61) to environmental abuse may be expressed in many languages. To see in statements about biomass, 'emergy', culture, livelihood, a lack of understanding or an *a priori* rejection of the techniques of economic valuation in actual or fictitious markets, is to fail to grasp the existence of value pluralism. Different interests can be defended either by insisting on the discrepancies of valuation inside the *same* standard of value, or by resorting to non-equivalent descriptions of reality; that is, to *different* value standards. We may write, 'shrimp exports are a *valuable* item of world trade' and, also, '*valuable* ecosystems and *valuable* local cultures are destroyed by shrimp farming'. Which is then the true value of farm-raised shrimp? The legitimacy of this question itself, let alone the answer, depends on the outcome of the conflict. The reduction of all goods and services to actual or fictitious commodities, as in cost–benefit analysis, can be recognized as one perspective among several, legitimate as a point of view and as a reflection of real power structures. Who, then, has the power to impose a particular standard of valuation?

NOTES

1. Message from Fundecol@ecuanex.net.ec of 11 March 1999. *Concheras* are women who collect shellfish (*Anadara tuberculosa*) mostly for selling, also for subsistance. Camaroneros are the owners of the shrimp ponds (*camarón* being the shrimp). *Carboneros* are charcoal makers. *Concheras* get across *esteros* (the swamps) by boat to get to the mangroves and collect the shells at low tide. The coastal population of the province of Esmeraldas in Ecuador is, in its majority, of African descent.
2. Journal *La Tribuna*, section 'Ecocomentarios', 29 October 1997; also website Environment in Latin America at CSF, 9 November 1997.
3. Email from Grupo Ecológico Manglar, San Blas, Nayarit, 27 April 1998.
4. Letter from Matthew Gianni, Oceans Campaign Coordinator, Greenpeace International, to Hon. Rafael Villalta Loaiza, 5 October 1998.
5. There is a description of the origins of African people on that coast in Manfred Max-Neef's *From the Outside looking in: Experiences in 'Barefoot' Economics* (1992: 62–3). A ship commanded by the Sevillian Alonso de Illescas went aground on that coast in 1553 with a cargo of 17 male and 6 female slaves sent to Peru from Panama. The Spaniards left on foot through the swamps, the Africans remained, led by a native of Cape Verde who also took the name of Alonso de Illescas, and who in alliance with local Indian groups repeatedly defeated colonial expeditions until 1570. Then he was caught, but released again by a young novice of the order of the Mercedarios by the name of Escobar. Other shipwrecks added more Africans to the group. In the late 1580s an agreement with Quito was reached, and a Christian missionary, Pedro Romero, settled among the local population.
6. Interview by Martha Luz Machado, reported in Patricia Falla, '*Estado actual y tendencias en el manejo del ecosistema manglar por comunidades del Pacífico colombiano*', master's thesis, Universitat Autónoma de Barcelona, July 2000. Also in Martha Luz Machado, 'Las flores de los manglares', *Ecologia Politica*, 20, 2000, 31.
7. *Shrimp News International*, an industry publication issued by Bob Rosenberry, San Diego, California 1996.
8. Raja Siregar (Friends of the Earth), 'Indonesia to intensify shrimp farming', *Link*, 90(6), 1999. Also Raja Siregar and Emmy Hafild (Friends of the Earth International/WALHI), 'Global Shrimp Trade and Indonesian Shrimp Farming Policies', typewritten report, Jakarta, November 1999 (20 pages).
9. The Supreme Court decisions in India, in this and other 'green' cases throughout the present book, are collected in Divan and Rosencranz, 2nd edn, (2001).
10. E-mail from Thomas Kocherry, coordinator, World Forum of Fish-Harvesters and Fish-Workers.
11. ET News, the Newsletter of the Journalists' Environmental Association of Tanzania, November 1998, and e-mail from Alfredo Quarto, Mangrove Action Project, 28 April 1999.
12. *Business Times*, 1 June 1993.
13. Gurpreet Karir and Vandana Shiva, 'A cosmetic ban – why the U.S. shrimp ban will neither save turtles or people'; sent by e-mail to environmental groups, 22 June 1996.
14. Ann Swardson, 'Turtle protection law overturned by WTO', *Washington Post*, 13 October 1998, p.C2, cited by Shabecoff (2000: 163); also French (2000: 121–3).
15. Kevin G. Hall, 'Shrimp farms harvest aquaculture clash', *Journal of Commerce*, 24 October 1997.
16. Oficio 0960380, Instituto Nacional de Pesca, Guayaquil, 10 May 1996, from Franklin Ormaza, PhD to Lic. José Vicente Maldonado, Quito.
17. CIEL, IUCN, WWF, 'Protecting marine and coastal biodiversity under the Convention on Biological Diversity', April 1996, 36–7.
18. Suthawan Sathirathai, 'Economic Valuation of Mangroves and the Roles of Local Communities in the Conservation of Natural Resources', Centre for Ecological Economics, Chulalongkorn University, January 1999.

6. The environmentalism of the poor: gold, oil, forests, rivers, biopiracy

GOLD MINING

One leitmotif of the present book is that consumption drives the economy. Several objections arise. Are not profits made in production rather than consumption, and is it not the profit rate that is the essential driver of capitalism? Are not investments essential as outlets for capital, whether in resource extraction, in the production of capital goods or in consumer goods? Are not changes of techniques the real drivers of capitalism, and are they not introduced in production, rather than consumption, because of the pressures of competition on profits? Moreover, could not enough consumption to maintain production levels be secured already by the incomes gained in relatively dematerialized activities – a Seattle economy without Boeing? These are interesting but premature questions, because the economy is not dematerializing and because consumption has a life of its own; it is not determined by the necessity to sell production. If the economy is driven by the profit rate, by investments and technical change, it is *also* driven by conspicuous consumption or the wish to obtain positional goods (Hirsch, 1976), which is more a cultural than a biological trait. Hence the use of increased incomes in order to buy more and more gold, a habit of the human species in which the east and the west truly meet. Gold mining is similar in a way to shrimp farming, or to the extraction of tropical wood like mahogany or to exports of ivory and diamonds from Africa. About 80 per cent of all gold that is dug out of the ground ends up as jewellery.

Gold is sometimes produced together with other metals such as copper but is often the primary objective. The price of gold makes it still profitable to open new mines. Gold lasts a very long time but the existing stock of gold in the world, counting also the central banks' reserves, does not seem to satisfy humankind's desires, and there is pressure to open new mines, not to replace for gold which is lost but to accumulate new stocks. Why do the central banks not sell the gold they hold? Some religions forbid consumption of shrimp or pork or beef, or other types of food. Is there a religion that forbids the mining and accumulation of gold? Gold mining is particularly destructive, both when it is small-scale (as with the *garimpeiros* in

Brazil) or when it is large-scale, by corporations such as Placer Dome, Newmont, Freeport, Rio Tinto or Anglo-American. Gold leaves behind enormous 'ecological rucksacks', and also pollution from mercury or cyanide.

The participants at a Peoples' Gold Summit in San Juan Ridge, California, held on 2–8 June 1999 (www.moles.org (Project Underground)), asked for a moratorium on the exploration for gold because commercial gold mining projects are mainly on indigenous lands. By violating their land rights, mining companies are denying the right to life of those indigenous peoples, whose relationship to land is central to their spiritual identity and survival.

> We need to support the self-determination of indigenous peoples and the recovery, demarcation and legal recognition of campesinos, tribal and indigenous peoples' lands . . . Large-scale and small-scale, toxic chemical-dependent gold mining damages landscapes, habitats, biodiversity, human health and water resources. Water especially is contaminated by cyanide, acid mine drainage, heavy metals and mercury from gold mining. Additionally, the hydrological cycle is changed and water sources are grossly depleted by pumping water from aquifers.

This is indeed a true description. The participants added:

> Life, land, clean water and clean air are more precious than gold. All people depend on nature for life. The right to life is a guaranteed human right. It is, therefore, our responsibility to protect all of nature for present and future generations. Large-scale gold mining violently uproots and destroys the spiritual, cultural, political, social and economic lives of peoples as well as entire ecosystems. Historic and current destruction created by gold mining is greater than any value generated.

I would myself frame the issue in terms of incommensurability of values, because from a chrematistic perspective the value of gold might indeed be higher than the value of the destruction.

In Peru, there are large conflicts in 2001, in Tambo Grande (Piura) (see Chapter 11) and in Cajamarca (where Atahualpa met Pizarro) between the Yanacocha mine and local communities that belong to the Federación de Rondas Campesinas. In Cajamarca peasants have been evicted from lands that they sold for a few dollars to the company. They complain that they did not know then what they know now. As families are displaced by the mine and forced into the city of Cajamarca to look for somewhere to live, they find themselves in a situation where they have to pay rent and have no way of making a living. The concession to the mine is for 25000ha. The Yanacocha gold mine is owned by Newmont, and also by a local company, with a 5 per cent share belonging to the International Finance Corporation of the World Bank. 'At the mine, the ore is loosened by daily dynamite blasts, and then piled on to large leach pads to be sprayed twenty-four hours a day with cyanide solution.'[1] Sodium cyanide used in gold mines can kill fish and cause other ecological damage. There is pollution of rivers downstream, and pollution of local water sources. The cyanide technique has been presented as an alternative to amalgamation with mercury. It consists of spraying a solution of cyanide over crushed ore heaped into open piles. Mercury is also used. In June 2000, a truck travelling from the Yanacocha gold mine spilled mercury in the village of Choropampa. 'Residents scooped it up, and dozens were poisoned. The government fined the company around US$500000 and ordered it to clean the area'. (*The Economist*, 22 June 2001). In such mines, the voluminous tailings, if left on open ground with no vegetation cover, become a nightmare when wind blows the dust away.

In other recent cases in Latin America (in northern Costa Rica against Placer Dome, in Imataca, Venezuela against various Canadian companies), gold mining was successfully stopped, at least for the time being. In Venezuela, under the government which preceded that of President Hugo Chavez, Decree 1850 of 1997 tried to open up the forest reserve area of Imataca of three million ha to gold mining. A movement which comprised the sparse local indigenous Pemon population, some environmental groups such as Amigransa (the friends of the Gran Sabana, led by two women), some anthropologists and sociologists, and some members of Parliament, all using different languages in the service of the same cause (from Indian demonstrations in the streets of Caracas to legal appeals to the Supreme Court), managed for the time being to stop mining in Imataca. The environmental commission of the Chamber of Deputies of Venezuela appealed to the Supreme Court against Decree 1850, quoting a figure between US$7000 and 23000 per hectare for the restoration of the vegetable cover affected by exploitation, a useful if moderate figure in order to calculate some environmental liabilities that gold mining, with its toxic effects and large ecological rucksacks, implies.[2]

OIL IN THE NIGER DELTA, AND THE BIRTH OF OILWATCH

The powers of persuasion of the American administration were brought to bear on OPEC governments in 1999, to obtain increases in oil extraction and a lower price for oil which, as President Clinton said at a press conference on 29 March 2000, 'was good for the economy and for the American people'. The local and global environments were not mentioned. As oil extraction increases, local conflicts flare up.

The USA has already consumed nearly half of its available reserves of oil. In the world we are burning oil twice or three times faster than we are finding it. Because of such fossil fuel 'addiction', the oil frontier is reaching fragile natural habitats, and endangering the health and survival of local communities. It would be possible to put such frontiers out of bounds to the oil industry, increasing instead the use of other sources or energy, or even increasing the extraction of oil and gas in other areas, or increasing energy efficiency. The fact is, however, that the oil and gas frontier is moving outwards. Extraction of oil from wilderness areas in Alaska is only one particular case. Behind this fact there is the trend towards exhaustion of reserves and/or increasing extraction costs in older areas.

The language of the conflicts on oil extraction is sometimes the defence of wilderness but more and more often is that of human rights and indigenous territorial rights. On 10 November 1995, the military dictatorship of Nigeria killed nine dissenters, the most prominent of whom was the poet and playwright Ken Saro-Wiwa. Their crime had been to draw attention to the impact of drilling by the Anglo-Dutch oil company, Shell. The MOSOP, Movement for the Survival of the Ogoni People, founded by Saro-Wiwa in 1991, had organized the opposition to Shell and its military backers. The generals in Lagos responded with threats, intimidation, arrest and, finally, by judicially murdering Saro-Wiwa and his colleagues. (Saro-Wiwa, 1995; also *The Guardian Weekly*, 12 November 1995; cf. Guha, 2000: 102). Human rights violations related to oil exploration and production in the Niger delta continued after 1995. Internationally known environmental activists such as Nnimo Bassey and Isaak Osuoka were arrested. Many people have been killed. Major multinational oil companies, not only Shell but also Chevron, Agip and Elf, are involved in those violations because they sometimes ask for the intervention of the police and the military. A Human Rights Watch's report for February 1999 stated:

> The Niger Delta has for some years been the site of major confrontations between the people who live there and the Nigerian government security forces, resulting in extra-judicial executions, arbitrary detentions, and draconian restrictions on the rights to freedom of expression, association, and assembly. These violations of civil and political rights have been committed principally in response to protests about the activities of the multinational companies that produce Nigeria's oil. Although the June 1998 death of former head of state Gen. Sani Abacha and his succession by Gen. Abdulsalami Abubakar has brought a significant relaxation in the unprecedented repression General Abacha inflicted on the Nigerian people . . . human rights abuses in the oil producing communities continue and the basic situation in the delta remains unchanged.

The Kaiama Declaration was signed in December 1998 by members of youth movements belonging to the Ijaw, a larger ethnic group than the Ogoni. The Kaiama Declaration stated that 'all land and natural resources (including mineral resources) within the Ijaw territory belong to Ijaw communities and are the basis of our survival'. It demanded 'the immediate withdrawal from Ijawland of all military forces of occupation and repression by the Nigerian state'. Accordingly, 'any oil company that employs the services of the armed forces of the Nigerian state to 'protect' its operations will be viewed as an enemy of the Ijaw people'. The Kaiama Declaration asked that Nigeria become a federation of ethnic nationalities. Linking the issue of global warming to local grievances against oil companies – because of human rights abuses, oil spills, land and water pollution and gas flaring – the Kaiama Declaration finally announced that a direct action 'Operation Climate Change' would be launched on 1 January 1999, which would include extinguishing gas flares. Oil wells extract water and gas together with the oil, the water they throw into ponds or they reinject back into the soil, the gas they often flare when there is no market nearby. This implies local pollution, and also CO_2 emissions. If the gas is not flared and it escapes unburnt, the greenhouse effect from methane would be even greater. The objective of the Ijaw youths was not to increase methane emissions into the atmosphere but rather to force the oil companies to stop operations altogether by a spectacular action. Local and global issues were thus brought together in the Kaiama Declaration.

The focus for action is the flow stations, where oil, extraction water and gas from the wells is collected and separated. Almost one year later, in early November 1999, an international meeting on 'Resistance as the Road to Sustainability' took place in Quito, a few days before the general assembly of Friends of the Earth International. Nnimo Bassey was not present, but he sent a paper in which he stated:

> In the Niger Delta area of Nigeria a strategy of stopping oil and gas exploration and production will radically transform the terrain of the struggle and also qualitatively change the character of the possible outcome. And the flow stations can be closed, effectively shut down. We can generalise the Ogoni experience across the entire Niger Delta . . . And the Ijaws demonstrated with the Kaiama Declaration the immense potential of this strategy. This requires the activists to organise a Niger Delta-wide platform of struggle and a Niger Delta-wide forum to articulate and harmonise the views, programs and demands of the people of the region. The people would then need to organise Niger Delta-wide days of action to build up to a climax which would be represented in continuous mass action around oil and gas installations effectively shutting the flow stations and paralysing the activities of transnational capital. The ultimate platform for resolving the constitutional strictures that have deprived the people of their basic rights and access to a safe and satisfactory environment can only be at a

Sovereign National Conference. The SNC is perceived as the forum for the achievement of self-determination through restructuring of Nigeria into genuinely federating nations. Through it the people would also achieve the ownership, control and democratic self-management of our resources. Resistance through mass action appears to be the only way through which dialogue will come about.

The conflict in the Niger Delta continues, as the Ogoni, the Ijaw and other ethnic groups battle against the oil companies and the Nigerian state, deploying vocabularies of human rights, livelihood, territorial rights for minorities, federalism and environmentalism. Events such as the death of the 'Ogoni Nine' in 1995 and other struggles in the Delta, and the long struggle in Ecuador against Texaco and other oil companies, led to the birth of OilWatch. This is a network based on southern countries, which grew out of and is fed by local movements of resistance against oil or gas extraction. In 1995, its newsletter, *Tegantai* (an Amazonian butterfly, in Huaorani language), announced Saro-Wiwa's death months in advance, while European environmentalists were focusing on the Greenpeace victory over Shell in the Brent-Spar case.[3]

Also in West Africa, which is one of the frontiers of oil extraction, the World Bank supports the US$3·5 billion pipeline between Chad and the coast of Cameroon to be built by Exxon and other companies. In Cameroon, the pipeline will cross forest areas inhabited by the Bakola. One official argument for the project is that it will speed up the integration process of the Bakola into modernity, provided of course that they survive it.[4] On 6 June 2000, the executive directors of the World Bank representing 181 governments approved the pipeline, which will be used over 30 years to export a total amount of about one billion barrels of oil. A jubilant advertisement by Exxon (*New York Times*, 15 June 2000) foresaw that the revenues for both countries could help transform their economies, if they are managed properly. 'To ensure that they are, Chad's Parliament and president have enacted an unprecedented revenue management program. This law imposes strict controls on the government's share of oil revenues and places project funds in special accounts that will be subject to public reviews and World Bank audits.' Thus the World Bank has become not only a proponent of 'weak sustainability' but a manager of it.

OilWatch provides information on such conflicts over oil extraction in fragile tropical areas from its secretariat in Ecuador, and through members in other southern countries and also in Europe. There is a wealth of local knowledge and documentation to be explored on conflicts over oil extraction, including papers from court cases, such as the Texaco case in Ecuador. In 1993, a class-action suit was started in the USA in slow motion by a group of indigenous people and settlers from the northern part of the

Amazonian region in Ecuador, claiming that Texaco had contaminated their water, killed their food supply and caused disease. Nobody really can dispute that Texaco, whose official abode is in White Plains, NY, through its subsidiary in Ecuador, between the early 1970s and the late 1980s polluted the water and the soil. It could plausibly be argued that its successor, Petroecuador, has inherited the same practices. The area is dotted with viscous black pools of water which was extracted with the oil, later deposited into these pools which sometimes overflow, or suddenly catch fire and fill the air with black particles. There are reports of increased cancer rates, humans becoming bioindicators of environmental damage. Texaco also opened up roads which facilitated the arrival of settlers in the forest, damaging the livelihood of the indigenous Cofans and other tribes. It built the trans-Andean pipeline to Esmeraldas, which has had many leaks. The question of whether Texaco used different standards in the USA and abroad, on reflection does not even arise, in the sense that the USA has no Amazonia. The lawyers argued their case in the framework of the Alien Torts Claims Act (ATCA) of 1789, intended to provide a federal forum in the USA for aliens suing domestic entities for violations of the law of nations. The District Judge in New York, Jed Rakoff (who took over the case after the death of the initial judge), at first dismissed the case on grounds of *forum non conveniens.* The government of Ecuador, through its ambassador in the USA, Edgar Terán, had claimed sovereignty rights. Later, Ecuador (in the short period of 1997 when Bucaram was the populist and corrupt president, a strange ally for the environmentalists) reversed its position, and its attorney-general officially accepted the US court's jurisdiction. An appeal against the first dismissal was then successful. The *New York Times* (19 February 1999) stated that the case should be heard 'in the only forum that can provide a fair trial and enforce penalties, an American court' but it was likely that the case would be sent back to Ecuador. In September 1999, the NGO, Rainforest Movement gave support to an advertising campaign in the USA on this case, and there were rumours in October 1999 that an out-of-court settlement for US$400 million would be reached. Initial claims were of the order of US$1·5 billion.[5] Other recent conflicts in Latin America are those between the Ashaninka and Elf, between Shell and the Nahua (both in Peru), between Maxus (later YPF, later Repsol) and the Huaorani in Ecuador, between Repsol and Amazonian populations in Bolivia, and between Occidental Petroleum and the U'Wa in Colombia.

Such ecological distribution conflicts over the actual or potential damage from oil extraction may be fought inside one single standard of valuation, as when monetary compensation for externalities is asked for. This is the case with the indemnity for US$1·5 billion demanded initially from Texaco in the Ecuador case (which, in legal parlance, would cover both compensatory and punitive damages). The logic of environmental economics is relevant here, as it was for the *Exxon Valdez* case in Alaska in 1989. Technical questions are: Is contingent valuation acceptable to the courts? Are valuations of externalities from other cases transferable to the Texaco case in Ecuador? How to value the loss of unknown biodiversity?

The conflicts may also be fought across plural values. Thus, as will be seen next, a common unit of valuation is not available in the conflict on oil extraction in the Laguna del Tigre in the Peten, in Guatemala, which pits an oil company supported by the IFC-World Bank against international wilderness organizations and local settlers who claim community rights based on the promise of sustainable forest management.

OIL IN GUATEMALA

Perhaps one of the least appropriate sites in the world for extracting oil is the Peten in Guatemala, the northern region which borders on the Selva Lacandona in Mexico, and which still contains much primary forest and wetland, and also Maya ruins (such as Tikal) that are a major tourist attraction. The region was designated as the Maya Biosphere Reserve in 1990. Preservation has been helped by USAID money for the Guatemalan National Environmental Commission (CONAMA), which divided the reserve into zones, with core zones assigned the highest priority for protection. The largest core zone of the Maya Biosphere Reserve is the Laguna del Tigre national park, covering 1300 square miles, recognized also by the Ramsar Convention on wetlands. Precisely in that area, the International Finance Corporation (IFC) of the World Bank supported plans by the oil company Basic Resources to extract oil and build a pipeline to the port of Santo Tomás de Castilla.

Some local settler communities, not of pre-Hispanic origin but recent arrivals, since the Peten started to be colonized only in the last decades, have learnt to defend their interests through the language of community rights and sustainable development. They claim to practise sustainable forest management, and after 1990 they founded ACOFOP, an organization of local forestry communities led by Marcedonio Cortave, a long-time political activist who is now also an environmentalist. ACOFOP opposes oil extraction in the Peten, and the pipeline which inevitably produces oil spills. It has been helped by the NGO, Madre Selva, which is also active against oil extraction in the region of Lake Izabal together with local tourist operators, and the Kekchi indigenous people who consider the lake sacred. There is here a confluence of the environmentalism of wilderness with the environmentalism of the poor, both currents sharing the scepticism concerning economic valuation.[6] Just across the Mexican border there seems to be lots of oil, as many people have learnt from the neo-zapatista Marcos.[7]

THE CASE AGAINST UNOCAL AND TOTAL BECAUSE OF THE YADANA GAS PIPELINE

In the late 1990s, Unocal (based in California), Total (based in France) and national corporations from Burma and Thailand were developing the Yadana natural gas field in the Andaman Sea, and building a gas pipeline to Ratchaburi in Thailand for the production of electricity. This was a large project (the capacity of the gas-to-electricity plant will be 2800MW). It was also a controversial project. The pipeline in Thailand goes through forests, and threatens biodiversity. In Burma (or Myanmar, as the military rulers call their country), the pipeline goes though the southern area of Tenasserim. There was large-scale displacement of people in order to ensure the security of the pipeline. Certainly, the environment of some human groups (such as the Karen) was being disrupted. Moreover, the ruthless use of forced labour, and the forced dislocation of people, led to many complaints by human rights groups, and also by groups supporting democracy in Burma.

A successful preliminary case against Unocal in California claiming jurisdiction of US courts was argued by lawyers Cristóbal and John Bonifaz (Cristóbal Bonifaz was a lawyer also in the Texaco-Ecuador case) in terms of deprivation of internationally acknowledged human rights. Judge Richard Paez granted jurisdiction to a US court to proceed against Unocal for actions in Burma (25 March 1997), under the Alien Torts Claims Act (ATCA). The government of Burma was excluded from the court case, because of its sovereign immunity. Unocal was a partner of the Burma government, and tried to hide under its sovereign skirts. However, the judge stated that Unocal could be liable on its own. The liability of both defendants (one immune, the other not) could be separated. Total, the French company (which had a large participation in the Yadana project) had not been brought to court in France, but perhaps it may be considered liable also in the USA jointly with Unocal. This is a case, as in Nigeria and elsewhere, where there are damages against both human rights and the environment, since it is impossible to separate Nature from human livelihood, and livelihood from human rights.

The Unocal-Burma case is similar to the Texaco-Ecuador case in that the main issue is the preliminary one of whether US courts have jurisdiction.

But the case is different on two counts. First, it was accepted by the judge that, in Burma, forced labour being like slavery or perhaps torture, the case belonged to a peremptory international law which is immediately applicable. In Ecuador, the question under discussion was not forced labour but damage to the environment and to human health. Moreover, in Ecuador the plaintiffs asked for reparation of damages caused by Texaco between 1970 and 1990, and it could be argued that this would not be possible without the participation of Petroecuador, Texaco's successor, a state company which owns the wells and the oil pipeline running over the Andes to the port of Esmeraldas on the coast.

In contrast, in the Unocal case, the plaintiffs said in 1996–7 that, if granted jurisdiction in a US court, they would not ask for reparations at this stage but only for an injunction stopping Unocal from giving money to the military rulers, and obliging it to withdraw from Burma. This Unocal could do by itself (according to judge Paez), separately from any decisions by the military rulers of Burma, and by the Burma gas and oil company.[8] The court order was something of a shock. There were reports in business journals that, in view of the current growth of major infrastructure and natural resources projects in emerging economies in which the host governments usually play a significant role, companies should be aware of the novel application of the ATCA legislation, not against foreign governments or their agents, or foreign individuals, but against American companies.[9] In April 1997, one month after judge Paez's ruling, President Clinton put Myanmar in the same category as Cuba, Libya, Iraq, North Korea and so on, a clear-cut case of a country where no new American investment is allowed. It appears, however, that the gas pipeline will be finished. Whether a court case claiming retrospective damages will be heard in the USA is uncertain. As in other cases in this book related to mining in Indonesia, South Africa and Namibia, and related to oil in Nigeria, perhaps the new democratic governments, including one day in Burma–Myanmar itself, will help to establish claims for the payment of compensatory retrospective damages to their own citizens in foreign courts, in many cases already too late. Or, perhaps, democratic or not, such governments will not wish to antagonize the multinational companies.

Several such court cases have become bogged down irremediably already at the first stage, that of asking for jurisdiction in the courts. From a purely juridical point of view, there is much to be said for judging the cases where the damage has been done and where many of the direct witnesses reside, rather than where the damage has been planned (or acquiesced to); hence the doctrine of *forum non conveniens* has been repeatedly applied. However, court cases held in the USA, Europe or Japan would bring into the open the environmental and social injustices much more than court cases in

Third World countries would do. Also the documentary evidence of decisions by Texaco, Unocal, Union Carbide, Repsol, Elf, Shell or Freeport are in their main offices. The advantages of a 'northern' court case apply even to countries such as India, which enjoy an independent judicial system and a large free press. The case against Union Carbide for the Bhopal tragedy will be analysed in Chapter 10.

Once jurisdiction was granted, such court cases would be heard in the USA as 'class-action suits', that is, the 'class' of the people who have suffered damages must be certified (perhaps some tens of thousands of people). Now it is implausible that tribal peoples themselves would know about the possibilities of international litigation, and that they would decide to hire a particular lawyer from New York, Los Angeles, London, Paris or Tokyo. In some cases, their own governments would not allow this. Moreover, tribal peoples, or rural peoples in general, speak the languages of the Third World. Unless there is outside intervention by activists, or perhaps directly by outside lawyers (as in the DBCP case regarding sterility in banana plantations in Costa Rica and in Ecuador), a 'class-action' suit would never materialize.

In the Unocal case in March 1997, the plaintiffs from Burma were described in the Californian court under the unlikely names of John and Jane Doe, and Baby Doe – because of the peril of reprisals by a dictatorial government. In the Texaco-Ecuador case, which I know well, the plaintiffs (Aguinda *et al.*) are not just a group of Cofan and Secoia people and of settlers who one day got together by themselves, and phoned, faxed or e-mailed US lawyers instructing them to start a case in White Plains, NY where Texaco was domiciled. The idea of the court case came from outside. Where else could it come from? Now, eight years later, some of the local people have learnt about the procedural intricacies of such litigation, they have been several times to New York. The weaker part must quickly attempt to understand the aliens' system of justice.

The Indian communities of Peru learned how to draw up petitions to the Viceroy in Lima and to the King of Spain (written not in local languages but by intermediaries who knew the appropriate forms of Spanish). There is no larger cultural difference in the world today than that between the CEO of Texaco or Freeport McMoRan and tribal peoples in Ecuador or West Papua, polluted by the water from oil extraction or by mine tailings dumped into rivers. In general, such court cases (which arise through the intervention of NGO and lawyers) do not invent environmental and human rights conflicts, they represent them in one particular language. The discourses are indeed remarkable; they should not make us forget the social and environmental grievances behind them, and the clashes in value systems.

Other actions have been tried against Unocal. Thus, in September 1998, a coalition of activists' groups asked the attorney-general of California to begin proceedings to revoke the charter of Unocal (Union Oil Company of California) on the grounds that the company had polluted the environment in California itself and around the world, violating occupational and health regulations, and violating also human rights not only in Burma but also in Afghanistan (the allegation is that Unocal worked with the Taliban regime to build an oil pipeline, later abandoning this plan). The attorney-general denied the petition.[10] Also the government of Massachusetts sought to forbid Unocal from doing business in Burma, but the US Supreme Court ruled on 20 June 2000 that foreign policy was a federal prerogative.

Litigation against multinational companies *inside* their countries of origin for damages done abroad is, then, becoming a hot issue.[11] The calculus of damages in such civil litigation will provide interesting ingredients for the valuation of the environment and of human rights. While economic logic, north and south, is that 'the poor sell cheap', judicial logic in awarding punitive damages beyond reparation costs might be different.

PLANTATIONS ARE NOT FORESTS

One hundred years after Pinchot introduced 'scientific forestry' to the USA, the conflict between plantation forests and 'true' forests is coming into the open in the Third World. Scientific forestry for sustainable wood yields (going back to German forestry science, and Faustmann's rule of 1849) is, no doubt, in all its variations, 'a complex, multilayered discourse formation that was historically and contingently produced' (Sivaramakrishnan, 1999: 280). Beyond discourse analysis, we can identify a structural conflict across cultures and politico-administrative systems. In many regions of the tropical world this is a conflict of monospecific tree plantations against biodiverse forests with many species of trees (sometimes as many as one hundred per hectare). In other regions (at southern latitudes in South America, for instance), the native forest is almost monospecific, and the conflict is between this native forest (old, slow-growth forest) which is cut, turned into chips and exported, and new plantations of quickly growing pines after deforestation has taken place.[12] Given the increased export of paper pulp from the south, there is an increasing number of social conflicts over logging and subsequent tree plantation (mainly, but not only, eucalyptus), such as that going on in the later 1990s against Smurfit in Portuguesa, Venezuela, where the actors are not indigenous populations but local settlers. One can combine in-depth study of particular conflicts with the comparative information available from international networks (such as the World Rainforest Movement) that support such widespread conflicts.

Until recently, the bulk of the raw materials for the paper industry were produced in northern countries. Wood and paper pulp production is growing in the world, and moving towards the south, where the land is cheaper (because there is an ample supply of land mainly in Latin America and Africa, and because the people are poorer). But old-growth raw material is not enough; there are many new tree plantations. Although only one-third of world wood production goes to paper pulp, wood production for paper pulp is increasing faster than wood production for sawn logs. The slogan that sums up the resistance to such trends is 'plantations are not forests' (Carrere and Lohman, 1996).

Trained into doctrines of export-led growth, pressed to earn foreign exchange, the state Forest Department of Thailand initiated in the late 1970s the conversion of tens of thousands of hectares of natural forests into plantations of eucalyptus, in order to provide chips for paper mills, mostly owned by Japanese companies. 'Eucalyptus is like the state,' some peasants from a small, remote village in the northeast told the anthropologist Amare Tegbaru in 1990. 'It sucks and takes everything for itself' (Tegbaru, 1998: 160). In order to defend themselves against government-sponsored plantations, the peasants resorted to the language of sacredness appropriate for *pi puta* forests, and also to the newly-acquired language of environmentalism. Peasants in Thailand believed that their rice fields would be affected by the proximity of the water-guzzling and soil-depleting Australian tree; they also mourned the loss of the mixed forests from which they harvested fodder, fuel, fruit and medicines. Peasant protesters were mobilized by Buddhist priests, who led their delegations to public officials and also conducted 'ordination' ceremonies to prevent natural forests from being turned into regimented tree plantations (Guha, 2000: 100; Lohman, 1991; 1996: 40).

Regimented lines of single-species tree plantations, although often classified as forests in Europe and the USA (following the 19th-century management rule: maximum sustainable wood yield), have lost the characteristics of the true forests. The introduction of plantations means that many of the ecological and livelihood functions of the forest are lost, and poor people tend to complain accordingly. There are recent attempts to claim short-run carbon-sink functions for some eucalyptus, pine or acacia plantations (in 'joint implementation' or 'clean development mechanism' projects) (see Chapter 10). This would make the economics of plantations even more favourable, although some guarantee must be given that the carbon sequestered will not become carbon dioxide too soon. Other functions lost (degradation of the soil, loss of fertility and water retention, loss of grass for pasture) are never included in the profit-and-loss accounts of the paper pulp firms.

Resistance movements to tree plantations have developed in many countries. Another widely known case is that of the Penan, a tiny community of hunters and farmers who live in the forests of the Malaysian state of Sarawak. In the 1980s, they were steadily encroached upon by commercial loggers, whose felling activities had fouled the rivers, exposed their soils and destroyed plants and animals which they harvested for food. The processing of sago as food, as Pete Brosius explains (Brosius, 1999b), requires clean water. In watersheds affected by deforestation, existing sago, even if not destroyed, cannot be processed because of lack of clean water. Beyond this material loss, there was a deeper loss of meaning, for the Penan have a strong cultural bond with their river and forest landscape. Helped by Bruno Manser, a Swiss artist who lived with them, the tribe organized blockades and demonstrations to force the chainsaws and their operators back to where they came from. The Penan struggles were taken up and publicized by the Penang-based group, Sahabat Alam Malaysia, and by transnational organizations such as Friends of the Earth, Greenpeace and the Rainforest Action Network (Guha, 2000: 100). In contrast to hundreds of forgotten similar cases across the tropical world, this became a case in which the number of outside activists approached the number of people directly involved.[13]

STONE CONTAINER IN COSTA RICA

On 7 December 1994, the young and vital leaders of AECO (Asociacion Ecologista Costarricense) Oscar Fallas, Maria del Mar Cordero and Jaime Bustamante died in the night in a fire at their home in San José. The official verdict was accidental death. Time will perhaps tell whether there was an attempt to frighten or even kill them, but this is an issue which cannot be pursued here. Maria del Mar and Oscar (whom I met several times) had been involved throughout 1993–4 in the conflict against Stone Container in the Osa Peninsula and Golfo Dulce in south-west Costa Rica, and they were getting ready for a fresh conflict in northern Costa Rica against Placer Dome, the noted Canadian gold mining company.[14] They were practitioners of a popular environmentalism, outside mainstream Costa Rican environmentalism so much influenced by US conservationist organizations and personalities. Their loss is still felt among environmental groups in Latin America loosely allied since the Rio de Janeiro NGO summit of 1992.

Maria del Mar and Oscar had just achieved a partial victory in their conflict with Stone Container; they had placed themselves at the intersection between local livelihood interests and international groups such as the Rainforest Action Network and Greenpeace. AECO was the Costa Rican member of Friends of the Earth International. They learnt how to manoeuvre inside the permeable Costa Rican state, a democracy with such a degree of internal consensus among the social forces and the main political parties that sometimes it feels closed to dissidents. They profited from the environmental image that President Figueres (1994–8) and his Minister for the Environment, René Castro, wanted to promote. The early 1990s was a time when 'reforestation' was still a good word from any point of view, when, precisely in Costa Rica, the discussion on forest environmental services was being pioneered, when the critique against tree plantations had not yet really begun even within most environmental organizations (Carrere and Lohman, 1996).

The conflict with Stone Container had to do with both terrestrial and marine ecology. Chips from new plantations would be exported through industrial facilities which would perhaps damage the ecology of Golfo Dulce. In this case, the species chosen was *Gmelina arborea* (melina), which started to be planted by Stone on rented land in the area around Golfo Dulce in 1989, some of it degraded pastures or forest lands, some of it former agricultural land used for rice but cheap to rent because of the policy of discontinuing subsidies for domestic basic grains production under IMF advice. Stone initially obtained permission to build a dock and a factory to process the trees into chips for export. These industrial facilities would be located at Punta Estrella, in the innermost part of the Golfo Dulce, 30 km from the mouth of this tropical fiord, which has little circulation of water. It was foreseen that 180 truckloads per day would reach the factory at Punta Estrella, coming from the 24 000 ha of melina plantations. Apart from pollution of the sea, Punta Estrella was located in a biological corridor connecting two wilderness reserves on both sides of the Golfo Dulce, the Corcovado Park and the Esquinas or Piedras Blancas park. At the end, instead of 24 000 ha of melina in six years, Stone Container planted some 15 000 ha over ten years. New threats of tree monoculture now come from oil palm plantations. Permission for the chips factory and dock at Punta Estrella was withheld at the end of 1994. Stone exported roundwood instead of chips, and it did not use the permission it obtained to build the chip factory nearer the mouth of Golfo Dulce, at a place called Golfito, where there is already a dock (and a disused railway) from the days of United Fruit's banana plantations from the 1930s to the 1980s.

Before coming to Costa Rica, Stone Container had invested successfully in plantations in Venezuela but it had had recent trouble in Honduras. Pamela Wellner, of Rainforest Action Network, had been active in Honduras, and later she was active against Stone's plans in Costa Rica from her new position with Greenpeace. The *Rainbow Warrior* visited the Golfo Dulce in September 1994. European groups from Germany and Austria were also mobilized. Letters were written to the authorities, and claims were made in Costa Rica (for instance by Max Koberg, a politician and businessman who was the head of the Stone's subsidiary in Costa Rica) that there was a conspiracy of foreign environmentalists against the national interest. However, Costa Rica is so much involved in global environmental politics that a general diatribe against foreigners was not useful politically. Even Maurice Strong, the secretary of the UN Rio de Janeiro conference of 1992, had also written a letter to the authorities against Stone.

There was a difference (it was argued in Costa Rica) between good environmentalists and radical environmentalists who were nothing else but recycled communists, 'water melons', red inside and green outside, looking for trouble with American firms now that the Cold War was over. Indeed, some members of AECO had been leaders in left-wing student organizations. Maria del Mar Cordero had taken part in the Sandinista alphabetization campaign in Nicaragua as a teenager.

Outside support was successfully mobilized by the local alliance in Golfo Dulce. This alliance consisted of AECO activists and local people (many of them women, put into action by Maria del Mar) who made a living by small-scale fishing, peasant agriculture and tourist services, three sectors endangered by Stone's plans. They constituted a Committee for the Defense of the Natural Resources of the Osa Peninsula. They also got support from some permanent foreign residents on that beautiful coast. They enlisted the services of some scientists, biologists who were members of AECO, and one high-powered marine biologist from France, Hans Hartmann, who in the summer of 1993 surveyed the Golfo Dulce and recommended (without success) that it be declared a 'marine national park'. Stone employed other scientists who dismissed so-called 'non-scientific emotional arguments' (Hombergh, 1999: 206) and praised the virtues of reforestation with melina, also discounting threats to the marine environment.

AECO found support in two state agencies, the Contraloría (that supervises state expeditures) and the Defensoría (the Ombudsman, a woman at the time), in the sense that they wrote reports against the industrial facilities although not against the plantations themselves. AECO encountered a negative reaction in the executive (before Figueres' election in 1994). The Ministry of Natural Resources declared tree plantations equivalent to reforestation, and this this was true 'sustainable development'. A couple of members of parliament supported the opposition to Stone, and they helped to organize useful local open discussions in the Golfo Dulce area, where Stone representatives lost the debates.

The government commission for the technical revision of Environmental Impact Assessments was dominated by industry, and it accepted too easily the EIAs submitted by Stone. There was still no discussion in Costa Rica on alternative valuation frameworks, whether in terms of integrated assessment or of multi-criteria evaluation. Stone also obtained a 'green' certificate from the USA, and was trying to get an ISO-14000 accolade. The environmentalists had to learn all these new words. In at the end, the Figueres government called for a commission to be formed, including government representatives and outside experts such as Daniel Janzen, and the solution was reached (a few days before Oscar's and Maria del Mar's deaths) of supporting the plantations while displacing the industrial facilities towards Golfito at the mouth of the Golfo Dulce. AECO took this as a partial victory. Many local people interviewed by van den Hombergh spontaneously declared that '*las plantaciones son monocultivos*'. So a victory was also won for environmental education.

SAN IGNACIO

As expected, there was no role in this Costa Rican conflict reserved for the army (Costa Rica has no army). Neither did the Catholic church play a role, although it has helped in other environmental conflicts. The languages of human rights or territorial rights did not come into play. There are parallels and contrasts with the following case in northern Peru, also in the early 1990s, remarkable on several counts.[15] The main actors were settlers and local townspeople, including the local authorities of the Catholic church. This was not an indigenous population. The fight was against commercial deforestation of the regional forest of podocarpus, a conifer locally called *romerillo*, which is not common in the Andes (Gade, 1999). The town of San Ignacio was founded in 1941 by ex-soldiers sent as settlers to establish a national presence near the border to Ecuador. The Chaupe forest is a cloud forest in the *ceja de selva*, going down towards the Amazon basin, and it is the habitat for a number of endangered species, including the spectacled bear. There is pressure on the forest from itinerant agriculturalists, but the new threat came from Peruvian commercial timber companies, not transnationals.

In this case, as in so many others in the present book, we see that the idea that there is environmental mismanagement because the property rights are not clearly defined, is naive beyond redemption. Clearly established property rights were twisted around as opportunities for commercial gain developed in opposition to local livelihoods and expectations. Under General Velasco Alvarado's government, efforts were made to preserve, or rather sustainably exploit, the podocarpus forest, and on 2 May 1973 the San Ignacio Forest was established, enlarged the following year to include all forested areas in the districts of Jaen and San Ignacio. The exploitation rights were first given to a sort of cooperative or social property company. Later, in the 1980s and 1990s, the trend in Peru was towards privatization and towards large-scale commercial exploitation of natural resources, certainly not a novelty in Peru's economic history. In San Ignacio this meant that a new company, Incafor, owned by Carlos Muncher (whose money came from the building and public works industry), obtained a concession to exploit the *romerillos* and sell the timber to Japan. Some local administrators complained, but they were overruled from Lima in 1991. Meanwhile,

> the authorities and inhabitants had begun to worry about the impact of the depredation of the forest on the quality of village life and on the town's future survival. Seasonal farming had already reduced the forest to such a point that the supply of drinking water in the town had been seriously affected and it was feared that changes in the microclimate as a consequence of the forest's disappearance could result in soil erosion and agricultural ruin. It was feared that the activities of a company the size of Incafor would hasten the disappearance of the forest. Faced with this situation, on 12 May [1991] a forest defense committee was formed in an open meeting chaired by Celedonio Solano, mayor of San Ignacio. (Scurrah, 1998)

This was followed on 1 October by an injunction sought by Manuel Bure Camacho on behalf of the defence committee and which was favourably received by the San Ignacio judge, Emiliano Perez Acuña. Over the next nine months the conflict increased in intensity as the company opened roads into the forest. Also, in the years 1991–2, the Shining Path insurrection was at its peak in Peru (in September 1992 its leader was captured and Shining Path rapidly lost its strength).

Circumstances were difficult in Peru in 1992. There was much tension.[16] In the night of 26–7 June, there was an attack on the Incafor company's camp located some three to five hours' drive from the town of San Ignacio. It was reported that some 20 to 30 heavily armed men with blackened faces had killed two security men; others were wounded and two tractors were burnt.

> During the morning of the 27th, members of the police department in San Ignacio proceeded to arrest the principal leaders of the San Ignacio Forest Defense Committee. They tortured them, obliged them to sign incriminating statements and accused them of murder, property damage, rioting and terrorism. The local judge and doctors were impeded from entering the police station and the accused were taken to Chiclayo, the regional capital . . . It seemed that through luck or design (or a combination of both) the company had not only obtained the right to proceed with the logging of the forest, but had also managed to place its main opposition in prison. (Scurrah, 1998)

Spokesmen for environmental groups felt desolate at the alleged connection with Shining Path or other armed groups. One commission formed by members of universities and environmental groups gave up the fight, recommending 'rational exploitation of the forest by means of a forest management plan which would include reforestation that would not require the same kind of flora to be maintained', thus opening a window for tree plantations. It seemed as if Incafor had won the day. Other environmental groups still criticized the contracts made with Incafor. Meanwhile, the local bishop of Jaen and San Ignacio, the Jesuit José Maria Ezuzquiza, and his secretary, became tenacious defenders of the accused, asking that they be not considered 'terrorists', and subject therefore to special legislation, but normal civilian prisoners. The Catholic local Radio Marañón took a clear position in their defence. Pressure was exercised by Peruvian human rights organizations such as Aprodeh and also by Amnesty International.

The environmental conflict was totally unrelated to the Shining Path insurrection. The people imprisoned had not carried out the violent attack. While the environmental groups buckled under pressure, the human rights groups took the high ground in order to defend procedures in the courts less drastic than those currently practised (and which had resulted in many other innocent people being jailed as presumed Shining Path members). Indeed, tens of thousands of people in Peru were killed in the 1980s 'by mistake'. The human rights groups had enormous experience of such cases, and did the little they could to stop and denounce the killings. The authorities in Lima, including the president, who inspected personally the San Ignacio forest, moved towards protection of the forest, logging concessions being suspended on 22 December 1992 (but in 1993 attempts were made to renew them, which prompted a strong response from the Peasant Confederation of Peru and from the new executive of the Forest Defense Committee of San Ignacio). New charges of poppy growing and Colombian influences were bandied about. Congress and the press also started to defend the imprisoned members of the Forest Defense Committee. Although there were attacks on 'agitators sheltering under an ecological soutane' (Scurrah, 1998), the Chiclayo court judgment of 5 March 1993 acquitted all the accused of all charges on the grounds of lack of evidence. The judgment stated that a large part of the evidence had been invented, and included strong criticism of the behaviour of the Incafor company.

In San Ignacio, there was no intervention by international environmental groups. Some officials of the state administration (at local level and in Lima) believed in the necessity of environmental protection for that special type of forest (in neighbouring Ecuador, near Loja, there is a podocarpus national park) in a general framework of increasing privatization and exploitation of natural resources but also of increasing international debate on conservation. The Incafor company had Peruvian nationality but it was external to the region, and even to forest exploitation itself. The army was eventually open in this case to arguments from the Catholic church leaders and even from human rights organizations; it also helped the general sense of relief in the country after the Shining Path leader was captured. The judiciary acted quickly enough. National environmental groups used the opportunity to present to the national public the problem of forest depredation and its most spectacular social consequences, but they felt embarrassed by the initial hypothesis of a violent attack in defence of the forest with Shining Path's or other armed groups' intervention. Lima environmentalists 'felt more comfortable defending "nature" conceived in biological terms than when it was associated with the complexities of social and political conflicts involving human beings' (Scurrah, 1998). There were no local explicitly environmental groups in San Ignacio. The Forest Defense Committee emphasized the non-commercial functions of the forest for the water cycle, but its members still refused a green label in 1992. Absent in San Ignacio was the discussion in terms of cost–benefit analysis and compensation, or even an Environmental Impacts Assessment, while in the Stone Container case in Costa Rica many of the arguments had hinged on the quality of the EIAs produced by the company. The issue of international 'green' certification of podocarpus exports never arose.

TREE HUGGERS AND RUBBER TAPPERS IN INDIA AND BRAZIL

Many cases of social conflict support the thesis of an 'environmentalism of the poor', that is, the activism of poor women and men threatened by the loss of the environmental resources and services they need for livelihood. The languages they use are, perhaps, those of indigenous territorial rights, or the language of sacred values, though they are not 'deep ecologists'. Certainly, the environment provides the raw materials for the production of commodities, such as wood or paper pulp. The rich buy more of such commodities than the poor. The environment does also provide the recreational amenities particularly appreciated by those with leisure and money to enjoy them. More relevantly, the environment provides, apart from commodities and amenities, and outside the market, essential services needed for livelihood.

It is true that the defence of old-growth forests, and the opposition to industrial tree plantations, the defence of Amazonia or the Sunderbans against oil exploration, and the defence of mangroves against shrimp farming, are supported by the environmentalism of the IUCN, the WWF and similar international groups and their local branches. However, poor and indigenous people are often found in the forefront of many of such struggles, from Ecuador, Peru or Chile to Indonesia, from the Philippines to Brazil. The uprooting of eucalyptus, and the planting instead of a variety of fruit trees and native trees, has become a common practice of such movements in places distant from each other. As we have seen, the languages that such struggles adopt may be very diverse, such as in Thailand the tying of yellow Buddhist monks' robes to protect old trees in danger of being cleared to make way for tree plantations, or the new insistence on an Afro-American past in mangrove and oil palm conflicts in Ecuador and Colombia. These are structural conflicts, they are not simply instances of the politics of place and identity. The use of local idioms of resistance is compatible with appeals to northern NGOs and judicial courts, and with the increasing networking of the actors of such struggles through the Internet.

One current Mexican case is that of Rodolfo Montiel, who started his Organización de Campesinos Ecologistas de la Sierra de Petatlán following the steps of thousands of peasants who have opposed the depredation of 'their' resources. For seven years, Montiel's group stopped deforestation on that region in Guerrero state, finally throwing out the firm Boise Cascade. In Mexico, there is normally a high level of governmental rural violence. Montiel was tortured and put in prison. There is now, however, an alternative globalization of cultural products, subversive information and human rights, and Montiel was awarded in San Francisco an environmental Goldman Prize for the year 2000. He was featured in *Time* magazine, Hillary Clinton expressed her sympathies, the Mexican goverment was embarrassed. In his comment on such events, Victor Toledo concludes:

> The solidarity with Nature and with today's and future humankind, eagerly sought after by environmentalists around the world, is found already in the cultures of many rural populations that have escaped so far the dangerous 'pollution' of exaggerated individualism and competitiveness. There is no difference at all between former peasant martyrs in rural conflicts and the new rural champions of Nature, except that represented by fashionable concepts. The *zapatas* of one century ago are today's environmentalists of the poor. (Toledo, 2000)

Fascinating historical cases in Sri Lanka show how 'ecological discourse was used by the state to repress *chena* cultivation in order to foster the interests of the planters' (Meyer, 1998: 816). The colonial administrators, here as elsewhere, tried for a long time to suppress shifting cultivation (*chena*) as a barbarous attack on the forests. The dispossession of native forests, on the excuse of the practice of chena, led to the establishment of coffee and tea plantations. There was no organized resistance movement but isolated instances of rebellion. For instance, according to one contemporary observer, a land surveyor was surrounded by natives who

> talked and bewailed as only natives can do. They would not go away, but surrounded his tent after it was pitched. The next morning he commenced with theodolite and chain, but the natives stood in front of the former, and threw themselves down on the ground before the course of the latter, saying: 'pass over our dead bodies, before you measure and sell the hunting grounds of our forefathers'. So, without any actual violence being used, the work was stopped. (Meyer, 1998: 815–16)

As Ramachandra Guha indicates, to these old struggles against environmental degradation one must add today struggles for environmental renewal, the numerous and growing efforts by communities to better manage their forests, conserve their soil, replant mangroves, sustainably harvest their water or use energy-saving devices like improved stoves and biogas plants. Indeed, struggles of resistance imply a fight for sustainability which does not focus on theory, or even only on technology, but also on practical institution building of community management (Berkes and Folke, 1998). One such struggle of environmental reconstruction was Kenya's Green Belt Movement founded by Waangari Maathai. In 1977, Matthai abandoned her university position to motivate other and less privileged women to protect and improve their environment. Starting with a mere seven saplings planted on 5 June 1977, the movement had by 1992 distributed seven million saplings, planted and cared for by groups of village women spread over 22 districts of Kenya (Guha, 2000: 102). Pressure on the forests continues in Kenya. As reported in February 1999,[17] the allocation of land in the Karura Forest outside Nairobi 'to well-connected people and the greedy suckers who bought it from them' gave rise to much opposition among university students, environmental activists and ordinary *wananchi* (citizens), who were talking not only of defending the forests but also of reclaiming the forests. While the president of the country attributed the controversy to tribalism, Professor Maathai did not agree with this view, and attributed the attack on the forest to corruption.

Wangaari Matthai and Ken Saro-Wiwa are well known African names. In this section, two other famous cases of environmentalism of the poor, one in India, one in Brazil, are examined and compared.[18] Lesser-known examples are numbered in their thousands in the countries of the south. These two top Third World environmental struggles started in the 1970s, one in India, one in Brazil. On 27 March 1973, in a remote Himalayan village high up in the upper Gangetic valley, a group of peasants stopped a group of loggers from felling a stand of hornbeam trees. The trees stood on land owned by the state Forest Department, which had auctioned them to a sports goods company in distant Allahabad, on whose behalf the loggers had come. Forests in India are used by local peasants or by tribal groups but since colonial times they belong to the state. The peasants prevented felling by threatening to hug or 'stick' to (*chipko*) the trees. This episode sparked a series of similar protests through the 1970s whereby hill peasants stopped contractors from felling trees for external markets. These protests collectively constitute the Chipko movement.

Prior to any discussion on efficiency in forest management, the criteria with which to evaluate the production of the forest must be established. Chipko made clear to the eyes of the world that forests are multifunctional, and essential to human livelihood. It also made clear that the state was an enemy of livelihood, by allowing private enclosures. Finally, this region-specific debate led in turn to a national debate on the direction of forest policy in India as a whole. Chipko also produced many international lessons, not only in forest management strictly, but also on the interplay between communities, state and private industry, and on the use of a new environmental idiom for the description and analysis of a type of conflict with many historical precedents. Chipko was simultaneously a peasant movement of resistance and an environmental movement. Its environmental aspects would not have been visible a few decades earlier.

The interpretation of Chipko as an environmental movement opened up a vast territory of socioecological historical research on forest conflicts in India and elsewhere. Many peasant conflicts may now be seen retrospectively also as environmental conflicts. This movement of Himalayan peasants may be compared to the struggle in the Brazilian Amazon in the late 1970s and 1980s associated with the name of Chico Mendes. In the Amazon, a massive expansion of the road network opened the way for settlers and entrepreneurs in a vast enclosure movement. Cattle ranchers burnt vast expanses of primary forest. In 30 years, the Brazilian Amazonian forest which was almost untouched since the conquest, lost 10 per cent of its territory. An estimated 85 per cent of this had been converted into pastures for livestock, a most inappropriate form of land use in poor soils which were exposed and further impoverished by the next downpour of rain. All in all, this was a colossal ecological disaster. Previous attacks on the rainforests for wood or rubber extraction, whether in the Belgian Congo or in western Amazonia at the beginning of the 20th century, had been savage enough towards nature and humankind, but the scale of destruction of forests in Brazil in the 1970s and 1980s had few precedents on a similar scale – though this in a country which had already managed to destroy most of the Mata Atlantica, the rainforest along the Atlantic coast (Dean, 1995).

Not only indigenous groups, but also collectors and harvesters of forest produce such as rubber (from scattered trees) and Brazil nuts, were affected by the devastation. They were called *seringueiros*, rubber tappers. They were not indigenous peoples of pre-European origin, they were rather first or second generation inmigrants from the impoverished north-east of Brazil, left alone to procure their own livelihoods long after the large-scale commercial exploitation of rubber had collapsed. These people often had no firm legal titles to the land and forests they worked, whereas the invading Brazilian ranchers and loggers had on their side the powers of military capitalist dictators from 1964 onwards determined to 'develop' the region rapidly. In the state of Acre, ranchers acquired six million hectares between 1970 and 1975, in the process displacing thousands of rubber tappers. Led by men such as Chico Mendes, a rubber tapper himself, the *seringueiros* resorted to an innovative form of protest: the *empate* or stand-off. Children, women and men marched to the forest, joined hands, and dared the workers and their chain-saws to proceed further. The first *empate* took place on 10 March 1976, three years after the first Chipko protest. Over the next decade, a series of stand-offs helped save nearly one million hectares of forest from conversion into pastureland.

The rubber tappers of Acre started a vigorous union, and in 1987 they joined hands with the indigenous inhabitants of Amazonia to form a Forest Peoples' Alliance. This alliance pledged to defend the forest and land rights of its members. It also worked with some success, not only for the demarcation of traditional indigenous territories to be excluded from enclosures, but also for the creation of new forms of community holding, called 'extractive reserves' (an idea attributed to the anthropologist Mary Allegretti), areas where rubber tappers and others could sustainably harvest what they needed for direct subsistence and for the market, without affecting the forest's capacity for regenerating itself. This was then an instance of new institution building for natural resource management at its most genuine. It was not another example in Latin America of communities with social and sometimes legal existence since 'time immemorial' defending themselves against the modernizing assaults of mining or agricultural enterprises. It was the invention of a new community tradition in the midst of Amazonian territory by non-indigenous people, a useful precedent for today's struggles in Brazil and in other other countries in defence of mangroves (which could also become 'extractive reserves'), in defence of artisanal fishing, certainly in defence of other forests. But as the rubber tappers became more organized, the ranchers became more determined in their efforts to drive them off the land. In 1980, ranchers and their agents had assassinated Wilson Pinheiro, a prominent union organizer. Eight years later, on 22 December 1988, they finally eliminated Chico Mendes, shot dead as he came out of his house. Simply one more rural union leader killed in Brazil, one could think. Literally hundreds of rural union leaders have been killed in the last 30 years, particularly in western and northern states (Padua, 1996). However, the explicitly environmental contents and language of this struggle, and the alternative proposals born within it, made of Chico Mendes and the men and women who fought with him worldwide symbols of the environmentalism of the poor. Today there are three to four million hectares in Brazil demarcated as 'extractive reserves'.[19] It is now accepted that, from economic, social and environmental viewpoints, it is advisable to keep forest cover in Amazonia.

Both the Chipko movement and Chico Mendes' struggle drew on a long history of resistance to the state and outsiders. In the Himalayan case, peasant resistance stretched back a hundred years or more. Both showed the habitual women's involvement in environmental conflicts. Neither struggle was merely content with asking the loggers to go home: the Forest People's Alliance proposed sustainable reserves, whereas Chipko workers have successfully mobilized peasant women in protecting and replenishing their village forests. Both movements have had recourse to an ideology that carries wide appeal in their societies. Two life-long Gandhians, Chandiprasad Bhatt and Sunderlal Bahuguna, led the Chipko movement. Likewise, Catholic priests and nuns from the Theology of Liberation movement supported the rubber tappers – there was no appeal to the sacredness of Nature but to the needs of the poor.

While Himalayan deforestation has had disturbing ecological effects – soil erosion, increased flooding – the clearing of the Amazon represents an enormous loss of unexplored biodiversity, the exposure of leachable soils to rain downpours, the substitution of one cow per hectare for over one hundred tons of forest biomass per hectare, and the loss of a very large carbon deposit and water evaporation capacity (Fearnside, 1997). Not only local livelihoods but also regional and world life-support systems in general, are involved. On the social side, in both cases the decisions for the unsustainable exploitation of natural resources at the cost of local livelihoods came from outside the immediate region but within national borders. They were not cases of intrusion by transnational corporations that escape national jurisdiction (as in so many other instances in the present book), but rather the intrusion of the national consumer goods industry of India itself, and of loggers and cattle ranchers from Amazonia or from the south of Brazil. Non-violent direct action was used in both cases, understandably so in India because of the Gandhian tradition, and remarkably so in Brazil where the military were still in government at the time, and the level of violence against the rural poor is high. True, there is also endemic rural violence in some regions of India, but traditions of democracy were more robust than in Brazil. It is admirable how, in such a context, the Chico Mendes movement managed to develop a non-violent form of struggle such as the *empate*.

DEFENDING THE RIVERS AGAINST DEVELOPMENT

In this section, two types of conflicts over use of water in rural areas will be explored: first, conflicts over dams (McCully, 1996); second, conflicts over the extraction of groundwater for irrigation (with examples from India).

If the wood and paper industry has its own lobbies and professional consultants and associations (often from Finland, otherwise a small, admirable country), the global dam-building industry is also internationally organized. It has been under attack, and it has had to submit to the outside scrutiny of the World Commission on Dams. From the 1930s to today, dams have been built in most rivers in the world. The Amazon still flows freely, though no longer some of its tributaries. The mighty Paraná was dammed at Itaipú (over 10 000 MW of installed capacity, at the cost of flooding spectacular landscapes). Yaciretá has also been built (about 3100 MW) leaving behind a large financial debt. In Chile, in 1999, the Pehuenche 'strong women against the Bio-Bio dams', fought internally and internationally against the Spanish company Endesa.[20]

The world movement in favour of the building of large dams was initially based in the USA. The defence of large dams, in terms of the new technique of cost–benefit analysis of multi-purpose river development, spread out from the USA from the 1940s, especially via the World Bank. By this peculiar accounting technique, all present and future values obtained or sacrificed by building a dam are reduced to a money numeraire, and discounted at present value. Cost–benefit analysis is complemented more recently, in a two-tier process, by the cosmetics of Environmental Impact Assessments (which exclude money values). An integrated economic, ecological, social and cultural assessment is not normally practised. The World Commission on Dams, which encompassed different viewpoints, discussed such decision procedures in its report published in late 2000. In countries with less respect for purported economic rationality and/or for environmental values than the USA, large dams have been promoted nevertheless with similar enthusiasm, from the Soviet Union for many decades after 1920 (with a misguided water policy which led to the Aral Sea disaster), through Nehru's India, Nasser's Egypt, Franco's Spain, the Brazil of the military dictators of the 1970s and 1980s, to Mao's and post-Mao's China, which today boasts the biggest dam of them all, and the largest number of displaced people: the Three Gorges under construction on the Yangtze. Resistance to large dams is often resistance against the state.

Only one-fifth of all electricity produced in the world is hydroelectricity, but the environmental and social effects of dam building have been enormous (Goldsmith and Hildyard, 1984; McCully, 1996). In some countries, like the USA, little unused potential is still available, and there is even talk of 'decommissioning' some dams in the west of the country in order to restore the natural flow of rivers and recover beautiful landscapes and recreational salmon fisheries.[21] Decommissioning is also discussed in Third World countries. In Thailand, Thongcharoen Sihatham, a leader of the aptly named Assembly of the Poor, after fighting for years against the Pak Mun Dam, claimed success in June 2000 when the government agreed to keep open the dam's sluice gates so as to allow the fish to come back to the river.[22]

In the world at large, the damage from further possible large dams is larger than that already done. Thus the Sardar Sarovar dam, being built on the Narmada river in central India, will stand as a showpiece of Indian economic development. This is one of several dams to be built. One other dam would do even more damage in terms of displaced people than the Sardar Sarovar. The potential 'oustees' have come together under the banner of the Narmada Bachao Andolan (Save the Narmada Movement), led by a woman in her mid-forties, Medha Patkar. She and her colleagues have fasted outside provincial legislatures, camped outside the Indian prime minister's house in New Delhi, and walked through the Narmada valley to raise awareness of the predicament of the to-be-displaced villagers (Baviskar, 1995). They also announced their willingness to stay put in the rising water until drowned, and every monsoon season, in July and August, as the waters rise, they patiently wait on the banks of the river in their annual *satyagraha*, deciding whether the time has arrived to get drowned in a *jal samahdi*. In the meantime, in August 2001, Medha Patkar and Arundhati Roy (the novelist) were threatened with jail sentences for contempt of court because of the tenor of their comments on the Supreme Court's decisions allowing continuation of work at the dam beyond the 90 metres height, provided there is proof of resettlement of oustees (*The Hindu*, 3 August 2001).

The early social hopes placed on hydroelectricity (a renewable energy amenable to municipal development, non-polluting when compared to coal) which made of it a favourite technology for some of the first European ecological critics of capitalism, such as Patrick Geddes ('palaeotechnics' meant coal; 'neotechnics' would be hydroelectricity), have been betrayed. Hydroelectricity has been associated with water use for enormous irrigation schemes, or for making water available for sprawling urban growth, as in southern California. Thus water from the Colorado River (where the Hoover Dam is located, which unleashed the big dam era), no longer reaches the delta in Mexico, a potential international ecological distribution conflict, were the Mexicans not so meek. Hydroelectricity is also associated in southern countries with the export of aluminium, as in Tucurui, Guri or Akosombo (in Brazil, Venezuela and Ghana, respectively). Tucurui's electricity is sold at about one cent of a US dollar per kwh to the aluminium smelters – Brazil subsidizes Japan and other importers.

There is a new awareness of the perils from dams (loss of sediments and silt in the deltas, increased local seismicity, salinization of soils in irrigation schemes, loss of fisheries, new illnesses, methane emissions, degradation of water quality, loss of fertile agricultural land, loss of the riverine biodiversity, loss of cultural monuments, risk of dam failure, and so on). There is also a new awareness of the large number of people displaced by dams, prompted by struggles such as that of the Narmada in India, or by the massacre in the Chixoy dam in Guatemala at the time of the civil war. Cost–benefit analysis cannot provide a rational answer either for the commissioning or the decommissioning of dams because the money values are contingent upon the acceptance of a given structure of social and environmental inequality. Thus the cost of displacing people will depend on their degree of poverty, and also on their degree of resistance should they refuse to accept the distribution of property rights on the environment which the state and the electricity companies defend as being legal. Prices (in actual or fictitious markets) depend on distribution. Moreover, prices are only one type of value. There are other values. Thus human life has a monetary value in the insurance market, but it has other, non-monetary values in other scales. One may say, 'where human dignity is affected, economic values do not count'. One may say, as reportedly one Gujarat politician said in the 1980s, with respect to the Sardar Sarovar, 'when the waters rise, the tribals will either drown or they will be flushed out of their holes like rats'.[23] One may also say, 'when an endangered species or an irreplaceable landscape is lost, equivalent compensation is impossible'.

Often ecological distribution conflicts over dams and water policy pit some regions against others, and different interests and values are brought into play. For instance, in Spain, regarding use of water from the Ebro river, the conflict over property rights, not only on the water but also on the river sediments, has now reached public discussion. As dams have been built in the Ebro basin over the last 80 years, one of the unaccounted costs has been the loss of sediments reaching the delta, contributing to its subsidence. Ecologists have tried to introduce in the last ten years a new water policy in

Spain and elsewhere, whose main plank is ecosystemic river management, away from the economists' and engineers' approach. Rivers must have at all times a sufficient amount of water, and also periodically large floods. This is their required regime. At present, not only do most sediments not reach the Ebro delta, but also massive water transfers from the Ebro towards Barcelona and south-east Spain are foreseen. Monetary compensation for the lost sediments to the inhabitants of the delta (who are totally immersed in a market economy) would in this case resolve the social conflict between upstream and downstream, but it would not solve the problem of delta subsidence, and the consequent ecological losses. A photovoltaic energy revolution which would make hydroelectricy less necessary, and sea-water desalination cheaper (in economic and environmental terms), would resolve both the conflict and the problem.

The Ebro delta is geographically and also socially to the south of Barcelona. Demonstrations in Barcelona against water transfers from the Ebro in 2001 by groups from the delta carried banners stating *Lo sud diu prou* – the south says this is enough! More dramatically than in today's Ebro battles in Spain, there are people in northern countries who have lost their lives in dam failures, or have lost their livelihoods because of dam building. Kate Berry (in Camacho, 1998) gives a moving account of the damage caused to Native American groups by the Pick-Sloan development plan, a massive project which went on from the 1940s to the 1960s in the upper Missouri basin throughout Montana, Wyoming, Nebraska, North Dakota and South Dakota. Not only homes and rich lands were lost, but also cemeteries and shrines. Both livelihoods and non-material values were sacrificed in the quest for flood control and improved navigation.

Similar resistance movements to those against dams also exist against other forms of river 'development' – for instance, against the Paraguay–Paraná Hidrovia, led by a coalition of environmental groups called Ríos Vivos, itself affiliated to the International Rivers Network. The Hidrovia was meant to facilitate the export of about 20 million tons of soybeans per year, to be produced in Matogrosso, eastern Bolivia, Paraguay and Argentina. The *scale* on which the project was proposed had a great influence on the forms of resistance. It was planned as a single waterway of 3000km. The project was officially assessed by cost–benefit analysis and environmental impact assessment, not by multi-criteria evaluation. Against such evaluation, claims were presented on behalf of the indigenous groups still living at the riverside in some parts of the Hidrovia. Initially, the project was publicly explained as a single project, which would possibly affect the water level in the Brazilian Pantanal, a very large wetland of great natural value. It now seems that the project would practically start downstream, little by little, segment by segment, inside national borders along both rivers from Uruguay upwards.[24]

The engineers of the hydroelectric and nuclear age have been among the 'modernizers' of this century, totally alien to any of the environmental currents analysed in the present book. Sometimes hydroelectric and nuclear engineers worked together, as in the pumped-storage plants, where the water which passes down through turbines in the peak hours is then pumped back uphill again using cheap night-time nuclear electricity. The enthusiasm for nuclear power in the 1950s and early 1960s should be recalled. The symbol of the Brussels World Exhibition of 1958 was the Atomium, which still stands. It promised cheap energy, atoms for peace, a monument to the misperception of risk. Such technological optimism had a lasting influence on mainstream resource and environmental economics. The old concern with the intertemporal allocation of exhaustible resources (as in the analytically pioneering work of Gray, 1914, and Hotelling, 1931) and with the sustainable use of renewable resources such as wood or fisheries, was replaced by the concern for the natural amenities because no important environmental costs were associated with the production of commodities such as energy (Krutilla, 1967). Technological change meant that there was no scarcity of resources for the production of a commodity like electricity. However, beautiful landscapes threatened by hydroelectric dams, geomorphological wonders such as the Grand Canyon and Hells Canyon and irreplaceable biological diversity, would be increasingly scarce and increasingly valued. So Krutilla defended mountain landscapes against hydroelectricity by arguing that the electricity would be cheaply available in the future, while landscapes would become more valuable with time. Therefore Krutilla applied a cost–benefit logic to the conservation of nature. His main assumption, that technical progress was environmentally harmless, was doubtful.

Which values do 'riverkeeper' activists involved in local struggles against large dams bring into play? Sometimes, in the north, they bring forward concerns related to 'amenity' values, or 'deep ecology' values in defence of the sacredness of nature, while in the south human material livelihood is often a supreme value compatible with aesthetic concerns and with respect for other forms of life. In the north, the opposition to dams has often come from groups of people concerned by the loss of the beauties of nature, or by the loss of pleasures such as rafting down a river. In the south, the opposition also comes, as in the movement by the *atingidos por barragens* in Brazil, from poor people in danger of losing their livelihood: 'An argument often used by dam builders and backers in developing countries . . . is that concern for the environment is a "first world luxury" which they cannot afford. In fact the opposite is the case' (McCully, 1996: 58).

UNDERGROUND WATER IN INDIA

There are basically three systems of irrigation in India: first, the traditional tank system in southern India; second, the system based on canals (as in the Punjab, of colonial origin); third, the system based on underground water, where water is an exhaustible resource. David Hardiman has long studied this last system. Water scarcity in Gujarat provides the rationale for the Narmada dams. His description of well irrigation in Gujarat (Hardiman, 2000) makes clear how matters of life and death are being played out. His explanation of rural water use in India is grounded in the inequalities of caste.

Underground water, which used to be abundant in some regions of Gujarat, was not in open-access. The British changed the structure of property; landowners enjoy the right to draw groundwater from their property with no limit imposed on the amount that may be extracted. The techniques of water extraction, based on energy from oxen, were such that the wells never ran out of water, and even overflowed during the monsoon. However, starting in the early 20th century and with great impetus in the 1970s because of water demands by 'green revolution' crops, deep wells have been dug by the development of tube wells and submersible pumps which use oil or electricity for energy. Private ownership of the wells and the change in techniques have meant that the water table has been lowered, and water has become more scarce. In order to get water, farmers must bore wells deeper and, to recoup the investment, they have to get and sell more water. In some coastal regions, the vicious circle is aggravated by the inflow of sea water as the aquifer is depleted. Access to underground water is even more concentrated than access to land, and the upper caste (the Patidars or the Rajputs, depending on the area of study) control the water. Some of it they sell, but only to some chosen people in the villages. So the externality of being deprived of water is shifted upon the disadvantaged members of the villages.

A tax on water had already been discarded by the British, on the grounds that what was desired was the boring of more wells in order to irrigate more land. The state has discussed a licensing system. The ecological situation is now different from colonial times, but the interests of the upper farmer and peasant castes prevent taxing or licensing water. According to Hardiman, in Gujarat some NGOs have been successful at playing at inter-caste disputes: the NGO Utthan Mahiti, from Ahmedabad, encouraged Koli women to assert their water rights against dominant Rajputs, being supported by local Patidar politicians, the Rajputs' traditional rivals. Another approach is that of the religious Hindu group, Swadhyaya Parivar, in Gujarat and Maharastra, with two million members, which emphasizes equality (for Hindus) and collective voluntary manual labour for the replenishment of wells.

Whether water is made available through wells (as we have seen) or through canal irrigation, or even in irrigation tanks in the south of India, water use and water management are determined by caste and gender inequalities. This thesis is supported by David Mosse (1997) who explains that, in the areas of Tamil Nadu where tanks provide the main source of irrigation, the pre-colonial system was reaffirmed by the British. The tanks are rain-fed but they are often linked in larger systems, and therefore a supra-village level of control is often involved. The water 'zamindars' continued during the colonial period to treat the tanks as political assets to be presented as gifts, exchanged and redistributed, rather than as market resources for a capitalist-style agriculture. Irrigation from tanks depended on the maintenance of water channels and distribution by sluice operators of a dalit caste, who were exploited but also backed by the zamindars, who often distributed water to some groups of people, by giving grants and leases to temples, pilgrim centres, relatives and creditors. With the end of this system of local chiefs and the emergence of the land-owning dominant peasant castes, it is increasingly common for farmers to draw water from the tanks using their own pumps and pipes. In the process, the dalit sluice operators are circumvented. Farmers thus may abuse the availability of tank water in a manner similar to those who pump water from their own wells elsewhere. So the view often encountered of a well-managed, equitable, religiously based system of tank irrigation in South India is challenged by Mosse. In fact, people who are poor, mainly the poor women, cannot find satisfaction of their water needs at the local level, whether for subsistence crops or even for domestic needs; they must use the judicial system, or depend on their own direct action with support from NGOs. In conclusion, access to water is represented as an egalitarian challenge to the caste system.

Now, however, if caste meant and means in colonial and post-colonial India unequal access to water, and also exhaustion of the resource in some circumstances, a capitalist agriculture does certainly not imply social (or gender) equality, or conservation of underground water. Sugar cane plantations attempt to get more water (as they did in Morelos, Mexico, at the time of Zapata), depriving poor families of the water they need for their livelihood. Women are often at the forefront of the ensuing complaints.

To conclude, river basin development was the original home of cost–benefit analysis, and customary systems of irrigation have often been studied as paradigms of peaceful community resource management. Looking at rural water use from more conflictive perspectives, this brief section has shown the variety of actors involved. The powerful (in terms of international or regional power and in terms of market power, or in terms of caste privilege) intensify the use of a resource which is becoming more scarce. The complaints by those on the losing side are expressed in diverse idioms of valuation, far from economic reductionism.

INTERNATIONAL BIOPIRACY VERSUS THE VALUE OF LOCAL KNOWLEDGE

The word 'biopiracy', introduced by Pat Mooney of RAFI (Rural Advancement Foundation International) in 1993, has been popularized by Vandana Shiva and other authors. I would love to have invented it myself, it is so easy, appropriate and successful. 'Biopiracy' emphasizes not only the robbery of the biological raw materials (genetic resources, as they are called) but also of the knowledge about the use of such resources, whether in agriculture or medicine. This type of ecological distribution conflict is not new at all, but it has become well known in the last ten or 15 years.

I was lecturing on ecological economics in June 1999 in the city of Loja in southern Ecuador. Loja is the botanical garden of America, in Humboldt's phrase. Life is peaceful and slow, few outsiders come to Loja: some eco-tourists and ecologists going to the podocarpus park, and some post-hippies going to the beautiful Vilcabamba valley where old people abound. Whether longevity is due to the quality of the water or of genetic origin is disputed locally and it might become relevant to our topic. The lectures had been well advertised, the audience was large and sleepy but it suddenly became alive when I mentioned a time-worn episode of Andean history which I have explained at other times, too often, to imperturbable audiences. In 1638, the Countess of Chinchon, the viceroy's wife, was cured for a time of an attack of fever by using the bark of a tree sent from Loja to Lima by local officials who had acquired this knowledge from indigenous people. The viceroy was the Count of Chinchon, a village near Madrid. Loja is now in Ecuador, Lima was the capital of the viceregal territory, and it is now the capital of Peru, both countries recently in conflict because of a contested border.

The quinine tree figures in the coat of arms of the Republic of Peru because it was such an important export at the time of independence, the 1820s. Its bark was much used against malaria all around the world until the Second World War. The tree was given the botanic name of *chinchona officinalis*. So the *chinchona* (rudely misspelled in English as 'cinchona') was not baptized with the name of the indigenous experts who knew its properties but with the name of an illustrious patient. It was overexploited around Loja. The Spanish Crown attempted until the independence of America to keep a monopoly on its exports. The tree became locally known in Spanish as *cascarilla*, named after the bark (*cáscara*). Later, the same or other similar species were overexploited in Bolivia, Peru and Colombia, this being an Andean tree which grows at medium altitudes. Still later, there were plantations in the East Indies (as would happen also with rubber) and even later, in the 1940s, the isolated and synthetized active principle was used in pharmaceuticals for malaria. This is a case where both the raw material was exploited, with very little local profit because of the patterns of colonial and post-colonial trade, and the knowledge was also used, at zero price and without recognition. *Chinchona* trees were not common in the Andes, and did not exist elsewhere. There was some false trade. Rio de Janeiro pharmacists, who had to reimport *chinchona* expensively from Europe, accepted from 1808 bark from Minas Gerais sent by a gentleman called Correa de Senna, who was awarded a knighthood of the Order of Christ and a pension. Indeed, 'cinchona was a remarkable and historically decisive medical discovery, because it was a native plant truly effective against an introduced disease' (Dean, 1995: 131). They are proud of this, in Loja!

Also in Ecuador, in the summer of 1998, it became known that Abbot Laboratories, near Chicago, had patented the active principle epibatidine, with a view to developing a painkiller as effective as morphine. Epibatidine is similar to the secretion of the frog *Epipedobates tricolor* found in Ecuador and Peru, and possibly in other neighbouring countries. Interest in the frog arose because the physiological effects were known locally. The frog chemical was isolated by John Daly, a scientist at the National Institute of Health in the USA, this information then being used by Abbot Laboratories. In order to isolate the active principle, a large sample of frogs was obtained and exported from Ecuador in the 1970s, apparently without permission. This was before the Rio de Janeiro Convention on Biodiversity of 1992 was operative, which anyway has not been ratified by the USA.

The Convention of 1992 gives states sovereignty over genetic resources in their own territories, and foresees internal legislation or regulations which will allow mercantile access to genetic resources by attributing concrete ownership over them (whether to the state, indigenous communities, private owners or otherwise). The Convention demands the equitable sharing of benefits between outside companies and host countries (and the actual owners of the genetic resources, if different from the state) and theoretically recognizes in article 8J the importance of indigenous knowledge, making it necessary to obtain the prior informed consent of concerned partners before genetic resources are taken out. The Biodiversity Convention arose from a double pincer movement: the southern historic disgust at the old practice which recently has come to be known as biopiracy, and the northern wish to regulate mercantile access, using payments as an incentive for conservation, and also incidentally as proof of legitimate resource acquisition in inter-company disputes on patenting.

An increasing number of countries, including the Philippines, the Andean Pact countries (Decision 391 of 1996 which applies to Ecuador), India and Brazil, among others, have enacted the regulations foreseen in the Convention or are about to enact them. More to the point in the Ecuadorian frog case, CITES, that is the international convention banning traffic in threatened species, was operative in the 1970s when the frogs were exported. The frogs were in the CITES lists.[25] Abbot Laboratories said that it owes nothing to Ecuador because it merely got the inspiration for its drug by reading a scientific paper about the frog chemical (Pollack, 1999). But why and where were the frogs' skin secretions investigated to start with? Acción Ecológica's announcement of the Abbot Laboratories' patent in 1998 carried the title *Los sapos se llevan a las ranas*, the toads take the frogs away ('toad' meaning also a sharp person).

Events such as this one are interpreted, from a southern point of view, as one more instance of biopiracy about which one had better joke than cry and, from a northern point of view, as a confirmation of a self-defeating trend, in the tropical countries where biodiversity is mostly located, towards imposing restrictions on access to genetic resources, unless there is compensation. 'When the world mentality was that natural resources were common ownership, then there was a fertile utilization of natural resources for drug discovery. The Rio convention destroyed it.'[26] The red tape is as or more bothersome than the actual payments or promises of royalties: this is one of the reasons why the Costa Rica model is so much praised from outside. Costa Rica's Institute of National Biodiversity (InBio) demanded moderate compensation in an orderly manner, allowing access to locally made inventories – certainly different from dealing with INEFAN in Ecuador, whose head changed once a year on average in the 1990s for no particular reasons. Because of the trend towards restricting access, drug companies are reported to be cutting back on natural drug discovery programmes, using instead combinatorial chemistry. The sad little stories of Shaman Pharmaceuticals and also of the *ayahuasca* patent (see below) seem to corroborate the lack of commercial value of the indigenous knowledge of medicinal plants.

INBIO-MERCK

Is biopiracy becoming something of the past? The InBio agreement with Merck in 1991 became well known because it was the first in its genre, and because it was trumpeted as a model. InBio was formed by academic biologists and became a parastatal organization in Costa Rica. It had inventories of classified samples it had collected (with money from foundations) in the conservation areas of Costa Rica. No legislation existed at the time on the ownership of genetic resources. This is a small country, which exports bananas (grown in the territory of former rainforests) and coffee, with a very small indigenous population. Rainforests are preserved in about one-fifth of the country, about one million hectares. InBio used 'parataxonomists' to collect the samples, a word which would be insulting in many other tropical countries, where local indigenous knowledge is most relevant, but which was accepted in Costa Rica. Merck gave InBio a little over one million dollars, and the promise of a small royalty on potential profits from patents, in exchange for access to several thousand samples. The agreement between InBio and Merck was reached, on the part of InBio, by Dr Rodrigo Gámez and Dr Daniel Janzen, with support from Dr Thomas Eisner, from Cornell University, who had coined in 1989 the term 'bioprospecting' (Gámez, 1999: 143). The contract could be criticized because a small royalty on net profits from potential patents was promised, instead of a larger royalty (say, 10 or 15 per cent) on gross revenue from such patents.

This is not my main point. The point is that Costa Rica, of its own accord, decided to preserve about one-fifth of its territory as forests, after a long history of deforestation because of banana plantations and cattle raising, to which today there are added threats from mining and also from population growth. Then, until new legislation was enacted, the biodiversity in the preserved forests was mostly ceded de facto to InBio, which made some money from putting biodiversity in the market in its contracts with Merck and other companies. The decision to keep the forests untouched was based on the non-commercial values of biodiversity, and helped by other considerations such as ecotourism, water retention and carbon absorption. It is a good decision, but it is not a decision produced by the market. The Merck money is more a tip than a price. I might still be wrong if Merck or any other of the companies which have bioprospecting contracts with InBio obtain a profitable patent based on InBio's materials. The beauty of the agreement is that it can be repeated, with other firms. Samples and taxonomy are being sold, no raw materials in bulk.

The decision to conserve the rainforest is taken *outside* real markets. One can argue, of course, that the role of the forest as carbon deposit, in the water cycle, as sustainable source of renewable wood, mushrooms and nuts, as an attraction for ecotourists and as a repository of biodiversity with high though uncertain option values for the future, if *properly* valued in money terms, are worth far more that the revenue to be gained by deforestation. This is the point, actually: the uncertainties on the proper money values to be given to tropical forests when internalizing their discounted positive externalities, plus the existence of other intrisic values, opens up enough political space for a decision favourable to conservation. The decision of conservation is taken outside real markets. It is either based on intrinsic non-monetary values, or based on uncertain potential utilitarian values (fictitiously monetized, if one wishes). Once the decision is taken, then tips are welcome.

The contract with Merck, and later other contracts with other firms, have certainly been useful for the conservation of InBio, as also have the revenues InBio has obtained from foundations and international prizes, and more recently from visitors to its botanical garden in San José. Merck paid a cheap price because Costa Rica is relatively poor, and also because Merck has a relatively short time horizon. Moreover, since most of Costa Rican interesting biodiversity is not endemic but shared with the neighbouring countries, the question arises of the geographical scope such contracts ought to have. Joe Vogel (2000) has repeatedly proposed the constitution of cartels among neighbouring countries for the purpose of selling the access to their biodiversity on better terms. In such transactions, the information component is more important than the raw material component, and since knowledge will be more useful to the buyer the more organized it is, there is a possibility of cartels being established more easily than, say, for coffee or for bananas because sellers will tend to be more specialized, and in lesser numbers. Here InBio shows the way by selling access to already catalogued samples. Why not, for instance, other regional multinational InBios under the auspices of indigenous confederations from Amazonian countries?

'Bioprospecting' contracts are better for the tropical countries than straight biopiracy. Now, however, the contracts are justified, not only on grounds of equity, but also on the expectation that bringing biodiversity to the market will be a powerful incentive for conservation, and at the same time that buying access to genetic resources is an economically attractive proposition for commercial firms. All these points remain to be proved. The InBio-Merck agreement, so bandied about, must not be interpreted as a real business transaction. From Merck's point of view, it was a public relations expenditure, and from InBio's point of view it was a useful addition to their finances, which mostly came and still come from foundations and foreign governments' donations, and not from placing their inventories in the bioprospecting market. InBio does not live off the market. It has been given donations and prizes for its ideological role in promoting market-based conservation, but paradoxically only a small fraction of its finances (one-fifth, at most) comes from the market (I include in this the Merck contract and other contracts with corporations). (See Gámez, 1999.) InBio's argument would be in any case that remunerated bioprospecting is better than straight biopiracy. The counter-arguments are that bioprospecting is the modern form of biopiracy, and that, if the rationale for conservation is market remuneration, and this (at least for the time being) is not forthcoming or very small, then enemies of conservation will feel strengthened. Biodiversity has values which the market does not capture.

SHAMAN PHARMACEUTICALS

Let us now turn to the case of Shaman Pharmaceuticals, founded in 1989 in San Francisco by Lisa Conte, a graduate in business studies from Dartmouth College (King and Carlson, 1995; King *et al.*, 1996). The firm flourished for a time on promises of patents on drugs which would be derived from the knowledge of local healers in the tropical forests. Inside or outside rainforests, most people in the world resort at least in part to local health traditions, such as the Ayurvedic system in India. Shaman emphasized tropical forest conservation. Very few plants, of the very many species in the tropics, have been investigated for their potential use in pharmacy. There were two possible approaches. The first, that of the large firms, would be either to abandon natural products in favour of techniques of combinatorial chemistry or, if still interested in natural products, to perform a random collection of plants that were investigated in high throughput screening programmes. The second, novel approach, that of Shaman Pharmaceuticals, would favour collection programmes geared to medicinal plants already known by indigenous people. Hence the name of the company. The plants were not merely going to be collected; research would be conducted on them with a view to isolating active principles and taking out patents. Shaman was not in the business of selling herbal remedies, but in the patented drug business.

Of course, many important chemical compounds, such as morphine and quinine, were originally discovered through their use by indigenous cultures. This was not so new, therefore. What was new was the faith in local informants and local use, and also the promise of an attitude of reciprocity from the business back to the communities. Already before the Merck–InBio deal in Costa Rica in 1991 (which anyway did not involve indigenous groups), already before the Rio de Janeiro Convention on Biological Diversity of 1992, Shaman Pharmaceuticals stated that a logical means of compensating indigenous people for their role in drug discovery would be to give them a share in the profits from the potential drugs to be developed. This would be enacted through a foundation, The Healing Forest Conservancy, which would be fed by future profits. The promise of compensation would be an incentive for indigenous peoples to maintain the forest, or at least to maintain sustainable practices of raw material collection (prior to the chemical synthesis of the active principles). Now, however, everybody knew that a long time would elapse between investigating a plant on a cue from a local shaman, and getting a patented medicine out in the market through all the hurdles of research and clinical trials under the rules of the Federal Drug Administration – perhaps ten years, in the best of cases. Therefore short-term and medium-term reciprocity was also envisaged.

In practice, Shaman Pharmaceuticals had no financial success. The closest it came to bringing patented drugs into the market was in 1998 with Provir and Virend, whose safety was not challenged but whose curative properties (for genital herpes, watery diarrhoea and other ailments) were not established, in the exacting trials demanded by the FDA, in time for Shaman Pharmaceuticals to keep its attractiveness to investors. Shares which had stood at 15 dollars in the early 1990s dropped to a few cents. Shaman Pharmaceuticals itself dropped out of Nasdaq. *The Economist* (20–26 February 1999) concluded gleefully that, whatever the debt for past contributions from local knowledge, nowadays such knowledge (whether free or remunerated) was superfluous for modern pharmacology. Ethnobiology was a sweet, useless anthropological discipline.

In 1999, Shaman recycled itself into a company selling, not patented drugs, but herbal remedies and dietetic supplements, which is a different market with a different sort of structure. For instance, a company from Austin, Texas (*raintree.com*) sold, in 2000, *sangre de drago* on the Internet, and this market is totally open. Shaman could have channelled its conservationist feelings, from the beginning, in a different direction, as a Californian company selling intriguing rainforest products, such as *ungurahua, uña de gato, sangre de drago*, adding value in the package and the labelling, and giving back a share of the gross revenue to indigenous people both for the raw materials and for their information. Fair-trade groceries, not patented drugs, perhaps a fair-trade fast-food chain selling Brazil nuts, some varieties of cassava and other tubers cultivated in Amazonia, some of the many fruits, and meatburgers from capibara and tapir raised in the Fatima wildlife farm of OPIP, the Organization of Indigenous Populations of Pastaza.

Sangre de drago (as it is called in Ecuador, or *sangre de grado*, as it is called sometimes in Peru), is the latex of *croton lechleri*, an Amazonian tree. This latex has an active principle, taspine, described in the scientific literature years before Shaman Pharmaceuticals was founded, which has cicatrization properties. This scientific research on taspine was done because of the local use of *sangre de drago*, which, as any tourist can see, is sold everywhere in the Amazonia of Ecuador, not at all a secret shamanic product. It is supposed to be good for many things. The cicatrization properties are not in doubt. It is also a fungicide. This is public knowledge and cannot be patented. Both Provir and Virend were derived from *sangre de drago*. Had the patents resulted in viable expensive commercial drugs, no doubt local indigenous federations in Amazonia (such as the OPIP, from Pastaza) would have raised a scandal and, if able, would have challenged the patents. Shaman Pharmaceuticals' charade of reciprocity would have been laid bare even more than it has. The commercial unviability of Shaman Pharmaceuticals prevented the threatening scandal. For the fact is that Shaman got freely the knowledge about *sangre de drago* which was widely available, and cheap to get, and it never really gave much back in Ecuador which was (together with Peru) the source of its supplies. In Ecuador, in the province of Pastaza, Shaman tried but did not succeed in getting the agreement of the locally decisive indigenous confederation, OPIP, in order to collect *sangre de drago*, and went instead on its own accord to a dissident evangelical community, Jatun Molino (unmentioned in Shaman's publications). Shaman's choice of Jatun Molino recalls the collaboration also in Ecuador between the Maxus oil company in the early 1990s and dissident evangelical Huaoranis, converted by Rachel Saint. But Maxus was merely an oil company.

One can be sure that Shaman (staffed by ethnobiologists, academic chemists and medical doctors) would have liked to do things properly but it tried to take a quick and easy road, perhaps pushed by the urgency of getting a promising patented drug in order to keep investors on board. Let us imagine for a moment that InBio of Costa Rica was a private company, and that it would have had to live and grow by attracting investors based on the promises of the royalties from the patents from Merck or other companies in the last ten years! In Shaman's case, they were not only collecting plants but doing chemistry, patenting and doing clinical trials, altogether a large investment. Losses of millions of dollars were reported per year, waiting for the moment to sell the patents of FDA-approved drugs to one of the big companies, or perhaps to develop and market the drugs directly. Hence the lack of patience and local diplomacy. The short-term compensation for Jatun Molino (there was no occasion for even medium-term compensation) consisted of expanding the local airstrip (a bit self-serving, since Jatun Molino can be reached only by a two-day canoe trip, or by air), buying a cow for communal eating and paying some salaries at local rates for the collection of *sangre de drago*. No contract was signed with OPIP (though, in Peru, an agreement was made with indigenous representatives).[27] The embarrassing list of compensation items for Jatun Molino was published by a young anthropologist, Viki Reyes (1996a), in an article on Shaman's activities in Pastaza, taken up at once by GRAIN in a shortened

English version in its journal *Seedling* of March 1996, widely publicized in print and on the Internet. Other versions of the same article were published in Ecuador. The meager compensation offered by Shaman in Jatun Molino became known in circles where Shaman Pharmaceuticals had had a good reputation up to then.

RAFI included Shaman's Provir and Virend in its list of the twenty worst patents. Another patent which also made it to RAFI's list was that for a cultivated variety of *ayahuasca*, another Amazonian dream (US Patent 5751, granted in 1986). The original variety was given in Ecuador to Loren Miller, not a big deal since *ayahuasca* (*Banisteriopsis caapi*) is commonly used, with different names, as a hallucinogen all over Amazonia. Some of its uses require the intervention of shamans, and have religious overtones. Miller, who developed a stable variety, set up a small company, International Plant Medicine, in the United States, and took out a patent, trying without success to interest big companies in the properties of the plant. Some years later, in the late 1990s, as things happen in the NGO world, RAFI became aware of this patent and made public its existence, causing an uproar in Amazonian countries including Brazil. Using language which emphasized their very strong feelings on the matter, Confederación de Organizaciones Indigenas de la Cuenca Amazónica (COICA) declared that patenting *ayahuasca* was like patenting the Holy Host, and that Miller was an enemy of indigenous peoples, persona non grata, and that his safety could not be guaranteed in Amazonian territories. Some of COICA's northern donors felt such language offensive, and COICA stated it was quite ready to do without their money: the value of Amazonian sacred symbols could not be measured in money terms. COICA got help from US lawyers, and the patent was first revoked in November 1999 by the US Patent Office and later reinstated. In January 2000, Waphisana Indians from the border between Brazil and Guyana were getting ready to start a lawsuit in Europe against patents taken out by the British chemist Conrad Gorinsky on chemicals isolated from tipir, a nut from the plant *Ocotea rodiati* locally used to stop haemorrhages and prevent infections in addition to being a contraceptive, and also from another plant called cunami (*Clibadium sylvestre*) used for fishing. There are about 16000 Wapishanas. They thought of starting a lawsuit after the success of the *ayahuasca* case. Brazilian Senator Marina Silva (from the Workers' Party in Acre, an ex-nun who had worked with Chico Mendes) was helping the Indigenous Council of Roraima on the Brazilian side, and international organizations helped the Wapishanas from Guyana.[28] Many Brazilians are familiar with famous cases of biopiracy in the history of their country.

Another example of unequal exchange, this time successful, is that of the Eli Lilly company which developed two drugs, vincristine and vinblastine, from a plant from African countries called rosy periwinkle. The drugs have proved effective against testicular cancer and childhood leukaemia, and earned Lilly hundreds of millions of dollars. African countries did not share in the profits. Another case is that of the 'J'oublie' berry, in Western Africa, used as a sweetener long before the French arrived in Western Africa. A protein isolated from this plant has been patented by University of Wisconsin scientists. Other recent examples of patents in the USA relate to Asian materials widely known for their health applications, such as turmeric from India and the bitter melon from China (Pollack, 1999). In India, spectacular cases in the last few years have been the attempts by foreigners to take out patents on some properties of products obtained from the very well known neem tree (*Azadirachta indica*) and on some varieties of chickpeas and basmati rice (by Rice Tec). Such cases, including the patents on some hybrid varieties of Bolivian quinua by University of Colorado scientists (Garí, 2000), have made of 'biopiracy' a well known notion. A widespread awareness has grown of the value of genetic resources, both medicinal and agricultural. Hence the reaction from NGOs, from communities and even from the concerned states. RAFI has published some estimates of the economic values expropriated by biopiracy. There are technical questions of how to calculate this item in the ecological debt, but, beyond economics, what is new is a sense of moral outrage, mixed with a feeling of *déjà vu.*

Irritation at biopiracy has reached its extreme in modalities related to the mapping of the human genome. One can well understand the scientific interest in collecting all genetic variations in the human species, which are more interesting the more isolated the human groups have been. Iceland, as a state, outdoing InBio, has made a commercial agreement with foreign laboratories making available the genetic composition of its population for research and potential commercial use. This is a case where prior informed consent applies. There was an open debate in Iceland on the issue.

Consent was not obtained in the famous case of the Guaymi woman from Panama, some of whose genetic material was patented without her knowledge, and it is not obtained in a meaningful way in the many hasty collections of genetic materials from indigenous groups around the world over the last few years under the Human Genome Project. In 1998, the government of China temporarily halted a project run partly by US scientists that 'sought clues to longevity by studying the genes of 10000 elderly Chinese' (Pollack, 1999) until agreement was reached on how publications and patents would be shared with Chinese scientists and organizations.

FARMERS' RIGHTS AND ECO-NARODNISM

The critique of biopiracy in agriculture, the fact that peasant varieties of crops and peasant knowledge have been up for grabs while 'improved' seeds are increasingly protected by regimes of intellectual property rights, is reinforcing a view of agriculture favourable to agroecology, food security, and the *in situ* conservation or coevolution of plant genetic resources. In the 'centres of agricultural diversity' (for instance, the Andes for the potato, Meso-America for maize), named after the Russian geneticist Vavilov, there has been over the last thousands of years a large amount of experimentation by peasants (women and men) in order to produce the thousands of varieties adapted to the different conditions. These varieties have been shared freely. In India, as Kothari puts it (1997: 51), a single species of rice (*Oryza sativa*) collected from the wild some time in the distant past has diversified into approximately 50000 varieties as a result of a combination of evolutionary/habitat influences and the innovative skills of farmers. This contribution to genetic diversity is a fact that the modern seed industry conveniently sidesteps, and that the consumers of industrialized countries have ignored until recently.

Agricultural biopiracy is a topic which the Food and Agriculture Organization of the United Nations (FAO) has been discussing with no noticeable results for 20 years under the name of Farmers' Rights. Some governments from poor countries say that

> if a company takes a seed from a farmer's field, adds a gene and patents the resulting seed for sale at a profit [or otherwise 'improves' the seed by traditional methods of crossing, and then protects it under the Union for the Protection of New Plant Varieties (UPOV) rules], there is no reason the initial seed should be free. They also say patents ignore the contributions by indigenous peoples, who often are the true discoverers of useful plants and animals, or of farmers who improve plants over the generations. The negotiation run by the Food and Africulture Organization [on Farmers' Rights] is weighing whether to compensate traditional farmers for work on improving crops and maintaining different varieties. Malaysia has proposed an international fund of $3 billion but the United States opposes it. (Pollack, 1999)

Notice that US$3 billion would represent not more than two dollars per member of the still existing peasant families in the world today, a negligible incentive to continue with their task of *in situ* conservation and coevolution of seeds. Twenty dollars per year could start to make a difference, if they reached the grass roots. But, then, who wants the Third World farmers to continue growing and locally freely sharing or selling their own low-yielding, low-input seeds? From the point of view of international capitalism, replacing their seeds with commercial seeds would be more conducive to economic growth. A new commodity, the seed, would definitively leave the sphere of oikonomia to enter into chrematistics. Should not traditional seeds be really be forbidden on grounds of lack of sanitary or yield guarantees? (See Kloppenburg, 1988b, for a pioneering study.)

There is, then, growing alarm in southern countries which are centres of agricultural biodiversity, or close neighbours to them, because of the disappearance of traditional farming. This new awareness, which goes totally against the grain of development economics, is helped by the social and cultural distance between the seed companies (often multinationals) and the local peasants and farmers. The languages of social exploitation and national security have been added to the agronomic language of defence of domesticated biodiversity against genetic erosion. While conservation of 'wild' biodiversity in 'national parks' is often seen as a 'northern' idea imposed on the south (as, to some extent, is really the case), the conservation of *in situ* agricultural biodiversity was for many years left aside by the large wilderness northern organizations. It was pushed instead by specific NGOs such as RAFI and GRAIN, also by southern scientists and by southern groups which develop pro-peasant ideologies. Countries are seen as increasing their national and food insecurity as they increase their dependence on outside seeds, technologies and inputs. This feeling of insecurity will increase with techniques of genetic engineering.

There are deliberate attempts in India by groups and individual farmers to revive agricultural diversity. In the Hemval Ghati of the Garhwal Himalaya, some farmers under the banner of the Beej Bachao Andolan (Save the Seed Movement) have been travelling in the region collecting seeds of a large diversity of crops. Many farmers grow high-input high-yield varieties for the market but also other varieties for their own families. The movement emphasizes the economic costs of inputs, and the health and ecological implications of using chemicals, and tries to spread some varieties like thapachini that performed well and produced more fodder. An important issue is to promote not only the survival of many varieties of the main crops (wheat and rice) but also to keep alive other food crops which have been not subject to 'Green Revolution' seed substitution, such as bajra, ramdana and jowar, and also pulses in general. In the south of the country, the somewhat grandly named 'seed satyagraha' of the Karnataka Rajya Raitha Sangha (KRRS), became well known in the early 1990s.[29]

Monsanto has used the loopholes in legislation or in effective regulation to introduce transgenic crops outside the USA. Thus there is a feeling in some parts of India against the introduction of Bt cotton (that is, cotton seeds into which the bacillus thurigiensis has been genetically engineered to act as an insecticide, which in principle looks a good idea, except that gene transfer might occur). In Andhra Pradesh, the farmers' movement APRS uprooted and burned two crop sites in 1998, and alerted the state parliament and government to ban further field sites, while in Karnataka the leader of the farmers' movement KRRS transparently called on the company to reveal the exact locations of its field tests of transgenic Bt cotton. Monsanto has been more successful elsewhere. There was little opposition in Argentina to transgenic soybeans (Pengue, 2000). The Ukraine and Bulgaria have been described as 'Monsanto's European Playground for Genetic Engineering',[30] because of the introduction of Bt potatoes and also transgenic maize and wheat in countries where not only are there no clear rules on liability and compensation but the regulatory structure is weak and/or corrupt, and there are no strict biosafety rules to regulate imports of GM seeds and crops.

In India, on 30 November 1999, the first day of the WTO conference in Seattle, several thousand farmers gathered in Bangalore at the Mahatma Gandhi statue in the park. They issued a 'Quit India' notice to Monsanto, and they warned the prestigious Indian Institute of Science not to collaborate with Monsanto in research. The company was urged to leave the country or face non-violent direct action against its activities and installations. Agribusiness had already been warned with the destruction of Cargill installations in one district back in 1993. The KRRS leaders have travelled around the world, much involved in the debates and actions against the World Trade Organization (WTO) because the new regulations on international trade bring in their wake the enforcement of property rights on commercial seeds, which unjustly do not recognize the original raw material and knowledge, while preventing farmers' local gifts or sale of such commercial seeds. In 2001, the KRRS was still trying to prevent the wholesale introduction of transgenic Bt cotton in India.[31]

Also in India, Navdanya is a large network of farmers, environmentalists, scientists and concerned individuals which is working in different parts of the country to collect and store crop varieties, evaluate and select those with good performance, and encourage their reuse in the fields (Kothari, 1998: 60–61), certainly a more participatory strategy than that of *ex situ* cold storage. What other name but 'ecological neo-narodnism' to give to such initiatives? Reality is contradictory, and movements against Cargill and Monsanto are combined in India with movements for subsidized industrial fertilizers. The new issue however, is, whether a movement consciously based on praise for traditional organic agriculture, and against transnational companies, such as the KRRS, can inspire other agrarian movements of poor peasants and landless labourers in India and elsewhere. Who would have thought, 20 years ago, that praise for organic agriculture would be expressed, not by professional ethnoecologists or agroecologists or by Northern neo-rural environmentalists, but by real farmers from India in international trade meetings? This is not homespun oriental wisdom combating northern agricultural technology, it is not identity politics only. On the contrary, it must be interpreted as part of an international world-wide trend with solid foundations in agroecology towards an *alternative modernity* (to use Victor Toledo's favourite formulation).

Changing continent, what is the strategy that the Quechua and Aymara peasantry could bring into play, in order to survive and prosper against the forces of modernization, development and rural depopulation? In the land reforms of the last 50 years, they got the land by fighting against the modernization of the haciendas. The hacendados wanted to get rid of them, they stayed put, and increased their holdings. There are more established communities and more community (pasture) land in the Andes now than 30 or 40 years ago. This bothers the neoliberals. The peasantry has not yet decreased in numbers, despite migration, but now the birth rate is coming down. Will Quechua and Aymara communities survive as such? Only 40 years ago, integration and acculturation was the destiny traced for them by local modernizers (such as Galo Plaza in Ecuador) and by the US political–anthropological establishment. Their resistance today would be helped by improvement in the terms of trade for their production, if subsidized imports of agricultural products from the USA and Europe were stopped, if they could get subsidies (in the form of payments for farmers' rights, for instance, and subsidies for use of solar energy), and if they could exercise organized political pressure for this purpose, not only as peasant and indigenous confederations but as nationalist movements, as is taking place in Ecuador and in Bolivia earlier than in Peru. I heard Nina Paccari, who is a lawyer and not an agronomist, vice-president in the late 1990s of the Congress of Ecuador, a member of CONAIE (the indigenous confederation), name publicly with feeling and knowledge, switching from Spanish into Quechua, the varieties of different crops she knew from her grandmother, in order to explain the concept and the reality of genetic erosion to a large environmental conference in Quito in 1995. Nationalist movements revive and even invent traditions: the language, of course, if still available, specific forms of civil law, some religious peculiarity, or, as we shall perhaps see explicitly for the first time in the Andes and also in Mesoamerica, an agroecological pride which provides a foundation for an alternative development or, as Arturo Escobar would put it, for an alternative *to* development.

If not this, what then? Should Andean peasants, with low-yielding agriculture, give up farming and livestock raising as the economy grows, give up their communities and their languages? Perhaps some will be forced to do so anyway because of desertification due to climate change. Should, then, some of their grandchildren, as the economy still grows more, come back in small numbers as subsidized mountain caretakers, making music and dancing as Indians for the tourists? In the final analysis, *in situ* agricultural biodiversity and local food security could be saved as part of a movement which would put a much higher value also on the preservation of cultural diversity. This is what Pratec in Peru, founded by the dissident agronomist Eduardo Grillo, tried to do, building on the work by agronomists from remote provinces such as Oscar Blanco who long defended cultivated species such as quinua and many tubers (the 'lost crops of the Incas') against the onslaught of imported subsidized wheat, and also defending *in situ* coevolution of varieties of potatoes and all the other species. Pratec is romantic and extremist, but the subject it puts on the table is realistic and down-to-earth. It is not Pratec's fault that it is not considered worthy of attention in multilateral banks or even in universities (Apffel-Marglin, 1998). For, under the discussion on agricultural biodiversity coevolution, lurks a large question, which is still outside the political and economic agenda. Has the march of agriculture in the last 150 years in western countries been wrong? What is the agronomic advice that should be given, not only in Peru or Mexico, but even more in India or in China: should they preserve their peasantries or should they get rid of their peasantries in the process of modernization, development and urbanization? How to stop not only agricultural genetic erosion but also the loss of animal races? FAO often quotes a figure of 75 per cent of agricultural varieties already lost *in situ* (though there is not enough research to substantiate a precise quantitative claim) and it has also asserted that 30 per cent of all races of domestic work or edible animals have disappeared or are about to disappear (*Financial Times*, 15 September 1998). Hence the Indonesian chicken disaster in 1998, a failure of food security, when the economic crisis, the devaluation of the rupee and the previous substitution in better times of imported chicken races fed with imported feedstuffs, for local, vanished chicken races, led to a great scarcity of chicken in the markets.

The usual explanation for the disappearance of the agricultural active population in the process of economic development is that, as agricultural productivity increases, production cannot increase *pari passu* because of a very low income elasticity of demand for agricultural produce as a whole (though not for specific items, such as cut flowers or, initially meat, compensated by negative income elasticity for potatoes and pulses directly consumed by humans). Therefore the active agricultural population decreases not only in relative but also in absolute terms, and indeed this has been the path of development – in Britain even before the First World War and in Spain since the 1960s, though not yet in India. Now, however, agricultural productivity is not well calculated, nothing is deducted from the value of production on account of chemical pollution and genetic erosion, and the new inputs are valued too cheaply because fossil energy is too cheap, and because unsustainable use is made of soils and some fertilizers (such as phosphorous). What the ecologically correct prices should be, nobody knows. The important point is that the ecological critique of the economics of agriculture opens up a large space for neo-Narodnik argument, a space which is being increasingly used around the world (and even in Europe by José Bové and the French Confédération Paysanne). Issues of global environmentalism, such as biodiversity conservation, threats from pesticides and energy saving, are transformed into local arguments for improvements in the conditions of life and for cultural survival of peasants, who are learning to see themselves no longer as doomed to extinction. Such arguments have become widespread in new networks such as the Via Campesina (the Peasant Way), which has instituted an international Peasants' Day, the 17 April, the anniversary of the massacre of 19 members of the Movement of the Landless in 1996 in El Dorado, Parà, Brazil. This is not a phenomenon of post-modernity, in which some live (or try to make a living) by buying Monsanto shares, others eagerly eat hogs grown on transgenic soybeans, others are macrobiotic, and still others do organic farming. It is rather a new route of modernity, away from Norman Borlaug, a modernity based on scientific discussion with, and respect for, indigenous knowledge, improved ecological–economic accounting, awareness of uncertainties, ignorance and complexity, and, nevertheless, trust in the power of reason.

Mexican peasant agriculture is under threat because of food imports from the USA under the North American Free Trade Agreement (NAFTA), particularly of maize. Eco-Zapatism was overdue in Mexico. In the early 1990s, President Salinas got Mexico into the OECD. Guillermo Bonfil had published his deeply moving account of vanishing indigenous Mexico (Bonfil Batalla, 1996). It has now become general knowledge in Mexico that indigenous cultures and bioversity go together (Toledo, 1996, 2001). Biodiversity is valuable even when it has no market. The Chiapas rebellion came out into the open against the NAFTA on the day it became operative. It is helping to make the indigenous peasantry a political subject. Mexican peasants never thought of patenting or instituting other types of intellectual property rights on the varieties of maize that have been collected in public or private *ex situ* repositories, and then used by the commercial seed industry either domestically or in the USA or other countries. Mexican peasants never thought of patenting varieties of beans (*Phaseolus vulgaris*), but one US based company was suing Mexican bean exporters at the end of 1999, charging that the Mexican beans they are selling in the USA infringe a patent taken out by Larry Proctor, the owner of a small seed company, Pod-Ners. The patent (n. 5894079) is on a yellow bean variety. Proctor called this variety Enola, and acknowledges that it was developed from Azufrado and Moyocaba beans from Sonora, yellow landraces (or rather 'folkseeds', as Pat Mooney likes to call landraces since they do not grow by themselves on the land). Proctor selected yellow beans of a particular hue and planted them again and again, several crops since 1994 when the original stock was imported from Sonora, and obtained a uniform and stable population of beans of a particular shade of yellow. No genetic engineering was involved. RAFI called this 'a textbook case of biopiracy', and stated that at CIAT in Cali (one of the CGIAR research centres and *ex situ* deposits) there are scores of yellow Mexican bean varieties which are 'in trust' germplasm under the the 1994 agreement between CGIAR and FAO, therefore not patentable. Why, then, can the Pod-Ners variety be patented when it is probably genetically identical to some of these other varieties? Mexican agricultural authorities have said that they would fight the patent, though this will be expensive.

How to combat biopiracy? Should there be a rush in southern countries to impose intellectual property rights on crop varieties, animal races and medicinal knowledge? In India, Anil Gupta has long confronted this question with a pioneering large-scale ground-level effort to document the local communities' knowledge regarding old and innovative resource uses in the form of local registers. The objectives are manifold: the exchange of ideas between communities, the revitalization of local knowledge systems, the building up of local pride in such systems, and protection against intellectual 'piracy' by outsiders (Kothari, 1997: 105). The protection arises because prior registration and publication would stop patenting. As Anil Gupta has said repeatedly, if somebody is to patent some properties of neem, why not ourselves, Indian farmers and scientists? The main thrust of his work, however, has been to enhance local pride in the existing processes of conservation and innovation, and to stop outside advantage being taken gratis from this work.

One could argue that registration is not enough, that trade secrets, proper patents or other forms of intellectual property rights are needed as an incentive to *in situ* conservation and *in situ* innovation. Now, really, are patents and the money that patents might bring a necessary stimulus to innovation? Moreover, what is the cost of worldwide patenting? The technical innovations at CERN in Geneva which led to the development of the Internet were not patented, nor were the mule or the windmill patented. Cooking recipes are not patented, not even protected as trade secrets. Honours, prizes and social recognition have been powerful incentives to creativity. Moreover, important artists have often failed in their lifetime.

Finally, a comment is needed on what is wild and what domesticated.

Continued enhancement of a diverse and reliant agriculture depends on the continued availability of wild relatives of crops, which sometimes are found very near the agricultural fields themselves but sometimes are in the 'wild' areas. The difference between domesticated biodiversity and 'wild' biodiversity disappears in studies such as that of Descola, on the cultivated and civilized Amazonian forest (Descola, 1994).

In summary, agricultural policy should balance environmental, economic, social and cultural values on different geographical and time scales. In some interpretations, modern agriculture is characterized by lower energy efficiency, genetic and soil erosion, and ground and water pollution. From another point of view, in the language of economics, modern agriculture achieves increased productivity. Another non-equivalent description of agricultural development will emphasize loss of indigenous cultures and knowledge. There is here a clash of scientific perspectives, also a clash of values. How to integrate the different points of view? How to decide on an agricultural policy in the presence of such opposite, legitimate points of view?

WHO HAS THE POWER TO SIMPLIFY COMPLEXITY?

This is a book of political ecology, a field (born at the intersection between human ecology and political economy) which studies ecological distribution conflicts. It is also a book of ecological economics, for the following reasons. First, such conflicts are born from the contradiction between economic growth and environmental sustainability. Ecological economics examines, it is hoped in a dispassionate way, whether such contradiction really exists, hence the technical debates on absolute and relative 'delinking' and on 'Kuznets environmental curves'. Second, popular resistance to environmental degradation often implies alternative proposals, and there the question is asked, how are such proposals to be assessed in terms of (indicators and indexes of) sustainability? Third, the language of ecological distribution conflicts is in some cases that of economic valuation: for example, how to put a price on environmental services, how to compensate for damages, how to substitute for exhaustible resources so that the sum of 'natural capital' and 'human-made capital' stays at least constant in a 'weak sustainability' framework. Thus a conflict over a dam may be expressed as a dispute over the proper economic values to be used for cost–benefit analysis.

Pigou was among the first economists who, as early as the 1920s, tried to bring the environment into the measuring rod of money. Economists are still fighting this battle, though they are losing it because of the 'protest' answers of citizens who refuse to behave as fictitious consumers in contingent valuation surveys (Sagoff, 1988), the existence of what economists call 'lexicographic' preferences such as livelihood requirements or deeply held environmental values, and the lack of interest by poor people in an allocation of environmental impacts in actual or fictitious markets where their own health and livelihood will be valued cheaply. Thus, despite 'the unwillingness or inability of authorities to understand messages encoded in terms other than those of the dominant economic discourse',[32] the idioms in which ecological distribution conflicts are fought are often alien to the market (or fictitious market): the ecological value of ecosystems, the respect for sacredness, the urgency of livelihood, the dignity of human life, the demand for environmental security, the need for food security, the defence of cultural identity, of old languages and of indigenous territorial rights, the aesthetic value of landscapes, the injustice of exceeding one's own environmental space, the challenge to the caste system, and the value of human rights. In this chapter we have seen the deployment of such languages in cnvironmental conflicts.

In the USA, the 'bottom-line' means the lowest line in a financial statement that shows net loss or profit, and, tellingly, also means the final outcome or the essential point in an argument. Conflict resolution and policy making often demand a forced reduction or simplification of complexity, thereby denying the legitimacy of some points of view. Exceptionally ecological distribution conflicts may be expressed as discrepancies in valuation inside one single standard of value, as when monetary compensation for externalities is asked for. The question is then of the following type: how to calculate the indemnities that Texaco should pay back in dollars for damages in Ecuador? However, ecological distribution conflicts are also expressed as 'value system contests', as clashes of incommensurable standards of value.

The monetary values given by economists to negative externalities or to environmental services are a consequence of political decisions, patterns of property ownership and the distribution of income and power. There is thus no reliable common unit of measurement, but this does not mean that we cannot compare alternatives on a rational basis through multi-criteria evaluation. Or, in other terms, imposing the logic of monetary valuation (as in cost–benefit analysis in project evaluation, or GNP growth arguments in political decisions at state level) is nothing more than an exercise in political power. Eliminating the spurious logic of monetary valuation, or rather relegating it to its proper place as just one more point of view, opens up a broad political space for environmental movements. Nobody ought to have the exclusive power to simplify complexity, dismissing some perspectives, giving weight to some points of view only.

NOTES

1. The source is Project Underground (www.moles.org).
2. *The Economist*, 12 July 1997, p.30; *El Universal* (Caracas), 3 August 1997, pp. 1–12.
3. One example of south–south networking: the Kaiama Declaration issued by the conference of Ijaw Youth Movements, 11 December 1998 was included, in Spanish, in Lorenzo Muelas, *Los hermanos indígenas de Nigeria y las compañías petroleras. Conociendo las tierras de los indígenas negros del Delta del Niger*, issued by OilWatch. Lorenzo Muelas, a former senator, is a leader of the Guambiano people in Colombia. See also *Tegantai*, 14 October 1999, monographic issue on Human Rights and Petroleum Exploitation, with an account by Isaac Osuoka on human rights abuse in the Niger Delta.
4. Samuel Nguiffo, in *Tegantai*, 14, 1999, p.29; see also *The Guardian*, 11 October 1999.
5. See the website *texacorainforest.org*, with information from both sides.
6. Witness for Peace, '*A crude awakening. The World Bank, US policy, and oil in Guatemala*', Washington, DC, 1998. Also, talk by Marcedonio Cortave at Amherst College, Mass. 18 October 1999, and Luis Solano, 'Guatemala: en lucha contra la explotación petrolera', *Ecología Política*, 19; 2000, 155–9.
7. For instance, letter from Marcos to José Saramago, December 1999, in *Ecología Política*, 18, 1999.
8. Information in *Tegantai*, no. 14, October 1999, pp.18–24; in Oilwatch, *The oil flows: the earth bleeds*, Quito, 1999, report from Noel Rajesh from TERRA (Thailand), pp.148–59; and, for Judge Paez's decision, the website *diana.law.yale.edu* (a project on international human rights, at Yale University Law School).
9. Cf. Yves Miedzianogova, Stuart T. Solsky and Rachel Jackson, 'The Unocal case: potential liabilities for developers for activities in foreign countries', *The metropolitan corporate counsel*, July 1997 (available at www.kelleydrye.com/prfin3.htm).
10. *Rachel's Environmental and Health Weekly*, summary of 1998 news.
11. There is a European university project on such cases, led by Sam Zarifi, University of Rotterdam (www.multinationals.law.eur.nl).
12. For an updated account of conflicts on deforestation and new tree plantations around the world, see the website wrm.org.uy.
13. The Penan struggle is the subject of a book being prepared by Pete Brosius, of the University of Georgia. See also Brosius (1999b). Bruno Manser disappeared and probably died in the region in 2000.
14. This conflict with Stone Container (a US paper company) has been narrated by Helena van den Hombergh (1999) in an excellent book which is a tribute to the activists of AECO and at the same time a detailed reconstruction based on careful fieldwork over four years for a doctoral thesis at the University of Amsterdam.
15. A good source on this conflict is Scurrah (1998). I am grateful for information to Manuel Boluarte of Aprodeh, Lima, Peru. See 'Represión contra el ecologismo popular en el Norte de Perú', *Ecología Política*, no.5, 1993.
16. I remember frightening nights in July 1992 in Lima, with bombs exploding not too far away, and a terrifying day at Lima airport (which was a threatened place) waiting for a plane to Piura to attend a meeting of Andean specialists on agricultural biodiversity, watching President Fujimori on TV haranguing the troops on Peru's national day.
17. John Githongo, 'The Green Belt and the Fading Green Ink', *The East African*, 8–14 February, 1999, p.11.
18. The following two pages are closely based on Guha (2000: 116–17). For Java, see Peluso (1993), for Burma, Bryant (1997).
19. On Chico Mendes, see Hecht and Cockburn (1990) and the interview with him published posthumously in *Ecología Política*, 2, 1991.
20. For up-to-date information on such conflicts around the world, see the website of the International Rivers Network.

21. *New York Times*, 17 October 1999, article by Sam Howe Verhovek on the cost–benefit analysis including so-called 'existence values' relevant to the proposed breaching of four hydroelectric dams in the Snake River.
22. Vasana Chinvarakorn, *Bangkok Post*, 17 June 2000. I owe this reference to Clemens Grunbuhel.
23. Jail Sen, 'Effects of the Narmada verdict', *The Hindu*, 31 July 2001.
24. Taller Ecologista (Rosario), 'Los mitos de la Hidrovia', *Ecologia Politica*, 16, 1998, pp.147–9.
25. Acción Ecológica, in *Ecologia Politica*, 16, 1998, p.151.
26. W. Fenical, director of the Center for Marine Biotechnology and Biomedicine, University of California, San Diego, reported by Pollack (1999). 'Common ownership' is taken to mean open access, in post-Hardin parlance.
27. Documents sent on 11 October 2000 by S.R. King to me in Barcelona, after a first version of this section was posted on the web when I gave a talk at Harvard in 1999, clarify the sort of contract Shaman had in Peru. A first document of 18 December 1992 granted Shaman permission for eight months to prospect and commercialize unspecified medicinal plants; this was signed by the Aguaruna-Huambisa council and a large number of representatives. In a letter of 23 November 1993, Shaman asked the Aguaruna-Huambisa council for eventual permission for patenting (*sacar una patente sobre el látex de croton de la sangre de drago*). This letter was apparently never answered.
28. *Istoe* magazine, S. Paulo, 19 January 2000, and GRAIN's Bio-IPR server.
29. Cf. the letter from M.D. Nanjundaswamy, 'Farmers and Dunkel Draft', *Economic and Political Weekly*, 26 June 1993, and the e-mailed newsletter of the KRRS. Also Akhil Gupta (1998, last chapters), for a description of the KRRS up to the mid-1990s.
30. Iza Kruszewska, International Programmmes Co-ordinator ANPED, Northern Alliance for Sustainability, paper for the Permanent People's Tribunal on Global Corporations and Human Wrongs, University of Warwick (School of Law), 23 March 2000.
31. Interview with Professor Najundaswamy in Bangalore, 25 July 2001.
32. Roy Rappaport, 'Distinguished Lecture in General Anthropology: The Anthropology of Trouble', *American Anthropologist*, 95, 1993: 295–303.

7. Indicators of urban unsustainability as indicators of social conflict

Urbanization increases because of productivity increase in agriculture, coupled with low income elasticity of demand for agricultural produce as a whole. Therefore agriculture expells active population. As we have seen, the ecological critique is that increases in agricultural productivity (which today depend on increasing inputs into agriculture and on the externalization of environmental costs) are not well measured because they do not take into account the decreased energy efficiency of modern agriculture, the genetic erosion that takes place and the effluents produced. So both cities and countryside nowadays tend to push environmental problems to higher spatial scales and longer temporal scales. But, while it would technically be possible to return to a pattern of 'organic' agriculture, large prosperous cities are irremediably based on fossil fuels and on the externalization of environmental costs. A world where urbanization is increasing fast is consequently a more unsustainable world. Cities are not environmentally sustainable; by definition, their territory is too densely populated with humans to be self-supporting. Do cities produce anything of commensurable or comparable value in return for the energy and materials they import, and for the residues they excrete? What are the internal environmental conflicts in cities, and are they sometimes successfully pushed outwards to larger geographical scales? These are the points of departure for the present chapter.

THE CENTURY OF THE MOTOR CAR?

Among the interpretations of the 20th century published in the last days of 1999, one seemingly uncontroversial one was that this had been the century of the triumph of the automobile. First in the USA, then in Britain and continental western Europe, also in Japan, in Korea and in Spain, production of cars was at different moments or still is the leading sector of the economy. In the 20th century, the industrial working class of some countries, regimented on workdays on Taylorist lines, was able to buy cars and to enjoy them over miles of new motorways leading to the parking lots of shopping malls or holiday resorts. In other words, modernity in the 20th century had meant the troika of Ford, Taylor and Le Corbusier. The number of private cars in the world exceeded 550 million in the year 2000; in some countries there was a car for every two people. Now, in the rich countries, the industrial working class seems to have vanished. Towards the end of the century we had entered 'post-fordism'.

There was also a strong movement against state regulation, despite the new environmental awareness. Reliance on the unregulated market and environmental concern were reconciled by the belief that the economy could grow with fewer and fewer environmental impacts, since the leading growing sectors of the New Economy were now informatics, and many forms of services. Conventional wisdom was that we were moving into a 'dematerialized' economy because of the increasing weight of the service sector in terms of employment and in terms of economic value added. A British film like *The Full Monty* captured the plight of unemployed post-fordist, post-industrial workers in Sheffield, trying to make a living in the entertainment industry. Was dematerialization a reality? True, incomes were increasingly gained not in factories but by providing services which required directly low energy and material inputs. Incomes might be obtained, for that matter, by trading immaterial financial derivatives at home on the Internet. One question was the increased electricity required by using computers as domestic appliances. Another more weighty question was, on which items would the increased incomes gained by economic growth be spent? Probably on well-heated and well-refrigerated houses, much recreational travel, and computers and cars, indeed cars with computers.

There was perhaps a permanent trend in the rich economies towards relative 'delinking'; that is, the rate of growth of energy and material input was lower than the rate of growth of GNP. There was not yet absolute 'delinking'. Moreover, relative 'delinking' was to some extent a consequence of a geographical displacement of sources of energy and materials, and also of sinks for waste (such as carbon dioxide emissions), an effect which was not properly taken into account in the statistics. Instead, in the age of coal of the long 19th century until 1914, Europe and the USA had by and large both mined and consumed *in situ* the coal they required. Also hydroelectricity had rarely travelled outside the country of production. Now, oil and gas travelled far from the places of extraction. By the year 2000, even the USA was importing over half the oil it consumed. Moreover, though the 20th century had seen coal decrease in importance compared to oil and gas, five times more coal was mined in the world in 1990 than in 1900 (McNeill, 2000: 14).

World population had grown fourfold in the 20th century, reaching

6 billion in the year 2000. It will perhaps grow still further to 10 billion, by 2050, though human demography is difficult to predict. Would a prosperous world then have a stock of 5 billion cars, almost ten times as many cars as in the year 2000? *Would the 21st century be the real century of the motor car?* Would the car become an object of mass-consumption worldwide, or would its expansion encounter ecological limits? Was the car, not economically but *ecologically*, a positional good, a sign of oligarchic wealth which could not spread widely? A new car in the year 2000 cost at least ten times as much as a personal computer. Its building and maintenance required an energy and material input, and also a labour input, higher than the personal computer. The car thus remained undoubtedly one main factor in economic growth. Although new techniques were promised which would reduce some forms of pollution from cars, such as fuel cells, the fact that the car industry would remain a leading sector of the growing economy implied, without need for much other research, that it would be most difficult to decrease the inputs of energy and materials into the economy. What would be the implications of extending to the whole planet this gigantic technological lock-in, in terms of settlement patterns, energy consumption, air pollution and climate change?

The car is one main item of technological tranference from rich to poor countries. As the environmental journalist Daryl D'Monte puts it, urban investment in a growing metropolis like Bombay (Mumbai) is determined by the '9 per cent rule'. Motorways and flyovers are for the 9 per cent of car owning families. 'In most cities, policy makers have endorsed large-scale construction of fly-overs and widening of roads, ignoring the basic issues, namely, that more cars mean more pollution, and that unless the growth of vehicular traffic is checked, congestion and traffic snarls will continue to be prominent features of urban India' (Indian People's Tribunal, 2001: 1).

This is not a book about energy sources, nor is it particularly against cars. As a result of population growth, the absolute number of traditional peasants and landless labourers in the world was larger in the year 2000 than in 1900. Their disappearance (there are nearly two billion, including their families), together with the disappearance of their agroecological knowledge and innovative capacity, is even more irreversible and possibly a more important trend than the proliferation of the motor car. The two trends go together, since loss of population on the land combines with a trend towards a pattern of urbanization based on the car, which has not yet overwhelmed India, Indonesia or China at the beginning of the 21st century. This will probably be the century of irreversible urbanization. Many ecological distribution conflicts have nothing to do with cars. When oil and gas are not used as sources of energy, either nuclear energy or hydroelectricity from large dams come to the rescue – annoying the environmentalists, who are hard to please. Before the age of the car, there were strong environmental movements in the 19th century against sulphur dioxide. This problem has been solved in many places, but new conflicts arise. Today, despite computers and the Internet, there is an increasing use of paper in the world. This is one cause of increasing deforestation, and of new plantations of pines and eucalyptus. The environmentalists keep complaining. There is an increasing consumption of small edible or non-edible items which carry large ecological and social rucksacks, such as cultivated shrimps, gold or diamonds. The economy is driven by consumption. In the USA, the year 1999 broke the record in the number of new cars and light trucks sold, over 19 million, many of them imported.

A Mexican government minister argued early in 2000 that oil exports from Mexico to the USA should increase, against OPEC's restrictions and at the risk of lowering the price of oil, because car production for exports and for the internal market was becoming the driving force of the Mexican economy. Selling cheap oil was (he said) in Mexico's best interests. In the summer of 2000, there was some electoral debate in the USA both on the increased greenhouse effect and on the increased price of petrol, some politicians declaring themselves against both at the same time, other politicians deconstructing the greenhouse effect out of the political agenda. In the winter of 2000–2001, Green circles in Europe, pleased with the advances of eco-taxation, were acutely embarrassed by the revolt by farmers, lorry drivers, fishermen and ordinary citizens against the high price of oil.

LEWIS MUMFORD'S RELEVANT VIEWS

Ecological economics assumes that there is a clash between economic growth and the environment. This cannot be made good by simply wishing for sustainable development, or by hoping for ecological modernization and increased eco-efficiency. There is one way of confronting the conflict which consists of giving money values to negative (or positive) externalities. Another more comprehensive way is to consider at the same time money values and physical and social indicators of (un)sustainability, in a muti-criteria framework. This is the way of ecological economics, using indicators such as the consumption of water per capita, the production of sulphur dioxide, the production of carbon dioxide, the production of NO_x, VOC and particulates, the per capita expenditure of energy for transport, the per capita production of solid residues and the percentage of it that is recycled, and so on. We observe contradictory trends in such indicators. We set targets for them, and we implement what we hope is the most cost-effective policy in order to reach such targets. We can also construct indices which combine several indicators into a single figure, such as composite indices of air quality, or the 'ecological footprint'.

This ecological view of cities, today well known, has roots in the chemistry and physics of the 19th century, as when Liebig lamented the loss of nutrients in cities which did not return to the soil. Before the Athens Charter and the height of Le Corbusier's influence, the ecological view was influential in urban planning, most significantly in Patrick Geddes' work, and later in the work of Lewis Mumford in the United States and Radhakamal Mukerjee, a self-described social ecologist, in India. Geddes was a biologist and urban plannner. Writing to Mumford from Calcutta on 31 August 1918, he had succintly made one main point regarding ecological city planning. In his City Report for Indore he wanted to break with the conventional drainage of 'all to the Sewer' replaced by 'all to the Soil'. Shiv Visvanathan has powerfully asserted that today's Gandhi would not be so uniquely concerned with the virtues of the rural village.

> Gandhi would . . . make the scavenger the paradigmatic figure of modern urban India . . . Gandhi argued that waste has not been fully thought through by city science . . . sewage rather than becoming a source of pollution would become a source of life and work. The classic example of city sewage use was Calcutta. This much maligned city uses its sewage to grow the finest vegetables . . . By focusing on waste, the city sciences of today can recover an agricultural view of the world. (Visvanathan, 1997: 234–5)

One of the favourite indicators of urban unsustainability is W. Rees' and M. Wackernagel's 'ecological footprint', a notion which one could already find in H.T. Odum's works of the 1960s and 1970s. This is not merely a neutral index of the ecological (un)sustainability of a given territory, it also has a clear distributional content. Is there an unavoidable conflict between cities and the environment? Or, on the contrary, are cities the seat of the institutions and the origins of the technologies which will drive the economy towards sustainability? Why has the Agenda 21 movement taken deeper roots at the city level than at the regional, national or international levels? Who are the social agents active in cities in favour of or against sustainability? Are indicators of urban (un)sustainability to be seen also as indicators of (potential or actual) social conflicts? Is there a new debate on 'disurbanization', remembering that in Moscow around 1930, which was stopped by Stalinism with the help of Le Corbusier (read his mocking letter to Moses Ginzburg, of 1930)? Or, on the contary, is there a new praise for the cities?

Indeed, the role of the city as the origin of technological and cultural innovations is the guiding line of Peter Hall's *Cities in Civilization* (1998).

Armed with beliefs in the blissful kingdom of economic growth at compound interest as announced by Keynes, and in Kondratieff's long cycles of
investment, Peter Hall produced a fascinating, dramatic book which culmi-
nates in the triumph of the 'new economy'. As with the initial cluster of car
manufacturing in Detroit, so with personal computers, a local constellation
of technical ability and 'garage' entrepreneurship develops into a new
leading sector of the economy. Peter Hall pays lip-service to the notion of
ecological sustainability, mentioning 'sustainable urbanism' (p.965) and
even 'sustainable urban development' (p.620) whatever that may mean, but
the main thrust of his book goes against Lewis Mumford's ecological pessimistic view of large-scale urbanization.

There are two main questions to be discussed here: one, the increased
urbanization of the world population; two, the form adopted by cities,
whether they are compact cities or whether, on the contrary, they sprawl.
There was a close relation between the 'garden city' movement born from
Ebezener Howard's proposals of 1900 for green belts to stop the growth of
conurbations, and Mumford's regional planning of the 1920s against sub-
urban overspill. (Urban 'sprawl' was invented in 1956 by W.F. Whyte; it was
not yet used by Mumford.) Howard's 'garden city' idea, or rather his terminology, was often used for totally opposite objectives – to justify private
middle-class suburbs. Mumford wrote to Geddes on 9 July 1926, trying to
find new words for Howard's approach: 'We are attempting to discard the
word, Garden City. And Regional City is our present substitute, which
must carry with it the notion of a balanced relation with the region, as well
as a complete environment within the city for work, study, play, and domes-
ticity.' Three decades later, Mumford was still making a spirited defence of
Howard's proposal to build relatively self-contained, balanced communities, supported by their local industry, with a permanent population of
limited number and density, on public land surrounded by a swath of open
country dedicated to agriculture, recreation and rural occupation.

> Howard's proposal recognized the biological and social grounds, along with the
> psychological pressures, that underlay the current movement to suburbia . . . The
> new kind of city he called the 'garden city', not so much because of its internal
> open spaces, which would approach a sound suburban standard, but more
> because it was set in a permanent rural environment . . . making the surround-
> ing agricultural area an integral part of the city's form. *His invention of a . . .*
> *green belt, immune to urban building, was a public device for limiting lateral growth*
> *and maintaining the urban–rural balance.* (Mumford, in Thomas, 1956, pp.395–6;
> emphasis added)

The Garden City approach was based on an ecological understanding of
the city within its region.

The ecological conflict over green belts is also an economic conflict over the appropriation of the potential differential rent from the preserved green spaces as they are consumed by urban sprawl. When the economic conflict is solved in favour of realizing the potential rents by sprawling and building over the green belt spaces, then unaccounted negative environmental effects arise.

Mumford was the most universal and historically significant American ecological writer of his time because his subject was the ecology of cities, particularly of New York, and the ecological critique of technology. He was in the vanguard of a new epoch, building on the work of authors such as G.P. Marsh, Patrick Geddes and Ebenezer Howard who constitute a coherent line of ecological thought. Mumford also liked to acknowledge Kropotkin's influence. Mumford's moderate anarchist sympathies, and later his early opposition to nuclear power, isolated him from the political mainstreams of his time.

Although Mumford was indeed aware of Patrick Geddes' ecological view of the city as a centre for the gathering and dissipation of energy (and for the intensification of the cycles of materials), nevertheless he did not develop Geddes' vision into an empirical energy analysis of cities (Bettini, 1998). This type of analysis had to wait until the 1970s, when the study of 'urban metabolism' (by authors such as S. Boyden and K. Newcombe, in their research on Hong Kong) became an established field of study. When one looks at reality, one sees that the innovative cities, for instance Seattle, are also examples of car-based urban sprawl. And many other cities are not innovative. Large-scale urbanization is still before us. The largest cities are not yet in India and China, they are Tokyo, New York, São Paulo and Mexico. If the hierarchy of cities in China and India does not change, if their active agricultural population goes down to 20 per cent, conurbations of 40 or 60 million inhabitants will develop. As humanity becomes more and more urban, are we moving towards economies which use less energy and fewer materials per capita? Certainly not.

RUSKIN IN VENICE

Geddes died in 1932 in Montpellier, the year of the Athens Charter when CIAM (the International Congress of Modern Architecture) under Le Corbusier, fresh from his polemics against the disurbanization of Moscow, enacted the principles of modern urban planning, totally contrary to the garden city – regional planning ideas. The romantic appreciation by Geddes (also by Camillo Sitte) of historic city centres, crooked streets and small piazzas, against a rationalized grid pattern, had been anticipated in

Ruskin's *Stones of Venice*. Such a nostalgic outlook, based on cultural conservation and on the conviviality of small city life, seems funny in retrospect. Almost all European cities have witnessed an increasing destruction of the old mediaeval street pattern, but in Venice, the mediaeval layout has been preserved, as Ruskin wished, and many houses have been restored. Here again the romantics had been more scientific than the 'rationalists'; they asked questions about the ecology of the city, they also questioned the increased transport needs when cities would be split up into zones of work, residence and recreation. We know that, while the endosomatic energy consumption of a citizen is about 2 500 kcal per day, that is, a little over 10 megajoules per day, that is 3·65 gigajoules per year, the expenditure of energy of one person during one year only in individual transport in an urban region characterized by urban sprawl, such as Los Angeles, is about 40 gigajoules. In comparison, in compact cities, with metro or bus, one person will spend 4 gigajoules per year in urban transport. And, should the person travel by foot or bicycle, then we have already included his/her energy expenditure in the endosomatic account.

Venice is still a pedestrian city: children walk to school or play all over some piazzas without fear of being run over. Cars cannot come into the island, because of the decision to keep the canals. Ruskin wanted Venice to be a general model for so many mediaeval cities in Europe which still had time to keep their character. However, cities in Europe changed in their patterns because of rationalist planning even in the 19th century, and later the motor car and the bombs of the Second World War, and the Corbuserian fury. Venice is a singular exception in Europe. Instead of a model to be restored and copied, Venice appears now so quaint that large parts of it are now a European historic thematic park, where instead of Mickey Mouse you may find Vivaldi's musicians dressed up as such among the throngs of tourists.

SCALE AND FOOTPRINTS

As conurbations grow by urban sprawl into metropolitan regions, and as the throughput of energy and materials increases over the region, environmental indicators and indexes may show different trends at the municipal and regional levels. This is a familiar phenomenon in Europe, where core areas improve their environmental quality (with some exceptions still, such as Palermo) while exporting pollution and importing environmentally costly materials and energy (Figure 7.1). There are many other cases in the world (Lima, for instance) where trends have been negative on all scales. Such phenomena are paralleled at world level where metropolitan countries are sometimes able to displace environmental loads to the periphery (see Chapter 10).

Taking the case of Barcelona, this is a nice city which in the strict administrative sense occupies only 90 square km, with a population of 1·5 million. The city is booming in economic and cultural values, and the population has decreased in the strict municipal territory in the last ten years, allowing a process of renewal and (partial) gentrification in the old city centre. Water consumption has also decreased, green spaces have increased (new beaches in the Olympic village, new parks) and visits by tourists have increased. Are we to say that we are more sustainable, better adapted to increasing scarcities of energy and materials? Who has the power to privilege one analytical point of view (the economic, the social, the environmental) on a chosen time–space scale? The conurbation is a half circle with a radius of about 30km, with a population of about 4 million people. This constitutes a single daily labour market. The improved private and public transport network facilitates travel. In fact, the largest Olympic investment was, in 1992, the building of a circular motorway which facilitates getting in and out of the city by car. All this constitutes a familiar pattern of urban sprawl. While some environmental indicators have improved in the city itself, there are increases in carbon dioxide produced in the conurbation. The agricultural green belt does not exist any longer. Water consumption is increasing in the conurbation, and Barcelona is contemplating importing water from the Ebro or the Rhône. The conurbation is fed by oil and gas imported from Algeria and elsewhere, hydroelectricity from the Pyrenees and nuclear power imported from three large stations in southern Catalonia, 160km to the southwest of Barcelona. In February 2001, a strong local movement independent of political parties stopped the plans for another power station in this region of Ribera d'Ebre, this time a combined cycle gas power station of 1600MW to be built by Enron.

On what scale(s) should (un)sustainability be assessed? In contrast to the deterioration of some North American city centres because of the process of urban sprawl, in Barcelona (as in many other European cities) urban sprawl has been compatible with increasing the economic and cultural values of the core of the conurbation. Tourism certainly helps. What are the main environmental conflicts? On what geographical scale should they be apprehended? Should we travel to the nuclear landscape of southern Catalonia; should we go to Algeria and Morocco to see the gas pipeline; should we trace the route of the CO_2 emissions from the Barcelona conurbation as they sink into the oceans or stay temporarily in the atmosphere; should we travel around the outlying quarters of the conurbation and listen to the complaints about noise from the motorways, about the threats of garbage incineration?

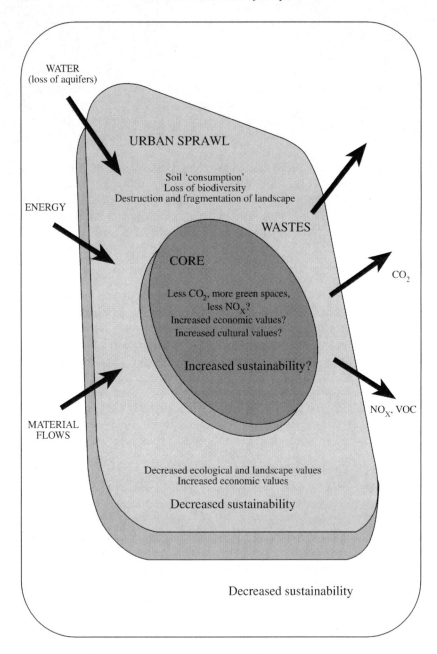

Figure 7.1   Urban (un)sustainability on different scales – European model

Coevolution, as the term is used by Richard Norgaard in ecological economics, denotes a process in which human culture evolves, agriculture is invented, new varieties of plants are selected and new agrarian systems develop, all in a context of sustainability and (perhaps) increased complexity. There are no similar examples of technological change in cities on which one could construct a theory of *sustainable* endogenous technical change. There is no spontaneous internal trend towards use of sustainable forms of energy, for instance, or towards less production of material residues, because the internal complaints against 'externalities' in cities are often displaced elsewhere by changes in scale. London smog no longer exists in London, and fish swim again in the Thames, but on other scales London's environmental indicators indicate more pressure than before.

Against the main thesis of this chapter, it might be argued that city growth contributes by itself to ecological sustainability, not perhaps because of technological innovations but because city life allows the freedom of birth control. I do not want to dispute this view too strongly. It has merit. Historically, there are urban versus rural differences in demographic behaviour, but there are also cases of neo-Malthusian rural populations.

ENERGY AND EVOLUTION

In the 1880s, the views on biological evolution and on thermodynamics, which seemed to point in two opposite directions (evolutionary improvement or at least increasing complexity, and thermodynamic entropy) coalesced in Boltzmann's famous dictum, 'the struggle for life is a struggle for available energy'. Lotka took this up in his 1925 book on the physics of biology and, moving from biology into human affairs in some incidental passages, he asserted that Boltzmann's idea could be applied to nations which would gain a competitive advantage by the use of more energy, though on second thoughts he also wrote that the more efficient use of energy could also represent a competitive advantage. The study of energy (and materials) flows, taking into account the qualities of the different energy inputs, is indeed relevant for the study of human history, both rural and urban. Can one say that the increasing importance of a city is due to increasing net energy flows into the city? If both things happen together, which is cause and which is effect?

We observe how cities and city centres concentrate energy flows. Such energy concentrations are a consequence, and not a cause, of the growth of cities, and they will depend on the affluence of their populations, on transport systems and so on. Cities do not grow and outcompete other cities because they have more energy available. Cities grow in size and political power, and therefore they are able to pull more energy in. If they are not able to do so, they certainly cannot grow. The analysis of the social and economic causes of growth or failure to grow must be combined with the physical analysis of energy and material inputs, and also the physical analysis of excretion, in order to understand the social metabolism of cities.

H.T. Odum's interpretation of Lotka in terms of a so-called 'maximum power principle' (a principle of evolution) is of doubtful significance for a history of nations and cities, and for a prescriptive analysis or urban ecology. If the throughput of energy in a system (a nation, a city) is higher than in another system, are we going to say that the first system (nation, city) is better adapted? Or is it badly adapted? Better New York than Calcutta, or vice versa, from an evolutionary viewpoint? We know that humans are able to use extremely different amounts of exosomatic energy, and therefore human ecology is a history of intra-human conflict. Can this be rephrased in terms of evolutionary adaptability and advancement?

Is the information created by such energy throughput (possibly at a high cost in 'emergy' or embodied energy, as Odum's 'transformities' for information show) able to compensate the extra expenditure of energy, thus reinforcing the system? Are we dealing with metaphors or with historical explanations? Does it matter what the content of the information is? Is the information contained in biodiversity similar in quality to the information produced in cities, in its significance for ecosystem functions and complexity? Are cyborgs real?

We can assert that, if a city grows nowadays by cultural or technological competitive innovations, it will probably use more energy and materials. The same would happen if it grew by naked political power. It was different in a distant past, where technologies of energy and materials consumption were different in different places – this is clear in the studies of the ecology of old Edo in Japan.

There is no spontaneous evolutionary trend to ecological sustainability linked to the growth of cities, rather the reverse. Nevertheless, social movements against some of the 'externalities' produced in cities which are not shifted elsewhere could help in the movement towards sustainability. The final section offers some examples from India.

POLLUTION STRUGGLES IN INDIA AND BRIMBLECOMBE'S HYPOTHESIS

Being still truly a minority, environmental activists cannot cope with every issue. Hence there is no strong movement against cars in most cities in the world. The environmental chemist and historian Peter Brimblecombe (Brimblecombe and Pfister, 1990) has argued that sulphur dioxide emissions usually provoke social reactions because they come from *visible* single-point sources (coal power stations, smelters), while other forms of air pollution (NO_x and VOCs from cars, precursors of tropospheric ozone) are more dispersed and they are more peacefully accepted. Brimblecombe's hypothesis is really helpful in explaining movements against sulphur dioxide. Does the hypothesis also explain why there is not, anywhere, a popular spontaneous environmentalism against cars, even in polluted cities of the south (including China) where most people have no cars? Is this a missed opportunity for the environmentalism of the poor? Is this situation changing, with the perception of an increasing incidence of infantile asthma in cities, and with the (successful) movements against leaded gasoline? Have we looked close enough?

Why is the reaction against 'London smog' usually stronger than against 'Los Angeles smog'? One answer is that London smog, largely sulphur dioxide, usually arises from easily identifiable sources. Hence, for instance, the 'chimney wars' in 19th-century Germany. Los Angeles smog is largely produced by cars running all over the conurbation: it is diffused.

In India, the colonial authorities enacted regulations in Bombay and in Calcutta as long ago as the 1860s, curbing air pollution. The problem was worse in Calcutta than in Bombay because of lack of wind during a good part of the year. Starting with the ready availability of Raniganj coal, Calcutta had witnessed a sudden change in the character of its atmosphere. Anderson (1996) applies Brimblecombe's hypothesis to Calcutta. It was not so much that the aggregate levels of haze increased (that haze being due to the widespread burning of wood and dung in poor households across the city) but rather that there were now easily identified sources of black smoke from the industrial chimneys of the jute mills and also from the ocean steamships. Opposition to these visible sources of pollution explains the new legislation, promoted by the colonial power with general support. Nevertheless, such general support against industrial air pollution cannot be taken for granted. An environmental improvement, if gained at the cost of a worsening economic distribution, will be opposed by poor people, as in Shiv Visvanathan's account (1999) of pollution struggles in Delhi.

Workers were confronted by industrial closures or the displacement of industries outside the limits of Delhi because of Supreme Court's decisions, especially under the 'green' judge Kuldip Singh, starting in 1985 with the petition filed by the advocate M.C. Mehta against tanneries which polluted the river Ganga. Foundries, fertilizer factories, steel mills, paper and pulp factories, even textile mills were hit by the active role of the court, whose decisions were directed to visible industrial installations more than to diffuse sources of pollution. Compensation to the displaced labour in Delhi was ordered but tens of thousands of workers were not on the rolls, being casual subcontracted labour.

A junior textile employee at Swatantra Bharat Mills complained about the displacement of this industry outside the so-called 'National Capital Region' (NCR):

> In this world the divide is between the rich and the poor and it is the poor who have to die for they are cheaper! We will have to shift to Tonk [the new site] for the law is of the rich man . . . The management is powerful, the government is of the rich. This is an attempt to throw the poor out of the city. *Pollution in the city is vehicular, not industrial.* Does the government think how a poor man will feed his wife and child? . . . These wise intellectual men of law Kuldip Singh and Saghir Ahmad have brought people to ruin . . . Whatever Kuldip Singh did, he did not think of the poorer sections of society. What was the need of leaving the NCR and going to Tonk, where there is nothing at the moment. With one stroke of the pen he wrote away lives of thousands of people in difficult times. (Visvanathan, 1999: 17)

To this textile employee and other workers like him in Delhi, contrary to Brimblecombe's hypothesis, diffuse pollution due to traffic became now more visible than point-source pollution! The debate on asthma became more relevant politically than sulphur dioxide or than water pollution.

Figures from a combined pollution index show that in Delhi over 75 per cent of the air pollution is vehicular (from private and public transport, with over 3 million vehicles, including two-wheelers), 12 per cent domestic, 10 per cent industrial (of which two thermal power stations account for a major share) (Visvanathan, 1999: 5). Official actions were directed to visible industrial installations. The new social visibility of vehicular air pollution in Delhi, fuelled by the controversy over industrial dislocation and by a strong campaign from the Centre for Science and Environment, led to a decision by the Supreme Court on 28 July 1998 that all city buses and all autorickshaws should convert to CNG fuel (compressed natural gas) by 31 March 2001. When the fateful date arrived, there was pandemonium in Delhi since most buses had not yet converted, and did not circulate for one or two days. Debate still continues on the cost efficiency of converting to CNG instead of ULSD (ultra-low sulphur diesel) or LPG (liquid petroleum gas). It now seems that vehicular pollution from buses and autorickshaws will start to decline in Delhi. Nevertheless, the traffic and pollution from private cars and motorbikes is on the increase.[1]

One may well ask, in agreement with the major theme of the present book, why there is not an environmental movement by pedestrians and cyclists against private cars, not only because of the pollution they produce but also because of their disproportionate use of urban space. This in cities around the world where most people are poor and have no cars; nor do they expect to have cars soon. While the use of the bicycle is a 'post-materialist' luxury in rich cities, perhaps a Sunday pleasure for car-owning families, or a convenient and healthy means of transport for short distances in well-regulated cities, everyday cycling to work in cities in India among the fumes and threats of buses and private cars is the risky daily obligation of many people who perhaps cannot afford the small fee for public transport.

In the next chapter, in a different cultural and economic context from that of India, in the USA, other urban ecological conflicts will be considered under the heading of 'Environmental Justice'. Do local conflicts in the USA on the siting of incinerators belong to a different system than the complaints against the foreseen location of nuclear waste in Yucca Mountain, Nevada, shipped there from nuclear power stations that produce electricity for cities? Do the complaints by the Ogoni and the Ijaw in the Niger Delta against oil extraction belong to the same system as the cities in rich countries where the oil exported by Shell fuels cars, and indeed where Shell has its headquarters? What are the limits of the city?

NOTE

1. Report in *India Today*, 16 April 2001, pp. 52–7.

8. Environmental justice in the United States and South Africa

Since the late 1980s and early 1990s, 'environmental justice' has come to mean an organized movement against 'environmental racism'. The movement has been succesful. In principle, this description of environmental justice applies only to the USA although, as we shall see in this chapter, it has also been used in South Africa and it could be extended to the world.

There are books on ethics with the title 'environmental justice' (Wenz, 1988) that discuss the norms to be applied to the allocation of environmental benefits and burdens among people including future generations, and between people and other sentient beings. The subject includes the extension of Rawls' principles of justice to future human generations (under the somewhat fanciful assumption that we are behind a veil of ignorance as to which generation we belong to), and the discussion on whether animals have 'rights'. However, 'environmental justice' is an expression which belongs more to environmental sociology and to the study of race relations than to environmental ethics or philosophy. For instance, the catalogue of the Yale University Library states (in 1999–2000) that, under environmental justice, 'are entered works on equal protection from environmental and health hazards for all people regardless of race, income, culture or social class'. Works on animal rights are entered elsewhere. Librarians are not worshippers of fashion. They acknowledge what they hope will be permanent classificatory realities. Environmental justice is, then, the organized movement against 'environmental racism', that is the disproportionate allocation of toxic waste to Latino or African–American communities in urban–industrial situations and in the USA. It is also applied to Native American reservations, particularly in the context of uranium mining and nuclear waste. Indeed, 'environmental justice' could subsume historic conflicts on sulphur dioxide, the Chipko and Chico Mendes cases, the current conflicts on the use of carbon sinks and reservoirs, the conflicts on oustees from dams, the fight for the preservation of rainforests or mangroves for livelihood, and many other cases around the world which sometimes have to do with 'racism' and sometimes not.

Ecological distribution conflicts, as analysed in the present book, are conflicts over the principles of justice applicable to the burdens of pollution and to access to environmental resources and services. For instance, are there moral and legal duties for greenhouse gas emissions beyond national borders (as there are duties regarding the 200 mile fishing zone, or for CFC emissions)? Do such duties arise only from ratified treaties, that is positive law, or are there general principles of international environmental justice? Do they apply to corporations such as Unocal or Texaco? For instance, could the allocation of CO_2 allowances inside the European Union be seen as an internal application of a principle of environmental distributive justice (by allowing increases per capita to Portugal, Spain, Greece and Ireland)? On the other hand, does the European Union total carbon allowance represent internationally an injustice because all countries, including Portugal, Spain, Greece and Ireland, are already much above the per capita world average for CO_2 emissions? No doubt, the sociological concept of 'environmental justice' opens up a wide terrain for philosophical debate on principles of environmental justice. In the present book, I stay in sociological territory.

FIGHTING 'ENVIRONMENTAL RACISM'

The environmental justice movement in the United States (Bullard, 1990, 1993; Pulido, 1991, 1996; Bryant and Mohai, 1992; Bryant, 1995; Sachs, 1995; Gottlieb, 1993; Szasz, 1994; Schwab, 1994; Westra and Wenz, 1995; Dorsey, 1997; Faber, 1998; DiChiro, 1998; Camacho, 1998; Taylor, 2000) is quite different from the two previous currents of environmentalism in this country, namely, the efficient and sustainable use of natural resources (in the tradition of Gifford Pinchot), and the cult of wilderness (in the tradition of John Muir). As a self-conscious movement, environmental justice fights against the alleged disproportionate dumping of toxic waste or exposure to different sorts of environmental risk in areas of predominantly African–American, or Hispanic or Native American populations. The language employed is not that of uncompensated externalities but rather the language of race discrimination, which is politically powerful in the USA because of the long Civil Rights struggle. In fact, the organized environmental justice movement is an outgrowth, not of previous currents of environmentalism, but of the Civil Rights movement. Some direct collaborators of Martin Luther King were among the 500 people arrested in the initial episode of the environmental justice movement, in the town of Afton in Warren County in North Carolina in 1982 (Bullard, 1993). Governor Hump had decided to locate a dump for PCB residues (polychlorinated biphenyls) in Warren County, which in 1980 had 16000 inhabitants of whom 60 per cent were African–American, most of them under the poverty line. A NIMBY struggle escalated into a massive non-violent protest with nationwide support when the first trucks arrived in 1982. The protest was not successful and the dumping ground became operative; however, the self-conscious movement for environmental justice was born there. Its roots are in the African–American Civil Rights movement of the 1960s, also in the United Farm Workers' movement of Cesar Chavez which had gone on strike in 1965 against grape growers (who used pesticides which are now banned) and which worked together in 1968 with the Environmental Defence Fund in a short marriage of convenience for the prohibition of DDT to the benefit of birds' and human health. Martin Luther King's last journey to Memphis, Tennessee in April 1968 had been related to the improvement of working conditions of garbage disposal workers subject to health risks.

In the Third World, the main socioenvironmental question in the 1980s was whether an indigenous, independent environmentalism of the poor existed, a question first theorized in India and South-East Asia, later, in Latin America, because of episodes of defence of common property resources against the state or the market. In the USA the question was whether the buoyant mainstream environmental movement would deign to consider the existence of 'environmental racism', whether it could accept and work with 'minorities' which were mainly concerned with urban pollution. Why were black people so totally absent from the governing bodies of the Sierra Club and other main environmental organizations, collectively known as the 'big ten'? The 'people of colour' environmental justice movement, fed up with 'white' environmentalism, pronounced itself initially against slogans such as 'Save the Rainforest', insisting on urban issues, and ignoring the fact that many rainforests are civilized jungles. Only some mainstream organizations, such as Greenpeace and the Earth Island Institute (founded by David Brower in San Francisco), responded quickly and favourably to the challenge of the environmental justice movement.

In 1987, the United Church of Christ Commission for Racial Justice published a study of the racial and socioeconomic characteristics of communities with hazardous waste sites. Subsequent studies confirmed that African–Americans, Native Americans, Asian Americans and Latinos were more likely than other groups to find themselves near hazardous waste facilities. Other studies found that the average fine for violations of environmental norms in low-income or people of colour communities was significantly lower than fines imposed for violations in largely white neighbourhoods. Under the banner of fighting 'environmental racism' (the term itself was introduced by the Reverend Benjamin Chavis), low-income groups, members of the working class and people of colour constituted a movement for environmental justice, which connected environmental issues with racial and gender inequality, and with poverty.

There are many cases of local environmental activism in the USA by 'citizen-workers groups' (Gould *et al.*, 1996) outside the organized environmental justice movement, some with a hundred years' roots in the many struggles for health and safety in mines and factories, perhaps also in complaints against pesticides in southern cotton fields, and certainly in the struggle against toxic waste at Love Canal in upstate New York led by Lois Gibbs (Gibbs, 1981, 1995) who also later led a nationwide 'toxics-struggles' movement showing that poor communities would not tolerate any longer being dumping grounds (Gottlieb, 1993; Hofrichter, 1993). In the 'official' environmental justice movement are included celebrated episodes of collective action against incinerators (because of the uncertain risk of dioxins), particularly in Los Angeles, led by women. Cerrell Associates had made known a study in 1984 in California on the political difficulties facing the siting of waste-to-energy conversion plants (such as incinerators of urban domestic waste), recommending areas of low environmental awareness and low capacity for mobilizing social resources in opposition. There were surprises when opposition arose in unexpected areas, such as the Concerned Citizens of South Central Los Angeles in 1985. Also in the 1980s, other environmental conflicts gave rise to groups such as People for Community Recovery in South Chicago (Altgeld Gardens), led by Hazel Johnson, and the West Harlem Environmental Action (WHEACT) in New York, led by Vernice Miller. In 1989, the South-West Network for Economic and Environmental Justice (SNEEJ), led by Richard Moore, was founded, with its main seat in Albuquerque, New Mexico, out of grievances felt by Mexican and Native American populations. Richard Moore was the first signatory of a famous letter sent to the 'big ten' environmental organizations in the USA in January 1990 by the leaders of organizations representing African–Americans and Hispanic Americans. The letter warned that the 'white' organizations would not be able to build a strong environmental movement unless they addressed the issue of toxic waste dumps and incinerators in 'Third World communities' inside the USA. It also pointed out the absence of 'people of color' in the main environmental organizations.

In October 1991, the First National People of Color Environmental Leadership Summit took place in Washington, DC. The principles of environmental justice were proclaimed. The movement for environmental justice became well known. In the USA much statistical effort has been made by environmental justice activists to prove that race is a good geographical predictor of environmental load. President Clinton's Executive Order 12,898 of 1994 on Environmental Justice was a triumph for this movement. It directed all federal agencies (though not corporations or private citizens) to act in such a way that disproportionate burdens of

pollution do not fall on low income and minority populations in all territories and possessions of the USA. Thus both poverty and race are taken
into account, and nothing is said about impacts outside the USA. Happy
the country where 'low-income' people are regarded as a minority (along-
side or overlapping with racial 'minorities').[1]

'Environmental justice' has become an established way of representing
urban pollution issues in the USA, and this is to the credit of this movement. Outside the USA, 'environmental racism' has usually not been part
of the explicit vocabulary of protest deployed in order to oppose the disproportionate burden of pollution, or the privatization or state takeover of
communal resources. Racism is not a universal language. Thus Ken Saro-
Wiwa did not use the language of 'environmental racism' against the military government of Nigeria. He used the language of indigenous territorial
rights and human rights. He could have used the language of environmental racism against Shell. To repeat, ecological distribution conflicts are
fought with different vocabularies; the language of 'environmental racism'
is powerful, it can be used in many cases of environmental injustice, though
not in all. For instance, the Narmada struggle is not being fought in terms
of 'environmental racism'.

The insistence on 'environmental racism' is sometimes surprising to ana-
lysts from outside the USA. In fact, some foreign academics refuse to
acknowledge the racial angle, and have boldly stated: 'If one were asked to
date the beginning of the environmental justice movement in the United
States, then 2 August 1978 might be the place to start. This was the day
when the CBS and ABC news networks first carried news of the effect of
toxic waste on the health of the people of a place called Love Canal'
(Dobson, 1998: 18). However, the Love Canal people, led by Lois Gibbs,
were not people of colour, they were white, as such categories are understood in the USA, and therefore were subject only to metaphorical, not real
'environmental racism'. Their grievance was also about PCB dumping.
Other non-US academics agree with the interpretation that environmental
justice in the USA is a movement against 'environmental racism'. I also
agree. Thus the seminal moment (Low and Gleeson, 1998: 108) was in 1982
in Warren County, North Carolina. Of course, one could also argue that
the world environmental justice movement started long ago on a hundred
dates and in a hundred places all over the world: for instance, in Andalusia
on 4 February 1888, when miners and peasants at Rio Tinto were massacred by the army; or when Tanaka Shozo a hundred years ago threw himself
in front of the Emperor's carriage with a petition in his hand; or, in the
USA, not in North Carolina but in the struggles against mining corporations in Wisconsin conducted by alliances of Indian tribes and environmentalists in the 1970s and 1980s (Gedicks, 1993), and in many other struggles

of resistance by Native Americans, from Canada to Tierra del Fuego. Which will be the worldwide First of May or Eighth of March of Environmental Justice and the Environmentalism of the Poor? Chico Mendes' assassination day, Ken Saro-Wiwa's, or perhaps the day the *Rainbow Warrior* was sunk by the French secret services in New Zeland, and its Portuguese cook died? Or when Karunamoi Sardar died defending her village in Horinkhola, Khulna, Bangladesh, on 7 November 1990?

As Bullard wrote in 1994:

> The environmental justice movement has come a long way since its birth a decade ago in rural, mostly African–American, Warren County, North Carolina ... Although the protestors were unsuccessful in blocking the PCB landfill, they brought national attention to waste facility sitings inequities and galvanized African–American church and civil rights leaders in support for environmental justice.

Indeed, the movement *invented* the socially extremely potent combination of words, 'environmental justice' (or eco-justice: Sachs, 1995), it shifted the whole discussion about environmentalism in the USA away from preservation and conservation of Nature towards social justice, it destroyed the NIMBY image of grassroots environmental protests by turning them into NIABY protests (not in anyone's backyard), and it expanded the circle of people involved in environmental policy.

By emphasizing 'racism', environmental justice emphasizes incommensurability of values. This is its greatest achievement. If I pollute a poor neighbourhood, by applying the polluter pays principle (PPP), I may compensate the damage. This is more easily written than done, because, how much is human health worth? On which scale of value? Nevertheless, the PPP implies that a worsening ecological distribution is in principle compensated by an improving economic distribution. The objective is of course to make pollution expensive enough, so that its level will decrease by a change in technology or by a lower level of polluting production. Whatever the objective, the principle implies a single scale of value. Now, the same problem phrased in terms of 'environmental racism' becomes a different problem. I can inflict damage on human dignity by using a racial epithet or by racial discrimination. Paying a fine does not entitle me to repeat such conduct. There is no real compensation. Money and human dignity are not commensurate.

Bullard, who is both an academic and an activist, realizes the potential of the environmental justice movement beyond 'minority' populations, asserting in 1994:

> Grassroots groups, after decades of struggle, have grown to become the core of the multi-issue, multi-racial, and multi-regional environmental justice

movement. Diverse community-based groups have begun to organize and link their struggles to issues of civil and human rights, land rights and sovereignty, cultural survival, racial and social justice, and sustainable development . . . Whether in urban ghettos and barrios, rural 'poverty pockets', Native American reservations, or *communities in the Third World*, grassroots groups are demanding an end to unjust and non-sustainable environmental and development policies.[2]

Notice, then, the clear awareness that environmental justice is functional to sustainability, and that it concerns poor people everywhere, including, indeed, Third World communities; that is, billions of people.

The importance of the link between the increasing globalization of the economy and environmental degradation of habitats for many of the world's peoples has been emphasized not only by Bullard but also by other actors in the US environmental justice movement. There is a worldwide link between environmental degradation, and human and civil rights:

In many places where Black, minority, poor or Indigenous peoples live, oil, timber and minerals are extracted in such a way as to devastate eco-systems and destroy their culture and livelihood. Waste from both high- and low-tech industries, much of it toxic, has polluted groundwater, soil and the atmosphere. Environmental degradation such as this, and its concomitant impact on human wealth and welfare, is increasingly seen as violation of human rights.

As mining, logging, oil drilling and waste-disposal projects push into further corners of the planet, people all over the world are seeing their basic rights compromised, losing their livelihoods, cultures and even their lives. 'Environmental devastation globally and what we call 'environmental racism' in the United States, are violations of human rights and they occur for similar reasons.'[3]

In the USA, Louisiana is one of the best places for 'environmental racism'. It contains 'Cancer Alley' between New Orleans and Baton Rouge. There are communities in Louisiana such as Sunrise, Reveilletown and Morrissonville, which were on the fence-lines of Placid Refinery, Georgia Gulf and Dow Chemical, respectively, and which 'were literally wiped off the map, and the people suffered the permanent loss of their homes after many years of struggles'.[4] In some other cases in Louisiana, victories have been reached, for instance against Louisiana Energy Services Inc. (May 1997) when the US Nuclear Regulatory Commission denied a licence to a proposed uranium enrichment plant sited between two African–American communities, Forest Grove and Center Springs, and in the case of Shintech (September 1997), a Japanese company which proposed the siting of a very large polyvinyl chloride plant in a small African–American rural community called Convent. The communities struggled for years (nine in one case, three in the other) to stop such plans. The legal strategies incorporated the Executive Order 12,898 of 1994. This Order is not directly enforceable as law, but the regulatory agencies are supposed to take it into account when approving or disapproving siting decisions. The alleged pattern of continuous environmental racism, where the right to an environmentally healthy surroundings is curtailed by policy decisions that facilitate the location of hazardous industrial facilities and waste sites in communities that are predominantly African American (or Native American or Latino), has led some lawyers to suggest the application of international agreements on human rights to the USA.[5]

Nevertheless, granting the increasing internationalization of the US environmental justice movement, granting its awareness that environmental injustices are not only directed against African–Americans, why is Lois Gibbs not 'officially' credited within the environmental justice movement as being its founder in the 1970s in Love Canal, why is the official birth located in North Carolina in 1982? The answer is race, an important principle of the American social constitution.[6] In America there is racism, and there is *also* anti-racism. Race is of practical importance in order to explain not only the controversial geography of toxic dumps or incarceration rates but also residential and school patterns. Moreover, to establish a link between the non-violent Civil Rights movement of the 1960s and the increasing environmental awareness of the 1970s and 1980s proved attractive for instrumental reasons. The legislation against racism (such as Title VI of the Federal Civil Rights Act of 1964) forbids discrimination based on race. However, in order to establish the existence of racism, it is not sufficient to prove that environmental impact is different (for instance, that lead in children's blood level is different according to racial background), it must also be shown that there is an explicit intention to cause harm to a minority group.

Because of the uncertainties of environmental hazards which have been mentioned in Chapter 2 under the rubric of 'postnormal science', and because of the statistical difficulties in separating racial and economic factors in toxic waste location decisions (statistically distinguishing between environmental racism and Lawrence Summers' Principle), the attempts to prove environmental racism have given rise to a rich practice of 'popular epidemiology' (Novotny, 1998). Lay persons gather scientific data and other information, and they also process the results offered by official experts in order to challenge them in cases involving toxic pollution, a clear case of 'extended peer review'. It might be difficult to prove that race more than poverty correlates with toxic waste, but if this is convincingly shown, then the chances of redress are higher.

The environmental justice movement is thus specifically a product of the

USA. Internally, it has shifted the debate on environmentalism away from the emphasis on 'wilderness' (preservation) or the emphasis on 'eco-efficiency' (conservation) towards emphasis on social justice (Gottlieb, 1993). Though structured around a core of people of colour activists, it encompasses also conflicts on environmental risks affecting poor people of whatever colour. Internationally, it is slowly linking up with Third World environmentalism (Hofrichter, 1993). I have, then, only one minor quarrel with the 'official' environmental justice movement in the USA, and this is its emphasis on 'minority' groups. The movement worked with the Clinton–Gore administration in order to diminish environmental threats to minority groups in the USA; becoming somewhat enmeshed in governmental commissions, it has not led a worldwide movement for environmental justice. It was not a main actor at the environmental NGO mass celebrations of the 1990s such as Rio de Janeiro, 1992, Madrid, 1995 (the campaign, 50 Years is Enough against the IMF and World Bank) and Seattle, 1999, but it will probably have a strong presence in the Rio plus Ten meeting in Johannesburg in 2002. It does not yet speak loudly on global climate change, or globalized *Raubwirtschaft*. The 'minority' focus detracts from its usefulness worldwide, unless we decide to look at the world through US lenses, applying the language of race universally, and classifying the majority of humankind as 'minorities'.

There are ecological distribution conflicts in the world (the European conflicts over nuclear risks as expressed at famous fights in Gorleben or Creys-Malville, or the European conflict against US 'hormone beef' and transgenic crops, or the current conflict over the Three Gorges dam in China, for instance), for the analysis and resolution of which, the metaphor of 'environmental racism' is not useful. On the other hand, we could retrospectively apply 'environmental racism' to the Spaniards in America, who imposed a terrible load of mercury poisoning on indigenous workers in silver mines (Dore, 2000) and who in some areas destroyed indigenous agriculture through the 'plague of sheep' (Melville, 1994). Research could profitably be done on specific cases of Dalit (and tribal) environmentalism in India, while in Latin America environmental racism might become a useful language for conflicts which have been fought up to now under the banner of indigenous territorial rights.

Activists and lawyers in the class action suit against Texaco from Ecuador, blamed Texaco in advertisements in US newspapers in 1999 for 'environmental racism'. Notice that this language, so effective in the USA, was not used when the case started in 1993, and it would be problematic though not impossible to apply it to Texaco's successor, Petroecuador, which has used similar technology, damaging not only indigenous people but also average mestizo Ecuadorian settlers. Perhaps 'internal colonialism'

(Adeola, 2000) could be used against Petroecuador, as against the Nigerian authorities, while 'racism' could be reserved for Texaco (or Shell, in Nigeria). Profiting from the publicity against Texaco because of a court case for internal racism against black employees in the USA (settled out of court in 1997 for US$176 million), sympathizers with the Ecuadorian plaintiffs placed an advertisement in the *New York Times* (23 September 1999) which stated:

> The lawsuit alleges that in Ecuador, Texaco dumped the poisonous water pro-duced by oil drilling directly onto the ground, in nearby rivers, and in streams and ponds. The company knowingly destroyed the surrounding environment and endangered the lives of the indigenous people who had lived and fished there for years. These are people of color, people for whose health and well-being Texaco shows only a cavalier disregard . . . It's time that Texaco learns that deval-uing the lives and well-being of people because of the color of their skin is no longer acceptable for any American company.

The USA houses the most polluting transnational companies, it has the highest per capita production of carbon dioxide, the most potent move-ment for the preservation of wilderness in the world, and probably the strongest eco-efficiency movement (competing with Europe in this line). Why not also the most forceful environmental justice movement? Everything is best in America. There are the best capitalists, but also the best anarchists. However, lacking in the USA are some natural amenities such as wild elephants, lions and tigers. Lacking also are some cultural amenities, and, most relevantly to our theme, lacking is also a movement of *peasant* struggles to keep control and manage sustainably communal resources threatened by private enclosure or state takeover. The environ-mental justice movement in the USA has included complaints about pesti-cide exposure among immigrant farmworkers, but it has not actively promoted agroecology in the USA and in the world. The large majority of 'organic' farmers in the USA are neo-rural white folks. There are calls by Wendell Berry, Wes Jackson and other authors to go back to farming, and recreate rural communities. There is a long tradition of criticism of 'facto-ries in the field'.

> Most of the writers who condemned the vast monocrop plantations stretching across the West were aware of the link between the robbing of the soil and the robbing of the farm worker, but perhaps none expressed it so clearly and pow-erfully as Carey McWilliams (1939, 1942) . . . While intensive agriculture depleted water supplies and exhausted soils, while stoop laborers died of dehy-dration and pesticide inhalation, McWilliams fought for the workers' right to organize and bargain collectively, and for celebrated radical utopian land settle-ments like the one at Kaweah, whose residents established cooperative gardens

and pioneered methods of sustainable forestry. Twenty-five years later, Cesar Chavez and Dolores Huerta would draw directly on McWilliams' radicalism in their struggle against the grape growers.[7]

Despite these struggles of past decades, the USA lacks a peasantry. In California and in Florida, agriculture relied on immigrant workers. In the south, there was no radical land reform after the Civil War, but, on the contrary, reconstruction. Anyway, the southern peasants left the land long ago. In contrast, in Latin America, not only in Mexico, Guatemala or the Andes, but also in a country such as Brazil (which lacks the long massive tradition of indigenous farming of these other countries), we now find the Movimento dos Sem Terra (MST), the powerful movement of landless labourers which until recently put forward a productivist platform against the latifundia, finally coming round in 1999 to an environmental viewpoint (see below, Chapter 10). The USA is a peasantless nation, although some fights by Native Americans against mining and toxic waste (such as the Navajo or the Soshone against uranium mining and nuclear waste), or for the control of water or the control of remaining communal pastures by Hispanic people in the west, are close to 'ecological narodnism'.

Aldo Leopold, in his posthumous *Land Ethic* (1949), asked whether in the agriculture of the USA one could discern a cleavage between economic and ecological viewpoints similar to that which existed in the management of wilderness and in the management of forestry. A similar conflict between economy and environment had long been noticed in urban planning by Patrick Geddes and Lewis Mumford, but urban ecology was not among Leopold's interests. Leopold wrote: 'In the large field of agriculture I am less competent to speak, but there seem to be somewhat parallel cleavages' to those in forestry and wilderness management. Leopold had been raised in Iowa, and he spent a large part of his professional life in Wisconsin, combining his devotion to wilderness with scientific ecological knowledge – mostly based on biogeography – but becoming also keenly aware of the new ecological energetics. Leopold had also lived for a while, and married, in New Mexico, but he was at a loss to find examples of agroecological management, writing: 'The discontent that labels itself 'organic farming' while bearing some of the earmarks of a cult, is nevertheless biotic in its direction, particularly in its insistence on the importance of soil flora and fauna', thus referring perhaps to Rudolf Steiner's followers more than to peasant agroecologists. Now, across the border in Mexico (also perhaps among the pueblos of New Mexico?), the majority of 'organic' farmers and foresters were peasants belonging to indigenous groups, including today the 'organic' coffee growers (Moguel and Toledo, 1999). In contrast, in the

USA there are some ecological neorurals but there is no 'organic' peasantry because there is no peasantry.

On the other hand, lacking in the Third World eco-agrarianism, eco-*zapatismo* and environmentalism of the poor, and in the literature on political ecology from anthropology and geography, has been the strong urban emphasis of the environmental justice movement in the USA, extremely relevant for a world of increasingly urban poor populations. There is then not only a north–south but also a rural–urban complementarity among both approaches. Will they come together in a global environmental justice movement against pollution by mining companies in Irian Jaya or in southern Peru, in Third World urban movements against pollution and disproportionate land occupation by private cars, in complaints againt biopiracy of 'wild' or medicinal or agricultural genetic resources, against the environmental and health risks from GMOs, pesticides and nuclear waste, against damage from oil extraction in Louisiana or Nigeria, and indeed in the attempts to stop the disproportionate use by the rich of the carbon sinks and reservoirs?

WILDERNESS VERSUS THE ENVIRONMENTALISM OF THE POOR IN SOUTH AFRICA?

In South Africa, race is even more important socially and politically than in the USA. The country also has a strong wilderness movement. These are common traits. But South Africa is very different from the USA. In South Africa, environmental justice is not a movement in defence of 'minority' populations, as it has evolved in the USA. On the contrary, the majority of the population is potentially concerned. An Environmental Justice Networking Forum in South Africa with substantial township and rural organizational membership (Bond, 2000: 60) is trying to mobilize a new constituency focusing attention on a range of urban, environmental health, and pollution-related problems, and also land and water management problems, which had not been considered by the 'wilderness' NGOs. In their view, good environmental management involves protecting people as well as plants and animals.

True, until recently, 'the dominant understanding of environmental issues in South Africa was an authoritarian conservation perspective. This focused exclusively on the preservation of wilderness areas and particular species of plants and animals. Within this perspective, 'overpopulation' was often identified as the main environmental problem' (Cock and Koch, 1991). Attempts have been made in South Africa, as elsewhere, to discard the old colonial and post-colonial idea that preservation of Nature cannot be achieved unless indigenous people are removed, and instead to involve local people in managing reserves through offering them economic incentives, in the form of a share of eco-tourist (or even controlled hunting) revenues. Beyond this, a powerful environmental movement will perhaps emerge in the new South Africa which will link the struggle against racism, social injustice and the exploitation of people with the struggle against the abuse of the environment. For instance, land erosion is interpreted as a consequence of the unequal distribution of land, when African populations were crowded into 'homelands' under apartheid. The expansion of tree plantations for paper and paper pulp creates 'green deserts', in a country where a large proportion of the population depends on fuelwood for cooking (Cock and Koch, 1991: 176, 186).

Environmental conflicts in South Africa are often described in the language of environmental justice (Bond, 2000; McDonald, 2001). Thus a conflict in the late 1990s placed environmentalists and local populations against a project near Port Elizabeth for the development of an industrial zone, a new harbour and a smelter of zinc for export, owned by Billinton, a British firm which would guzzle up electricity and water at cheap rates while poor people cannot get the small amounts of water and electricity they need, or in any case must pay increasing rates under current economic policies. The Billinton project had costs in terms of tourists' revenues because of the threats to a proposed national elephant park extension nearby, to beaches, estuaries, islands and whales (Bond, 2000: 47). There were also costs in terms of the displacement of people from the village of Coega. This point was emphasized in a letter sent by the Southern Africa Environment Project to Peter Mandelson, then British Secretary of State for Trade and Industry: 'We are writing on behalf of those who have historically lacked the capacity to assert their rights and protect their own interests but who now seek to be heard and to call to the attention of the international community the injustice that is now about to be inflicted upon them.' The life of the people of Coega was already full of memories of displacements under the regime of apartheid. Although Billinton could no longer profit from the lack of voice of the people under apartheid, now – it was alleged – it sought 'to take advantage of the region's desperate need for employment to enable construction of a highly polluting facility that would never be allowed adjacent to a major population centre in the UK or any other European country'.[8] A small improvement in the economic situation of the people would be obtained at high social and environmental cost, because of displacement of people, and also because of increased levels of sulphur dioxide, heavy metals, dust and liquid effluents. An appeal was made to the British minister to take into account the OECD's guidelines for multinational enterprises, which include a chapter on environmental protection since 1991, but which are no more than recommendations which the authorities cannot enforce directly. The minister was asked in any case to exercise his influence upon Billinton informally.

The environmental impacts which the apartheid regime left behind are now surfacing. There are large liabilities to be faced. Best known is the asbestos scandal, which includes international litigation initiated by victims of asbestosis against British companies, particularly Cape. Thousands of people asked for compensation because of personal damages as a result of Cape's negligence in supervising, producing and distributing asbestos products. The lawyers argue that Cape was aware of the dangers of asbestos at least from 1931 onwards, when in Britain asbestos regulations were introduced. Nevertheless, production continued in South Africa with the same low safety standards until the late 1970s. Medical researchers have found that 80 per cent of Penge's black miners (in Northern Province) who died between 1959 and 1964 had asbestosis. The average age of the victims was 48. Cape operated a mill for 34 years in Prieska, Northern Cape, where 13 per cent of workers' deaths were attributed to mesothelioma, a very painful asbestos related cancer. Asbestos levels in this mill in 1948 were almost 30 times the maximum UK limit. There are other cases in South Africa of asbestos contamination, by companies such as Msauli and GEFCO, at locations such as Mafefe, Pomfret, Barberton and Badplass (Felix, in Cock and Koch, 1991).

Contaminated abandoned mines and asbestos dumps must nowadays be rehabilitated by the post-apartheid South African governments. Simultaneously, court cases were started against Cape in the UK, and the House of Lords (in its judicial capacity) ruled for a while that such cases could be heard in London rather than in South Africa. It seemed that British companies could be sued in British courts. At the end of 1999 (*Financial Times*, 6 December 1999) the Court of Appeal in Britain refused to give 3000 South African asbestos victims leave to pursue their case against Cape. Citing the precedent of the Bhopal disaster of 2 December 1984, where the US courts refused jurisdiction because the claimants were Indian residents, the British court said that the public interest lay in the Cape action being heard in South Africa. A further appeal was foreseen. Against WTO doctrine, the asbestos court case and similar ones, if successful, would show that international regulation is required not only about the safety and quality of the final products but also on the process of production and its side-effects. When regulation failed or was non-existent, and when effective protest was impossible because of political repression, there are then retrospective liabilities to be faced. The courts will perhaps institute little by little a sort of international Superfund obligation for the transnational companies.

*   *   *

Wilderness enthusiasts sometimes assert that economic growth, modern agriculture, urbanization and industrialization do not present unavoidable environmental threats because of the march of technological progress, Kuznets environmental curves and a post-industrial service-based economy. According to this view, the main environmental threats are not in industry and in cities. They come from the expansion of the human population and human activities into wild areas. Hence the possible alliance between the currents of environmentalism described in this book as the 'cult of wilderness' and the 'gospel of eco-efficiency' in order to enjoy simultaneously economic growth in industrial–urban society while salvaging some natural spaces by keeping people out of them.

There is a possibility of another alliance. The wilderness enthusiasts might come to recognize that economic growth implies stronger and stronger material impacts, and also the disproportionate appropriation of environmental resources and sinks, thus damaging poor and indigenous people whose struggles for livelihood are sometimes fought in idioms (such as the 'sacredness' of Nature) which should be attractive to the wilderness enthusiasts themselves. Such an alliance is not always easy, because often population growth, poverty and, possibly, cultural traditions which do not contain 'wilderness' values lead to encroaching upon and poaching the great wilderness reserves whose preservation has been so much a product of 'white' civilization, notably in eastern Africa and South Africa. Indeed, 'the preoccupation of some whites with wildlife preservation at the expense of, for example, dispossessed rural communities may be historically demonstrable – but this should not blind us to the fact that South Africa now has one of the best systems of protected areas anywhere in the world. This is a national treasure from which all future South Africans will benefit' (Ledger, in Cock and Koch, 1991: 240). From what is still the opposite viewpoint, 'minority group campaigners against pollution accuse mainstream US environmental organizations of obsession with 'elitist' goals such as wilderness preservation. A similar chasm has opened up in South Africa recently as radical activists influenced by the American environmental justice movement have rediscovered ecological issues' (Beinart and Coates, 1995: 107), such as the dangers of asbestos and herbicides, the health conditions in mines and the lack of water in black urban settlements. Thus the subaltern third current of environmentalism (environmental justice, the environmentalism of the poor) is consciously present nowadays both in the USA and in South Africa, First World and Third World, two countries whose dominant environmental tradition is the 'cult of wilderness' but where anti-racism and environmentalism are now walking together.

THE BASEL CONVENTION

The South African apartheid state was blind to damage to black workers. The asbestos and mining companies most probably fulfilled internal South African laws as regards safety, wages and taxes. Nevertheless, they should be held accountable for the 'externalities' that they left behind. Given the chance, workers and their families would have complained, not so much because they were environmentalists but because their health was threatened. The law firm which represents the asbestosis victims (Leigh, Day) also brought actions in London for damages to workers at Thor Chemicals in KwaZulu-Natal on behalf of victims of poisoning by mercury, and on behalf of cancer victims from Rio Tinto's Rossing uranium mine in Namibia.[9]

In April 1990, massive concentrations of mercury had been detected in the Umgeweni River near the Thor Chemicals' Cato Ridge plant. This was reported in the national and international press. Thor Chemicals imported mercury waste into South Africa, partly supplied by Cyanamid, an American company. South African environmental groups, mainly Earthlife under Chris Albertyn's leadership, allied themselves with the Chemical Workers Industrial Union, the local African residents under their chief, and also white farmers from the Tala Valley who had already endured a bad experience of pesticide spraying from the neighbouring sugar industry. A true 'rainbow' alliance, which also incorporated US activists against the Cyanamid plant in question, complained against such 'garbage imperialism' or 'toxic colonialism' by asking: 'Why did Thor, a British company, decide to build the world's largest toxic mercury recycling plant on the borders of KwaZulu in a fairly remote part of South Africa? Why not build it closer to the sources of the waste mercury in the United States or in Europe?' (Crompton and Erwin, in Cock and Koch, 1991: 82–4).

Actually, 'the practice of exporting hazardous wastes for disposal in developing countries has been described as environmental injustice or environmental racism on a global scale' (Lipman, 1998). The Basel Convention of 1989 forbids the export of hazardous waste from rich countries except for recovery of raw materials or for recycling. It was complemented on 25 March 1994 by a full ban on all exports of hazardous waste from the 24 rich industrialized countries of the OECD. The agreement was reached over the opposition of the richest countries, which received from Greenpeace, in this context, the name of the Sinister Seven. Some defections inside the European Union (Denmark, and later Italy) helped an alliance among China, eastern European countries and in general all southern poor countries in order to close the 'recycling' loophole of the initial 1989 convention though which 90 per cent of the waste was flowing. Thus, pending ratification and domestic implementation of this agreement, and assuming also that article 11 of the Basel Convention (which allows for bilateral or multilateral hazardous waste exporting agreements provided they comply with 'environmentally sound management') is not abused, a sad chapter of industrialization will be closed. Rich countries would not be able to exploit the weaker regulations of poorer countries to avoid their own responsibility for minimizing waste.

Clearly, the issue is far from over. The pressure for the export of toxic waste is still increasing, although the Basel Convention has had a positive effect. This is the context in which, in November 1998, it was announced that nearly 3000 tons of Taiwanese toxic waste from the group Formosa Plastics had been dumped in a field in the port of Sihanoukville in Cambodia. Taiwan is not a party to the Basel Convention. The waste was scavenged by poor villagers, many of whom later complained of sickness; one died quickly. Local people panicked, and thousands left the city. Demonstrations took place, and the authorities arrested Kim Sen and Meas Minear, members of a Cambodian human rights group, Licadho. The arrests sent a chilling message to environmental and human rights acti-vists. Later, the government ordered the removal of the waste, and approved an order in April 1999 which bans the import of toxic waste in the future (Human Rights Watch, 1999b).

Another example: Delta & Pine is an American company which holds the patent for the 'Terminator' technology which would prevent seeds from rep-licating themselves. This is its major claim to fame, but not the only one. Its attempted merger with Monsanto raised much alarm. It failed at the end of 1999, and Monsanto had to pay a US$81 million indemnity. Delta & Pine is the leading provider of cotton seeds in the USA. In this capacity it became involved in a notorious case of waste dumping in 1998–9 in Paraguay, when a deposit of 600 tons of lapsed cotton seeds treated with toxics was discovered near Ybicuí, in Rincon-i (which in Guarani means 'little corner') and in Santa Agueda. With support from environmental and labour organizations such as Alter-Vida and UITA (a union of food indus-try workers), a national and international scandal was raised after the death of Agustin Ruiz Aranda in December of 1998, and after hundreds of people in the neighbourhood of the contaminated sites became ill (Amorin, 2000).

The logic of Lawrence Summers' Principle still remains compelling:

> The measurements of the costs of health impairing pollution depend on the forgone earnings from increased morbidity and mortality. From this [strictly economic] point of view a given amount of health impairing pollution should be done in the country with the lowest cost, which will be the country with the lowest wages. I think the economic logic behind dumping a load of toxic waste

in the lowest wage country is impeccable . . . I've always thought that under-populated countries in Africa are vastly under-polluted, their air quality is probably vastly inefficiently low [*sic*, meaning 'high'] compared to Los Angeles or Mexico City. Only the lamentable facts that so much pollution is generated by non-tradable industries (transport, electrical generation), and that the unit transport costs of solid waste are so high prevent world welfare enhancing trade in air pollution and waste.[10]

Also new opportunities for dumping waste might develop in the vastly underpolluted oceans.[11]

It might also happen that, as a consequence of the ban on exporting hazardous waste, industries relocate to poorer countries where environmental resistance is weakened by people's powerlessness and by corrupt government. 'The products are then being shipped to the home country where consumers enjoy the benefit of the product while shifting the environmental costs to the developing countries. Greenpeace is investigating a shift in new organochloride related industries from developed to developing countries and have identified at least fifty new facilities in Brazil, India, Indonesia and Thailand' (Lipman, 1998).

ENVIRONMENTAL LIABILITIES AND UNCERTAIN RISKS: SUPERFUND

When enough information is available on the probability of risk, and when an agreeement is reached on the economic values to be given to damages (not a trivial question in itself), then externalities can be internalized into the price system by insurance. Thus, in many countries, the economic costs of motor traffic accidents are indirectly included in the price of travelling through compulsory insurance which is based on sufficient statistical information. In other countries, such as India, car owners pay for traffic accidents directly as they happen. Usually, they do not pay very much, given the low average economic value of life. In any case, other effects of car traffic, such as changes in land use, air pollution and the global greenhouse effect, are not internalized. It would be possible, of course, to try and approximate the costs of some such externalities through eco-taxes, or through markets in pollution permits.

When risk probabilities are unkown, and cannot really be subjectively estimated, as is sometimes the case with new technologies, other instruments have been suggested in order to implement the 'precautionary principle': for instance, compulsory posting of bonds (Costanza and Perrings, 1990) which would cover the maximum damage in case of accident, and which would be paid back with interest should no accident occur during the lifetime of the project. This is a system which would be appropriate for nuclear power stations, or for new biotechnologies, though it still requires an estimate of the maximum damage (could the cost of Chernobyl have been anticipated?) and also a financially impracticable time horizon (hundreds, perhaps thousands of years).

Different instruments of environmental policy are thus applicable to different situations, depending on whether the probability distribution of risks is known or unknown. A certain level of risk can be deemed acceptable and the discussion is then on cost effectiveness. Naturally, what the acceptable level of risk should be is itself polemical.[12] In the USA the Superfund legislation was enacted in the late 1970s (at the end of President Carter's administration). Its official name is the Comprehensive Environmental Response Compensation and Liability Act (CERCLA). As in Europe after the Seveso alarm (dioxin release from a chemical firm near Milan), in the USA after the Love Canal scandal near Niagara Falls in upper state New York, there was a feeling that something should be done to remedy damage done, and to make future damage costly by imposing strict norms of private or public liability. Superfund may also be interpreted as a government response to the first stirrings of the environmental justice movement. Cleaning-up operations under Superfund are financed by special charges on the oil and chemical industries, when the sites are 'orphaned'. When the companies are identified and still active, they have to pay for the cleaning up. The Environmental Protection Agency (EPA) must not act in an 'arbitrary and capricious' manner but it has no obligation to prove that there is actual damage, only that there is a risk of damage. Critics of Superfund point out that the costs, including administrative costs, are too high compared to benefits and that the communities near the waste sites cleaned up do not always benefit economically because the improved environmental situation is countered by the adverse environmental image.

In the Superfund practice, even when the costs are high, cleaning up is worth doing because the risks are deemed to be high. From another perspective (Stroup, 1997), the fact that 'knowledge about harms such as cancer from environmental pollution is extremely uncertain' becomes an argument for *not* doing anything, or rather for leaving reparation costs to private negotiation or litigation under common law, and not under Superfund regulation. Thus neither a cost–benefit approach nor even a cost-effectiveness approach is appropriate when uncertainties prevail. In fact, often the situation is such that risk is not even perceived. Even today, it is still difficult to get people to agree on the reality of environmental damage such as loss of agricultural biodiversity, the consequences of the proliferation of the motor car, the increased greenhouse effect or the thinning of the ozone layer. There is agreement, however, on the danger from the use of DDT and other pesticides (such as DBCP) which were for a time believed to be relatively harmless to wildlife and to humans. Agricultural pesticides are still used in northern modern agriculture in much greater quantities (despite colder climates) than in traditional tropical agriculture. Similarly, regulatory authorities believed some decades ago that there was no important risk involved in the use of asbestos or lead paint in buildings, or lead in petrol. Risks are not perceived or they are perceived too late.[13] Scientific uncertainties and faulty legislation (which puts the burden of proof of damage on the users of the products or on the government regulators, and not on the producers and sellers) are often blamed for the delay in risk perception. However, the elimination of scientific uncertainty is not a realistic objective. The perception of risk changes with time, sometimes because scientific research produces clear results, sometimes because, on the contrary, scientific uncertainties cannot be dispelled, and a feeling of danger creeps in. Then the question is asked: who is responsible for cleaning up the (newly perceived) mess, or for paying indemnities or making reparations? How to assign *environmental liabilities*, granting that restoration may be impossible when irreversible damages or deaths are involved?

Thus the Superfund legislation in the USA is supposed to achieve the cleaning up of hazardous waste sites (chemical dumps, mine tailings and so on). The burden of proof lies rather with polluting companies than with the polluted citizens or with the regulatory agency. Companies have to prove against EPA allegations that no risk of damage exists from the waste they have abandoned. However, nuclear waste is excluded from the Superfund legislation. Will current controversies in the USA over the environmental dangers from transgenic crops (from Monsanto or other companies – see Chapter 10) be conducted inside the framework for liability which the 'Superfund' determines for companies in the chemical or related industries? Or will the Superfund legislation be scrapped under President Bush?

Why the delay in risk perception? Sometimes, the groups affected by environmental impacts (such as future generations) need vicarious representation, which may not be forthcoming. True, 'wilderness' organizations sometimes intervene on behalf of other species, either because they believe in their right to exist, or simply because they support the enjoyment of wildlife by humans. Some risks can fall disproportionately on children, as forcefully argued by John Wargo regarding pesticide residues in food (Wargo, 1996). Sometimes the social groups negatively affected or threatened can get their act together in a collective social protest or in a judicial action, but favourable political and social conditions are required for this. Such groups become active because environmental risks are not randomly spread out. They may fall disproportionately on the poor or on some racial minority groups. Also women can be more subject to risk than men. Another example: the enhanced greenhouse effect (largely due to the excessive use of free carbon sinks and reservoirs) will have an impact on relatively dry areas and also on populated low-lying areas by the sea, mainly in poor countries. Even if the risks are perceived, regions and countries which will suffer damage, and which are at present modest contributors to the greenhouse effect, are not powerful internationally. They are so far unable to press a case for environmental liability or ecological debt against rich countries, as will be discussed in Chapter 10. Notice also that there is *no international Superfund* to which appeal can be made, should judicial actions fail against Texaco, Freeport MacMoRan, Dow Chemical, Cape, Shell, the Southern Peru Copper Corporation, Union Carbide, Unocal, Elf, Repsol and others.

The European situation as regards international environmental liability is more favourable to firms than is the case in the USA. Despite attempts to the contrary by the European Parliament, all that the European Union has been able to produce in this field is non-action. Still in 2001, the European Commission blandly wrote that 'European businesses are urged to demonstrate and publicise their world-wide adherence to the OECD guidelines for multi-national enterprises, or other comparable guidelines' – this, instead of imposing legally binding rules of environmental accounting and liability not only in Europe but also abroad.[14]

YUCCA MOUNTAIN

Nuclear waste is an environmental issue related to risk perception, and to the question of liability. Nuclear power plants worldwide are running out of room to store the waste they have generated, and safe repositories have not been found (Kuletz, 1998: 81). This issue has been discussed since the 1950s and 1960s, when the nuclear power industry started in the USA, Britain, France and Japan. The disposal of highly radioactive waste nuclear fuel has been done up to now on the site of the nuclear power stations themselves. There is also some trade in nuclear waste, to extract the plutonium (as happened early on with waste from the Magnox power stations in Britain, sent to the USA) and nowadays happens in Britain and France. In the USA, given the history of nuclear power, including the close military–civil links, it is appropriate that the western states (New Mexico, Nevada) should be today the site of environmental conflicts regarding the disposal of nuclear waste. This region is also a site of conflict over the risks from uranium mining, and from uranium mine tailings, particularly for the Navajo. New Mexico was the state where the largest spillage of low-level radioactive waste in the USA took place, on 16 July 1979, near Church Rock in the Rio Puerco, when the United Nuclear uranium mill tailings dam broke. The Rio Puerco ('Pig River') was a major water source for the Navajo and their livestock. The environmental justice movement in the USA was involved from its beginning in the public airing of this and other instances of 'environmental racism' against Native Americans.[15] As many as 3000 Navajo men were employed in the uranium mining boom of the late 1940s to the 1970s, both for military and for civilian purposes. In 1990, the US Congress passed the Radiation Exposure Compensation Act, authorizing cash awards to workers and families affected by disease and death from uranium mining, and also from radioactive fallout from nuclear testing, but many claims have not been resolved positively for lack of documentation showing family links with the deceased, or for lack of statistical proof of causality. In any case, money cannot undo the suffering and deaths.

Radioactive fallout from bomb tests and from bomb production facilities has affected people particularly in Nevada, New Mexico and Washington State. 'For example, between 1944 and 1956, approximately 530,000 curies of radioactive Iodine-131 were released into the air at the Hanford Nuclear Reservation in Washington State, neighbor to the Yakima Indian nation, resulting in the largest known public radiation exposure in U.S. history' (Erickson and Chapman, 1993: 5). Certainly, 'prior informed consent' from the victims was lacking.

If a nuclear Superfund existed, it would be confronted in the USA by a clean-up bill of some US$500 billion (Kuletz, 1998: 82). The costs include decontamination of radioactive sites, but they do not include the costs of 'safely' disposing of the waste. Some of this waste is military, most of it is civilian, coming from the nuclear power reactors (aproximately one hundred are still operating) in 20 states. The amount of nuclear waste increases despite the halt in the construction of new nuclear power reactors after the Three Mile Island incident of 1979. The companies ask what they should do with the waste, after the provisional period of storage at the power stations themselves. Will the companies be held liable for 'safe' disposal? In fact, the liability of the nuclear industry in the event of an accident is limited in the USA by the Price–Anderson Act, while the nuclear companies are not concerned with the long-term disposal of the residues.

Did these utilities post a bond which will now cover the costs? They did not. What they did was to charge consumers one-tenth of a cent per kwh, which should now finance 'safe' disposal. But, what really are the costs of 'safe' disposal, when safety refers to a period of thousands of years? Should the future be discounted; should it be undervalued? 'Scientists have been searching for a place to bury nuclear waste since 1954, when the Atomic

Energy Act permitted commercial nuclear reactors to generate electricity. The federal government was made responsible for disposing of spent nuclear fuel. Since then, nuclear waste has piled up in holding tanks at reactors nationwide' (Alvarez, 2000). Current *in situ* storage of nuclear waste in large pools of water, or in dry-cask storage, requires no transport of spent fuel, and there is no reason to think it is less safe than putting it all together in one place (Erickson *et al.*, 1994). Once spent nuclear fuel is suffciently cooled in water (for some five years), dry storage entails placing bundles of spent fuel rods in stainless steel canisters and then in concrete vaults (Erickson *et al.*, 1994: 97). Why, then, the attempt to find a few temporary monitored retrievable storage (MRS) facilities in Indian country, or a final disposal site in Yucca Mountain? The answer is clear: the nuclear industry is interested in saving costs of *in situ* storage, and it is also most 'interested in eliminating its liability and responsibility for spent fuel. Together or separately, an Indian country MRS facility or a Yucca Mountain depot would exempt manufacturers of the waste from subsequent liability for damage it may cause. The time period for potential liability is probably between 250,000 and 500,000 years' (Erickson and Chapman, 1993: 6).

The Department of Energy in the USA (not the EPA, or the Department of the Interior) must, then, find a way of disposing of the nuclear waste. The problem is similar in European countries and in Japan. The solution to the conflict (if not to the problem itself) should be easier in the USA, because it is a large country. However, some of the areas in the west, even desert areas, are inhabited by Indian groups, or belong to them. They are marginalized people who inhabit so-called 'wastelands'. If Indian people were not in these desert regions to begin with, they were driven there by the US government and by white settlers (Kuletz, 1998: 114). Some of the land already belongs to the state, not as natural parks in this instance but as military installations such as the Nevada (Nuclear) Test Site.

For the temporary deposit of spent nuclear fuel (pending final disposal in Yucca Mountain), initial MRS proposals in the mid-1980s focused on the site of the Clinch River Breeder Reactor, in the neighbourhood of Oak Ridge, Tennessee, not only because of the local experience with nuclear materials management but also because of the intention, later abandoned, to locate there a breeder reactor using plutonium as fuel (as with Creys-Malville in France). Pressure from the state of Tennessee and the community of Oak Ridge, and the threat of a veto by the state's governor, led to a different option. The US Congress in 1987 revoked the MRS plans for that site and other proposed sites in Tennessee (Erickson *et al.*, 1994: 78). The federal government set up the office of Nuclear Waste Negotiator in August 1990, a distinct federal agency, separate from the Department of Energy, accountable to the president and Congress, headquartered in Boise, Idaho.

Attention turned to Native American reservations. Attempts were made in the 1990s to reach agreements with Indian groups, such as the Mescalero Apache (an offer to study the proposition was first accepted, but later opposed partly because of the activism of several women, including Rufina Laws) (Kuletz, 1998: 107). Other 'volunteer' sites considered for MRS (applying Lawrence Summers' Principle internally to the USA) belonged to the Skull Valley Goshute in Utah, and to the Fort McDermitt Paiute–Shoshone in Nevada.

In many environmental conflicts, security in the access to natural resources and complaints against pollution are expressed in the language of indigenous territorial rights. In the USA, this pro-environmental use of indigenous territorial rights has been prominent in mining conflicts (Gedicks, 1993). Examples of indigenous territorial rights being used as a bulwark against the oil industry in Nigeria and in Colombia, have gained worldwide fame. In the MRS case, the US nuclear industry and the federal government took the opposite line, trying to use the loophole of tribal sovereignty, which allows US Indian tribes to open casinos even in states where there are anti-gambling laws. The sovereignty over their territory was here used by the authorities to encourage these remaining Indian tribes to accept nuclear waste. There was also an official appeal to Indian long time horizons, which would make of them careful trustees of nuclear waste: 'With atomic facilities designed to safely hold radioactive materials with half-lives of thousands of years, it is the native American culture and perspective that is best designed to correctly consider and balance the benefits and burdens of these proposals.'[16]

However, acceptance of MRS of nuclear waste by Indian tribes has proved to be more difficult than originally planned. Almost all nuclear power stations are in the east of the USA, while repositories are being sought in the west. Moving both low-level and high-level radioactive waste into repositories out in the west implies crossing state boundaries, so that states still have something to say. Moreover, the very few Indian tribes which initially accepted grants for MRS feasibility studies later became internally divided (Erikson and Champman, 1993; Erickson *et al.*, 1994). Valery Kuletz (1998: 110) concludes: 'The environmental justice movement has emerged to combat the inequitable burden of environmental degradation placed on poor communities and communities of color. The targeting of Native American lands for temporary nuclear waste storage can be seen as a form of environmental racism and what Indian people themselves call nuclear colonialism.' Money compensation is no longer the issue, when such words come into play.

For final deposit of nuclear waste, the designated site is Yucca Mountain, very near the Nevada Test Site and also near to Death Valley (a well-known 'wilderness' area), where a deep geological burial is planned. Given the longevity and the lethality of nuclear materials, this would be literally the burying of uncertainty (Kuletz, 1998: 97). The state sees itself as having planning powers and foresight quite out of the ordinary, while the market failure in nuclear electricity pricing is evident. More than 15000 truck and rail shipments through 43 states over a period of 30 years would be required to move the nation's waste from nuclear power plants to Yucca Mountain (Kuletz, 1998: 116), should this finally be the national repository. It is possible that foreign waste would also be accepted (reversing in this case the normal flow of waste), in order to prevent its military use abroad, thus making possible a continuation of the policy by the USA and also some European countries and Japan, of favouring nuclear power while trying to discourage its military use.

On 25 April 2000, President Clinton vetoed a bill passed by Congress that would have required the Energy Department to move nuclear waste to Yucca Mountain in Nevada within 18 months of the time that a licence was granted, and set deadlines for other steps. The plans for a repository to be built there have not been completed. Under current commercial contracts between the nuclear electric companies and the US government, the Energy Department was supposed to begin accepting waste for disposal in January 1998. Current plans delay the date to 2010. But the plan for developing a repository at Yucca Mountain, which lies 90 miles north-west of Las Vegas, 'has an uncertain schedule and cost'.[17] There has been a local movement of protest against the use of Yucca Mountain. Such protests are led by western Shoshone, aided by anti-nuclear grass-roots groups (Kuletz, 1998: 147). This is part of the environmental justice movement, and no doubt President Clinton's veto was related not only to the technical debate on the safety of nuclear waste but also to concerns about social resistance.

Yucca Mountain and its immediate surroundings are not seen as a desert or wasteland by the Indians. There is water in a number of springs; the approaches to the mountain were used in a pattern of seasonal migrations by the western Shoshone and other groups; there are also human burial grounds. Whether the state of Nevada will strongly oppose to the end the use of Yucca Mountain as a repository for high-level nuclear waste remains to be seen. In 2000, strong opposition came from Senator Richard H. Bryan, and other legislators in Nevada itself and in neighbouring states oppose trucking the waste through their territories: this could become a 'mobile Chernobyl' (Alvarez, 2000). Corin Harney, a western Shoshone spiritual leader, agreed: the waste should be kept where they made it, because transport would put 50 million people at risk of contact with this most toxic poison. Whether the central government will eventually impose its will over the Indian groups and the state of Nevada also remains to be seen. In the meantime, Raymond Yowell, chief of the Western Shoshone National Council, reiterated that Yucca Mountain is a sacred place. His point was not only that the Shoshone should have legal title to the land, but that the land is sacred, and Shoshone are 'the land's caretakers'. Sacredness might help mobilize white 'deep ecologists'. Resistance has been weak: 'Though the Western Shoshone as a nation stand at the forefront of active protests, not all Western Shoshone are interested in nuclear politics; many are busy with other sovereignty struggles on land rights. Some couldn't care less, and many balk at making any kind of political alliance with white people, even those supporting them' (Kuletz, 1998: 147).

The government contends that the western Shoshone lost the land through encroachment as early as the 19th century, and it offered compensation in the 1950s of 15 cents per acre for 24 million acres through the Indian Lands Claim Commission. The western Shoshone refused this monetary compensation and still refuse it to this day, claiming instead title to the land (which includes many gold mines). Title was denied them by the US Supreme Court's decision in 1985 upholding the proposed monetary settlement.[18] Money, sacredness, indigenous territorial rights, uncertain future environmental and health hazards, national security and indeed the international norms which favour indigenous groups (such as Convention 169 of the International Labor Office) are available languages for fighting this dispute that will perhaps intensify under President Bush's pro-nuclear stand. Solving the social conflict would not in any case solve the problem of nuclear waste.[19]

NOTES

1. A public meeting on 20 June 2000, held by the Asthma Committee Forum a few blocks away from where I was writing this book, asked 'Why is New Haven's child asthma rate more than three times the national average?' More information would be provided by the New Haven Environmental Justice Network.
2. R. Bullard, *Directory. People of Color Environmental Groups 1994–1995*, Environmental Justice Resource Center, Clark Atlanta University, Georgia; emphasis added.
3. Deborah Robinson, executive director of International Possibilities Unlimited, Washington DC, 'Environmental Devastation at Home & Abroad: The Importance of Understanding the Link', 1999 (www.preamble.org/environmental-justice).
4. Kathryn Ka Flewellen and Damu Smith, 'Globalization: reversing the global spiral', 1999 (www.preamble.org/environmental-justice).
5. Monique Harden, Nancy Abudu, and Jaribu Hill, 'International Law: a Remedy for U.S. Environmental Racism', 1999 (www.preamble.org/environmental-justice).
6. For instance, when asking for a Social Security card in the USA, one is asked to classify oneself in one racial group, and, at least until recently, *only* in one.
7. Aaron Sachs, 'The Routes of Environmental Justice', draft paper, December 1999: pp.24–5.

8. Letter from Norton Tennille and Boyce W. Papu to Peter Mandelson, 7 September 1998 (www.saep.org).
9. Ronnie Morris, 'UK court demolishes double standards', *Business Report*, 4 March 1999, and subsequent information downloaded from the website *saep.org*. A UN report stated in 1990 that the Rossing uranium mine in Namibia was 'a theft under the law and must be accounted for when Namibia becomes independent'. There is a flow of exports of uranium out of Africa.
10. Internal World Bank memo, as reported in *The Economist*, 8 February 1992, under the title 'Let them eat pollution'. This has become a canonical text for the environmental justice movement.
11. Sources used are the website Basel Action Network, and reports from Greenpeace; for ocean dumping, *Journal of Marine Systems*, 20, 1998, monographic issue on 'Abyssal Seafloor Waste Isolation: a technical, economic and environmental assessment of a waste management option' (I owe this reference to Ramon Margalef and J.M.Naredo).
12. It is alleged, for instance, that the US EPA 'tries to make sure that a person near a Superfund site faces a risk of death from cancer that is lower than the risk of a person on the ground dying from a falling airplane' (Stroup, 1997: 134).
13. The European Environment Agency is about to publish in 2002 a book entitled *Late lessons from early warnings* on such 'false negative' cases, when the Precautionary Principle was *not* implemented, tracing the history of denial of risk far beyond the time when the first alarms were raised.
14. Commission of the European Communities, 'A Sustainable Europe for a Better World: A European Union Strategy for Sustainable Development', Brussels, 15 May 2001, COM (2001) 264 final.
15. W. Paul Robinson, 'Uranium Production and its Effects on Navajo Communities along the Rio Puerco in Western New Mexico', in Bunyan Bryant and Paul Mohai (eds), *Proceedings of the Michigan Conference on Race and the Incidence of Environmental Hazards*, Ann Arbor: University of Michigan School of Natural Resources, 1990.
16. David H. Leroy, U.S. Nuclear Waste Negotiator, speaking to the National Congress of American Indians, 4 December 1994, quoted in Erickson and Chapman (1993: 3).
17. Matthew L. Wald, 'President vetoes measure to send nuclear waste to Nevada', *New York Times*, 26 April 2000.
18. Evelyn Nieves, 'A Land's Caretakers Oppose Nuclear-Dump Plan', *New York Times*, 23 April 2000, p.12.
19. Under President Bush, and after the events of 11 September 2001, the disposal of nuclear waste may become ever more closely linked to national security concerns and less open to social debate.

9. The state and other actors

In other nuclear countries, a similar pattern of unfair sharing of environmental risks is to be found as that in the United States described in Chapter 8. For instance, French nuclear testing in Mururoa compares with US testing in other Pacific islands, and in or near Indian country in the continental USA. Horrific stories of radioactive pollution, both from military and civil sources, are known from the ex-Soviet Union, and are bound to come to light in other countries still following the same path. A 'nuclear' state, as Robert Jungk remarked 30 years ago, tends towards dictatorship, though one could argue that the Chernobyl accident of 1986, which questioned the generalized belief in technical progress in the ex-Soviet Union, had a most important role in accelerating political change away from dictatorship.

In India, as in France, an alliance between scientists and technocrats in government has given support to the nuclear industry. Thus, in 2001, the government of India is proposing a breeder reactor fuelled by plutonium to be built on the coast of Tamil Nadu, amidst general acquiescence – perhaps because of the distance between proposals and reality – except for complaints from the Fishworkers' movement. At the other end of the nuclear 'life' cycle, the Uranium Corporation of India, a state enterprise, has heavily contaminated since the mid-1960s the miners and miners' families in some areas of Jharkhand, but national controversy has only arisen recently (Bathia, 2001: 129–35, Wielenga, 1999: 93–6).

The state has played everywhere a decisive role in the development of nuclear power, because of the links to military power, and because it has enacted legislation which diminishes the nuclear power companies' liability. Shall we then conclude that the state is usually an anti-environmental actor? I am myself inclined towards this view, objections to which will be discussed in this chapter, where states will be disassembled into different pieces, and the interplay between state actors and other actors of environmental conflicts will be analysed. Popular resistance to environmental degradation acts sometimes in opposition to the state, sometimes with allies within the state.

There is a common southern pattern of cooperation between the upper levels of the state and foreign private corporations for the use of natural resources of the national territory, and this encounters resistance by local groups that try to link up internationally under the banners of indigenous rights, human rights and environmentalism. States like Nauru have enthusiastically cooperated in the spoliation of their own territory, mined for phosphates (McDaniel and Gowdy, 2000). Often opposition to the state has gone together with the defence of natural resources, as we saw in the case of Bougainville. In large countries like India and China, the main environmental clashes are still with their own governments or public corporations rather than with multinationals. Thus, in India, despite sharp memories of colonial exploitation and current movements against Cargill, Monsanto or Enron, there is not the pervasive sense of outside exploitation of natural resources that one finds in Indonesia, Nigeria or Peru.

GOVERNANCE AND ENVIRONMENTAL POLICY

After Seattle in late 1999, in a decade which also saw the joyous gathering of NGOs at Rio de Janeiro in 1992 and their negotiation of a number of sensible environmental 'treaties', it could no longer be believed that world environmental policy depends exclusively or mainly on the internal policies of states and on the regimes they institute by their agreements (Wapner, 1996: 152). The success of transnational environmental activist groups demonstrates that states do not monopolize environmental policy. States share the international stage with other actors. States sometimes get into disagreements with each other (even within the G7, even within the European Union), or different parts of states get into conflict with each other. Opportunities appear for a transnational environmental movement, as happened with the Basel Convention (see above, p. 183), and as also happened with the Biosafety Protocol of 2000.

There are other actors in environmental policy besides states and transnational environmental activist organizations, and none more important than transnational corporations, as anybody will soon find who does research on the mining, oil and gas, pharmaceutical, agricultural and forest sectors. Corporations have in theory no political power, they operate only in the economic sphere. One may choose to emphasize how reality squarely contradicts this theory, or one might choose to highlight instead the fact that they often operate in countries distant from their home base, and have difficulties in exercising power. Bribery and corruption often arise from lack of direct political power.

Corporations have been trying to organize a common position on the conflict between economy and environment, pushing the view that eco-efficiency will solve all problems, as proposed by the Business Council for Sustainable Development in Rio in 1992. While some firms take an active role in proposing new policies on the increased greenhouse effect, others such as Exxon still deny its existence. Corporations such as Shell have great difficulties in acquiring a green image despite their publicity campaigns. Rules on environmental liabilities vary from country to country. In some respects (mine tailings, greenhouse gases, nuclear waste) corporations manage in general to eschew liability altogether. Nevertheless, there is a trend for important corporations to include such environmental liabilities (moral, so far, more than economic) in their reports to shareholders. Local firms, such as those operating in the shrimp export sector or wood extraction in countries like Ecuador or Indonesia, usually operate with fewer environmental restrictions than transnationals. Here there is a role for overseas consumers' movements to stop the environmental degradation.

Although at first sight eco-efficiency depends on decisions by firms, the states or the international regimes agreed by states are crucial in determining property rights on the environmental resources and sinks, and in organizing markets in emission permits or introducing eco-taxes. Also environmental auditing of firms and the regulation of environmental liabilities require state intervention. The environmental quality of a process of production or a product is rarely left only to the self-management of Chambers of Industry or bodies which certify ISO-14000 standards. Who certifies the certifiers? Quality is socially constructed. State or international sanction is normally required to separate pure 'greenwashing' from genuine environmental improvement.

While not as powerful as states, or as corporations (taken as a whole), networks of environmental groups such as Friends of the Earth, or the big conservationist organizations (WWF, Nature Conservancy, IUCN), or transnational environmental entities such as Greenpeace, or the specific networks (such as the International Rivers Network, or OilWatch) significantly shape behaviour as it relates to environmental issues. They refrain from taking head-on the capitalist world as a whole, and they have no grand coherent blueprint or scheme for the future of humankind and nature. They rather focus on particular issues, and on particular rogue corporations that behave in extremely offensive ways. They try to undermine the support of the World Bank and associated regional banks for controversial projects such as dams, and oil and mining projects. They play an important role in influencing the agenda of contemporary world environmental politics. Their activities go far beyond lobbying governments. Lobbying still leaves states as main actors but the international networks also exercise power, they mobilize collectivities and individuals, they enrol members (in the millions) and get money (in the hundreds of millions of dollars) and they use the power of the media. However, international environmental groups do not always agree on the line to be taken, and they tend to lecture to southern grass-roots groups instead of learning from them. (One example we have seen in some detail is the failed boycott on cultivated shrimps – see Chapter 5. Another example is the emphasis of northern groups on domestic eco-taxes, rather than on the damages caused by coal, oil and gas extraction in poor countries.)

In 'greenhouse' politics, an international scientific body, the International Panel for Climate Change (IPCC), has become an important actor, and it has recommended cutting emissions of greenhouse gases by half within a reasonable time. States, including southern states (with the exception of the Alliance of Small Island States), also tend towards the status quo on this matter. This is true even for Brazil and India, whose resources of diplomacy would allow them to play a much stronger international role. Often southern states still believe in a doctrine of economic growth at any cost, where environmentalism is seen as a luxury of the rich more than a necessity of the poor, and then fail to profit from the opportunities opened up by environmental conflicts. Oil and gas corporations long refused to believe in the very reality of the enhanced greenhouse effect, as did also oil exporting states.

At times, environmental groups become enmeshed in the details of international environmental agreements (such as the Kyoto Protocol) and they forget the 'carbon debt'. Remarkably, until 2001, there was still no organized social movement (though there were competent intellectual voices) in favour of a policy of 'equal rights to carbon sinks and reservoirs' whose potential constituency is enormous. The IPCC may be seen (or could be seen, before President Bush), at the international level, in two lights: one, the old idea of a body of scientists establishing the facts for the politicians (decision makers) to take well-informed decisions; the other, as a negotiating body for international governance which will talk with and listen to a multitude of participants in order to reach some sort of policy consensus by integrating the analyses at all levels (scientific, economic, social) and relevant time-and-space scales. Thus the emphasis is not on advice to decision makers but on interventions in a collective decision-making process. Will politicians relinquish for the sake of governance the power they have over the decision-making process? Many environmental problems are complex, with contradictory scientific, economic and political facets, and this makes it possible to press forward different points of view, sometimes finding unexpected allies. Now choosing the procedure for the integration of the different perspectives is still a matter of power more than consensus. State power does not always translate into a power to simplify complexity, imposing a single perspective on the problems thrown up by the contradiction between the economy and the environment.

How important are environmental issues for states? When the environment became a political issue, state administrations already had many ministries and departments. States, if they could, would like to consider environmental policy as only one more branch of policy. The environment was a new arrival of the 1980s and 1990s, just as in most universities. States now have ministries for the environment. Now, however, the environment cannot be separated from agriculture, transport, industry, urban planning or even public finance (because of eco-taxes). Hence the call by the European Commission (from the Cardiff summit of 1998 to Gothenburg in 2001) for the integration of environmental policies into other sectorial policies, so that, for instance, transport policy or agricultural policy take the environment into account, it is hoped in a win–win outcome. Whether win–win is the rule or the exception depends on empirical practice, and also on how long policies may be delayed. Environmental NGOs believe that win–win solutions are not so frequent, and therefore environmental policies should predominate. Although sectoral integration of environmental policies is the acknowledged principle, there is not a single case to my knowledge of a combined ministry for the environment and the economy, where the minister would explain to the journalists that the GNP grew by so much, the HANPP and TMR also grew, but air quality in cities improved. Would the journalists be able to do their own sums?

Governments, faced with an environmental agenda often not to their own taste, are forced anyway to make policy. Internally, in some countries and in some periods, policy can made dictatorially, often inspired by a doctrine of economic growth. (Big dams, at any cost.) In democracies, politicians in the very recent past liked to base their decisions on sound science, and to choose rationally the optimal option. Not big dams at any cost, but big dams after cost–benefit analysis with all the externalities factored in. Sometimes, faced by the uncertainties and urgencies characteristic of so many environmental issues, governments are now moving away from a strategy of legitimization of decision making, where sound science served policy, towards a different strategy, a call for *governance* defined as the capacity to draw upon a wide range of expert and stakeholder opinions, so that decisions are better informed and rest on a wide basis of consensus. Instead of optimal solutions, we settle for compromise solutions. The languages of valuation are more diverse. The state becomes more permeable.

ENVIRONMENTAL MOVEMENTS AND THE STATE

As we have seen, the claims to the rights to natural resources of poor communities, and their complaints about pollution, are an integral part of the environmental justice movement. However, it has been rightly said that, in the USA, 'most toxic activists avoid questioning the compatibility between capitalism and environmental ends, preferring to explore "clean" technologies and to argue that production processes could be changed to accord with environmental priorities without serious economic consequences, either for the corporations involved, or society as a whole' (Epstein, 2000). The environmental justice movement in the USA has been ready to work closely with the state. The EPA has a (small) office for environmental justice, which might survive, or not, under the Bush presidency. The demands of the movement against toxic contamination are a demand for a state that has more power to regulate the corporations, a state that responds to the public interest, in a tradition that goes back to the New Deal's regulation of economic conflicts (Epstein, 2000). The environmental justice movement is the most radical current of American environmentalism. Nevertheless, it is not a radical anti-state movement; it asks the state to regulate ecological distribution conflicts inside the USA, though not (yet?) outside the USA. Compare this, for instance, with the Ogoni and the Ijaw in the Niger Delta defending themselves against the Nigerian state and Shell, learning to combine local grievances with international greenhouse politics, linking up in the Oilwatch network and with other groups, combining indigenous territorial rights with the demands for a decentralized confederal state composed of Nigerian nationalities (see above, p. 103). The US scene is more conservative and domestic.

The benevolent environmental image of states has some shadows. States have armies. Greenpeace, an eco-pacifist organization, was founded in Vancouver in the early 1970s. It devoted itself mainly to the preservation of large marine mammals, though it soon spread out to many other issues. Its immediate origin was not whales but nuclear testing. A local Vancouver group got the idea in 1969 (which Quaker groups had practised before) of sailing a ship to the site of the tests, in this instance the Amchitka Island in the Aleutians. The ship, the *Phyllis Cormack*, never made it to the Amchitka because of bad weather and harassment by the US Coast Guard. However, returning to Vancouver, the crew were surprised to find thousands of people greeting them. These initial anti-nuclear activists organized themselves as the Greenpeace Foundation in 1972 (Wapner, 1996: 44–5). States have armies, and some states (in the north but also in China, India and Pakistan) have nuclear arms. Even without nuclear arms, armies, by the equipment they use, are directly heavy polluters even in peacetime. This is a point that environmentalists such as Matthias Finger have emphasized, but in the world of NGOs there is a division of labour between the pacifists and the environmentalists. Indirectly, armies of northern countries also damage the environment because they exist, to some extent, in order to secure the flow of energy and materials, while armies of southern countries have often been used to repress social movements against natural resource extraction and environmental pollution, from Rio Tinto in Spain in 1888 to Guatemala, Nigeria and Indonesia recently. Their personnel have profited from the extraction of raw materials, directly or through allocations in the state budget (as with the military in Ecuador and Chile, with fixed percentages of oil or copper revenues).

States are the main military entrepreneurs but, despite privatization policies, they are also active in other areas, as industrial entrepreneurs and builders of public works. All around the world, social movements oppose dams, pipelines and mines built by states themselves or by corporations sponsored by states. Thus, in India, as this book goes to press, the confrontation in the Western Ghats between the Kudremukh Iron Ore Company, owned by the state, and local environmentalists and tribals who defend the forests and the Tunga and Bhadra rivers, has reached an acute phase. Silent actors of this conflict are also the iron ore importers. Vocal opponents to the closing of the mines are the workers' unions. Exploitation of iron ore in this microcosm of biodiversity started under Indira Gandhi's Emergency rule, when dissent on such issues was almost suppressed. Now the extension of the lease (which lapsed on 24 July 2001) is in question. 'Both the Centre [that is, the New Delhi government] and we [that is, the Karnataka government] are waiting to see the Supreme Court's judgement on public interest litigation filed [by environmental groups] demanding stoppage of mining in the area.' The KRRS and other groups are leading the protests.[1]

Again, another current case from southern India shows the state in an unfavourable light. The Plantation Corporation of Kerala has been cultivating cashew in 4500 hectares in the Kasargod district, spraying an organochloride pesticide called endosulfan that has been banned in many countries. In the Philippines, Hoechst Chemical brought a court case for libel against Dr Romy Quijano, a toxicologist and human rights activist, who warned of the dangers of endosulfan through the mass media and also through the Pesticides Action Network for Asia and the Pacific. Hoechst's suit was dismissed in June 1994. Local inhabitants of Kasargod, Kerala, including one medical doctor, have pointed to the disproportionate incidence of cancer and malformations in the area. An Endosulfan Spray Protest Action Committee was set up, and denounced the case. Passivity at the state level was compensated by an appeal to outside allies, among which the Centre for Science and Environment from Delhi (led by Anil Agarwal) that carried out measurements of endosulfan concentrations in water, cow's milk and tissue, human blood and milk, and in the soils, showing very large values (reported in *Down to Earth*, 23 February 2001). However, even in a democracy like India, local poor people have so far been unable to stop the aerial spraying; moreover, the government asks them to prove the damage. The determination of the risk assessment procedure remains in the power of the state.[2]

Are states from the south ever mobilized for international environmental policy? There are some rare instances of this. Thus some Latin American states were instrumental in getting the international law on resources of the sea based on the 200 mile exclusive economic zone. Ecological distribution conflicts are then phrased in the language of international public law. As long ago as the 1940s, Bustamante y Rivero, the president of Peru, together with neighbouring governments, announced this policy to prevent overfishing by foreigners. Overfishing in Peru in the late 1960s was by local entrepreneurs. In Namibia (under South African administration) pilchard stocks plummeted in the 1960s and 1970s; there was overfishing without local political power to counteract it. Recently, the intervention of states against some patents has been essential in 'biopiracy' struggles, for instance against the patent on the yellow bean from Mexico, or against the patent on transgenic cotton by Agracetus, refused by India. However, to repeat, states from the south are not important environmental actors. For instance, on an issue which is of great importance for the south, they have been unable or unwilling to move forward the negotiations on farmers' rights boycotted by most northern governments. In this agrarian landscape of unresolved and almost unspoken conflict, there now enter some new collective actors, such as Via Campesina, proposing a new world agricultural policy. The field is wide open.

Domestically, for environmental groups to exist, there has to be a measure of democracy, or a phase of political struggle in transition towards democracy, when environmental groups, such as Walhi in Indonesia in the 1990s, prosper because they play several roles at the same time. In eastern Europe, political green activism peaked at the time of political transitions around 1990. In democracies, some organs of the state may be permeable to environmental movements, or may act as an umbrella for them. The sympathy, or at least the neutrality or neglect, of the state may be necessary in order to introduce environmental improvements at the local level. We saw in Chapter 6 the receptivity of the Costa Rican government, under local and international pressure, to modify the initial plans for wood exports by Stone Container in 1994. Also, in West Bengal, as in some other instances in India of successful joint forest management, several new village forest reserves have been reported (Poffenberg, 1996) which became possible because grass-roots leadership was effective in mobilizing the communities' potential commitment to forest protection. Tribal and low-caste leaders were intensely aware of the exhaustion of *sal* (*Shorea robusta*) forests because of the villagers' search for fuelwood for their own needs and to make a living by selling it. These leaders have successfully re-established village forest reserves of a few hundred hectares in each village. Vigilance against wood thefts by outsiders is carried out informally by the villagers themselves. All this has been possible in the concrete situation of West Bengal, under the government of the Communist Party (Poffenberg praises it as a 'populist government'), the reserves being supported by the West Bengal Forest Department's officials who themselves had repeatedly been unable to protect the forests on their own. New institutions of communitarian management have been born with the complicity of parts of the state. One may still complain that officialized Joint Forest Management often excludes women's participation (Sundar, 1998). One may feel nostalgia for other forms of biodiversity protection such as sacred groves well known in ancient and modern India – the Buddha himself is said to have been born in a *sal* sacred forest in what is now Nepal. But there is no doubt that some state organs have helped environmental movements.

In general, the wilderness movement relies almost everywhere on the state for the designation of natural parks, sometimes against the wishes of local populations, while popular environmentalists act against the state in cases of oil extraction, mining or dams, or they operate totally outside the state, as in the agroecological movements. There are other examples, some of them collected in this book, in which popular environmentalism uses the judiciary of the states by having recourse to internal courts, or to courts in northern countries. In India, as we have seen in Chapters 5 and 7, the judiciary power took a strong pro-environmental and pro-poor people stand in the attack on the shrimp industry; it was also pro-environmental, although socially controversial, regarding air pollution in Delhi. It is anti-environmental in the Narmada case, and it was too shy or perhaps overruled in the Bhopal case, analysed in the next chapter. In Brazil, the judiciary power, and regional executive powers, have been decisive in the case against exports of Monsanto GMO crops, also analysed in the next chapter.

THE ENVIRONMENT AND HUMAN RIGHTS

Southern environmental movements often use the language of defence of human rights, and have made practical alliances with organizations such as Amnesty (Sachs, 1995). From the wilderness branch of the environmental movement, the Sierra Club has also worked with Amnesty in recent years trying to reach a wide public in the USA by showing environmental conflicts through famous victims (such as Chico Mendes and Ken Saro-Wiva) depicted as individual heroes, the tip of an iceberg of environmental confrontation. The language of human rights implies a straight interpellation of the state because the state is supposed to respect, indeed must guarantee, human rights to life and freedoms.

Are infringements of human rights exceptional occurrences? They should be, but they are not. However, there is conceivably a trend towards fewer infringements. Sometimes statistics on crimes against human rights increase because of better coverage, as there is a fresh possibility of more thorough outside supervision. Nevertheless, there are fewer dictatorial governments in the world today than there were some years ago. Now, however, although governments make sincere efforts to improve the human rights situation, more and more environmental impacts and therefore also harm to human rights, may be expected because of economic growth.

Related to human rights, states have had population policies, sometimes outlawing neo-Malthusian movements (see Chapter 3) and forbidding abortion, at other times trying to stop population growth. Finally, and very importantly, states are essential to regulate and/or forbid international migrations, helping thereby to maintain international inequalities. One peculiarity of human ecology is that, on the borders of rich countries, there are a sort of Maxwell's Demons disguised in uniforms, which keep out most people from poor countries, thus being able to maintain extremely different per capita rates of energy and material consumption in adjoining territories: witness the many deaths per year of those trying to enter the USA or Europe from the south.

RESISTANCE AS THE PATH TO SUSTAINABILITY

Whatever idioms they use, whether 'external costs', 'human rights', 'territorial rights' or 'sacredness', southern environmental movements have tended to be more adversarial than northern movements with regard to their governments, opposing laws and policies deemed to be destructive or unjust, mistrusting the intermediation of the state in their conflicts with outside interests (Guha, 2000). Northern groups in all their variety, including the US environmental justice movement, have worked more with the governments. 'Conflict resolution' is more appreciated in the north than in the south, where it obvious to all that, in socially asymmetrical situations, pacifying a conflict is not the same as solving a problem.

In both north and south, there has now accumulated a rich body of reflective work to complement direct action. In poor countries intellectual reflection, for the most part, is prompted by or follows local resistance. In Brazil, the idea of 'extractive reserves' came out of the *seringueiros*' practice, and the movement was able to impose this new form of community property on the state at a time of transition to democracy in the late 1980s, when the state was more permeable than before. In India, which is the cradle of the notion of the 'environmentalism of the poor', the many instances of resistance by local communities to abusive modes of resource use (including the Chipko movement) were theorized from the 1970s onwards. In Latin America (in Mexico, in the Andes), there was a new intellectual perception, starting in the 1960s and 1970s, of the richness of traditional indigenous agroecology, and a few agronomists changed sides at that time. Every year thousands of environmental conflicts in southern countries go unreported, some of which are classified under a different heading. Invisibility is a trait that the environmentalism of the poor shares with feminism.

The line from practice to theory runs perhaps in an opposite direction in the north, where books like Rachel Carson's *Silent Spring* may even be said to have 'sparked off' the environmental movement of the late 1960s and 1970s, and where the writings of Thoreau, Muir, Leopold and G.P. Marsh had already inspired many followers. The intellectuals of the south are less well known, even in their own countries. Why are Anil Agarwal and Sunita Narain (who became environmentalists after Chipko) not the main advisors to NGOs and southern states on 'greenhouse' politics? Why is Kumarappa's peasant economics of permanence less well known than Schumacher's economics of smallness and beauty? True, everyday conflicts on the health impacts of pollution have constituted one common variety of environmentalism in north and south. However, only in the south have large masses of people engaged in environmental conflicts, while fending for themselves. They do not know how to mobilize immediately the resources of the environmental movement against business and the state. As explained by Ramachandra Guha (2000: 106), commercial tree plantations, oil drilling, gold, iron, coal and copper mining, and large dams all damage the environment, and they also, and to their victims more painfully, constitute a threat to livelihoods. The opposition to these interventions is thus as much a defence of livelihood as an 'environmental' movement in the narrow sense of the term. There is a prior claim to the resource in question – land, wetland, forests, fish, water, clean air – abruptly extinguished by the state or by the commercial sector working in concert with the state that has granted these outsiders oil, mineral, water or logging concessions. Civil society existed before the state. There is, then, manifest a palpable sense of betrayal, a feeling that the government has let the poor down by taking the side of the rich, whether nationals or foreigners.

There is, however, at first the hope that the government will come to see the error of its ways. These struggles thus most often begin by addressing letters and petitions to persons of authority, in the state administration, or in influential organizations (such as the Church in Latin America), as if the mere knowledge of injustice would, by itself, bring remedy to it. Geographical and social distance from the centres of power often prevents direct lobbying. When these pleas are unanswered, protesters turn to more direct forms of confrontation, and they also appeal to a wider national and international audience. Here NGOs play the role of translating the local vocabulary of the petitions into an environmental, human and territorial rights language which connects with international organizations and networks. Some such environmental networks born in the south or which work mainly towards the south, appear often in this book, an International in the making, without a politbureau.

On the ground, the forms of social protest may be diverse. In India, seven different forms have been identified: the *dharna* or sit-down strike, the *pradarshan* or mass procession, the *hartal* or general strike, forcing shops to down shutters, the *rasta roko* or transport blockade (by squatting on rail tracks or highways), the *bhook hartal* or hunger fast (conducted at a strategic site, say the office of the dam engineer, and generally by a recognized leader of the movement), the *gherao*, which involves surrounding an office or official for days on end, and, last of all, the *jail bharo andolan* or movement to fill the jails by the collective breaching of a law considered unfair or unjust (Gadgil and Guha, 1995). Many of these methods were perfected by Mahatma Gandhi in his battles with British colonialism, but they have equivalents in other peasant and indigenous cultures too. Chico Mendes invented the *empate*. In Amazonia (in Ecuador and Peru), the non-aggressive kidnapping of workers or, better, managers of the oil industry who enter indigenous territories has become common over the last five or ten years, with a view to negotiated outcomes.

Gandhi has given Indian environmentalists their most favoured techniques of protests as well as a moral vocabulary to oppose the destruction of the village economy. Thai peasants have recourse to Buddhism to remind their rulers, who publicly profess the same religion, that their policies are a clear violation of their commitment to justice, moderation and harmony with nature. It is notable that the anti-eucalyptus struggle was led by Buddhist priests, known appositely as *phra nakanuraksa*, or 'ecology monks'. In most of non-indigenous and even in some parts of indigenous Latin America, the ideology most conveniently at hand is popular Catholicism and its contemporary variant, liberation theology, which makes clear the commitment of part of the clergy and the Church to redirect their energies towards the poor. Thus Leonardo Boff, the Brazilian liberation theologist (a former member of the Franciscan order, now no longer a priest of the Catholic Church) has written books on ecology and the poor (Boff, 1998). 'There should be life before death,' according to the Christian churches which participated in the Jubilee 2000 campaign against the payment of the external debt. In the USA, the organized environmental justice movement from its beginnings in the early 1980s was closely linked to some churches.

Do such religious languages of social justice imply also a non-instrumental respect for other forms of life apart from humans? Has religion anything to say on HANPP? Buddhism perhaps, more than Christianity. Who will defend Nature when Nature is not directly linked to human livelihood? Which of the languages used by the environmentalism of the poor are close to the cult of wilderness? The truth is that such religious languages are often linked to sustainable agriculture more than to wilderness (for instance, the cult of Pachamama, 'Mother Earth', in the Andes) and still at other times the environmentalism of the poor does not use religious languages at all (Gosling, 2001).

THE RELEVANCE OF SEN

Development as conventionally understood has been attacked on a theoretical plane (Escobar, 1995; Latouche, 1991; Norgaard, 1994; Sachs, 1992) and critics have been forthcoming with down-to-earth sector-specific proposals as well. In South Asia, in the realm of water management, they have offered, to large dams, the alternative of rain harvesting, with small dams and/or the revival of traditional methods of irrigation such as tanks and wells. In the realm of forestry, they have asked whether community control of natural forests is not a more just and sustainable option when compared to the handing over of public land on a platter to industrial tree plantations. In the realm of fisheries, they have deplored the favours shown to trawlers at the expense of artisanal fisheries (Guha, 2000). The alternatives have been not merely technological but also institutional, reinforcing the old and creating new community systems of management of resources (Berkes and Folke, 1998).

Environmental movements of resistance carry within themselves programmes for alternative development projects. Is development still to be understood as 'modernization'? Are we thinking of development only in economic terms (as in 'weak' sustainability) or in physical and social terms (as in 'strong' sustainability)? For instance, agroecology in industrialized countries is a minority neorural movement, tolerated in a world where postmodern social experiments are not only allowed but positively encouraged (like cycling in northern cities, provided it does not threaten the car industry and urban sprawl). In the south, the fight for traditional agroecology and against the transnational seed companies is potentially relevant to hundreds of millions of members of peasant families. The ecological – economic rationality of peasant systems provides a practical departure point for an alternative modernization. In Latin America, environmental thought is marked by an awareness of outside exploitation and ecologically unequal exchange, going back to silver mining in Potosi and gold mining in Minas Gerais. This appears in essays and literary works, from José Bonifacio and the proto-ecologist Alberto Torres in Brazil (Padua, 1996, 2000) to José María Arguedas' *Todas las sangres* and Eduardo Galeano's *Venas abiertas*, through writings on the rubber voragine and the devil's metals. Recent ecological Latin American thought is also characterized by a tremendous respect (that recalls that of Alexander von Humboldt) for the wealth of a continent so unexplored in its ecological potential, so rich also in solar energy, biodiversity and water, so relatively empty of people. Hence the Bariloche Report, published as an answer to the Club of Rome report of 1972 (Gallopin, 1995). Hence also the promises of a future 'alternative ecological productive rationality' which can be perceived already in some existing indigenous communal management systems (Leff and Carabias, 1992; Leff, 1995). This line of thinking is absent from the local proposals of environmental movements in Europe, Japan and the USA.

We are witnessing a groundswell of popular environmentalism. Area specialists (Latin-Americanists, specialists on South and Southeast Asia, Africanists) still have difficulties in understanding its wide scope. Consider the attempt to classify the pioneering work on India by Ramachandra Guha and Madhav Gadgil, not as an interpretation relevant and influential also for Africa and America and indeed for European history, but rather as a purely local pro-community, anti-state, post-colonial discourse derogatorily described as the Indian 'standard environmental narrative' (SEN):

> in the days of yore vibrant local communities lived largely in balance with nature, prudently managing their common property resources to satisfy a variety of needs of the community. The British, however, expropriated the common property resources without compensating the local stakeholders in order to exploit these resources commercially, thereby undermining the resource base of the local communities. Through no fault of their own, these communities subsequently have had to exploit whatever resources they had access to, in a less sustainable manner. After Independence, the State and its main agent, the Forest Department, have been increasingly corrupted by politicians, forest contractors and timber mafias. According to the SEN, this has caused the contemporary environmental crisis. Consequently, the forest-dwellers and tribals must reassert their control over the commons to manage it on the basis of their indigenous knowledge, and in cooperation with NGOs. (Madsen, 1999: 2–3)

The SEN is also relevant in contexts where the market, more than the state, is the main agent of deforestation. Hence the relevance of the comparison between Chipko and the Chico Mendes' movement, between old communities and of new communitarian institutions, between state property and private concessions in the first case, enclosure by private owners in the second case, depriving the *seringueiros* of access to the forest. Moreover, Gadgil's work on 'sacred groves', and the insistence on the value of local indigenous knowledge, finds parallels in other continents, while Ramachandra Guha's main theoretical inspiration comes from the English social historian E.P. Thompson. Again, there are obvious parallels between SEN and the narratives of the defence of mangroves by (recently constituted?) communities in Latin America and elsewhere, or the struggles against oil and mining companies in countries other than India. Oil and minerals belong to the state according to most legal systems, and the state gives concessions to local or foreign firms. River water also belongs to the state, and the state directly or indirectly 'develops' the rivers by building dams. In other cases, water is appropriated privately: nothing different in principle or in practice to the forest conflicts which Ramachandra Guha studied in detail. The environmentalism of the poor cannot be pushed back into a South Asian forest. The idea was indeed born there in the 1970s and 1980s, but it has spread across the south because of its relevance; it is also relevant for European history, and it is now, it is hoped, linking up with the environmental justice movement in the United States.

It is professionally profitable today in sociology, anthropology and history, in North Atlantic universities and research institutes, to eschew general interpretations, and prefer instead little narratives contingent on place. To find a structure of cross-cultural environmental conflicts produced by the growing clash between the economy and the environment, as the present book does, to emphasize at the same time the growing movements of resistance expressed in different idioms across the world, undoubtedly does some violence to the bewildering variety of cultures and actors where such conflicts occur. So be it. Let other authors pick up the place-specific pieces.

GENDER AND ENVIRONMENT

The idea of an environmentalism of the poor first appeared in print in the late 1980s and early 1990s. For many years, the conventional wisdom was that the poor were 'too poor to be green'. 'If you look at the countries that are interested in environmentalism, or at the individuals which support environmentalism within each country, one is struck by the extent to which environmentalism is an interest of the upper middle class. Poor countries and poor individuals simply aren't interested' (Thurow, 1980: 104–5). 'It is not accident,' wrote Eric Hobsbawm (1994: 570) 'that the main support for ecological policies comes from the rich countries and from the comfortable rich and middle class (except for businessmen, who hope to make money by polluting activity). The poor, multiplying and under-employed, wanted more "development", not less.' This book challenges the view that societies of the Third World are too poor to be green, in a shift of perspective similar to that which the environmental justice movement caused in North American environmentalism. Furthermore, it has been argued (Rocheleau *et al.*, 1996), after the large output of publications on political ecology in the 1990s, that *today's conventional wisdom is the theory of the environmentalism of the poor, and what is really new is 'feminist political ecology'.* It might well be so, as will now be discussed.

The case in favour of peasant production because of its virtues in terms of conserving biodiversity and using direct solar energy might be convincing. Being pro-peasant resonates with some currents of contemporary environmentalism: 'small is beautiful', 'organic farming'. But, alas, peasant societies are patriarchal. The conflict betwen an ecological pro-peasant stand (such as I support) and the feminist viewpoint has been emphasized by several authors, including Bina Agarwal (1998) and Mukta and Hardiman (2000). In order to build an eco-feminist society we cannot look to a peasant past or to a peasant present; we have to look to the future (or perhaps to a distant, underpopulated, no longer relevant, hunter–gatherer past).

Women have a constructed social role of providers for the *oikos*, and therefore they have reacted strongly when water scarcity and pollution, or air or soil pollution, threaten the survival of families. Besides, poor women often depend on common property resources (for fuelwood, for pastures, for water) to a larger extent than men, who are more integrated into the market. Therefore women react againt the enclosure of such resources. Women rely more than men on common property resources because in many cultures they hold a smaller share of private property (Agarwal, 1992). Indeed, one feature of the environmental justice movement and the environmentalism of the poor has been the significant and sometimes determining part played by women. Women have assumed leadership roles. They have been harrassed, beaten, jailed or killed, whether in the struggles against Los Angeles urban refuse incineration, or in Bangladesh in the fight against farmed shrimps.

Among women in the countryside, there is often a deep awareness of the dependence of human society on a clean and bountiful environment. A tribal woman in the Bastar district of central India, herself active in a forest protection campaign, put it this way: 'What will happen if there are no forests? *Bhagwan Mahaprabhu* (God) and *Dharti Maata* (Mother Earth) will leave our side, they will leave us and we will die. It is because the earth exists that we are sitting here and talking' (Guha, 2000: 108, quoting Sundar, 1998). Taking off from such remarks, some feminists posit an intrinsic biological rapport between women and Nature which in their view is denied to men. This has been called *essentialist eco-feminism*. Many feminists are repelled by this position, which situates women close to Nature while men are close to culture, politics and the economy. Now, both men and women are close to Nature, whether we like it or not. It might well be that, in western scientific cultures, men more often than women have felt themselves to be masters and owners of Nature (to use Descartes' words). Neither men nor women should be alienated from natural realities in this way (Salleh, 1997), believing themselves to be 'dematerialized' angelical beings. In any case, other 'non-essentialist' eco-feminist scholars (Agarwal, 1992; Rocheleau *et al.*, 1996) have forcefully argued that the participation of women in environmental movements stems from their closer day-to-day involvement in the use of Nature and the caring for a healthy environment, and additionally from their greater awareness and respect for community cohesion and solidarity. In the division of labour typical of most peasant, tribal and pastoralist households, it falls on women and children to gather fuelwood, collect water and harvest edible and medicinal nuts and plants. Women are thus more easily able to perceive, and quickly respond to, the drying up of springs or the disappearance of forests.

In industrialized market economies, eco-feminist economists (Waring, 1988; Mellor, 1997; Pietila, 1997) have pointed out that, in national income accounting, even the destruction of natural resources is counted as production, while environmental and social reproduction is not. This is explained by social history, not by biology. The money economy is only a small island surrounded by an ocean of unpaid caring domestic work and free environmental services. It is also the case that women, more than men, are inclined to take the long view, to sense, for example, that mining or tree plantations or commercial shrimp farming might bring in some quick cash today but will undermine their economic security for tomorrow and the day after. Social eco-feminism is a movement of resistance against environmental degradation.

Bina Agarwal (1992) prefers herself not to use the term 'eco-feminism' at all (because of its essentialist connotations) and refers instead to 'environmental feminism'. Agarwal refuses the 'essentialist eco-feminist' idea (in Vandana Shiva's fanciful book on the Chipko movement: Shiva, 1988) that there was a time in the historical past when there was more equality between men and women, and when there was no domination of humans over Nature but rather a relationship of harmony. Particularly in India, because of caste, the subordination of women has been strong, in order to control marriages. 'Basically, for transforming the relationship between women and men and between people and nature, we need to enhance the bargaining power of women in relation to men, and of those seeking to protect the environment in relation to those causing its destruction' (Agarwal, 1998: 85). The emphasis on old systems of management of natural resources, against the state or the market, is dangerous to women because the traditional communities were internally unequal. What is needed is new communitarian institutions based on eco-feminist economics and values, rather than a return to traditions of discrimination against women. One cannot but agree.

The notion of the 'ecological debt', which in an international north–south context is examined in the next chapter, and which is a lynchpin of the present book, was first proposed in 1985 in an eco-feminist context. Eva Quistorp, a founding member of the German Green Party, wrote at the time, together with her colleagues, 'Women are creditors of economic debts arising from unpaid labour, they are also entitled to compensation for the political and social subjection they have suffered, also they are owed ecological debts caused by the plundering, pollution, and irreversible destruction of our natural resources which make it ever more difficult for women to secure the existential basis for their lives and those of their children'.[3]

NOTES

1. Sownya Aji Mahu in *The Times of India*, 27 July 2001, and 'Dharna against mining in Western Ghats', *The Hindu*, 10 August 2001.
2. *The Hindu* (magazine), 22 July 2001; *Down to Earth*, 15 August 2001.
3. Women in the Green Party (FRG), 'Women in Movement – West Germany. Current situation and activities, perspectives on international solidarity', 1985.

10.   The ecological debt

Internationally, the ecological debt arises from two separate ecological distribution conflicts. First, as we shall see immediately, the exports of raw materials and other products from relatively poor countries are sold at prices which do not include compensation for local or global externalities. Second, rich countries make a disproportionate use of environmental space or services without payment, and even without recognition of other people's entitlements to such services (particularly, the disproportionate free use of carbon dioxide sinks and reservoirs).

The ecological debt brings together many of the conflicts related to the environmentalism of the poor, and it also puts on the table the question of the languages in which such conflicts are to be expressed. The ecological debt is an economic concept. The first discussions on the ecological debt took place around 1990, largely because of the inputs from a Latin American NGO (the Instituto de Ecologia Politica from Chile). One of the alternative international 'treaties', at Rio de Janeiro's Earth Summit of 1992 was a Debt Treaty, which introduced the notion of an ecological debt in contraposition to the external debt. Fidel Castro was persuaded by Latin American activists to use this concept in his own speech at the official conference.[1] Virgilio Barco, the president of Colombia at the time, had already used the expression in a speech in the USA at an MIT commencement ceremony on 4 June 1990. One decade later, Friends of the Earth made of the ecological debt one of its campaigns for the following years.[2] The notion of an ecological debt is not too radical. Think of the environmental liabilities incurred by firms under the US Superfund legislation, or of the engineering field called 'restoration ecology', or the proposals by the Swedish government in the early 1990s to calculate the country's environmental debt.[3]

ECOLOGICALLY UNEQUAL EXCHANGE[4]

The Ricardian theory of comparative advantage showed that, if all countries specialized in the production which was internally cheaper to produce in relative terms, all could win by trade. Subsequent elaborations of the theory showed that, if countries specialized in productions which relied on the internally most abundant factors (say, natural resources as opposed to skilled labour or manufactured capital), all could win by trading. Critics pointed out that relying on comparative advantage would mean, in some cases, remaining locked into a pattern of production which excluded gains in productivity from economies of scale (that is, the infant industry argument for protectionism). Nowadays, the recognition that production also involves destruction and degradation of the environment bring us to a new perspective in the study of trade between regions and countries. We shall not argue for autarky, or for a strict 'bioregional' position. From a purely ecological point of view, there is an argument for importing elements the lack of which would limit production, in the sense of Liebig's law of the minimum. However, the ecological view of the economy as an open system which necessarily depends on nature for resources and sinks has given rise to a new theory of ecologically unequal exchange, building on earlier notions such as *Raubwirtschaft* or 'plunder economy' coined by geographers and almost forgotten in the discipline (Raumoulin, 1984).

Unequal exchange had already been pointed out in terms of undervaluation of labour and health of the poor and of deterioration of the terms of trade expressed in prices, and used as part of a theory of underdevelopment. By recognizing the links to the environment, the notion of unequal exchange can be expanded to include unaccounted, and thus uncompensated, local externalities, and the different production times exchanged when extracted products that can only be replaced in the long run (if at all) are traded for products or services which can be produced quickly. By ecologically unequal exchange we mean, then, the fact of exporting products from poor regions and countries, at prices which do not take into account the local externalities caused by these exports or the exhaustion of natural resources, in exchange for goods and services from richer regions. The concept focuses *on the poverty and the lack of political power of the exporting region*, to emphasize the idea of lack of alternative options, in terms of exporting other renewable goods with lower local impacts, or in terms of internalizing the externalities in the price of exports, or in terms of applying the precautionary principle to new export items produced with untested technologies.

Selling at prices which do not include compensation for externalities and for the exhaustion of resources can be described as 'ecological dumping'. This happens not only in the trade of natural resources from south to north but also sometimes from north to south, as with agricultural exports from the USA or Europe to the rest of the world which are subsidized directly, and also indirectly, because of cheap energy, no deductions for water and soil pollution and use of pesticides, no deductions for the simplification of biodiversity. We describe the first kind of ecological dumping (from south to north) as ecologically unequal exchange to emphasize the fact that most extractive economies are often poor and powerless, and therefore they are unable to slow down the rate of resource exploitation or to charge 'natural capital depletion taxes', unable to internalize externalities into prices, and unable to diversify their exports. 'Dumping' implies a voluntary decision to export at a price lower than costs, as with European exports of surplus agricultural products. When oil is exported from the Niger delta, power and market relations are such that there is no possibility of including the social, cultural and environmental costs of oil extraction in the price. Diamonds from Africa carry heavy unaccounted ecological and social rucksacks. When a country like Peru exports gold and copper, and much environmental and human damage is suffered internally, it is not appropriate to say that the social values of the Peruvians are such that they care little for health and the environment. Rather, we should say that they are unable to defend their interests for a better environment and a better health because they are relatively poor and powerless. In an economic model, whatever the causes, the result will be the same. The externalities (insofar as they are known) are not factored into prices. In the mathematics of the models, it does not matter whether this is a free choice or an imposed decision, whether there are inscrutable preferences or unjust social structures.

The study of the state-sponsored large projects in the 1970s in the Northern Amazonian region of Brazil (mainly iron and aluminium exports) led some authors (Bunker, 1985; Altvater, 1987, 1993) to the idea of ecologically unequal exhange. Bunker emphasized the lack of local political power in this region. Differing 'production times' together with the valorization (*mise-en-valeur*) of new territories are the notions that Altvater brought into play (see Chapter 3), in an ecological elaboration of Rosa Luxemburg's theory of the accumulation of capital. Capitalism necessarily incorporates new spaces by means of new transport systems in order to extract natural resources. Spatial relations being modified, temporal relations are altered as well, because production in the newly incorporated spaces can no longer be governed by the time of reproduction of Nature. Capitalism needs new territories and accelerates the production times. The antagonism (noticed long ago by Frederick Soddy) between economic time, which proceeds according to the quick rhythm imposed by capital circulation and the interest rate, and geochemical–biological time controlled by the rhythms of Nature, is expressed in the irreparable destruction of Nature and of local cultures which valued its resources differently. Nature is an open system, and some of its organisms grow sustainably at very rapid rates, but this is not the case of the raw materials and products exported by the Third World. By placing a market value on new spaces we also change the production times, and economic time triumphs, at least apparently, over ecological time. But, as Richard III put it after killing some of his relatives, what has been done cannot be now amended.

Overexploitation of natural resources is intensified when terms of trade worsen for the extractive economies which have to face payments of the external debt and have to finance necessary imports. This is in fact the trend for many of the Latin American, African and South-East Asian resource exporters, where a quantum index of exports was growing faster than an economic value index in the 1980s and 1990s. When coal used to be the main commercial energy source, production and consumption were geographically not far apart (in Europe and the USA). Now, although there is gas and oil extraction in Europe and the USA, large amounts of energy travel large distances with a predominant south-to-north direction. Similarly there are increasing net currents of iron, copper and aluminium from south to north (Barham *et al.*, 1994; Mikesell, 1988). There is displacement of production of materials from north to south, in a context of general increase of the material flows (Muradian and Martinez-Alier, 2001).

The inability to bring all externalities and the deterioration of natural resources into the measuring rod of money makes it hard to produce a measure of ecologically unequal exchange, in the fashion that conventional economics is familiar with. The key question is whether standard trade theory has adequately worked out the problems of externalities related to exports. The theory of incomplete markets tries to provide explanations why externalities might arise and what problems they might bring to known welfare propositions. A substantial part of the recent application of this framework to study trade and environmental issues focuses on the presence of incomplete property rights over natural resources and services to explain why trade might not be necessarily welfare improving for the exporting country. Shrimp farming destroys mangroves – never mind, the theory says that such losses could be monetarized through appropriate property rights and appropriate markets on the livelihood and ecological functions of mangroves, and then we could know exactly what the balance is. Another way of putting this point across is the following: negative environmental externalities derived from the export activity can be introduced in the standard trade theory approach by bringing in the distinction between private and social marginal cost of production or extraction. However, economic valuation will depend on relative incomes and on power relations. The problem only becomes harder when we consider that the externalities might reach the future as well as the present. In that case, the problem is to translate not only the externalities of the present period into money value but also those of the future periods, something that forces us to choose a discount rate, and therefore to choose an intertemporal distributional pattern of costs and benefits.

Standard economic theory points to the need to internalize externalities, something that, to the extent possible, is desirable in order to bring the costs of extraction and exporting of natural resources closer to the 'real' social costs. The applicability of standard economic reasoning necessarily implies aggregating the externalities, at present values, under a unique numeraire. The point is that it is precisely the social and political limitations in achieving this goal that pushes the analysis outside the neoclassical sphere, towards incommensurability of values (which means the absence of a common unit of measurement across plural values). As explained in Chapter 2, incommensurability of values entails the rejection not just of monetary reductionism but also of any physical reductionism.

Trade theorists are used to dealing with nominal, real or factoral terms of trade, or even with the notion of terms of trade in embodied labour units, as needed for Emmanuel's unequal labour exchange theory (Emmanuel, 1972). The environmental degradation caused by trade in exporting countries can be counted in physical units. H.T. Odum's theory of unequal exchange in terms of 'emergy' is an example. Emergy is defined as embodied energy. It is similar to Marx's concept of labour value, but in energy terms. Odum is concerned with exposing unequal exchange of emergy between regions or nations, and he discusses trade in terms of their emergy exchange ratio. The periphery is underpaid for the emergy content of its natural resources because they are not properly valued in the market. The problem, as Hornborg (1998) points out, is whether Odum intends to give us a normative or a positive approach: that is, whether the emergy content is something that should be used to determine how exports should be paid for, and thus we should aim at an emergy–equity trade, or is just something to be used descriptively, an indicator about imbalances in trade along with measurements in tons of materials and measurements in money values. Trade policy should then take into account several indicators which perhaps show different trends.

Hornborg also reviews the use of the concept of exergy to provide a different perspective on the relationship between energy and trade. Exergy stands for available energy. Hornborg argues that market prices are the specific mechanism by which world system centres extract exergy from, and export entropy to, their peripheries. Furthermore, it would be impossible to understand accumulation, 'development' or modern technology itself without referring to the way in which exchange value relates to thermodynamics, that is, the way in which market institutions organize the net transfer of energy and materials to world centres (Hornborg, 1998). One may add that the disposal of waste, such as carbon dioxide emissions, with zero market value, is also another key factor to understanding economic growth in the north. Hornborg's point is a crucial one because it stresses the importance of understanding the mechanism by which unequal exchange takes place. This is precisely something which a theory of ecologically unequal exchange has to provide, that is, an explanation why market prices and market mechanisms have not provided a fair and reciprocal exchange. Still, the use of concepts like emergy and exergy, aside from the difficulty in their calculation and application, would only account for one aspect of the link between extraction of resources and the environment. The important point is not the difficulty of calculation. The essential point, as argued above, is that incommensurability applies not only to money value but also to physical reductionism. Can 'biopiracy' be reduced to energy calculations?

At any rate, a theory of unequal exchange has to include a clear framework in which to describe how this kind of exchange arises. Theories more in accordance with standard economics would point to the existence of incomplete markets. This naive body of literature would then highlight the need for establishing property rights, and negotiations in actual or at least in fictitious markets, in order to avoid environmental problems. In ecological economics and political ecology, work is being done instead emphasizing the lack of political and market power of those suffering the externalities. The concept of 'environmental liabilities' arising from concrete instances of pollution in mining or oil extraction is significant in this respect. It is certainly implied in the Superfund legislation in the USA (see above, p. 185), which is not applicable internationally. After listing a number of cases in the USA in which indemnities have been paid by corporations such as Exxon Valdez, a Venezuelan journalist asked himself: 'Venezuela being a country dominated by the oil and mining industries, the question is, what is the *pasivo ambiental* [environmental liability] of all this oil and mining activity in our country?'[5]

It is fascinating to watch the diffusion of the term *pasivo ambiental* in a mining and oil extraction context in Latin America as one writes this book. Hector Sejenovich, from Buenos Aires, was perhaps the first economist to use this term when he calculated the environmental liabilities from oil extraction in the province of Neuquen, Argentina. The Argentinian Minister for the Environment was quoted on 6 February 2000 (journal *Rio Negro*, on line) as saying that regional incentives to oil companies in Neuquen would not include lowering environmental standards. The government, he added ominously, had in its possession the study made for UNDP which evaluated the *pasivos ambientales* from oil exploitation in Neuquen at one billion dollars. In Peru, a new law project was submitted to Congress in 1999 (project n.786) creating an National Environmental Fund – a sort of internal GEF (Global Environmental Facility, financed by the World Bank), as some congressmen put it. The Fund would finance environmental research, it would restore the environment, it would promote ecological agriculture. Its economic resources would come from a percentage of the revenues from the privatization of state enterprises. After complaining about the environmental deterioration because of mining and fisheries, after commenting also on increasing desertification and deforestation in the country, congressman Alfonso Cerrate remarked that the *pasivos ambientales* had been a factor in the lack of buyers at the auction which was to privatize Centromin (the state firm which was the successor of the Cerro de Pasco Copper Corporation). The question was, 'Who will pay for the ecological debt? Who will assume the environmental liability [*pasivo ambiental*] accumulated throughout the years by Centromin and other state firms?'

In Chile, new legislation on liabilities after mines are closed was being discussed in 1999 and 2000. The Sociedad Nacional de Minería was aware of a danger of being accused internationally of ecological dumping, and it was in favour of applying international environmental standards adapted, of course, to national realities. On the topic of the *pasivo ambiental*, it added, discussions were proceeding but the general feeling in the industry was that the state should assume such environmental liabilities.[6] The Bolivian Vice-minister of Mines, Adán Zamora, referring to the pollution in the river Pilcomayo (that flows down from Potosí towards Tarija and eventually Argentina), increased by the bursting of a tailings dyke at Porco belonging to Comsur, had said in 1998, '*la nueva política estatal minero-metalúrgica tiene como responsabilidad remediar los pasivos ambientales originados en la actividad minera del pasado*' (*Presencia*, 16 June 1998): 'the new state policy on minerals and metallurgy has the reponsibility of mitigating the environmental liabilities originated by mining in the past'. In fact, environmental liabilities in Potosí reach back to the 16th century, long before the Bolivian state came into existence.

Ecologically unequal exchange is born, therefore, from two causes. In the first place, the strength necessary to incorporate negative local externalities in export prices is often lacking in the south. Poverty and lack of power induce local environment and health to be given away or sold cheaply, even though this does not mean a lack of environmental awareness but simply a lack of economic and social power to defend both health and environment. In the second place, the ecological time necessary to produce the goods exported from the south is frequently longer than the time required to produce the imported manufactured goods or services. As the north has profited from an ecologically unequal trade, it is in a debtor position.

MEMORIES OF GUANO AND QUEBRACHO

Oversupply of primary commodities, forced by a doctrine of export-led growth and by the obligation of servicing the external debt, leads to low prices. This must not be mistaken for a trend towards material and energy 'delinking' in the importing economies. The point needs some emphasis. Thus an authoritative African view is that 'Current difficulties of such countries as Côte d'Ivoire and my own country, Cameroon, which until recently, were considered development models in Africa, can largely be explained by . . . the fall of prices of African commodities in the international market.' Agreed, but why should this be so?

> The main reason is that the quantity of raw materials now required for an industrial production unit represents only two fifths of what was needed in 1990, and this decline in demand for raw materials is accelerating. In this respect, the Japanese experience is particularly striking. In 1984, for each industrial production unit, Japan used only 60 percent of the raw materials it had used eleven years earlier, in 1973, for the same volume of industrial production. The example of some industries is also significant. Thus, it is possible to send as many telephone messages with a glass fiber of 50 to 100 pounds as with a ton of copper wire. However, the production of the 100 pounds of glass fiber does not require more than five percent of the energy needs for the production of the ton of copper wire. Similarly, plastic that is more and more replacing steel in automobile bodies is only half the cost of steel, energy and raw materials included. Reliance on raw materials as sources of income for exports cannot therefore be a wise long-term policy for African governments; to the contrary. (Doo Kingue, 1996: 41)

One agrees with the conclusion, that reliance on exports of raw materials is bad economic policy, without agreeing with the premise of 'dematerialization'. Witness in the region the controversial new Chad–Cameroon pipeline to ship oil for exports. The volume of materials exported from south to north, which is far higher than the volume imported, is not decreasing in absolute terms. True, some raw materials may become technologically obsolete, as happened to the exports of Chilean saltpetre (which had caused the War of the Pacific of 1879 between Chile, Bolivia and Peru), and which through the Birkeland-Eyde process and later the Haber process (during the First World War), was replaced by nitrogen taken from the atmosphere at a high energy cost. In other cases, exhaustion or at least substantial depletion occurred before substitution arrived, even though the resources themselves were renewable, like the *chinchona officinalis*.

Sometimes there are products which in principle would be ecologically sustainable but are not, such as *guano* in Peru between 1840 and 1880, and *quebracho* in Argentina from the 1900s to the 1950s. Guano is a Quechua word which has made it not only into Spanish but also into English. It is a substance that consists of the dried excrement of sea birds, and is used as a fertilizer. In the early 1830s, Charles Darwin in his diary on the voyage of the *Beagle* referred to the virtues of guano which were known since before the Incas. Guano existed in large stocks off the coast of Peru, where it never rains. It was not a commodity that had to be produced; its deposits already existed on small islands and promontories accesible to cargo ships. The large-scale commercial exploitation of guano was contemporaneous with the birth of agricultural chemistry in 1840, with Liebig's and Boussingault's publications. A chemical analysis of its contents had been made by Fourcroy and Vauquelin, as the science of plant nutrients was being born. In 1840, the new knowledge of agricultural chemistry, and the need to increase yields in Europe and the USA, came into play. A few influential Peruvians already thought of 'turning guano into railroads' (in a 'weak sustainability' perspective, if one may use such terms). One of them was the chemist Mariano de Rivero, born in Arequipa, who had been trained in Paris, and was a colleague of Boussingault. He was sent to America by Humboldt, together with Boussingault, with a letter of recommendation for Bolivar in the early 1820s, to discover new resources for export. About 11 million tons of guano were exported from Peru in four decades (Gootenberg, 1993; Martinez-Alier with Schlüpmann, 1987). Guano is the same resource as fishmeal (even though at a later stage of the trophic chain), which was also exported from Peru at a non-sustainable rate in the 1960s and early 1970s. Periodically, the warm waters of El Niño appear around Christmas (hence its name), provoking intense rains on the coast of Ecuador and the Piura desert in northern Peru; they also displace or destroy the fisheries of anchovy (*Engraulis ringens*) and other species, many birds dying of hunger. This natural phenomenon, locally well known (Lavalle, 1913: 97), is today world-famous because its global reach has been understood following the events of 1972–3. El Niño helps to explain the foretold collapse of the anchovy fishery in the early 1970s but not the near-exhaustion of guano in 1880. Guano is a favourite topic of Peruvian history. Good monographs have been written on guano (Maiguashca,1967; Bonilla, 1994; Mathew, 1981), more from the financial and political than from the ecological viewpoint.

A.J. Duffield, towards the end of the Peruvian Guano Age of 1840–80, estimated the guano deposits still existing in Peru. He transcribed an optimistic dispatch sent by Juan Ignacio Elguera, the Peruvian Minister of Finance, for the benefit of overseas bondholders, two years before the start of the war of 1879:

> However long the guano deposits may last, Peru always possesses the nitrate deposits of Tarapacá to replace them. Foreseeing the possibility of the former

becoming exhausted, the Government has adopted measures by which it may
secure a new source of income, in order that on the termination of the guano,
the Republic may be able to continue to meet the obligations it is under to its
foreign creditors. (Duffield, 1877: 102)

In today's ecological economics parlance, this was indeed extremely 'weak'
sustainability on the verge of the Chilean takeover of the saltpetre fields.[7]

The Peruvian guano economy, today a staple of ecological–economic
history, provided in the 1960s the model for the theorization by Levin
(1960) of the 'enclave' economy, defined as an economy where linkages were
lacking between the export sector and the internal economy. Peruvian
guano was extracted by some local labour, and by Chinese imported inden-
tured labourers. It was not produced, but quickly extracted and then 'com-
moditized' or merchandised by European merchants from London and
Paris (Gibbs and Dreyfus). The USA came late to the great guano rush
(Skaggs, 1994), no Monroe Doctrine applying here. The US Congress tried
to make up for the delay by passing an Act in 1856 (which apparently is still
in the current statutes) 'to authorize protection to be given to citizens of the
United States who may discover deposits of guano' in small islands, rocks
or keys off the coast of Africa, the Caribbean or the Pacific, or wherever
they might be, provided they did not belong to other states nor were occupied by citizens of other states. Nothing of much commercial value came
out of this attempt at enjoying the pleasures of open access to guano
through newly well-defined property rights (Skaggs, 1994).

The trade in *quebracho* (*Schinopsis balansae*) from Argentina is a story of
the 20th century.[8] It was used for railway sleepers, for posts, and for tannin
extract for export, at a non-sustainable rate. There are two types of quebracho, white and red. The extract from the red was used from the end of the
19th century for tanning. It is a hard wood, which grows in isolated strips.
The regions containing these slow growing trees were the Chaco and Santa
Fe, in Argentina. After some initial attempts by local entrepreneurs at
developing an export industry of extracts, Baron Emile Beaumont
d'Erlanger of London set up a company in 1906, known as La Forestal, for
the purpose of acquiring and further developing the business of the
Compañía Forestal del Chaco. By 1911, the new company owned 1·5
million acres, and leased 0·5 million acres, by 1913 growing to 5 million
acres freehold, and 0·6 leased (Hicks, 1956: 7, 16). In 1920–21, there was
much labour unrest, and the tannin factories in Argentina were locked out.
The 1920s became a period of expansion, the productive capacity of quebracho extract reaching in 1928 (for La Forestal and other minor companies) 430000 tons annually (Hicks, 1956: 45). The company sold land
cleared of quebracho for cattle rising, and for settlers. The official history

of the company remarks that 'of the vegetable tanning materials in common use at the end of the First World War – oak, chestnut, spruce, quebracho, etc – quebracho was not only by far the cheapest, it was, and it is still today, the tanning agent which most rapidly penetrates the hide' (Hicks, 1956: 22). Despite such advantages, La Forestal diversified its sources, developing black wattle and mimosa tree plantations in eastern and South Africa as a source of tannin.

Argentina forbade the export of roundwood quebracho in 1928, to foment the production of tannin extract in its own territory. Later, during the Peron government from 1946 onwards, the regulation of export of quebracho extracts (through state control) and its taxation (as on agricultural exports in general) were introduced. According to the official history of La Forestal, this attempt to increase export prices initially made Argentinian quebracho extract uncompetitive internationally, but by the early 1950s a successful accommodation had temporarily been reached. More than 200 000 tons of extract were sold annually during the Korean war years. Now, many of La Forestal's factories were in Santa Fe, where, in contrast to the Chaco, 'supplies of quebracho trees round the factories were becoming exhausted' (Hicks, 1956: 68). These factories had to be closed down. For the local populations, the abandoned settlements were to be regarded as the equivalent of mining ghost-towns. Large reserves of quebracho still existed in the Chaco, owned by the state, and new factories could be opened, though there was the threat from African plantations, and also a new threat: 'the full impact of leather substitutes [such as artificial rubber] on the sale of leather, which in its turn may influence the demand for tanning materials, has not yet made itself fully felt' (Hicks, 1956: 70).

Replanting quebracho was never contemplated. Liability for depletion was not in question. Exhaustion of the resource was limited by transport costs between field and factory, and also by occasional slumps in demand. Whether quebracho was used up too quickly, or not quickly enough, whether the benefits to Argentina were considerable or negligible, are topics still open to hot debate. The decisions were certainly not taken in Santa Fe and the Chaco (Acevedo, 1983; Garcia Pulido, 1975; Gori, 1999) but in London and Buenos Aires. Nationalist complaints against La Forestal's many sins have been often heard in Argentina.

Depletion is quicker than production in many old-growth forests. One of the most memorable Latin American cases was the export of mahogany from the Selva Lacandona in Southern Mexico from 1870 onwards (de Vos, 1988), a region famous today because of the Chiapas insurrection of 1994, but really inaccessible at the time. There, also, as in Argentina with quebracho, roundwood exports were forbidden in 1949 – much damage had already been done to the primary forest, and much more was to occur in successive decades because of cattle ranching and agriculture. A hundred years ago, mahogany was sent to Liverpool and other destinations from enormous timber concessions (one of them named after the Marquis of Comillas, from Spain) worked by debt peons. The wood was sometimes lost in the forest, the oxen being unable to pull it out. It was floated down the small rivers and eventually down the Usumacinta to the port of Tabasco, but sometimes the rains were heavier than expected, and the accumulated wood was lost before an organized shipment could be made. In any case, nobody ever thought of replanting mahogany, nor was there a concern about the destruction of parts of the forest because of the extraction and transport of isolated mahogany trees.

Here I shall use such cases in order to establish a typology regarding both *renewable* and *exhaustible* resources:

- resources which are exploited at particular locations and exported at such a rate that they become (almost) exhausted, whether they are renewable or not (guano, oil and certainly many metals, the costs of extraction of which grow too high as the concentration diminishes);
- resources which are exported at such a slow rate that substitution intervenes and they become economically obsolete long before they are exhausted (Chilean saltpetre, replaced by industrial fertilizers);
- resources which are exploited at a rate quicker than renovation, whose stocks are depleted locally (such as the *quebracho colorado*), but of which it can be argued that a slower rate of exploitation would have been unwise, because of the threat of substitution.

From the reality of many instances of substitution of particular raw materials we cannot argue that growth of the economy will always endogenously make available 'backstop' technologies. Against this view, there is also the reality of increasing flows of materials and energy coming into the world economy, and producing waste.

*   *   *

Larger and larger quantities of raw materials are exported, to a considerable extent to be able to pay back the interest of the external debt, so much so that the importance of the external debt is frequently assessed by the ratio of debt service payment to export income, thus leading to the conclusion that the external debt loses importance when that quotient diminishes. After the wave of neoliberalism of the 1980 and 1990s (which recalls other eras in the history of republican Latin America) the old issue of unequal trade is reappearing. How to achieve an alternative development, or an alternative to development, that is not based on unsustainable trade? It is true that the participation of Latin America in world exports measured in monetary terms has decreased, and it is also true that much of Africa looks economically superfluous to the world's economic growth. But figures in money are deceptive, we have to look to the flows of energy and materials. There are also the indirect effects. For example, in order to export one ton of aluminium, major inputs of bauxite are necessary, and in order to extract and move the bauxite a great deal of material and vegetation is destroyed. Then the large input of electricity for the smelting of the aluminium also has its own material 'rucksack'. The cultivation of coffee has been carried out at times at the cost of the original forest and erosion of the soil, as in Brazil. In order to export cocaine, a lot of soil is eroded (growing coca leaf on slopes under most precarious political conditions) and rivers are polluted by its production inputs (kerosene, sulphuric acid). Therefore, even high-price and low-volume products can involve large environmental impacts

These are repetitions of old stories. Thus, in Latin America, oil ('black gold') has been exported without concern for exhaustion, or the local environmental impacts, or the increased greenhouse effect. 'Green gold' has been stolen and it is now the object of new bioprospecting contracts which others call biopiracy. 'White gold' from hydroelectric plants which destroy forests and biodiversity goes to aluminium processing for export. 'Yellow gold', a product which goes straight to conspicuous consumption, requires the removal of huge quantities of material in order to obtain a few grams, its amalgam is sometimes still made with mercury (the same quicksilver which poisoned the miners of Potosí). Finally, there is 'pink gold', the shrimp that destroy livelihoods and mangroves, or that kill turtles. This is a long history of pillaging of nature, certainly not because of the pressure of population on resources in Latin America (and in Africa) but because of the pressure of exports.

It would appear that the export of agricultural products is a sustainable activity supported by photosynthesis (where the energy is the flow of current solar energy and not the stock of fossil fuels). However, such exports carry nutrients with them (like potassium in bananas), sometimes also (like sugar from Cuba or coffee in Brazil) a 'rucksack' of destroyed primary forests. Such is the paradox that Argentina appeared, together with Haiti, among the Latin American countries which use the least fertilizer per hectare, as she relies on the natural fertility of the Pampas. The Latin American economies depend to a considerable degree on an increase in exports of oil, gas, minerals such as iron, copper and gold, as well as wood and feedstuffs such as soybeans and fishmeal; even some 'non-traditional' export products such as flowers or shrimp are primary exports with some processing. True, some areas of Latin America, such as São

Paulo, are escaping the tendency to reprimarization. On the contrary, this is an area which imports energy and materials and exports industrial goods, such as cars. Another industrial area is the Mexican frontier with the USA which imports intermediate inputs for the *maquila* industry. Another part of Brazil, the North, is being turned (as we have seen) into a region of enormous new mineral extraction projects with rail links directly to the coast, in accordance with the old model of extractive 'enclaves' with few links to the regional economy. The Matto Grosso region in the southwest of Brazil is being turned into a region of agricultural exports, together with parts of Paraguay and eastern Bolivia, ready to export millions of tons of transgenic soybeans. Chile's economic growth has been based on primary exports such as copper, fish products and wood from old-growth forests such as larches made into chips for export to Japan, so that, with good reasons, Rayen Quiroga and her collaborators at the Institute of Political Ecology in Santiago started a debate on the environmental consequences of such trade by describing the Chilean economy as 'the Tiger without a Jungle' (Quiroga, 1994).

The Latin American theory of deteriorating terms of trade, as proposed in the later 1940s by the Argentinian economist Raul Prebisch, is still relevant. This theory was the backbone of CEPAL's proposals from the 1950s to 1973 on 'import substitution' – 1973 saw the fall of Allende in Chile, and the inauguration of economic neoliberalism under Pinochet's capitalist dictatorship. The theory, which has precedents in eastern Europe in the period between the world wars, explains that increases in productivity in the primary export sectors (that is, larger production per worker thanks to technological progress) are translated into lower prices, for two reasons. First, despite attempts at forming cartels, there are many international competitors; second, the workers are poor, often non-unionized, and there is an ample supply of unemployed labour. This was so in Central American banana plantations, and in Bolivian mines, not so much in the Argentina of Peron. In the meantime, the prices of imported manufactured goods and services do not drop in proportion to the increases in productivity, because the market structure is more oligopolistic, and the workers, unionized and already well paid, are in a strong bargaining position which allows them to obtain increases in salaries at least in proportion to the increase in productivity. Hence the trend towards worsening terms of trade for primary producers.

The theory is open to objections. For example, in some periods economies can grow on the basis of primary exports, and these open economies can create significant urban and industrial bases. This has been called the staple theory of economic growth, after the work of the Canadian historian Harold Innis, himself critical of this mode of development. It applies to some periods of the economic history of Canada, New Zealand, Australia and the Scandinavian countries, also to the regions of Buenos Aires and São Paulo. Another objection is that industrial products and services are also subject to competitive commercial pressures which lower their prices, as has occurred with cars and with information technology. However, the theory of the deterioration of the terms of trade was again relevant at the end of the neoliberal export wave of the 1980s and 1990s. There is a real deterioration in the terms of trade, and also (as Marxist economists such as Emmanuel have explained) many hours of badly paid work are 'exported' in exchange for well-paid hours. Moreover, there is ecologically unequal exchange, in terms of non-internalized environmental and health damages or risks, and in terms of exhaustion of resources.

QUANTIFYING THE ECOLOGICAL DEBT

Ecologically unequal exchange is one of the reasons for the claim that there exists an ecological debt. The second reason for this claim is the disproportionate use of environmental space by the rich countries. Putting both reasons together, and expressing the ecological debt in money terms, the main components are as follows.

Regarding Ecologically Unequal Exchange

- The (unpaid) costs of reproduction or maintenance or sustainable management of the renewable resources which have been exported: for instance, the nutrients incorporated in agricultural exports.
- The costs of the future lack of availability of destroyed natural resources: for instance, the oil and minerals no longer available, or the biodiversity destroyed. This is a difficult figure to compute, for several reasons. Figures on the reserves, estimation of the possible technological obsolescence because of substitution, and a decision on the rate of discount are needed in the case of minerals or oil. For biodiversity, knowledge of what is being destroyed would be needed.
- The compensation for, or the costs of reparation (unpaid) of, the local damages produced by exports (for example, the sulphur dioxide of copper smelters, the mine tailings, the harm to health from flower exports, the pollution of water by mercury in gold mining) or the present value of irreversible damage
- The (unpaid) amount corresponding to the commercial use of information and knowledge on genetic resources, when they have been appropriated gratis (see Chapter 6). For agricultural genetic

resources, the basis for such a claim already exists under the terminology of Farmers' Rights.

Regarding Lack of Payment for Environmental Services or for the Disproportionate use of Environmental Space

- The (unpaid) reparation costs or compensation for the impacts caused by imports of solid or liquid toxic waste.
- The (unpaid) costs of free disposal of gas residues (carbon dioxide, CFC and so on), assuming equal rights to sinks and reservoirs (see below).

One objection to the notion of an ecological debt is that debts are recognized obligations arising from contracts, such as a sale or a mortgage. A non-recognized debt does not exist, according to this view. However, there are cases in which debts have arisen without a contract. Witness, for instance, the obligation to pay reparations by a state after a loss, as with Germany after the First World War, or to pay some sort of indemnities for infringements of human rights, as with Germany after the Second World War (in the second case, with the agreement of most citizens of the country).

Another objection to the notion of the ecological debt is that it implies monetization of Nature's services. I confess, *mea culpa*. My excuse is that the language of chrematistics is well understood in the north. We know that the movement in Thailand that opposed eucalyptus plantations at times used a religious language by protecting the trees threatened by plantations with the yellow clothing of Buddhist monks and calling meetings with the ritual *pha pha ba* normally employed for the consecration of temples. This would not impress the IMF in its everyday business. Petitions for forgiveness of the external debt in the Jubilee 2000 campaign of Christian churches used a biblical language. The banks could reply, how many Brady bonds has the Vatican? Possibly some, but not enough to impress the creditors.

Are there other languages available? As we have seen (Chapter 8) the idiom of environmental justice has been employed in the USA in the struggle against the disproportionate amount of pollution in areas occupied by minority and low-income people. The disproportionate emissions of carbon dioxide are an example of environmental injustice at the international level. Another idiom might be that of environmental security, not in a military sense, but in a sense similar to the way we would speak of food security, as an agricultural policy which would ensure local availability of food through use of local human and land resources. However, such a definition of 'food security' could be contested. Environmental security is likewise a contested concept. It might mean the use of military force to impose a solution on environmental conflicts. In the literature it refers to the guaranteed access to natural resources (such as water) and to environmental services for all, not just the rich and powerful. Environmental security is a condition in which environmental goods and services are used at a sustainable rate, in which fair and reliable access to environmental resources and services is universal, and, finally, in which institutions are competent to manage the conflicts associated with environmental scarcity and degradation (Matthew, 1999: 13). So the south could argue that the north has produced and is producing a disproportionate amount of pollution, including the greenhouse gases, and that it takes an unfair amount of natural resources, which is not only counter to environmental justice, and it does not only give rise to environmental liabilities, but which also puts the environmental security of the south (or at least parts of the south) at risk.[9]

THE CARBON DEBT: CONTRACTION, CONVERGENCE AND COMPENSATION

How to decide the limit or target for emissions of greenhouse gases? How much is enough? Attempts at using cost–benefit analysis of the increased greenhouse effect are not convincing because of the arbitrariness of the discount rate (Azar and Sterner, 1996) and also because many items are not easily measured in physical terms, much less easily valued in money terms (Funtowicz and Ravetz, 1994). Moreover, the very pattern of prices in the economy would be different to start with, without the free access to carbon sinks. When (in the IPCC process, 1995) it was suggested that 'greenhouse' policy should be guided by a calculus of the economic costs of climate change, including an estimate of the economic value of human lives to be lost in some poor countries, there were loud complaints. Some said that a human life could not be so cheap. Nevertheless, if the existing distribution of property and income is accepted as a reality, then economic values of an average human life 15 times greater in the USA or western Europe than in Bangladesh are plausible. Ask insurance companies. The economists were right. The poor are cheap. However, will Bangladesh still be poor in 50 years? This is a different question, which could be factored into the economic cost-benefit analysis of the increased greenhouse effect.

There was another, more substantial, difference of opinion on whether economics holds the key to an integrated assessment. It does not. Uncertainties and complexities make it impossible to conduct an honest cost–benefit analysis. Moreover, a cost–benefit analysis goes against the poor, whose willingness-to-pay is necessarily limited. Hence the plausibility of the appeal to non-economic values. For instance, it can be stated that, while humans have different economic price-tags, they all have the same value in the scale of human dignity.

There are two methods to calculate the 'carbon debt'. First, costing the damage that will be done. Second, the 'abatement' cost. Consider the case of the environmental service provided by the permanent carbon sinks (oceans, new vegetation, soils) and by the atmosphere as a temporary deposit or reservoir where the carbon dioxide accumulates while waiting for a permanent sink. In this way the concentration of carbon dioxide in the atmosphere has increased from 280ppm to 360ppm. The decision of the European Union, discussed at Kyoto in December 1997, was to allow the concentration to increase to 550ppm, which would possibly involve a two degree Celsius rise in temperature, with much uncertainty about the range, and even more regarding local effects. That this is a 'safe' limit has been strongly disputed (Azar and Rodhe, 1997). The emissions per person per year in the USA are of the order of six tons of carbon, in Europe half of this, in India 0·4 tons. We all breathe in and out more or less the same, and it would be impracticable to reduce carbon dioxide emissions by slow respiration. There are livelihood emissions and luxury emissions. We are dealing here with one characteristic feature of human ecology, extreme intraspecific difference in the exosomatic use of fuels, differences which are much larger than such national per capita figures reveal. The global average is above one ton of carbon per person/year (global emissions, above 6000m tons of carbon), already excessive, though it will normally increase because of population growth and economic growth. The required reduction, in order to avoid further increase of concentration in the atmosphere, is of the order of half the present emissions, that is over 3000m tons of carbon per year. Although the dynamics of carbon absorption in the oceans, new vegetations and soils depend to some extent on the amounts produced (this is called 'CO_2 fertilization', for the growth of vegetation), it is not disputed that the use of the atmosphere as an open-access reservoir is increasing. The sinks (oceans, soils, new vegetation) are also used on a first come, first served basis, without payment. In Kyoto, in 1997, and afterwards, the European Union, playing the 'leadership game', proposed a slight reduction in emissions, which the USA found difficult to accept (partly because the population is growing in the USA) until President Bush's refusal of the Kyoto Protocol in early 2001. Kyoto would give 'grandfathered' rights to the USA, Europe and Japan equal to their 1990 emissions, on the promise of a reduction of 5·2 per cent by the year 2010.

There are many instances in which, through a change in industrial technology, or through conservation of forests under threat, or through new vegetation, there is a genuine gain in jointly implementing the objectives of carbon emissions reduction. How will such gain be shared? What will be the price of reduction of carbon emissions, or the price of the extra absorption? If the owners of carbon sinks are poor, the local selling price of carbon absorption will be low; then intermediaries would come into play, perhaps southern governments, perhaps northern financial institutions. When the commitment to reduce emissions is small, as at present, then, in principle, the price of a ton of carbon in joint implementation projects will be low because the demand for sinks will be small. Moreover, the price will be low if local negative externalities from the projects themselves are not factored into the price. The price will also be low when the supply of projects in the south (whether as additional sinks, especially when conservation of threatened primary forests is also accepted, or as changes in techniques which diminish carbon emissions such as substituting natural gas for coal) is large, compared to the demand. However, should the commitment to reduce be of the order of 3000m tons of carbon per year, as it should be, then the price would increase enormously. In other words, the stronger and quicker the commitment to reduce, the higher the marginal cost of the reduction. Instead, if there is not a reduction, this implies the persistent and disproportionate use of the sinks (oceans, new vegetations and the soils), and the atmosphere, as de facto property of the rich, and therefore a continuous increase, year after year, in the ecological debt, to the tune, say, of US$60 billion per year (3000m tons of carbon which should be reduced at the cost of US$20 per ton). The ecological debt arises on this count because, by not making the necessary reduction, the rich countries save themselves an amount which would be roughly of this order of magnitude. One could easily argue that the appropriate average cost to use should be US$100 per ton or even higher. In any case, as a term of comparison, the present accumulated Latin American external debt was in 1999 US$700 billion (equivalent to only 12 years of 'carbon debt' at US$60 billion per year).

A similar calculation was published in 1995 by Jyoti Parikh (a member of the IPCC), making in substance the same argument. If we take the present human-made emissions of carbon, the average was about one ton per person and per year. Industrialized countries produce three-quarters of these emissions, instead of the one-quarter which would correspond to them on the basis of population. The difference is 50 per cent of total emissions, some 3000m tons. Here the increasing marginal cost of reduction is again contemplated: the first 1000m tons could be reduced at a cost of, say, US15 per ton, but then the cost increases very much. If we take an average of US$25, then a total annual subsidy of US$75 billion is forthcoming from south to north (Parikh, 1995).

Such calculations are now being taken up and elaborated upon by NGOs concerned with the social and environmental burdens imposed on poor countries by the service and repayment of the external debt. Thus Christian Aid made available in 1999 a document on climate change, debt, equity and survival (with the title *Who owes who?* and pictures of Bangladeshi children with water up to their necks) that argues that, to mitigate the effects of climate change,

> we will all have to live within our environmental budget. The atmosphere can only absorb a certain amount of greenhouse gases before disruption begins. So, their emission needs controlling. As, each day, industrialized countries delay action on the 60–80 per cent cuts that are needed, they go over-budget and are running up an environmental or 'carbon' debt. Ironically those same countries today stand in judgement over much poorer countries who have comparatively insignificant conventional, financial debts.

Christian Aid's calculation of the 'carbon debt' was done in this way. The carbon intensity of GNP was (wrongly) taken as constant, a reduction of carbon emissions in rich countries of 60–80 per cent was assumed and the corresponding decrease in GNP calculated. The enormous decrease in GNP does not occur because the reduction in emissions does not take place: this is the avoided cost, that is, the debt. Christian Aid's figures are far too high because small reductions of carbon emissions can be achieved with small marginal costs (perhaps even with win–win opportunities), the marginal cost increasing with the volume and urgency of the reductions. One has to allow for changes in techniques and in the composition of output. What the 'proper' average cost would be, is not so obvious – in my estimate above, US$20 per ton of carbon has been used. The argument for a substantial ecological debt accumulating year after year would be valid even with a price of US$10 per ton.

Other Christian groups such as the Canadian Ecumenical Council for Economic Justice have also (in 2000) estimated the 'carbon debt' in the context of the growing discussion on the ecological debt (www.ecej.org). There are many uncertainties as to how the future energy systems will develop. Methods for injecting the carbon dioxide back into the earth or in aquifers might become practicable and widespread. Photovoltaic energy might become cheaper. The number of windmills is increasing in many places. If we look at the past century, we see that, at the global level, new energy systems are added on top of the existing ones, without replacing them. The world economy, and especially the rich countries' economy, will be based on fossil fuels for at least 30 or 40 years. Afterwards, we do not know. Hydrogen, to be used in fuel cells, should be seen as an energy carrier, not as an energy source, because much energy is needed to obtain the hydrogen. Meanwhile, the carbon debt accumulates.

To sum up, countries which are in a creditor position could give a sense of urgency to the negotiations on climate change (and also on other issues, such as Farmers' Rights), by claiming the ecological debt, which is admittedly hard to quantify in money terms. Perhaps the Alliance of Small Island States (AOSIS) and other countries will push this point, joining in a greenhouse politics based on contraction of emissions, convergence to about 0·5 tons of carbon per capita and per year, and in the meantime compensation, deploying also the language of their threatened environmental security.

The claim of the ecological debt, when it becomes an important topic in the international political agenda (perhaps the Green ministers in France and Germany could help), will contribute to the 'ecological adjustment' which the north must make. The point is not exchanging external debt for protection of Nature, as has been done in some anecdotal cases.[10] On the contrary, the point is to consider that the external debt from south to north has already been paid on account of the ecological debt the north owes to the south, and to stop the ecological debt from increasing any further.

In greenhouse politics this line of thinking is not called the 'leadership game' but the 'liability game', which up to now southern governments have been reluctant to take. Thus any Latin American audience is easily impressed by the dollar amount that a child of that continent already owes to foreigners at birth, but it is more difficult to awaken interest in the theoretical position as creditor which that same infant occupies in the ecological debt account. This is not yet on the political agenda.

LOSING FACE

It can be argued that, before making a commitment to carbon emission reductions, it is necessary to explore the reduction of other greenhouse gases, such as CFCs which have been emitted mainly by rich countries but which are now prohibited because of their effect on the ozone layer, or methane which, at least in the portion coming from garbage dumps, could be cheaply recycled through combustion, thus greatly diminishing the direct effect it has as a greenhouse gas. In the experimental cases of joint implementation (later also called the Clean Development Mechanism) which are designed to reduce carbon emissions or to produce additional carbon absorption, the costs per ton of carbon are estimated at a few dollars. Sometimes there are even negative marginal costs of greenhouse gas reduction, called 'win–win' opportunities which combine economic savings and dimished emissions. Costa Rica has (more as a gimmick than as a serious financial operation) placed some carbon dioxide absorption bonds at US$10 per ton (less than US$3 per ton of carbon, the relation between carbon dioxide and carbon being 3.7 to 1).

Ludicrously, 'lose–lose' situations also exist, as in the FACE project in Ecuador, which consisted of planting 75 000 hectares of eucalyptus and pines in the highlands to absorb the carbon dioxide which would be produced by a power station in the Netherlands of 650MW. The research group Ecopar (financed by FACE itself) has found out that, by the disturbing of the rich organic soil of the *páramo* when planting pines, more carbon is released than will be absorbed.[11] The chairman of FACE until 1999 was Ed Nijpels, a former Minister for the Environment of the Netherlands. FACE was set up by a consortium of electrical utilities in the Netherlands. The acronym is for 'Forest Absorption of Carbon dioxide Emissions'. It has operated with arrogant ignorance, stating in its Annual Report of 1995 (p.18) that in Ecuador at altitudes between 2400 and 3500 metres 'agriculture is no longer possible and livestock farming is less profitable'. Quito lies at 2800 metres; Cuzco, much farther south from the Equator, at 3400 metres; the Sacred Valley below Cuzco, a shrine of Andean agriculture, at about 3000 metres. FACE started out with a strong prejudice against Andean agropastoral practices, and against the indigenous inhabitants of such regions – perhaps a form of 'environmental racism'. The social and environmental externalities produced by pine and eucalyptus plantations were discounted by FACE from the beginning. Moreover, FACE has repeatedly asserted that 'knowledge of indigenous tree species has been lost, and local people prefer to reforest with such exotics as pine and eucalyptus' (*Annual Report, 1998*, Arnhem, June 1999: 17).

FACE's objective of planting 75 000 ha of pines and eucalyptus in the highlands of Ecuador will not be reached. Only 18 958 ha were planted up to 1998 (*Annual Report, 1998*). Nijpels, the chairman, left in 1999. His parting shot was incredibly upbeat. He wrote, in May 1999, that

> since its creation in 1990, Face has financed the planting of new forests for the benefit of electricity generating companies who can, at any moment, deduct the CO_2 sequestered by these forests from their emissions. Yet, although the outlook is good, the international debate on climate has not yet reached the stage at which crediting can actually occur.

SEP (the Dutch Electricity Generating Board), which initiated FACE (to compensate for Dutch carbon dioxide emissions) would no longer support FACE financially after 1999. FACE had to stand on its own feet, and spread its wings wider. No intimation of immediate collapse transpired from Nijpels' farewell address. On the contrary, FACE must put a clear product on the market, in order to achieve self-financing, whatever the outcome of the negotiations on joint implementation and the Clean Development Mechanism. FACE had therefore developed the new project 'certified CO_2 fixed in forests. This involves a certificate from an independent certifying institution that shows how much CO_2 a certain forest sequesters per year' (*Annual Report, 1998*). Firms would buy such certificates in order to put 'climate-compensated products in the market'. Nijpels concluded his speech of May 1999 by stating: 'A new fascinating period has started for FACE.' Indeed. The trouble is that one of FACE's products is net CO_2 produced by thousands of hectares of pine plantations in the *paramo* of Ecuador, thus slightly increasing the ecological debt of the Netherlands.

Projects for carbon sequestration were not new in Ecuador when FACE arrived in the early 1990s and set up PROFAFOR together with its local partners. The first attempt at selling carbon absorption was promoted by BOTROSA, owned by the notoriously deforesting Durini family, one of whose members was in 2000 a government minister. The intention was to use financing from the Global Environmental Facility of the World Bank. This became a controversial tree plantation project, not so much, at the time, because of greenhouse politics, as because it displaced shifting cultivators. Philip Fearnside wrote to the World Bank on 10 September 1992, acting as a consultant and arguing against this project: 'The idea of planting trees to sequester carbon is perfectly valid, and should be experimented with. A number of cautionary tales are necessary, however, including the priority that should be assigned to this approach when it is used in detriment of efforts to slow deforestation – a much more cost-effective means of avoiding net emissions as well as achieving other benefits.'[12] In Ecuador, a better idea than uniform tree plantations would be to preserve the forests in Amazonia, threatened by settlers and by the oil industry, and also coastal mangrove forests, although these are not additional sinks.

ECOLOGICAL CONDITIONALITY: SELECTIVE BLINDNESS

Governments in the south are often reluctant to take environmental politics seriously. The practice of the environmentalism of the poor is old, yet the theory is new and not generally accepted, not only in the north but also in the south. Quite often environmentalism is still seen, north and south, as a luxury of the rich rather than a necessity of the poor.

The south has allowed the north to occupy the moral high ground in the environmental field, and countries whose lifestyle cannot be generally adopted by the world at large have been allowed to lecture on how to achieve ecological sustainability. For example, Latin American fishermen were reprimanded because they killed dolphins while fishing for tuna for export. The lifting of the US tuna fish embargo placed on Venezuela, Mexico, Colombia and other Latin American countries brings to light this interesting case of environmental conditionality of exports. As we saw in Chapter 5, a similar argument is often made in the USA against imports of shrimp captured in the sea with fishing methods which cause the death of turtles.

The dolphin case ought to be dismissed under GATT–WTO rules, because the tuna fish were perfectly healthy, and unfortunately trade restrictions can only be justified by the quality of the product, not by the defects in the process of production. The standard argument on trade and the environment from GATT–WTO is that trade produces economic growth, and economic growth will produce an improvement in the environment and also in social conditions, so that to stop imports because of environmental damage, or child labour, or lack of human rights at the point of production, is in general (with the single exception of slave and prison labour) counterproductive. Nevertheless, the outcry was so large that the USA imposed an embargo on tuna fishing methods which cause the death of dolphins. In order to lift the tuna fish embargo, the fishing fleets were obliged to open themselves up for inspection by the US National Marine Fisheries Service, an obligation which undoubtedly smacked of 'eco-colonialism'. The fishing industries of the countries subject to the tuna fish embargo maintained this was 'green protectionism' in favour of the US fishing industry and its Asian partners.[13]

Killing dolphins is cruel and unnecessary, denounced by northern and southern environmental organizations. What is is fact surprising is the *selective blindness* in northern public opinion and environmental organizations against other cases of imports which have grave environmental impacts. Why pick on tuna fish, and not on oil from Mexico, Venezuela or Nigeria? When Austria attempted to impose an obligatory green 'certificate' on imports of tropical wood in 1992 in order to guarantee their origin in sustainably managed forests, it was confronted by a protest led by the Malaysian and Indonesian governments under GATT, and apparently it was not able to find influential internal allies in those countries. Instead, there are examples of harmonious collaboration between northern and southern NGOs aimed at stopping the export of cheap products from the south, as in the provisional victory in 1997 over the Trillium logging company in Chile whose logging concession was cancelled, much to the satisfaction of Chilean ecologists and to the irritation of the Frei government. It would be funny to tell the Chileans opposing Trillium: first, you let Trillium cut and export the old-growth forests as chips, then you become rich, finally you will be rich enough to become environmentalists. Then, it would be 'too late to be green'.[14]

Environmental standards linked to trade are seen by southern governments and business (though not by southern environmentalists) as blatant neo-protectionist devices designed to extinguish the competitive advantage of poor countries. Contrary to this view that environmental non-tariff trade restrictions are a manifestation of northern protectionism at the cost of southern producers, there have been southern demands for northern consumers to boycott southern exports because of their social and environmental effects. Such voices from the south are as yet largely unheeded, but they announce a different world where consumers will have information on the processes of production of the products they consume. So, instead of complaining about the ban on tuna fish imports, or on unsustainable tropical forest products, instead of becoming indignant at the 'green protectionism' of the north, which is really a 'red herring', it would be coherent with southern interests to emphasize the environmental damages, local and global, that the increase in international trade in oil and gas, copper and aluminium, gold and diamonds, wood and paper pulp, is producing, and also to emphasize the benefits which importers have long enjoyed by not paying for such damages, benefits which are part of their ecological debt. A couple of examples: the environmentalist Augusto Ruschi fought, to no avail, in the 1970s in the state of Espiritu Santo against the cellulose-exporting company Aracruz, which set up large plantations of eucalyptus (on old or newly deforested land) and which sent the effluents into the ocean (Dean, 1995: 304–13). Further south, in Porto Alegre, the fight against another cellulose factory was important for the birth of Brazilian environmentalism. External allies would have been welcome back in the 1970s.

The fact is, however, that conditionality, be it in the financial, environmental or human rights fields, is always imposed by the hegemonic states. Weaker countries resent conditionality, though at times, when international cooperation is conditioned on respect for human rights, it can happen that the civil society of the countries subject to conditionality, despite the political asymmetry, is pragmatically in favour of it in order to defend itself against its own government: this apart from the fact that the states imposing the conditionality may also be violators of human rights internally or abroad.

'Conditionality' is a concept that refers not so much to the environment, or to human rights, but to the conditions which are imposed by the World Bank and the IMF before making a loan or renegotiating a debt. Let us accept that many countries in the south needed lessons in the 1980s and 1990s, based on the so-called Washington Consensus, regarding the stabilization of their inflationary economies, and let us also suppose that the social and environmental costs of such 'adjustments' could be avoided. Should the south now also accept an environmental conditionality? There are two ways of rejecting such conditionality, which in Latin American language could be expressed as follows.

First, 'Here come the gringos again, messing around in our business, stopping our bananas or our tuna or tropical wood or flowers or strawberries or avocados from entering their markets, because they say that they are anti-environmental, and to boot they say that they will not make loans or re-negotiate the external debt unless each investment financed by them carries this lunacy of an environmental impact study.'

The second line of rejection of environmental conditionality would be based on the fact that there is an environmentalism of the poor which is hidden to many as it frequently expresses itself in non-environmental language. It should be understood in the south that the greatest threat to the environment is overconsumption in the North. And so, rather than unilaterally imposing its environmental conditionality on the south, the north ought to pay its ecological debt, and should 'adjust' its economy to its own environmental space. But the question would remain, who will put the 'environmental conditionality' bell on the cat of the rich economies? One way of imposing an 'ecological adjustment' on the north would be by way of much stronger south–south cooperation, trying to increase the price of oil and other materials, perhaps through 'natural capital depletion taxes', and also through other export taxes to compensate for externalities.

ECO-TAXES AND NORTH–SOUTH CONFLICT

The USA imports half the oil it consumes, and the figure is growing. In order to comply with the vague promises of Rio de Janeiro in June 1992, Clinton and Gore in their first mandate proposed the introduction of a tax on fossil fuel energy, the BTU-tax, in order to make its price a little higher, with lower demand and carbon dioxide emissions in consequence. That tax, as with the European eco-tax (which would have meant up to US$10 per barrel of oil, as discussed in 1992) has not been applied, even though there is a slight tendency in the fiscal system of some European countries towards increased taxes on energy. For each individual country, the introduction of an eco-tax can involve a loss of competitiveness. Now this signifies that the competitiveness was partially based on the externalization of environmental costs such as those from global warming, and therefore on the increase of the ecological debt which the rich and competitive countries already owe. Anyway, let us examine the question of the BTU-tax or the eco-tax from the point of view of the oil, gas or coal exporting countries, many of them poorer than the USA, the European Union or Japan. Such taxes are seen negatively, owing to their distributive impact. By lowering the demand through an increase in taxes, exporters would be forced either to export the same amount at a lower price, or to export less in order to maintain the price. In whatever way, their income would be lower. An international tax system could be designed in such a way as to recycle ecological taxes to the oil, gas or coal-exporting countries in order to improve the social situation of those which are poor, and to improve energy efficiency and substitution in all. Or something more radical could be proposed: that the fossil fuel-exporting countries themselves, instead of opposing and even boycotting the negotiations on the greenhouse effect as they have until now, should impose an ecological tax at source which would increase price: that is, exporting less at a higher price, thus contributing to a reduction in the greenhouse effect (though maintaining cooking gas subsidies, in order to protect against depletion of fuelwood). Naturally, in order to implement such a tax (which could have a 'natural capital depletion' component, and a local and global externalities compensation component), there would be a need for a collective agreement, within the framework of OPEC or another, similar cartel. However, for the governments and perhaps also public opinion in the gas, oil and coal exporting countries, it has been more convenient not to confront the north and to deny the enhanced greenhouse effect, and, lamentably, to divide the countries of the south, thus facilitating inaction in the north.

FAIR TRADE

The recent attempts to organize 'Fair Trade' networks by means of cooperation of the north with the south (consumers who, for example, are willing to pay a higher price for imported 'organic' coffee) stem from the awareness that consumption drives the economy and from a willingness to incorporate certain social and environmental costs in the price. Conversely, those costs are not internalized in the prices which apply in normal production and marketing. Apart from 'organic' coffee,[15] there are many other products which could attract the attention of environment-friendly importers. Boyce has analysed the case of Bangladeshi exports of jute, which, like cotton, wool, sisal and rubber, has lost international markets to synthetic substitutes. Polypropylene is the main synthetic substitute for jute. It is slightly cheaper, in market terms. However, life-cycle analyses of both products show the environmental virtues of jute compared to polypropylene, which are not factored into prices (Boyce, 1995, 1996). Similar reasoning could be applied to exports of Argentinian beef, still grown without hormones (in contrast to US exports) and in open fields. Instead of playing the 'organic' card, the Argentinian government, as we shall see, joined the 'Miami group' of countries led by the USA.

When 'conventional' coffee is exported, the international prices do not cover the environmental and social costs. The 'Fair Trade' movement shows, in practice, that in order to allow exported products to be produced in ecologically and socially sustainable processes, importers must be ready to pay a premium for a product which is certified as being sustainably produced. The Fair Trade networks are a modern NGO version, small-scale, with both social and environmental objectives, operative only for some products, of the international commodity agreements which Keynesian social democracy had proposed in the 1940s and 1950s: a tradition to remember, once the present neoliberal wave runs its course. Thus a proposal on International Commodity-Related Environmental Agreements was made by Henk Kox from the Netherlands (Kox, 1991, 1997). The proposal recognizes that there is unequal ecological exchange at present, and gives an incentive for a better environmental management, perhaps not taking sufficiently into account that environmental standards in the poor exporting countries are low because of lack of bargaining power to start with. In a move parallel to Fair Trade in 'organic' coffee, an international fund would be set up to pay more to commodity exporters who respect environmental standards, and who then produce 'green' commodities. Oil companies would then fancifully market 'green organic black gold', which presumably would still produce carbon dioxide on combustion.

Policies such as Fair Trade networks, the prohibition of mangrove destruction for shrimp exports, the real implementation of farmers' rights in order to ensure the *in situ* conservation and coevolution of agricultural biodiversity, the 'natural capital' depletion tax on exports, the conservation of forests in 'extractive reserves', the successful claim for payment of the ecological debt and its application to sustainable technologies, are policies which could improve environmental quality and simultaneously improve the economic situation of the poor in the south – true *win–win* policies that do not rest on the false expectations of the 'trickle-down' from economic growth.

RIO GRANDE DO SUL: A TRANSGENIC-FREE ZONE?

Brazil has long been a very large coffee exporter, but there is no significant production of organic shaded coffee in Brazil. This is not a land of traditional agroecological peasants but a land with a history of sugar and coffee plantations, slavery and almost total destruction of the Atlantic rainforest. Brazil is not a place for romantic agroecologists, like the Andean highlands or the Maya territories. The potato in Brazil is called *batata inglesa*. There are indigenous groups in Brazil who know about medicinal biodiversity. There is useful indigenous knowledge of edible insects. The whole issue of indigenous intellectual property rights has been closely linked to Brazilian anthropology through Darrell Posey. There are well-known Brazilian stories of biopiracy (the *ipecac* in colonial times, or nowadays the *jaborandi* for glaucoma, not to speak of rubber). There is not, however, a large agroecological peasantry in Brazil, or a widespread indigenous agroecological pride, though Brazil contains many interesting varieties of maize, and of course of manioc or cassava, a staple in the diet both of the indigenous tribes and of Brazilians today, and indeed of Africans who got the plant from America.

If not much of a traditional agroecological peasantry, there is instead in Brazil today the strongest movement in the world for land reform, the MST (the Movement of the Landless), whose social origins are in Rio Grande do Sul (RGS) though this is not the state with most land conflicts. Indeed, RGS has served as a relatively peaceful base for the MST. In 1999, the MST declared itself against transgenic crops and, in January 2001, the MST, together with Rafael Alegria and other leaders of Via Campesina, and with José Bové of the French Confédération Paysanne, became the media stars of the Porto Alegre World Social Forum when they symbolically destroyed some Monsanto experimental fields in the village of Nao-me-toques. The context was the prohibition of transgenic soybeans in RGS by the state government. Even if the valiant attitude of the government and judiciary in Rio Grande do Sul against transgenic crops was finally to fail because of federal overruling, it has served finally to propel the MST in an ecological direction. This is a movement started by the sons and daughters of small farmers of German and Italian ancestry; it has spread to the whole country; it has withstood violent armed repression in Paranà, Parà and other states. Its tactics consist of occupation, settlement and immediate cultivation of large idle properties. Land invasions are achieved by peaceful mass direct action, with emphasis on food production for subsistence, but also with a modernist and productivist technological outlook against absentee landlords and *grileiros* (speculators who illegally enclose large areas of land) who are taken to be so rich that they do not care to produce food. Many of the MST leaders belong also to the Workers' Party, though the MST is more to the left. The transgenic issue has sparked off a general discussion on agricultural technology inside the MST which was lacking until now in a country like Brazil, whose population is no longer growing rapidly and of which Ignacy Sachs once said, 'instead of turning into a rural paradise, which it could be, it is becoming an urban hell' (Padua, 1996). The MST is sponsoring return migration from urban shanty towns to new rural settlements.

The European alarm at GM foods is well known in the Americas. This is a movement led by consumers, worried about uncertain health hazards, strongly supported by some remaining peasant groups in France that believe that one defence of European agriculture lies in producing output with different standards of quality. There is a lingering suspicion that European policy against US 'hormone' beef, or against imported trans-genic crops, is motivated not only by uncertain health hazards but also by farmers' interests in hiding behind non-tariff barriers. However, the European Union has marshalled scientific evidence that high doses of some the hormones given to beef in the USA has carcinogenic effects and that other hormones might affect, as seems logical, the development of sexual organs (*New York Times*, 25 May 2000, C4). The USA retaliated by impos-ing tarrifs on some innocent European exports (such as Roquefort cheese), and the dispute went to the WTO. Both for hormone beef and for GMOs, we are in classic 'postnormal science' disputes. In a reputable American environmental journal, Robert Paarlberg adds further reasons for the European attitude. Since there is no credible evidence of a food safety risk linked to any GM food currently on the market in Europe, the issue arises from a post-traumatic stress syndrome because of the BSE ('mad cow') disease, plus an effort to assert 'culinary sovereignty' not only against GM foods but also against McDonald's and CocaCola. 'All this is to be expected among consumers in wealthy, postmaterialist [*sic*] market economies' (Paarlberg, 2000: 21). Clearly, there must be better explanations for atti-tudes to GM crops than 'post-materialism' in a Europe awash with materi-als and energy.

The conflict over the safety of imported or internally produced GM crops could apparently be solved by forcing companies such as Monsanto to take out insurance or to post a bond to compensate for possible future damages. However, the consequences of introducing GMOs are scientifically contested, while the decision is urgent. This helps to enhance the social legitimacy of a plurality of perspectives and social interests. Do the economic costs of introducing GM crops outweigh the benefits? Do we know how to give a present value to uncertain future costs to human health and the environment? Should we tamper with Nature in this way? Is nothing sacred? Should a precautionary principle be applied to such a new technology, and how should it be implemented? Should agricultural pro-duction move towards (or preserve) an 'organic' ideal, and which are the very different social forces in different countries which would support this? Who would pay the costs?

Not so well known around the world as the western European resistance to GM seeds and crops is the local resistance since 1998 to GM soybeans in Rio Grande do Sul. The state government imposed a ban on sowing transgenic soybeans from Monsanto that are able to withstand increased doses of the herbicide Roundup Ready, a glyphosate – this might lead to weed resistance. The opposition to transgenic crops in RGS is a case similar to that of opposition to logging, mining, shrimp exports or oil exports in other southern exporting countries. *It is not green protectionism but its reverse*, resistance to exports because of local damage or uncertain local environmental hazards. In this case, there is support not only from NGOs but also from both the judiciary and the (local) executive branch of government. The fact that a state in Brazil which is a leading producer of soybeans for export would forbid transgenic crops is of great interest. It offers a commercial opportunity to fill in the European import requirement for non-GM soybeans. Besides this, it gives arguments for a similar attitude towards transgenic maize, which is indigenous to the New World, and therefore with many wild relatives. Maize and soybeans are staple feedstuffs for the world food regime of increased meat consumption.

The so-called 'Miami Group' of agricultural exporting countries is similar to the Cairns group, active against so-called 'green protectionism'. Led by the USA, it includes Argentina, Australia, Canada, Chile and Uruguay. This transgenic sextet comprises 'staple theory of growth' countries, Alfred Crosby's 'neo-Europes', or Harriet Friedmann's 'settler agriculture states'. Chile is not really interested in soybeans or maize exports, but potentially in transgenic timber, and in any case it acts out of neoliberal principle and colonial fidelity. This is a coherent group that consistenly opposed the negotiation of an international Biosafety Protocol to be added to the Convention on Biological Diversity, insisting instead on unrestricted free exports of transgenic crops. Remarkably, the Miami Group did not include Brazil. In fact, Argentina is the number two producer of GM soybeans after the USA. The disagreement on the Biosafety Protocol hinged on the technical issue of prior informed consent to consume transgenic products. Article 19(3) of the Biodiversity Convention of 1992 states that 'the Parties shall consider the need for and modalities of a protocol setting out appropriate procedures including, in particular, advance informed agreement, in the field of the safe transfer, handling and use of any living modified organism resulting from biotechnology that may have adverse effect on the conservation and sustainable use of biological diversity'. The 'advance informed agreement' procedure would oblige countries to ensure that its exporters give prior notification to importing countries to enable them to make a risk assessment of the GM product before import is approved. Clearly, this would facilitate, if nothing else, the labelling of GM products, and the spontaneous development in the market of a two-tier price structure for transgenic and non-transgenic soybeans and maize, which the GM corporations fear as much as regulation *per se*.

In January 2000, the USA (which has not ratified the Convention on Biological Diversity of 1992), hampered through the Miami Group, at a meeting in Montreal as it had done one year earlier in Cartagena de Indias, attempts at regulating exports of transgenic foods. The argument is that concern for the environmental and health risks of transgenic crops cannot overcome the rights and obligations of countries under other international agreements, such as those under the WTO whose rules prevent countries from blocking food imports unless there are very clear health reasons. However, invoking WTO rules after the Seattle fiasco of 1999 was not an issue except for those belonging to the true neoliberal faith. In the end, the Biosafety Protocol was adopted, on an equal footing with WTO regulations.

In May 1999, the Brazilian federal Ministry of Agriculture had authorized Monsanto Roundup-Ready soybeans, but a federal court ruled that Monsanto and its Brazilian subsidiary, Monsoy, could not commercialize the seeds until the government issued biosafety and labelling regulations for GM organisms. This verdict was a response to the suit brought by the Brazilian Institute of Consumer Defence and by Greenpeace, arguing that the Constitution mandated environmental assessments for any innovation which has an impact on the environment. Judge Antonio Prudente (his real name) stated that 'the irresponsible haste in introducing the advances of genetic engineering is inspired by the greed of economic globalization'. Monsanto appealed, but the decision stood. So the situation in Brazil, in late 2001, is that GM soybeans are still forbidden in theory.

The Workers' Party has been in power in Porto Alegre, the capital of Rio Grande do Sul, for many years. It has conducted a famous social experiment called 'participatory budgeting' at the municipal level. By a narrow margin, it came to power in the state itself in January 1999, though it has a minority of seats in the legislative assembly. RGS is a state with a strong identity; people call themselves, and are known throughout Brazil as, Gauchos. Porto Alegre has a long tradition of environmentalism since the early 1970s through Jose Lutzenberger. The new governor, and before him the Secretary of Agriculture, became convinced by local NGOs (Centro Ecologico and others, including the Colmeia (Honey Bee Hive) consumer and farmer cooperative), that, in addition to environmental and health risks, the introduction of GM crops would result in the loss of sovereignty over seed production. NGOs were supported by experts from EMATER, the official agricultural extension service, such as Angela Cordeiro. International organizations such as RAFI (Rural Advancement Foundation International) and GRAIN (Genetic Resources Action

International) chimed in with information on environmental risks. Also Monsanto had been buying Brazilian seed companies, which used knowledge developed by Embrapa, a public corporation partly privatized not long ago. Monsanto was attempting to stop Brazilian seed production, and RGS is Brazil's largest seed producer. The state government also became concerned that patented industrial seeds, first of soybeans, later of maize, could not be freely used by small and medium farmers, who dominate the RGS agricultural scene. The head of the inspection programme in RGS, Marta Elena Angelo Levien, who in the 1999 planting season was trying to stop some non-compliant farmers from sowing transgenic soybeans seed smuggled from Argentina, stated that ensuring that regular non-transgenic soybeans are planted was a matter of national security since this 'is a technology that is dominated by a few big businesses forming a cartel. By adopting transgenic crops, Brazil would become dependent on an oligarchy for food technology'.[16]

The Brazilian enemies of transgenic crops were given encouragement at the end of 1999 by the class action suit brought against Monsanto in the US District Court for the District of Columbia on 14 December 1999 (reported in *The Wall Street Journal*, same date) on behalf of plaintiffs who are farmers from Iowa and Indiana, but also from France, and also potentially on behalf of other farmers in Canada and Argentina. The plaintiffs sought injunctive relief, meaning that Monsanto should stop what it is doing, and they also asked for compensatory and punitive damages. The main grounds for the suit were that of monopolizing or attempting to monopolize soybean and maize seeds, and that of failing to test adequately GM seeds and crops both for human health and for environmental safety, and for failing to disclose adequately the lack of testing. Jeremy Rifkin, president of the Foundation on Economic Trends, who together with the National Farm Coalition was instrumental in filing the class-action suit, remarked that, beyond issues of regulation of untested seeds and environmental and health hazards, there was also a broader issue of corporate concentration of power over world agriculture 'in the emerging bio-tech century'.[17] Agricultural biotechnology is by no means dead, but, as *The Wall Street Journal* wrote on 7 January 2000, 'With the controversy over genetically modified foods spreading across the globe and taking a toll on the stocks of companies with agriculture–biotechnology businesses, it is hard to see those companies as a good investment, even in the long term.'[18] Market values are embedded in the social perception of physical realities and in social institutions and struggles. Had the opposition been weaker, the shares would do all right despite all the uncompensated future uncertain externalities. Civil society was ahead of governments in applying the precautionary principle.

However, the flow of smuggled Monsanto transgenic soybeans proved unstoppable in 2000 and 2001. The government of RGS got no support from other states. Jaime Lerner, the governor of Paranà and a former mayor of Curitiba with an environmental reputation, did nothing against transgenic crops. By mid-2001, Monsanto appeared to be winning the war over transgenic soybeans in Brazil, and was getting ready to market also Bt maize.

A PROCLAIMED ABSCONDER: UNION CARBIDE

A notorious environmental accident where the issue of liability for the damages is still alive 17 years after it happened, was that of Union Carbide in India in 1984. I see this case as a failure of organized environmentalism (which I compare, for instance, to the success against the *Exxon Valdez* oil spill in Alaska in 1989).

The Bhopal tragedy put many issues on the table. There are trends in the environmental indicators of unsustainability; there are also *surprises* in the relation between economy and environment. What were the safety standards in the Bhopal plant and in the Union Carbide West Virginia plant which also used methyl isocyanate (MIC) as raw materials? How is corporate liability regulated and implemented around the world? How did a democracy like India, with a solid tradition of judicial independence, deal with the case, in comparison with cases in Nigeria, Indonesia or South Africa? Why did a democracy such as India first enact a norm by which the state became the sole representative of the victims in litigation, then demand that the case go back to India, then settle with Union Carbide for a sum smaller than would possibly have been awarded in court not only in the USA but also in India? Why was Warren Anderson not kept in prison when he visited Bhopal shortly after the accident? What were the conflicts between the executive and the judiciary, and inside the judiciary, which led in 1989 to the dropping of criminal charges, and in 1991 to reinstating them? Why did the Indian state assume liability for damages that would exceed the US$470 million settlement? May Warren Anderson be extradited from the USA to India as citizens of Colombia or Panama are extradited to the USA? Why is it so difficult to have accurate statistics in Bhopal on the number of deaths and injured, over the years? When do states become interested in producing accurate statistics, and when do they prefer vague numbers? What are the values of human lives and in which metrics should they be expressed?

The absence of reliable governmental services to take care of families of the dead and to nurse the injured in Bhopal has opened some space for local groups of victims to put forward their own views and their own practices. True, outside observers lamented that no vigorous movement of 'community epidemiology' has arisen that would provide its own statistics, not only on the number of damaged people, but also on the quality of the damage. An International Medical Commission bitterly complained in 1994 about the failure to use a community-oriented epidemiology (Bertell and Tognoni, 1996: 89). Nevertheless, the fact that after more than 15 years local associations and their outside supporters are still keeping the issue of corporate liability alive not only in the courts but also in the media, forcing Warren Anderson, the former Union Carbide CEO, to keep a very low profile, must be seen as a brave attempt at environmental justice.

As a consequence of the 40 tons of methyl isocyanate (MIC) and other gases leaked from the Union Carbide pesticide company in Bhopal, Madhya Pradesh, in 1984, different sources indicate that between 2000 and 8000 victims died immediately, over 10000 more have died since then, and 120000 survivors are in need of medical attention.[19] Many animals also died. A civil suit claiming monetary damages was settled in India in February 1989, for US$470 million. The initial class-action suit in New York had been dismissed because of *forum non conveniens*, and this is why, with the agreement of authorities of India and over the protests of representatives of the victims, the case went back to India, and provisionally ended with the US$470 million settlement of 1989. However, not only are criminal proceedings pending in India, but a new class-action suit was also filed on 15 November 1999 in the federal court in New York under the ATCA against Union Carbide.[20] The settlement of 1989 granted Union Carbide officials immunity from criminal prosecution, but the Supreme Court of India revoked the criminal immunity in October 1991. Since then, officers from Union Carbide, including the 1984 chairman, Warren Anderson, have refused to go to India to stand trial. Warren Anderson is, in the legal parlance of India, a 'proclaimed absconder', that is, a fugitive from justice. There were, then, two cases pending at the end of 1999: the criminal case in India and the new class action suit in New York.

Union Carbide, because of the nature of its business, and also because of negligent management, has a spectacular history behind it: the main cases, before Bhopal, were Hawk's Nest tunnel in West Virginia in the 1930s, where many black workers died of silicosis, and nuclear radiation incidents and massive mercury dumping at Oak Ridge, Tennessee, since the 1950s (Morehouse and Subramanian, 1986; Dembo *et al.*, 1990). Bhopal has been described as the greatest industrial disaster (except for Chernobyl). When Rachel Carson loudly complained in 1962 against the effects of pesticides in the countryside, she did not foresee what might happen one day inside a city. MIC was the main raw material for the manufacturing of a pesticide with the trade name of Sevin. MIC reacted violently with water, which should not have reached the MIC tank, and the gas escaped into the atmosphere and fell on heavily populated areas of Bhopal.

Numbers began to be bandied about on the indemnities that could be awarded in the New York class-action suit which was later dismissed. What was the value of a human average life in countries so dissimilar as India and in the USA? 'Estimates of possible compensation vary widely and depend in part on whether Indian or American standards are used' (Morehouse and Subramanian, 1986: 57). This is obvious knowledge for insurance companies. The issue is very much alive in the IPCC's deliberations on 'greenhouse' policy. Is the value of a 'statistical' human life in India well represented by the indemnities paid in case of death in accidents by the National Railway Company? Are all dead passengers priced equally, whichever class they travelled in? How much have Indian passengers in international aviation disasters been worth, compared to passengers of other nationalities? As discussed in Chapter 2, when we say that somebody is 'as valuable' or even 'more valuable' than somebody else, the immediate logical reply must be, 'on which standard of value?' In terms of money, in terms of lost affection over many years, in terms of human dignity, in kilograms of human grease? Passion-laden questions, and passion-laden answers:

> when it comes to calculating monetary amounts for such phenomena as loss of life, mental distress, and deprivation of companionship for the survivors, there can be no double standard if we truly subscribe to the proposition that human life is as valuable in the Indian subcontinent as it is in North America. Indeed, given the extended nature of the Indian joint family, it could well be argued that loss of life leads to even greater deprivation of companionship than with the American nuclear family and that, therefore, still more substantial awards are in order for survivors of the Bhopal victims. (Morehouse and Subramanian, 1986: 59)

Half a year after the Bhopal disaster, an article in *The Wall Street Journal* (by Douglas J. Besajrov and Peter Reuter, on 16 May 1985) discussed monetary compensation (Morehouse and Subramanian, 1986: 58). At the time, Indian yearly per capita income was about US$250, while US income was US$15000. The statistical value of a human life in the USA was half a million US dollars (this had been the award made by a jury in the plutonium-contamination case of Karen Silkwood, a noted environmental martyr). In India it would be, in proportion, US$8300. For sick people, in the USA an average payment of US$64000 was being paid as compensation to asbestos victims, which in proportion would be US$1070 in India. Taking such values, and assuming some 16000 deaths over ten years (which Union Carbide never admitted), and about 200000 injured, we would come to a figure of US$328 million, inferior to the settlement for US$470 million negotiated in 1989.

There are several ways of discussing such figures. For instance, the cost of a permanently disabled person is not only the opportunity costs of lost earnings but also the costs of taking care of him or her. In a way, permanently injured people are more expensive than dead people. It is known that many victims have lost their immune system, and they die of tuberculosis or other common illnesses. Also the whole city of Bhopal stopped for some weeks, and this is an economic loss to be taken into account. Moreover, although many of the dead and chronically sick people were very poor, one could nevertheless assume that average income in a large city like Bhopal would be higher than the Indian average. One could also factor in the expectation of increased future incomes because of economic growth, a relevant factor for estimating the value of so many dead or disabled children (the rate of growth of the Indian economy has lately been higher than international discount rates which would presumably be used to give present values to the loss of future incomes). Finally, uncertain future costs, for instance because of inherited genetic disorders, ought to be included. Morehouse and Subramanian (1986) estimated the total minimum economic compensation at US$4 billion, and concluded: 'While calculations of monetized damages are inescapable, it is not the payment of money as such that matters but rather the efforts made to restore the lives of the victims, to the extent possible, to what it was before and then to try to compensate them for loss and suffering which cannot really be covered by money.' They also foresaw that

> the award of damages against Union Carbide, amounting to a substantial segment of its assets, will deliver an unambiguous message to hazardous industries all over the world that they no longer can give the quest for profit priority over human life. On the other hand, if Carbide is allowed to settle for a fraction of the amount that a jury would award [in the United States] and an amount that does not materially affect its financial position, the opposite message will be conveyed (Morehouse and Subramanian, 1986: 69–70)

If an accident such as Bhopal is cheap to a company because the indemnities are cheap (and if criminal proceedings which might entail non-monetary penalties, such as prison sentences, are not successful), then the incentive to prevent other accidents will be lower than otherwise. When the October 1989 settlement was announced, Union Carbide shares went up two dollars.

There is no major problem in giving reasonable money calculations of the value of human life adopting an insurance company's mindset. The problem is not mensurability but commensurability. When one says that life is 'precious', or that there are 'intangible' values involved in the form of enormous pain and suffering, the implication is not necessarily that money values should be higher but rather that they do not capture other types of value. Thus, among the many reasons for trying to start the second class-action suit in New York against the Union Carbide Corporation and Warren Anderson in November 1999, one is the allegation that Union Carbide had a deliberate policy of systematic racial discrimination against the plaintiffs (who represent all the people damaged). Other reasons are violations of the rights to life, health and security of persons, violations of international environmental rights (the Stockholm 1972 declaration) and the need for continuous and costly medical monitoring. Paradoxically, despite the appeal to values such as human rights which are unalienable, a civil suit like this, if successful, would result in so-called 'compensatory and punitive damages' expressed in money.

Early in 2000, Paul Lannoye, a long-serving member of the European Parliament, president of the Green group, together with a fellow MEP, Patricia McKenna, wrote to the Directorate-General for Competition of the European Union regarding the proposed merger of Dow Chemical and Union Carbide. In strong language, they accused Union Carbide and Dow Chemical of having made brazen misrepresentations to US and European authorities when they had stated that 'there are no . . . criminal . . . actions, suits, claims, hearings, investigations or proceedings pending'. These statements did not correspond to reality, they were intentionally misleading and they constituted a criminal offence under US law. It was well known that the Bhopal District Court had repeatedly served summons on Union Carbide's officers in the USA and through Interpol to appear for criminal trial in India. 'Providing false information is thus a sufficient ground for refusal or suspension of approval of a merger under US law. Furthermore, as the claims for damages against Union Carbide in pending law suits amount to billions rather than millions of US dollars . . . the misrepresentations concern circumstances which are vital for a correct assessment of the assets and economic situation of Union Carbide.'[21]

A final word on the Bhopal case. Money valuation of damages caused by Union Carbide has been one main point of conflict. This was also the case with Exxon after the famous oil tanker *Valdez* accident in Alaska in 1989 which mobilized the resources of the big US environmental organizations. The *Exxon Valdez* damages were valued at about 15 times more than the 1989 Bhopal settlement. No person died in Alaska, where there was much loss of animal life and biological resources. Non-monetary languages have also been used in Bhopal – infringement of human rights, criminal liability, racism – with one notable absence (at least in the writings in English on the case): the language of sacredness, certainly not alien to India but which seems excluded in such urban chemical pollution contexts.

NOTES

1. Personal communication from Manuel Baquedano, the head of the IEP, Chile.
2. A large conference on the ecological debt took place in November 2001 in Benin, under the auspices of Friends of the Earth, with participation of the World Council of Churches.
3. See the website of the ecological debt campaign (www.cosmovisiones.com). For Sweden, see the reports of Arne Jernelov issued by the Swedish Environmental Advisory Council.
4. Cf. Cabeza Gutés and Martinez-Alier (2001).
5. Orlando Ochoa Teran, *Quinto Dia*, 18 January 2000, relayed by J.C.Centeno through the Environment in Latin America discussion list (ELAN at CSF).
6. Danilo Torres Ferrari, 'Los avances de la normativa sobre Cierre de Faenas Mineras', *Boletín Minero* (Chile), 1122, June 1999.
7. Chilean nitrates are not guano, they are not 'organic' excrement.
8. I am grateful to Elsa Marcela Guerrero for information and references.
9. Authors who have written on environmental security include Thomas Homer-Dixon, Peter Gleick and Norman Myers. See Deudney and Matthew (1999).
10. Following the proposal of Thomas Lovejoy, 'Aid Debtor Nations Ecology', *The New York Times*, 4 October 1984.
11. Verònica Vidal, 'Impactos de la aplicación de políticas sobre cambio climático en la forestación del páramo de Ecuador', *Ecología Política*, 18, 1999, 49–54, gives the original source for this finding: G. Medina and P. Mena, 'El páramo como espacio de mitigación de carbono atmosférico', Serie Páramo, 1. GTP/Abya Yala, Quito, 1999. See also *El Comercio* (Quito), 3 November 1999.
12. Memo in *Accion Ecologica*, Quito, forest campaign archives.
13. *El Nacional*, Caracas, 1 August 1997.
14. Jonathan Friedland, 'Chile leads the region with a new environmental movement', *The Wall Street Journal* – Americas, 26 March 1997. This article described the triple alliance between radical Chilean environmental groups such as RENACE (led by Sara Larrain), Douglas Tompkins, a US citizen founder of the clothing chain Esprit de Corps who lives in southern Chile where he practises his belief in 'deep ecology', having bought and protected a huge forest property, and groups based in the USA with their own grudges against Trillium because of its actions in the northwest.
15. See Patricia Moguel and Victor Toledo (1999), for a careful description of five different coffee farming systems in a multi-criteria evaluation framework.
16. The main sources for this section are *Seedling* (GRAIN), 16(3) and 16(4), 1999, the report by Silvia Ribeiro in *Ecologia Politica*, 18, 1999, and the article by Steve Stecklow and Matt Moffett, *Wall Street Journal*, 28 December 1999. I have also profited from my friendship with some of the actors in the conflict, and from the invitation by EMATER to lecture for one week in Porto Alegre in July 2001.
17. Monsanto Sued, *Multinational Monitor*, January/February 2000, p.6.
18. Cf. *Rachel's Environment and Health Weekly*, n. 685, 3 February 2000, 'Trouble in the Garden'.
19. 'More than 3,000 people were killed and 200,000 others were injured in Bhopal on December 3, 1984, when 40 tons of vaporous methyl isocyanate, hydrogencyanide, monomethylamine, carbon monoxide and possibly 20 other chemicals were released from the Union Carbide pesticide plant after an explosion. Many more have died since of gas-related illnesses. It ranks as one of the world's worst industrial accidents.' ('Where is Warren?', *The New York Times*, 5 March 2000).
20. Websites www.bhopal.net or www.bhopal.org.
21. Paul Lannoye and Patricia McKenna to European Commission, Directorate-General for Competititon, Directorate B S Merger Task Force, ref. COMP/M. 1671 S Dow Chemical / Union Carbide, 21 January 2000.

11. On the relations between political ecology and ecological economics

Against the hopes of many environmental economists and industrial ecologists, the economy is not 'dematerializing'. This has been a point of departure for the present book. Ecological economics provides the *theory* on the structural conflict between the economy and the environment. Without such a theory, this book would merely become an entertaining catalogue of environmental struggles, with a tendency to select anecdotal evidence showing a black-and-white picture of the good guys (and girls) against the bad guys. The conflict between economy and environment does not manifest itself only in the attacks on remaining pristine Nature but also in the increasing demands for raw materials and for sinks for residues in the large parts of the planet inhabited by humans, and in the planet as a whole. The fact that raw materials are cheap and that sinks have a zero price is not a sign of abundance but a result of a given distribution of property rights, power and income. The environmental load of the economy, driven by consumption and by population growth, is growing all the time, even when the economy (measured in money terms) is based on the service sector. Some impacts may decrease on some geographical scales, but then other impacts appear on other scales, with the resulting social conflicts. For instance, reduction of global carbon dioxide emissions may be obtained through local nuclear or hydroelectric energy projects, or by absorption of carbon dioxide through controversial local eucalyptus or pine plantations. Environmental improvements in some nations might occur because of the displacement of pollution to other nations. The case for a general 'win–win' solution (better environment with economic growth) is far from proven. On the contrary, since the economy is not 'dematerializing' in per capita terms, there are increasing local and global conflicts over the sharing of the burdens of pollution (including the enhanced greenhouse effect) and over the access to natural resources (including 'biopiracy').

Environmental preservation and protection have been understood as desires which could develop only after the material necessities of life were already well covered. The movement for environmental justice in the USA and the wider and more diffuse worldwide movement of the environmentalism of the poor have bankrupted this view, which was prevalent until recently. Consider, for instance, the following statement: 'The Health of the Planet survey [by R. Dunlap and the Gallup Institute] has revealed than *even* publics in developing countries, contrary to expectations based on ideas about their "hierarchy of needs", also often give priority to environmental protection over economic growth' (Broadbent, 1998: 290, emphasis added). Of course they do! Precisely, the hierarchy of needs among poor people is such that livelihood is given priority over marketed goods. Oikonomia is more important than chrematistics. Livelihood depends on clean air, available soil, clean water.

MATERIAL INTERESTS AND SACRED VALUES

Commitments or pledges towards Nature characterize the variety of environmentalism described as the 'cult of wilderness', while a material interest in the environmental resources and services provided by Nature for human livelihood characterizes the environmentalism of the poor. The very concept of ecological distribution conflicts, central to this book, implies conflicts of interests. Shall we then conclude that there is an environmentalism of values versus an environmentalism of interests? No. When the U'Wa in Colombia, in a famous conflict in the late 1990s, refused Occidental Petroleum entry to their land, threatening mass suicide, they claimed that not only the surface land but also the subsoil was sacred, and should not be defiled by oil exploration. This is a vocabulary of protest which implies a denial of nature as capital (M. O'Connor, 1993b), that is, the impossibility of compensation for externalities in monetary terms.

The U'Wa, a tribe of 5000 people, refused oil exploitation, being successful in getting the Supreme Court in Colombia to annul the permission granted to Occidental Petroleum because of lack of prior informed consent, and also being successful later in expanding their communal territory up to some 200000 hectares. However, the Colombian Minister of the Environment, Juan Mayr, a former environmentalist, granted Occidental Petroleum permission in 1999 to open its first oil well, just 500 metres away from the limit of the expanded U'Wa territory. In reply, the U'Wa (supported by numerous environmental groups inside and outside Colombia), invaded the site of the well, camping there at the end of 1999. The U'Wa appealed to their indigenous territorial rights (*resguardo indigena*) under the constitution of Colombia.

The U'Wa case is only one of perhaps a hundred indigenous communities threatened at present by the oil and gas industry in tropical countries. Certainly, the appeal to sacredness has contributed to its popularity. That the land is sacred, one may not doubt in Native America. That Sira, the creator, also declared that the subsoil is sacred, and that oil is like blood inside the arteries and veins of the Earth, seems perhaps a recent theological strategy which, pressed by their international audience, the U'Wa deployed to keep the oil company out. Actually, the mere existence of oil inside the earth, let alone its sacredness, is not so obvious before seismic exploration and drilling take place – this is precisely the point of confrontation. We realize, then, that different languages of resistance, of different vintages, are deployed at the same time. Are they compatible? The U'Wa did not say, but could have said, that they would bring a class action suit against Occidental Petroleum in the USA asking for economic compensation for damages once oil exploration starts. In 1999, as reported by OilWatch, one of the oil wells which long ago had been opened by Texaco in Ecuador, Dureno 1, was symbolically claimed back by the Cofans, who performed a religious ceremony for the occasion. No oil platform has ever been religiously sanitized in the North Sea. Traditions are invented, but not haphazardly.

DiChiro (1998) describes the feeling of puzzlement at the First Environmental Justice Summit in Washington, DC in 1991 among delegates from inner cities, when listening to statements from Native Americans about 'our brothers the whales'. In fact, the first Principle of Environmental Justice of a list of 17 principles approved at that 1991 meeting affirms the 'sacredness of Mother Earth, ecological unity and the interdependence of all species, and the right to be free from ecological destruction', though another principle incongruously asks for full (*equivalent?*) compensation for environmental damages. Zimmerer (1996) explains in a different context that one discourse on land erosion in Cochabamba, Bolivia, is couched by Quechua peasants in terms of anger from Pachamama because of lack of proper rituals to her. This is certainly not a 'post-materialist' appreciation for natural amenities, it is something older and deeper, perhaps the real 'deep ecology'. Berkes (1999) has given a brilliantly detailed account of the combination of indigenous ecological knowledge and sacred values brought to bear on resource management by the Cree in Canada and by other groups around the world. In conclusion, there are feelings of the sacredness of nature among many peoples of the Earth which in no way may be conceptualized as 'post-materialist' values in Ronald Inglehart's sense, because they are bound together with the immediate material use of nature's life-support systems.

In the debates on the preservation of wilderness, the old view that preservation implied the displacement of local human population far from the natural park has been replaced by participatory management (West and Brechin, 1991). Here the question arises, on which values will participation be based? For instance, will participation for a new programme of conservation of tigers or elephants be achieved by compensating local people for damage by animals, and by allowing them to share in the eventual benefits from eco-tourism? Thus Himba people at Purros in the Namibia desert, where there are elephants and lions, are reported to declare: 'It is as if we are farming wild animals. But instead of getting meat and skins from them, we get the money that the tourists pay to see them' (Jacobson, in Cock and Koch, 1991: 221). I remember visiting Tortuguero in Costa Rica, where every turtle landing to lay eggs on its native beach was confronted by the flash of a tourist camera under the remunerated guidance of local children.

What about the places without eco-tourism, such as 99 per cent of Amazonia? What about situations in which the economic damages from the animals to humans or to human-owned livestock are greater than the benefits from eco-tourism? Is management based on the monetary 'bottom-line' culture more effective than the enhancement of local wilderness values which can still be remembered? Notice that the theory of the preservation of wildlife areas by the 'totemization' of some big animals relies on anthropological notions. For instance, should local populations be induced not to kill the Andean bear by giving them monetary compensation for damage to their crops of maize and a share in eco-tourist traffic, or should a more effective appeal be made to their own traditions of respect for such an animal? Can populations in the Catalan Pyrenees be made to accept the reintroduction of brown bears (imported from the Balkans, since they were locally extinct) under a European LIFE programme only by being compensated monetarily for loss of sheep and loss of revenues for the non-development of ski resorts in land set aside for the bears? Or should an appeal also be made to their own appreciation of wildlife, to the roles of bears in their ancient songs and rituals in Carnival, and to their own children's new acquired values as students of forestry, biology or environmental sciences in the lowlands? Why cannot local rural people have contradictory values, simultaneously in favour of more money and more wilderness, as exhibited by many members of the governing bodies of IUCN and the WWF?[1]

The environmentalism of wilderness and the environmentalism of human livelihoods both may use the languages of sacredness; both may appeal to cultural values, both refuse the pre-eminence of economic value. They may become allies. Thus, as this book goes to press, an example of this alliance may be seen in the opposition in Kerala to hydroelectric projects such as Pooyamkutty that would submerge valleys in the Western Ghats at about 300 metres above sea level which contain a profuse variety of vegetation, and where reeds are collected by poor people for the commercial paper industry.[2]

TWO STYLES OF POLITICAL ECOLOGY

A discussion on environmental valuation brings together political ecology and ecological economics. Brosius has perceptively recognized two forms or styles of political ecology (Brosius, 1999a: 17) which are not (as it might seem) rural/urban, or local/global, or Third World/ First World but rather material/constructivist. The first style of political ecology is 'a fusion of human ecology with political economy . . . [it is the study of] a series of actors, differentially empowered but with different interests, contesting the claims of others to resources in a particular ecological context'. This is the style of political ecology of the present book, with its emphasis on material interests as much as social values, with its definition of political ecology as the study of ecological distribution conflicts in an economy which is ecologically less and less sustainable. The second style of political ecology consists of 'discourse analysis'. This has to do with queries about the meaning or lack of meaning of 'environmental resources and services' for different cultures, with the 'social constructedness or reinventions of nature'. Thus, the Chipko movement briefly described in Chapter 6 disintegrates in some armchair seminars on political ecology-cum-cultural theory taught in the USA into an analysis of the discourses by different authors who write on the discourses produced by the putative actors of the Chipko movement (which perhaps never did exist at all), certainly an economy of research effort compared to old-fashioned concern with checking the facts.

Nevertheless, a connection may be established between both styles of political ecology. It is the following one: the different actors of ecological distribution conflicts, differentially entitled and empowered, might contest the claims of others by appealing to different languages of valuation within their wide cultural repertoire. As Susan Stonich succintly put it,

> an overemphasis on constructivist discourse analysis may diminish the concern for the material issues that first provoked the emergence of political ecology. From the perspective of the political ecologist, the importance of understanding discursive formations lies precisely in what that understanding reveals about the behaviors [and the interests and values] of the diverse actors involved in social and environmental conflicts. (Stonich, 1999: 24)

In a discussion on the vocabularies of protests deployed against the enclosure of grazing and fuelwood grounds in Karnataka, this same point was made some time ago: 'in field or factory, ghetto or grazing ground, struggles over resources, even when they have tangible material origins, have always been struggles over meanings' (Guha and Martinez-Alier, 1997: 13). The two styles of political ecology must thus be combined.

While conventional economics looks at environmental impacts in terms of externalities which should be internalized into the price system, one can see externalities not as market failures but as cost-shifting successes which nevertheless might give rise to environmental movements (Leff, 1995; J. O'Connor, 1988). Such movements will legitimately employ a variety of vocabularies and strategies of resistance, and they cannot be gagged by cost–benefit analysis or by environmental impact assessments. Thus this book provides an answer to Raymond Bryant's complaint that 'political ecologists have yet to develop an alternative to the mainstream concept of sustainable development' (Bryant and Bailey, 1997: 4). The answer is 'the environmentalism of the poor and environmental justice (local and global) as the main forces for sustainability'. To exaggerate slightly, the focus should not be on 'environmental conflict resolution' but rather (within Gandhian limits) on conflict exacerbation in order to advance towards an ecological economy.

There is a gender dimension to ecological conflicts, as shown by the prominent role of women in many local environmental movements everywhere in the world. Women's role in provisioning and care of the household leads to a special concern with such issues as scarcity and pollution of water and lack of firewood. Women often have a smaller share of private property, and depend more heavily on common property resources. Also women often have specific traditional knowledge in agriculture and medicine which is devalued by intrusion of market resource exploitation or state control. That conventional economic accounting makes unpaid domestic work invisible is a well-known feminist economic argument. That women's freedom is closely related to lower population growth, and therefore to lower environmental pressure, is also an old argument, today more relevant than ever.

In conclusion, non-economic values and livelihood interests come into play in environmental decision processes, aided by the failures of economic valuation. This book therefore brings together environmental justice, popular environmentalism, the environmentalism of the poor, debates on sustainability and disputes on valuation. It contributes to theoretical discussions:

- on the sociology and history of the main, different but intertwined varieties of environmentalism,
- on the relations between local and global ecological distribution conflicts,
- on the meaning and measurement of unsustainability, with particular reference to the debate on the 'dematerialization' of the economy,

- on the valuation of environmental resources and services, on the links between valuation and distributional conflicts, and on comparability and incommensurability of values.

NAMING ECOLOGICAL DISTRIBUTION CONFLICTS

The following list of ecological distribution conflicts and related resistance movements constitutes the evolving agenda of political ecology. The names have been given by authors who have studied them, or have arisen from the world of NGOs. Take a name like 'biopiracy' – the fact is not new at all, a new, insulting name now reveals a sense of injustice felt by some and denied by others. This is, then, the list of conflicts and resistance movements which (as work in progress) summarizes the field of political ecology at the present stage in research.

1. *Environmental racism* (USA)   The disproportionate burden of pollution in areas inhabited by African Americans, Latinos, Native Americans. *Environmental justice* is the movement against environmental racism. *Environmental blackmail* has been used to describe situations in which either LULU (locally unacceptable land use) is finally accepted, or the local population stays without jobs. One well known source is Bullard (1993).
2. *Toxic struggles*   This is the name given in the USA to fights against risks from heavy metals, dioxins and so on. Sources are Gibbs (1981), Hofrichter (1993).
3. *Toxic imperialism*   Greenpeace, in 1988, used these words to describe the dumping of toxic waste in poorer countries (theoretically forbidden by the Basel Convention of 1989).
4. *Ecologically unequal exchange*   Importing products from poor countries or regions, at prices which do not take into account the exhaustion of the resources and the local externalities. *Raubwirtschaft* (Raumoulin, 1984), which means plunder economy, was used by German and French geographers a hundred years ago.
5. *Internalization of international externalities*   A name given to lawsuits against transnational companies (Texaco, Dow Chemical and so on) in their country of origin, claiming damages for externalities caused in poor countries.
6. *Ecological debt*   Claiming damages from rich countries on account of past excessive emissions (of carbon dioxide, for instance) or plundering of natural resources. Attempts are made to establish such

environmental liabilities. Sources are Robleto and Marcelo (1992), Borrero (1993), Azar and Holmberg (1995) (for the intergenerational context); Parikh (1995), Martinez-Alier (1997).

7. *Biopiracy* The appropriation of genetic resources ('wild' or agricultural) without adequate payment or recognition of peasant or indigenous ownership over them (including the extreme case of the Human Genome project). This word was introduced by Pat Mooney, of RAFI, in 1993.

8. *Land degradation* Soil erosion caused by unequal distribution of land, or by pressure of production for exports. Blaikie and Brookfield (1987) introduced the basic distinction between pressure of population and pressure of production on the sustainable use of land.

9. *Plantations are not forests* The movements against eucalyptus, pine or acacia plantations for wood or paper pulp production (often exported) (Carrere and Lohman, 1996).

10. *Mangroves v. shrimp* The movement to preserve the mangroves for livelihood, against the shrimp export industry, in Thailand, Honduras, Ecuador, India, Philippines, Sri Lanka and elsewhere.

11. *Defence of the rivers* The movements against large dams (such as the Narmada movement in India, the *atingidos por barragens* in Brazil) (Goldsmith and Hildyard, 1984; McCully, 1996).

12. *Mining conflicts* Complaints over the siting of mines and smelters because of water and air pollution, and land occupation by open-cast mining and slag. (A good source is R. Moody's *The Gulliver File*, 1992).

13. *Transboundary pollution* Applied mainly to sulphur dioxide crossing borders in Europe and producing acid rain.

14. *National / local fishing rights* Attemps to stop open access depredation by imposing (since the 1940s in Peru, Ecuador and Chile) exclusive fishing areas (200 miles, and beyond, as in Canada, for straddling stocks). The language here is international public law. Another conflict is that of the defence (or introduction) of local common fishing rights against industrial fishing (as in coastal India, or lower Amazonia).

15. *Equal rights to carbon sinks and reservoirs* The proposal for equal per capita use of oceans, new vegetation, soils and atmosphere as sinks or reservoirs for carbon dioxide (Agarwal and Narain, 1991).

16. *Environmental space* The geographical space really occupied by an economy, taking into account imports of natural resources and disposal of emissions. *Ecological footprint* is a similar notion: the carrying capacity appropriated by large cities or countries, measured in terms of space (Rees and Wackernagel, 1994).

17. *Ecological trespassers v. ecosystem people*   This is the contrast between people living on their own resources and ('omnivorous') people living on the resources of other territories and peoples. The idea comes from Dasman, and has been applied by Gadgil and Guha (1995) internally to India.

18. *Workers' struggles for occupational health and safety*   Actions (in the framework of collective bargaining or outside it) to prevent damages to workers in mines, plantations or factories ('red' outside, 'green' inside).

19. *Urban struggles for clean air and water, green spaces, cyclist and pedestrian rights* (Castells, 1983)   Actions, outside the market, to improve environmental conditions of livelihood or to gain access to recreational amenities in urban contexts.

20. *Consumers' and citizens' safety*   Struggles over the definition and the burden of risks from new technologies (nuclear, GMO and so on) in rich or in poor countries.

21. *Indigenous environmentalism*   Use of territorial rights and ethnic resistance against the external use of resources (for example, Crees against Hydro Quebec, Ogoni and Ijaw against Shell). Good sources are Gedicks (1993, 2001).

22. *Social eco-feminism, environmental feminism*   The environmental activism of women, motivated by their social situation. The idiom of such struggles is not necessarily that of feminism and/or environmentalism (Bina Agarwal, 1992).

23. *Environmentalism of the poor*   Social conflicts with an ecological content, today and in history, of the poor against the relatively rich, not only but mainly in rural conflicts (as explained in Guha's history of Chipko, 1989, rev. edn. 2000, and in Guha and Martinez-Alier, 1997).

LOCAL AND GLOBAL CONFLICTS

There is a chronology of such conflicts. When did they start, when were they identified, when will they disappear? For instance, claims of an ecological debt on account of CFC emissions are less and less valid, while claims on account of CO_2 will increase. There is also a geography of such conflicts. Some are local and some are global. Some are fought in an explicitly environmental language, and some in other languages. One thing is clear, however – there are closer and closer connections between local conflicts and explicit, global environmentalism. Thus the movements for the defence of mangroves on the Pacific Coast of Central and South

America have pointed out the role of mangroves as first coastline defence, increasingly important when confronted with recurrent Niños, plus the risk of greenhouse sea level rise. Local resistance movements reinforce the global networks, and in turn they profit sometimes by adding the language and the strength of global environmentalism to their own local idioms and forms of resistance. At other times, the conflict arises in the first instance because of the external global influence – witness the recent use of the language of biopiracy in conflicts over property rights on *uña de gato*, *ayahuasca*, *sangre de drago*, *neem* and also quinua, basmati rice, turmeric, or indeed human genes, in several Latin American countries and in India.

It could be claimed that the defence of indigenous groups against the oil or mining industries, or against large dams or logging, is part of a *politics of identity*, while the environmental justice movement in the USA, insofar as it fights against 'environmental racism', could also be seen in this light. However, the connections between local and global issues are increasingly obvious to the actors themselves. There exist international networks which grow out of local conflicts and which support them. Therefore to see ecological distribution conflicts as a manifestation of the politics of identity would not be convincing. It is rather the other way around, collective identity being one of the idioms in which ecological distribution conflicts are expressed.

Consider, for instance, the current conflict over bauxite mining in Orissa. In India, as in China, it is often state enterprises, or private corporations belonging to national owners, which abuse the environment. However, as the economy rides the neoliberal wave, the presence of multinationals increases. Thus Utkal Alumina International Ltd. (UAIL) is a joint venture promoted by ALCAN of Canada, Hydro of Norway and INDAL of India. UAIL plans to develop a one million ton per year aluminium refinery mainly for export, at Doragurha in Kashipur (Rayagada district), from the bauxite mined from the Baphlimali hills. There is opposition to this project from tribal groups supported by Achyut Das, head of the NGO Agragamee. The opposition is strengthened by the success in stopping a similar project in the Gandhamardhan hills in Bargarh district. These hills and the temple of Nrusinghnath are regarded as sacred. Tribal areas in India are not under the protection of convention 169 of the International Labour Office but they are protected under a special Fifth Schedule clause in the Constitution. Local peoples through their *gram sabhas* (general assemblies) are supposed to have an ambiguous veto power over the extraction of natural resources. The complaints by local people against government officers who wanted to hold local meetings in favour of the UAIL project led to police intervention and to the killing of three people by the police on 16 December 2000 in the village of Maikanch, 13km from

Kashipur. This village is the centre of the movement of Kondh adivasis against bauxite mining (Menon, 2001: 143–8). The defence of the environment thus reaffirms tribal identity and tribal rights, while mobilizing also international support networks against multinational aluminium companies.

In the USA, environmental justice is a movement in favour of so-called 'minorities', while the environmentalism of the poor is potentially a movement not of ethnic minorities but of the majority of the world at large. Inside this current, the relations between local and global concerns are established through single-issue networks such as the International Rivers Network, OilWatch, MineWatch, World Rainforest Movement, RAFI and the Pesticides Action Network, which to some extent overlap in membership, or through specific programmes and campaigns of confederal organizations such as Friends of the Earth, or thanks to the help of global environmental organizations such as Greenpeace. For example, OilWatch, born of community struggles against oil and gas extraction, provides south–south links among activist groups in tropical countries. OilWatch groups around the world complain about local impacts, but they also point out that more oil extraction means more carbon dioxide production. Thus, at Kyoto in 1997, OilWatch issued a carefully crafted Declaration eventually signed by over 200 organizations from 52 countries calling for a moratorium on all new exploration for fossil fuel reserves in pristine and frontier areas, making the point that the burning of oil, gas and coal is the primary cause of human-induced climate change, and that the burning of even a portion of known economically recoverable fossil fuel reserves would ensure 'climate catastrophe'. The evaluation of all power projects should involve consultation with the communities most affected by them, respecting their right to refuse projects, that would be constructed as a veto threshold in multi-criteria analysis, similar to the endangered species provision in environmental management in the USA. Simultaneously, OilWatch demanded that oil, gas and coal prices 'properly reflect the true costs of their extraction and consumption, including the best estimate of their role in causing climate change in order to apply the polluter pays principle to reflect the cost of carbon in the price'.

The Declaration also asked for full recognition of the ecological debt as it relates to the impacts of fossil fuel extraction, for a legally binding obligation to restore all areas affected by oil, gas and coal exploration and exploitation by the corporations or public entities that are responsible, and required that public investments (including World Bank funds) which at present go to subsidize fossil fuel extraction and consumption be used instead for clean, renewable and decentralized forms of energy with a particular focus on meeting the energy needs of the poorest 2 billion people.[3]

Two years earlier, in 1995, Sunita Narain from the Centre for Science and Environment of New Delhi, joint editor of the periodical *Down to Earth*, who in 1991 proposed with Anil Agarwal a platform of 'equal rights to carbon sinks and reservoirs' for everybody in the world, visited the USA to meet academics and activists of the environmental justice movement. As she herself reported, 'having worked for environmental justice at the national level, this group was attracted to the concepts put forward in the book by us, asking for justice in global environmental governance'.[4] Environmental groups in Venezuela ('Orinoco OilWatch') published a long open letter to President Clinton on 9 October 1997, on the eve of his visit to the country, complaining about American oil companies' operations in areas inhabited by the Waraos and other indigenous groups, and pointing out the incongruity between Clinton's and Gore's well publicized alarm at the increased greenhouse effects (shown recently at a press conference in Washington on 6 October 1997) and Venezuela's plans (later discarded) to increase oil exports with American support to 6 million barrels per day.[5] We see here repeated instances of combining local and global views in the defence of the environment. This is not NIMBY politics. And this is not identity politics.

ENVIRONMENTAL JUSTICE AS A FORCE FOR SUSTAINABILITY

Some of the conflicts analysed are modern, some historical. The historical component is crucial to the notion of the environmentalism of the poor. Many social conflicts today, and in history, have an ecological content, with the poor trying to retain under their control the environmental resources and services they need for livelihood, and which are threatened by state takeover or by the advance of the generalized market system. Actors of such conflicts are sometimes still reluctant to call themselves environmentalists. Though the social groups involved in such conflicts are often quite diverse, the 'environmentalism of the poor' is a convenient umbrella term used in this book for social concerns and for forms of social action based on a view of the environment as a source of livelihood. In 1991, Hugo Blanco, a former peasant activist in Peru and at the time a senator, evocatively distinguished this kind of environmentalism from its northern counterpart, described in this book as the 'cult of wilderness'. At first sight, wrote Blanco,

> environmentalists or conservationists are nice, slightly crazy guys whose main purpose in life is to prevent the disappearance of blue whales and pandas. The

common people have more important things to think about, for instance how to get their daily bread. Sometimes they are taken to be not so crazy but rather smart guys who, in the guise of protecting endangered species, have formed so-called NGOs to get juicy amounts of dollars from abroad . . . Such views are sometimes true. However, there are in Peru a very large number of people who are environmentalists. Of course, if I tell such people, you are ecologists, they might reply, 'ecologist your mother' or words to that effect. Let us see, however. Isn't the village of Bambamarca truly environmentalist, which has time and again fought valiantly against the pollution of its water from mining? Are not the town of Ilo and the surrounding villages which are being polluted by the Southern Peru Copper Corporation truly environmentalist? Is not the village of Tambo Grande in Piura environmentalist when it rises like a closed fist and is ready to die in order to prevent strip-mining in its valley? Also, the people of the Mantaro Valley who saw their little sheep die, because of the smoke and waste from the La Oroya smelter. And the population of Amazonia, who are totally environmentalist, and die defending their forests against depredation. Also the poor people of Lima are environmentalists, when they complain about the pollution of water on the beaches.[6]

As this book was drawing to a close in 2001, one of these Peruvian conflicts flared up again, this time with an explicitly environmental mise-en-scène. The National Peasant Confederation of Peru issued a declaration on 2 March 2001, under the signature of Hugo Blanco, Washington Mendoza and Wilder Sánchez (www.laneta.apc.org), explaining that there had been a general strike in Tambo Grande (Piura) against the Canadian company Manhattan Minerals. This easily accessible town, with its hinterland, has about 70000 inhabitants. An open-pit mine is planned, literally on top of the town, displacing many of its inhabitants. Tambo Grande lies about 75km from the provincial capital of Piura, about 120km from the harbour of Paita, in the irrigated valley of San Lorenzo, a success story of World Bank financing in the 1950s and 1960s. The main actors are the local agrarian population, who use scarce water for export products, some as exotic as mangoes, and the Canadian company. A young Canadian observer wrote:

Manhattan holds a Supreme Decree from the fallen Fujimori government to exploit the sizeable gold, silver and copper deposit at its Tambogrande concession in Northern Peru. Unfortunately for Manhattan, its El Dorado is located underneath the town of Tambogrande. Local residents do not want to be relocated to make way for the mine. They are also skeptical about the compatibility of an open-pit, heap-leach gold operation with the highly productive agricultural operations in the area. Tambogrande is located in a desert. Its export-quality agriculture, which supports an enormous proportion of the local population, is dependent on an irrigation system that was developed in the 1950s. Concerned about competing uses of scarce water resources and the potential for water contamination, locals perceive there to be much at stake. It's not entirely surprising then, that on February 27 and 28, between five and six thousand locals marched through the streets of Tambogrande, demanding that Manhattan leave. Unfortunately, a small group of the protestors turned violent, setting fire to Manhattan's camp.

They even burnt down the six prototype houses for the displaced which were on show. Then, on 31 March 2001, a local farmer, Godofredo García Baca, with an engineering degree from the Agrarian University of La Molina (Lima), a member of the Ecological Forum, president of the Association of Mango Exporters and leader of the citizens' group against Manhattan Minerals, was shot dead while driving to his farm.[7]

Beyond the town of Tambo Grande itself, there are concerns about the effects of mine tailings and water and air pollution on the desert ecology of the region of Piura. Recurrent El Niño phenomena allow the desert to have a permanent population of algarrobo trees (*Prosopis pallida*). The hydraulic regime and the production of biomass in the region changes totally when El Niño strikes (annual rains may then be of the order of 3000mm). How resilient are local ecological adaptations to large scale open-pit mining by Manhattan and, later, by other companies?[8]

*   *   *

Demand for gold has a high income elasticity. If not in Tambo Grande, gold will be mined elsewhere. No doubt a higher level of income allows people to buy more gold, but it also gives the means to correct some environmental impacts. However, in the world in general, the level of income at which economic growth produces enough wealth so that environmental cure may be provided, is such a high level of income that much damage has already accumulated, as happened in so many mining 'ghost towns' (Opschoor, 1995). Irreversible damage thresholds are crossed in the meantime: for instance, biodiversity may disappear because of economic growth, and, later, without possible replacement for such a loss, it might be 'too late to be green'.

Starting from the premise that economic growth damages the environment, we have seen ecological distribution conflicts which are not only conflicts of interest, but also conflicts of values. Quite often, conflicts over the access to environmental resources and services adopt languages which are not explicitly environmental. Much work remains to be done trying to identify the ecological content in social conflicts which have used non-environmental idioms.

These are movements born from the resistance (expressed in many different languages) to the lopsided use of environmental resources and services by the rich and powerful. Ordinary women and men strive to correct the wrong that has been done to the land, water and air around them. Until the problem is solved, why pacify the conflict? On the contrary, the publicity given to each of these struggles through their own traditional channels of communication, and through the new networks society, inspires others to do battle against the forces spoiling the local and global environments (Cock and Koch, 1991: 22). The Brundtland report emphasized environmental damages caused by poverty. The contrary view, called 'the environmentalism of the poor', was first proposed in the late 1980s to explain conflicts in which poor people defend the environment (in rural situations, but also in cities) against the state or the market. Well-known instances are the Ogoni, the Ijaw and other groups in the Niger Delta protesting against the damage from oil extraction by Shell; the complaints about the planting of eucalyptus in Thailand and elsewhere, because plantations are not forests; the movements of oustees from dams; or some new peasant movements in the 1990s such as Via Campesina, against seed multinationals and biopiracy. There are also historical instances, such as in Rio Tinto in Andalusia in the 1880s, against sulphur dioxide, and in the early 1900s against pollution of the Watarase river from the Ashio copper mine. The words 'ecology' and 'environment' were not used politically at the time. Until recently, the actors of such conflicts rarely saw themselves as environmentalists. Their concern is with livelihood. The environmentalism of the poor is often expressed in the language of legally established old community property rights. At other times, new communal rights are claimed. Thus local fishermen in the middle Amazon river invent new communal rights against outside industrial fishing boats, in a conflict similar to that in Kerala in India between artisanal fishermen (who assert community rights, and claim that the sea is sacred) and industrial trawlers.

The environmental justice movement in the USA, as we have seen, does not fit into mainstream northern environmentalism. Its urban constituency is not concerned with wilderness, and its main platform is not eco-efficiency but eco-justice. It is part of a renewed civil rights movement, and it grew in the 1980s out of local protests against toxic waste and occupational or residential health hazards. Civil rights activists, who still have a long row to hoe, explicitly incorporated environmental issues in the early 1980s into their own platforms. In a similar way, elsewhere in the world, union leaders have long 'appropriated' issues of health and safety; national governments translate conflicts about fishing in the high seas into a vocabulary of national interests and international public law, local indigenous communities (whether old or recently born in a process of ethnogenesis) establish territorial rights which include claims to minerals and to genetic resources; and anti-imperialist militants try to appropriate the fight against polluting transnational companies. These are all legitimate appropriations. Ecological distribution conflicts are fought in different languages. Were Shell an American and not a European company, the Ogoni and the Ijaw in the Niger Delta would perhaps have used long ago the language of 'environmental racism'.

Environmental justice is a great slogan. In the American context, it can still be understood, in a limited sense, as referring to a sectoral aspect (environmental pollution) affecting minority populations. Its scope is potentially much larger, as shown by the South African environmental justice movement. In fact, the movement for environmental justice has grown in the USA, but it is uniquely placed to overcome the intellectual and social gap between the environmentalisms of the north and the south. In order to do this, it must keep its original impulse against the *disproportionate* use of environmental resources and services – to the profit of some and the detriment of others – moving beyond the USA in order to consider issues such as carbon sinks and reservoirs, biopiracy, ecologically unequal exchange, the externalities caused by transnational companies inside and outside the USA, and the land, water and urban problems of the south which are of a different scale from those of the north. Then, and this is my conclusion, environmental justice will become a strong force in order to achieve sustainability.

VALUE SYSTEM CONTESTS

A second, related conclusion will be developed next, on the relations between ecological distribution conflicts and valuation. To repeat: driven by consumption, the throughput of energy and materials in the world economy has never been so great as it is today. Paradoxically, increases in eco-efficiency lead sometimes to increased demands for material and energy because their costs diminish (the Jevons effect). Also expectations of economic growth lead to discounting the future and therefore to more degradation of resources today, and to less growth in the future (the optimist's paradox). We are certainly not in a 'post-material' age. Externalities (that is, cost shifting) must be seen as part and parcel of the economy, which is necessarily open to the entry of resources and to the exit of residues. The appropriation of resources and the production of waste result in ecological distribution conflicts, which give rise sometimes to environmental movements.

Coming now to valuation, conflicts over the access to natural resources, or the exposure to environmental burdens and risks, may be expressed in two ways. First, they may be expressed within a single standard of valuation (usually monetary, but it could also be energetic, for instance). How should the externalities caused by a firm be valued in money terms, when asking for compensation in a court case? How could an argument for conservation of a natural space be made or contested, in terms of the number and biological value of the species it contains, or in terms of its net primary production? An appeal to the particular experts is appropriate here, economists versed in cost–benefit analysis and contingent valuation, in the first case, or biologists in the second instance.

The second possible means of expression is through a contest or dispute over the standards of value to be applied, as when losses of biodiversity, or of cultural patrimony, damage to human livelihoods or infringements of human rights are compared in non-commensurable terms to economic gains from a new dam, a mining project or oil extraction. There is a clash in standards of valuation when the languages of environmental justice, indigenous territorial rights or environmental security are deployed against monetary valuation of environmental risks and burdens. Non-compensatory multi-criteria decision aids, integrated assessment and participatory methods of conflict resolution are more appropriate for this second, very common, type of situation, than the mere appeal to the disciplinary experts. Indeed, such methods may be understood as applied political ecology.

Any social group can use simultaneously different standards of value in support of their interests. This is particularly true of subordinate social groups. That is, the claims to environmental resources and services of others who are differentially empowered and endowed can be contested by arguing within a single standard of value or across plural values. Appeal to different value standards comes from different cultural backgrounds and also from different interests.

So the relations between political ecology and economic valuation are as follows. First, the pattern of prices in the economy will depend on the concrete outcomes of ecological distribution conflicts. Second, ecological distribution conflicts (which often arise outside the market) are not fought only through demands for monetary compensation established in actual or fictitious market places; they may be fought out in other arenas.

Moreover, in complex situations marked by uncertainties and synergies, the disciplinary approach of the experts (each of them with her or his value standard) is not appropriate. So incommensurability of values arises also because of complexity. Thus, when a group claims that biodiversity has an intrinsic value which cannot be translated into money terms, this does not necessarily mean that they do not understand the language of monetary compensation. The theorists of postnormal science, Funtowicz and Ravetz (1994), write

In the first place monetary value will be seen as a measure of one aspect of value reflecting one particular sort of interest, that which is mainly expressed through the commercial market [or through fictitious markets as in contingent valuation]. To choose any particular operational definition for value involves making a decision about what is important and real; other definitions will reflect the commitments of other stakeholders . . . This entails a plurality of legitimate perspectives and values.

The ecological economists, O'Connor and Spash (1999: 5) write:

This divergence in valuation perspectives can be introduced in terms of two different conceptions of *internalization*. The diagnosis in both versions is that decisionmakers have failed to take proper account of the impacts of human activity upon the natural environment and the remedy is taking the environment properly into account. The two formulations are:
* Internalization of environmental damages in a narrow sense, referring to an idea of Pareto efficiency in resource allocation.
** Internalization in a broad sense, referring to political processes and institutions for expressing and resolving or accepting [or exacerbating] conflicts over environmental concerns.

VALUES FROM THE BOTTOM UP

Classical and neoclassical economics differed on theories of value. Classical economists saw value as a substance embodied in the commodities, as in the labour theory of economic value of Ricardo and Marx. (There was a faint echo of such theory in energy theories of value of the 1970s.) Moreover, classical economics linked up value theory and social relations of distribution of property and power. The neoclassical economists from the 1870s until today were socially neutral. They explained that value equals price. The economy could be seen as an isolated system where prices were explained by supply and demand. In its turn, in order to explain supply, appeal was made to production theory (firms maximize profits by equalizing marginal revenue with marginal cost) and, in order to explain demand, appeal was made to consumption theory (consumers maximize utility, on a single dimension, following an analogous rule). Neoclassical environmental and resource economists still wish today to close down the debate on value, claiming that the economy must be seen as a closed system. They try and bring negative externalities and positive environmental services into the measuring rod of money, and they have to use arbitrary discount rates to compare present and future utilities and costs.

Now ecological economics has opened up again the debate on value going beyond its economic dimensions. Ecological economists willingly accept that there are many values, and they devise decision aids and also methods of macroeconomic evaluation and integrated assessment, able to (weakly) compare alternative situations across such plural economic, physical, social and cultural values. There have been some doubts among practising ecological economists as to whether we were searching for a new value theory (perhaps embodied energy?) or whether we were, on the contrary, searching for the true economic value of environmental services (Costanza *et al.*, 1998). Recent years have seen an agreement being reached that ecological economics is built upon value pluralism. Its foundation is weak comparability of values as defined by O'Neill (1993), and as already discussed by Otto Neurath in the 1920s. In project evaluation, this is not implemented by CBA (which is reductionist) but by Multi-criteria evaluation (MCE) methods, without trade-offs. When people are forced to travel at the back of the bus, this cannot be compensated by a cheaper fare. In the present book, value pluralism has been put in the foreground, not so much by theoretical discussions of incommensurability and comparability of values (see Chapter 2), but by a different strategy of research, namely, that of looking at concrete ecological conflicts from the bottom up, bringing into the open the diverse languages of valuation deployed by different social actors when arguing their case in struggles characterized as 'the environmentalism of the poor'. Now the structural similarities in such conflicts around the globe must make it clear that this book, though very attentive to different vocabularies and idioms of valuation, is not a book of discourse analysis in the mould of cultural theory. It is rather a book on the relations between ecological economics and political ecology.

To conclude, the environmentalism of the poor, popular environmentalism, livelihood ecology, liberation ecology and the movement for environmental justice (local and global), growing out of the complaints against the appropriation of communal environmental resources and against the disproportionate burdens of pollution, may help to move society and economy in the direction of ecological sustainability. This is one connection between political ecology, as the study of ecological distribution conflicts, and ecological economics, as the study of the ecological unsustainability of the economy. Strong ecological distribution conflicts may promote sustainability.

Ecological distribution conflicts are sometimes expressed as discrepancies of valuation inside one single standard of value (as when there is a disputed claim for monetary compensation for an environmental liability), but they often lead to multi-criteria disputes (or dialogues) which rest on different standards of valuation. What is 'the cost of living?' asked Arundhati Roy in the Narmada Valley. In which currency must it be paid? What is 'the price of oil?' asked Human Rights Watch in a report of 1999 on the Niger Delta. *Todo necio/confunde valor y precio*, declared long ago an Andalusian poet, who died in 1939 in northern Catalonia. When the study of an ecological distribution conflict reveals a clash of incommensurable values, then we can say also that political ecology is contributing to the development of an ecological economics which moves beyond the obsession of 'taking nature into account' in money terms, and which is able therefore to cope with value pluralism.

PROCEDURAL POWER

The emerging field of political ecology analyses the links between power inequalities and environmental degradation. Not only non-human species and future generation of humans are damaged, but also some sections of humanity suffer disproportionate damage from environmental degradation today. Social movements born of such ecological distribution conflicts attempt to redress the balance of power, so heavily biased today in favour of multinational corporations. From the perspective of political ecology, the encounter between economic growth, inequality and environmental degradation must be analysed in terms of power relations.

Power, in this book, appears at two different levels: first, as the ability to impose a decision on others, for instance to steal resources, to locate an environmentally damaging plant, to destroy a forest, or to occupy environmental space and dispose of residues. Externalities are understood as cost-shifting. Second, as the procedural power which, in the face of complexity, is able nevertheless to impose a language of valuation determining which is the bottom-line in an ecological distribution conflict.[9] Governance requires the integration into policy (whether greenhouse policy or European agricultural policy or local urban policies) of scientific and lay opinions, sometimes contradictory among themselves, relevant for different scales and different levels of reality. Who then has the power to decide the procedure for such integrated analysis? Who has the power to simplify complexity, ruling some languages of valuation out of order? This is one basic issue for ecological economics and for political ecology.

NOTES

1. Cf. Mary Sol Bejarano, master's thesis on the Antisana National Park, FLACSO, Quito, 1999. Also, on the buffer zone of Aiguestortes and St. Maurici National Park in Catalonia, see Neus Martí *et al.*, 'Baqueira no? El proyecto Diafanis de evaluación ambiental', *Ecología Política*, 20, 2000.
2. *The Hindu*, 6 August 2001.

3. The OilWatch/NGO Kyoto Declaration of 2 December 1997 may be found in www.oilwatch.org.ec and in websites of many other organizations.
4. *Notebook*, a newsletter from the CSE, New Delhi, 5, April–June 1996, p.9.
5. Letter published in *Ecología Política*, 14, 1997.
6. Article in the newspaper, *La Republica*, Lima, 6 April 1991.
7. Kathleen Cooper, Canadian Environmental Law Association, www.cela.ca, May 2001. Also Allan Robinson, 'Peruvian mine site a political flashpoint', *Globe and Mail* (Toronto), 28 March 2001; 'Tambogrande: el oro de la disputa', *La Revista Agraria* (Lima), n.25, April 2001; *The Economist*, 23 June 2001. I visited Tambo Grande on 15 July 2001.
8. F. Torres Guevara, 'Desarrollo de Piura: Agro o Minería', Ms. May 2001, (botanic@mixmail.com).
9. 'Procedural power' has been used by Serafin Corral Quintana in this sense, in his doctoral dissertation, directed by Giuseppe Munda, on air pollution from power stations in Tenerife.

Bibliography

Acevedo, A.L. (1983), *Investigación a la Forestal*, Centro Editor de América Latina, Buenos Aires.

Adeola, F.O. (2000), 'Cross-national environmental injustice and human rights', *American Behavioral Scientist*, **43** (4): 686–706.

Agarwal, A. and S. Narain (1991), 'Global warming: a case of environmental colonialism', Centre for Science and Environment, Delhi.

Agarwal, B. (1992), 'The Gender and Environment Debate: Lessons from India', *Feminist Studies*, **18** (1).

Agarwal, B. (1998), 'Environmental management, equity and ecofeminism: debating India's experience', *Journal of Peasant Studies*, **25** (4): 55–95, July.

Ahmed, F. (1997), 'In defence of land and livelihood. Coastal communities and the shrimp industry in Asia', Consumers' Association of Penang, CUSO, InterPares, Sierra Club of Canada, Ottawa and Penang.

Altieri, M.A. and S. Hecht (eds) (1990), *Agroecology and Small Farm Development*, CRC Press, Boca Raton.

Altieri, M.A. and L.C. Merrick (1987), 'In situ conservation of crop genetic resources through maintenance of traditional farming systems', *Economic Botany*, **41** (1): 86–96.

Altvater, E. (1993), *The Future of the Market*, Verso, London.

Altvater, E. (1994), 'Ecological and economic modalities of space and time', in M. O'Connor (ed.), *Is Capitalism Sustainable? Political Economy and the Politics of Ecology*, Guildford, New York.

Altvater, E. (1987), *Sachzwang Weltmarkt. Verschuldungskrise, blockierte Industrialisierung, oekologische Gefaehrdung*, VSA, Hamburg.

Alvarez, L., 'Senate and Clinton still stalled on Nuclear Waste Disposal', *New York Times*, 11 February 2000.

Amorín, C. (2000), *Las semillas de la muerte. Basura tóxica y subdesarrollo: el caso Delta & Pine*, Libros de la Catarata, Madrid.

Anderson, M.R. (1996), 'The conquest of smoke: legislation and pollution in colonial Calcutta', in Arnold, D. and Guha, R. (eds).

Appfel-Marglin, F. and PRATEC (1998), *The Spirit of Regeneration: Andean Culture confronting Western Notions of Development*, Zed, London.

Arnold, D. and R. Guha (eds) (1996), *Nature, Culture and Imperialism: Essays on the Environmental History of South Asia*, Oxford University Press, Delhi.

Arrow K. *et al.* (1995), 'Economic growth, carrying capacity and the environment', *Ecological Economics*, **15** (2): 91–6.

Avery, D. (1974), *Not on Queen Victoria's Birthday: The Story of the Rio Tinto Mines*, Collins, London.

Ayres R.U., 'Industrial Metabolism', in J. Ausubel (ed.) (1989), *Technology and Environment*, National Academy Press, Washington, DC.

Ayres, R.U. and L. Ayres (1996), *Industrial Ecology: Towards Closing the Materials Cycle,* Edward Elgar, Cheltenham, UK and Brookfield, US.

Ayres, R.U. and L. Ayres (2001), *Handbook of Industrial Ecology*, Edward Elgar, Cheltenham, UK and Northampton, MA, US.

Azar, C. and J. Holmberg (1995), 'Defining the generational environmental debt', *Ecological Economics*, **14**: 7–19.

Azar, C. and H. Rodhe (1997), 'Targets for stabilization of atmospheric CO_2', *Science*, **276**: 1818–19.

Azar, C. and T. Sterner (1996), 'Discounting and distributional considerations in the context of global warming', *Ecological Economics*, **19**: 169–84.

Balvin, D. and J. Tejedo Huaman and H. Lozada Castro (1995), *Agua, Minería y Contaminación. El caso Southern Peru*, Labor, Ilo.

Barham, B., S.G. Bunker and D. O'Hearn (1994), *States, Firms and Raw Materials: The World Economy and Ecology of Aluminum*, University of Wisconsin Press, Madison.

Barnett, H.J. and C. Morse (1963), *Scarcity and Growth: The Economics of Natural Resource Availability*, Johns Hopkins Press, Baltimore.

Bathia, B. (2001), 'Jadugoda: Fighting an invisible enemy', *The Hindu Survey of the Environment 2001*, Chennai.

Baviskar, A. (1995), *In the Belly of the River: Tribal Conflict over Development in the Narmada Valley*, Oxford University Press, Delhi.

Beck, U. (1992), *Risk Society: Towards a New Modernity*, Sage, London.

Beckenbach, F. (1996), 'Ecological and economic distribution as elements of the evolution of modern societies', *Journal of Income Distribution*, **6** (2): 163–91.

Becker, E. and T. Jahn (eds) (1999), *Sustainability and the social sciences*, Zed, London.

Beinart, W. and P. Coates (1995), *Environment and History: The Taming of Nature in the USA and South Africa*, Routledge, London and New York.

Berkes, F. (ed.) (1989), *Common Property Resources: Ecology and Community-Based Sustainable Development*, Belhaven, London.

Berkes, F. (1999), *Sacred Ecology: Traditional Ecological Knowledge and Resource Management*, Taylor and Francis, Philadelphia.

Berkes, F. and C. Folke (eds) (1998), *Linking Social and Ecological Systems: Management Practices and Social Mechanisms for Building Resilience*, Cambridge University Press, Cambridge.

Bertell, R. and G. Tognoni (1996), 'International Medical Commission, Bhopal: a model for the future', *The National Medical Journal of India*, **9** (2): 86–91.

Bettini, V. (1998), *Elementos de ecología urbana*, Trotta, Madrid.

Blaikie, P. and H. Brookfield (eds) (1987), *Land Degradation and Society*, Methuen, London.

Boff, L. (1998), *Ecologia: grito de la Tierra, grito de los Pobres*, Trotta, Madrid.

Bond, P. (2000), 'Economic growth, ecological modernization or environmental justice? Conflicting discourses in post-apartheid South Africa', *Capitalism, Nature, Socialism*, **11** (1): 33–61.

Bonfil Batalla, G. (1996), *Mexico Profundo: Reclaiming a Civilization*, University of Texas Press, Austin.

Bonilla, H. (1994 [1974]), *Guano y Burguesia en el Peru*, 3rd edition, Flacso, Quito.

Borrero, J.M. (1994), *La Deuda Ecologica*, FIPMA, Cali.

Boserup, E. (1965), *The Conditions of Agricultural Growth: The Economics of Agrarian Change under Population Pressure*, Aldine, Chicago.

Boyce, J.K. (1995), 'Jute, polypropylene, and the environment: a study in international trade and market failure', *Bangladesh Development Studies*, **13**: 49–66.

Boyce, J.K. (1996), 'Ecological distribution, agricultural trade liberalization and in situ genetic diversity', *Journal of Income Distribution*, **6** (2): 263–284.

Boyden, S. (1987), *Western Civilization in Biological Perspective: Patterns in Biohistory*, Clarendon Press, Oxford.

Boyden, S., S. Millar, K. Newcombe and B. O'Neill (1981), *The Ecology of a City and its People. The Case of Hong Kong*, Australian National University, Canberra.

Brimblecombe, P. and Ch. Pfister (eds) (1990), *The Silent Countdown: Essays in European Environmental History*, Springer, Berlin.

Broad, R. and J. Cavanagh (1993), *Plundering Paradise: The Struggle for the Environment in the Philippines*, University of California Press, Berkeley.

Broadbent, J. (1998), *Environmental Politics in Japan: Networks of Power and Protest*, Cambridge University Press, New York.

Brosius, J.P. (1999a), 'Comments to A. Escoba; After nature: steps to an anti-essentialist political ecology', *Current Anthropology*, **40** (1).

Brosius, J.P. (1999b), 'Green dots, pink hearts: displacing politics from the Malaysian rain forest', *American Anthropologist*, **101** (1): 36–57.

Bruggemeier, F.J. and T. Rommelspacher (eds) (1987), *Besiegte Natur, Geschichte der Umwelt im 19 und 20 Jahrhundert*, C.H. Beck, Munich.

Bruggemeier, F.J. and T. Rommelspacher (1992), *Blauer Himmel ueber der Ruhr. Geschichte der Umwelt im Ruhrgebiet 1840–1990*, Klartext, Essen.

Brunhs, B-I. and K. Kappel (eds) (1992), 'Oekologische Zerstoerungen in Afrika und alternative Strategien', *Bremer Afrika Studien*, **1**, Lit Verlag, Munster.

Bruyn, S.M. de and J.B. Opschoor (1997), 'Developments in the through-put–income relationship: theoretical and empirical observations', *Ecological Economics*, **20**: 255–68.

Bryant, B. (ed) (1995), *Environmental Justice: Issues, Policies and Solutions*, Island Press, Washington, DC.

Bryant, B. and P. Mohai (eds) (1992), *Race and the Incidence of Environmental Hazards*, Westview, Boulder.

Bryant, R. (1997), *Political Ecology of Forestry in Burma 1826–1993*, Oxford University Press, Delhi.

Bryant, R. and S. Bailey (eds) (1997), *Third World Political Ecology*, Routledge, London.

Bullard, R. (1990), *Dumping in Dixie: Race, Class and Environmental Quality*, Westview, Boulder.

Bullard, R. (1993), *Confronting Environmental Racism: Voices from the Grassroots*, South End Press, Boston.

Bunker, S. (1985), *Underdeveloping the Amazon: Extraction, Unequal Exchange, and the Failure of the Modern State*, University of Illinois Press, Chicago.

Bunker, S. (1996), 'Raw materials and the global economy: oversights and distortions in industrial ecology', *Society and Natural Resources*, **9**: 419–29.

Cabeza Gutés, M. and J. Martinez-Alier (2001), 'L'échange écologique-ment inégal', in Michel Damian and Jean Christophe Graz (eds), *Commerce International et Développement Soutenable*, Economica, Paris.

Callicott, J.B. and M.P. Nelson (eds) (1998), *The Great Wilderness Debate*, University of Georgia Press, Athens.

Camacho, D.E. (ed) (1998), *Environmental Injustices, Political Struggles: Race, Class and the Environment*, Duke University Press, Durham and London.

Carrere, R. and L. Lohman (1996), *Pulping the South: Industrial Tree Plantations and the World Paper Economy*, Zed, London.

Castells, M. (1983), *The City and the Grassroots*, University of California Press, Berkeley.

Cleveland, C. and M. Ruth (1998), 'Indicators of dematerialization and the materials intensity of use', *Journal of Industrial Ecology*, **2**: 15–50.

Cock, J. and E. Koch (eds) (1991), *Going Green: People, Politics and the Environment in South Africa*, Oxford University Press, Cape Town.

Cohen, J. (1995), *How Many People Can the Earth Support?*, Norton, London and New York.

Common, M. (1995), *Sustainability and Policy: Limits to Economics*, Cambridge University Press, New York.

Conklin, H.C. (1957), '*Hanun'oo agriculture: a report on an integral system of shifting cultivation in the Philippines*', FAO, Rome.

Costanza, R. (ed.) (1991), *Ecological Economics: The Science and Management of Sustainability*, Columbia University Press, New York.

Costanza R. and C. Perrings (1990), 'A flexible assurance bonding system for improved environmental management', *Ecological Economics*, **2**: 57–76.

Costanza, R., C. Cleveland and C. Perrings (eds) (1997), *The Development of Ecological Economics*, Edward Elgar, Cheltenham, UK and Lyme, US.

Costanza, R., J. Cumberland, H. Daly, R. Goodland and R. Norgaard (1997), *An Introduction to Ecological Economics*, St. Lucie Press, Boca Raton.

Costanza R. *et al.*, (1998), 'The value of the world's ecosystem services and natural capital', *Ecological Economics*, **25** (1).

Cronon, W. (ed.) (1996), *Uncommon Ground: Rethinking the Human Place in Nature*, Norton, New York.

Daily, G. (ed.) (1997), *Nature's Services: Societal Dependence on Natural Ecosystems*, Island Press, Washington, DC.

Daly, H. (1999), 'The lurking inconsistency', *Conservation Biology*, **13** (4): 693–4.

Daly, H. and J. Cobb (1994), *For the Common Good: Redirecting the Economy Toward Community, the Environment and a Sustainable Future*, 2nd edition, Beacon Press, Boston.

Dean, W. (1995), *With Broadax and Firebrand: The Destruction of the Brazilian Atlantic Forest*, California University Press, Berkeley.

Dembo, D., W. Morehouse and L. Wykle (1990), *Abuse of Power. Social Performance of Multinational Corporations: The Case of Union Carbide*, New Horizons Press, New York.

Desai, S. (1998), 'Engendering population policy', in M. Krishnaraj *et al.* (eds).

Descola, P. (1994), *In the Society of Nature: A Native Ecology in Amazonia*, Cambridge University Press, Cambridge.

Deudney, D.H. and R.H. Matthew (eds) (1999), *Contested Grounds: Security and Conflict in the New Environmental Politics*, SUNY Press, Albany.

Devall, B. and G. Sessions (1985), *Deep Ecology*, G.M. Smith, Salt Lake City.

Diaz-Palacios, J. (1998), *El Perú y su medio ambiente. Southern Peru Copper Corporation: una compleja agresión ambiental en el sur del país*, IDMA, Lima.

DiChiro, G. (1998), 'Nature as Community. The Convergence of Environmental and Social Justice', in Michael Goldman (ed.), 1998.

Divan, S. and A. Rosencranz (2001), *Environmental Law and Policy in India: Cases, Materials and Statutes*, Oxford University Press, Delhi.

Dobson, A. (1998), *Justice and the Environment: Conceptions of Environmental Sustainability and Dimensions of Social Justice*, Oxford University Press, Oxford.

Doo Kingue, M. (1996), 'Prospects for Africa's economic recovery and development', in A.Y. Yansane (ed.), *Prospects for Recovery and Sustainable Development in Africa*, Greenwood Press, Westport CT and London.

Dore, E. (2000), 'Environment and society: long-term trends in Latin American mining', *Environment and History*, **6**: 1–29 (previous version in Spanish in *Ecologia Politica*, **7**, 1994).

Dorsey, M. (1997), 'El movimiento por la Justicia Ambiental en EE.UU. Una breve historia', *Ecologia Politica*, **14**: 23–32.

Downs, A. (1972), 'Up and down with ecology: the issue-attention cycle', *Public Interest*, **28**, Summer.

Draisma, T. (1998), Mining and ecological degradation in Zambia: who bears the brunt when privatization clashes with Rio 1992?', Environmental Justice and Global Ethics Conference, Melbourne, October 1997; revised version, August 1998.

Dryzeck, J.S. (1994), 'Ecology and discursive democracy: beyond liberal capitalism and the administrative state', in M. O'Connor (ed.), *Is Capitalism Sustainable?*, Guildford, New York.

Duchin, F. (1998), *Structural Economics: Measuring Change in Technology, Lifestyles, and the Environment*, Island Press, Washington, DC.

Duffield, A.J. (1877), *Peru in the Guano Age. Being a short account of a recent visit to the guano deposits, with some reflections on the money they have produced and the uses to which it has been applied*, R. Bentley & Son, London.

Ehrlich, P.R. (1968), *The Population Bomb*, Ballantine, New York.

Ekins, P. and M. Max-Neef (eds) (1992), *Real-life Economics: Understanding Wealth Creation*, Routledge, London.

Emmanuel, A. (1972), *Unequal Exchange: A Study of the Imperialism of Free Trade*, Monthly Review, New York.

Epstein, B. (2000), 'Grassroots environmentalism and strategies for social change', New Social Movements Network, updated 28 February 2000, downloaded from www.interwebtech.com/nsmnet/docs/epstein.htm.

Erickson, J.D. and D. Chapman (1993), 'Sovereignty for sale. Nuclear waste in Indian country', *Akwe:kon Journal*, Fall, 3–10.

Erickson, J.D., D. Chapman and R.E. Johny (1994), 'Monitored retrievable storage of spent nuclear fuel in Indian country: liability, sovereignty, and socio-economics', *American Indian Law Review*, University of Oklahoma College of Law, 73–103.

Escobar, A. (1995), *Encountering Development: The Making and Unmaking of the Third World*, Princeton University Press, Princeton, NJ.

Escobar, A. (1996), 'Constructing nature. Elements for a post-structural political ecology', in R. Peet and M. Watts (eds).

Faber, D. (ed.) (1998), *The Struggle for Ecological Democracy: The Environmental Justice Movement in the United States*, Guildford, New York.

Faber, M., R. Manstetten and J.L.R. Proops (1996), *Ecological Economics: Concepts and Methods*, Edward Elgar, Cheltenham, UK and Brookfield, US.

Faucheux, S. and M. O'Connor (eds) (1998), *Valuation for Sustainable Development: Methods and Policy Indicators*, Edward Elgar, Cheltenham, UK and Lyme, US.

Fearnside, P. (1997), 'Environmental services as a strategy for sustainable development in Amazonia', *Ecological Economics*, **20** (1): 53–70.

Ferrero Blanco, M.D. (1994), *Capitalismo minero y resistencia rural en el suroeste andaluz. Rio Tinto 1873–1900*, Diputación Provincial, Huelva.

Finn, J.L. (1998), *Tracing the Veins: Of Copper, Culture and Community from Butte to Chuquicamata*, University of California Press, Berkeley.

Fischer-Kowalski, M. (1998), 'Society's metabolism: the intellectual history of materials flow analysis', *Journal of Industrial Ecology*, Part I: 1860–1970, vol. 2 (1), Part II: 1970–1998 (with Walter Huettler), **2** (4).

Fischer-Kowalski, M. and H. Haberl (1997), 'Tons, joules and money: Modes of production and their sustainability problems', *Society and Natural Resources*, **10** (1): 61–8.

French, H. (2000), *Vanishing Borders: Protecting the Planet in the Age of Globalization*, Norton, New York.

Friedman, J. and H. Rangan (eds) (1993), *In Defense of Livelihood: Comparative Studies in Environmental Action*, UNRISD, Kumarian Press, Hartford, CT.

Funtowicz, S. and J. Ravetz (1991), 'A new scientific methodology for global environmental issues', in R. Costanza (ed.).

Funtowicz, S. and J. Ravetz (1994), 'The worth of a songbird: ecological economics as a post-normal science'. *Ecological Economics*, **10** (3): 189–96.

Gade, D.W. (1999), *Nature and Culture in the Andes*, University of Wisconsin Press, Madison, Wisconsin.

Gadgil, M. and R. Guha (1995), *Ecology and Equity: The Use and Abuse of Nature in Contemporary India*, Routledge, London.

Gallopin, G. (ed.) (1995), *El futuro ecológico de un continente. Una visión prospectiva de la América latina*, vols 1 and 2, Fondo de Cultura Económica, Mexico.

Gámez, R. (1999), *De biodiversidad, gentes y utopías. Reflexiones en los 10 años del INBio*, Instituto Nacional de Biodiversidad, San Jose.

Garcia, X. (1990), *La Catalunya nuclear (la Ribera d'Ebre: centre d'una àmplia perifèria espoliada)*, Columna, Barcelona.

Garcia Pulido, J. (1975), *La explotación del quebracho e historia de una empresa*, Librería y Papelería Casa García, Resistencia.

Garcia Rey, J. (1996), 'Nerva: No al vertedero. Historia de un pueblo en lucha', *Ecologia Politica*, **13**.

Garí, J.A. (2000), 'The political ecology of biodiversity', DPhil thesis, University of Oxford.

Gedicks, A. (1993), *The New Resource Wars: Native and Environmental Struggles against Multinational Corporations*, South End Press, Boston.

Gedicks, A. (2001), *Resource Rebels: Native Challenges to Mining and Oil Corporations*, South End Press, Boston.

Georgescu-Roegen, N. (1971), *The Entropy Law and the Economic Process*, Harvard University Press, Cambridge MA.

Ghai, D. and J.M. Vivian (eds) (1992), *Grassroots Environmental Action: People's Participation in Sustainable Development*, Routledge, London.

Gibbon, P. (1997), 'Prawns and piranhas: the political economy of a Tanzanian private sector marketing chain', *Journal of Peasant Studies*, **24** (4): 1–86.

Gibbs, L.M. (1981), *Love Canal: My Story*, State University of New York Press, Albany.

Gibbs, L.M. (1995), *Dying from Dioxin: A Citizen's Guide to Reclaiming our Health and Rebuilding Democracy*, South End Press, Boston.

Gilbert, A.J. and R. Janssen (1998), 'Use of environmental functions to communicate the values of a mangrove ecosystem under different management regimes', *Ecological Economics*, **25**: 323–46.

Goldman, M. (ed.) (1998), *Privatizing Nature: Political Struggles for the Global Commons*, Pluto, London.

Goldsmith, E. and N. Hildyard (1984), *The Social and Environmental Effects of Large Dams*, Sierra Club Bks, San Francisco.

Goldstein, K. (1992), 'The green movement in Brazil', in M. Finger (ed.), *Research in Social Movements, Conflicts and Change: Suppl. 2, The Green Movement Worldwide*, JAI Press, Greenwich, CT.

Gootenberg, P. (1993), *Imagining Development: Economic Ideas in Peru's 'Fictitious Prosperity' of Guano, 1840–1880*, University of California Press, Berkeley.

Gopinath, N. and P. Gabriel (1997), 'Management of living resources in the Matang Reserve, Perak, Malaysia', in C.H. Freese, *Harvesting Wild Species: Implications for Biodiversity Conservation*, Johns Hopkins University Press, Baltimore.

Gordon, L. (1976), *Woman's Body, Woman's Right: A Social History of Birth Control in America*, Grossman, New York.

Gori, G. (1999), *La Forestal: La Tragedia del Quebracho Colorado*, 2nd edition, preface by Osvaldo Bayer, Ameghin, Rosario-Buenos Aires.

Gosling, D.L. (2001), *Religion and Ecology in India and Southeast Asia*, Routledge, London and New York.

Gottlieb, R. (1993), *Forcing the Spring: The Transformation of the American Environmental Movement*, Island Press, Washington DC.

Gould, K.A., A. Schnaiberg and A. Weinberg (1996), *Local Environmental Struggles: Citizen Activism in the Treadmill of Production*, Cambridge University Press, New York.

Gowdy, J. (1992), 'Georgescu-Roegen's utility theory applied to environmental economics', in J.C. Dragan, M. Demetrescu and E. Seifert (eds), *Entropy and Bioeconomics*, Nagard Publishers, Milan.

Greenpeace (1988), *International Trade in Toxic Waste*, Brussels.

Greenpeace (1994), *The Database of Known Hazardous Waste Exports from OECD to non-OECD Countries, 1989–94*, Washington, DC.

Grove, R. (1994), *Green Imperialism: The Colonial Expansion, Tropical Island Edens and the Origins of Environmentalism 1600–1840*, Oxford University Press, Delhi.

Grove, R., V. Damodaran and S. Sangwan (eds) (1998), *Nature and the Orient: The Environmental History of South and Southeast Asia*, Oxford University Press, Delhi.

Grueso, L., C. Rosero and A. Escobar (1997), 'El proceso organizativo de comunidades negras en Colombia', *Ecologia Politica*, **14**.

Guha, R. (2000), *The Unquiet Woods: Ecological Change and Peasant Resistance in the Himalaya*, University of California Press, Berkeley, 1989; revised edn 2000.

Guha, R. (2000), *Environmentalism: A Global History*, Longman, New York and Oxford University Press, Delhi.

Guha, R. and J. Martinez-Alier (1997), *Varieties of Environmentalism: Essays North and South*, Earthscan, London and Oxford University Press, Delhi.

Guha, R. and J. Martinez-Alier (1999), 'Political ecology, the environmentalism of the poor and the global movement for environmental justice', *Kurswechsel* (Vienna), **3**, 27–40.

Guha, R. and J. Martinez-Alier (2000), 'The environmentalism of the poor and the global movement for environmental justice', in Werner G. Raza (ed.), *Recht auf Umwelt oder Umwelt ohne Recht?*, Brandes und Apsel, Frankfurt, Südwind, Vienna.

Guimaraes, R. (1991), *The Ecopolitics of Development in the Third World: Politics and the Environment in Brazil*, Lynne Rienner, Boulder.

Gupta, A. (1996), 'Social and ethical dimensions of ecological economics', in R. Costanza, O. Segura and J. Martinez-Alier (eds), *Getting Down to Earth: Practical Applications of Ecological Economics*, ISEE, Island Press, Washington, DC.

Haberl, H. (1997), 'Human appropriation of net primary production as an environmental indicator: implications for sustainable development', *Ambio*, **26** (3): 143–6.

Haberl, H. (2001), 'The energetic metabolism of societies', Parts I and II, *Journal of Industrial Ecology*.

Haberl, H., K.H. Erb and F. Krausmann (2001), 'How to calculate and interpret ecological footprints for long periods of time: the case of Austria 1926–1995', *Ecological Economics*, 38, 25–45.

Hall, C., C. Cleveland and R. Kaufman, (1986), *Energy and Resources Quality: The Ecology of the Economic Process*, Wiley, New York.

Hamilton, L.S. and S.C. Snekader (eds) (1984), *Handbook for Mangrove Area Management,* Environment and Policy Institute, East–West Center (Hawai), IUCN, UNESCO.

Handberg, H. (1998), 'A study of people's conception of the social consequences of the shrimp farming industry in two local communities in coastal Ecuador', Department of Anthropology, University of Oslo, November.

Hanna, S. and M. Munasinghe (1995), *Property Rights and the Environment: Social and Ecological Issues*, Beijer International Institute of Ecological Economics and World Bank, Washington, DC.

Hardiman, D. (2000), 'The politics of water: well irrigation in Western India', paper for a seminar on Environment and Development, Yale University, 14 February.

Hayek, F. von (ed.) (1935), *Collectivist Economic Planning*, Routledge, London.

Hayek, F. von (1979), *The Counter-Revolution of Science: Studies on the Abuse of Reason*, 1952; Liberty Press, Indianapolis.

Hays, S. (1959), *Conservation and the Gospel of Efficiency: The Progressive Conservation Movement 1898–1929*, Harvard University Press, Cambridge, MA.

Hays, S. (1998), *Explorations in Environmental History*, University of Pittsburgh Press, Pittsburgh.

Hecht, S. and A. Cockburn (1990), *The Fate of the Forest: Developers, Destroyers and Defenders of the Amazon*, Penguin, London.

Hicks, A.H. (1956), *The Story of the Forestal,* published by The Forestal Land, Timber and Railway Company, Ltd., Shell-Mex House, Strand, London, produced by Newman Neame, London.

Hille, J. (1997), *The Concept of Environmental Space. Implications for Policies, Environmental Reporting and Assessments*, European Environment Agency, Experts' Corner no. 2, Copenhagen.

Hirsch, F. (1976), *Social Limits to Growth*, Harvard University Press, Cambridge, MA.

Hobsbawm, E. (1994), *Age of Extremes: The Short Twentieth Century 1914–1991*, Michael Joseph, London.

Hofrichter, R. (ed.) (1993), *Toxic Struggles: The Theory and Practice of Environmental Justice*, foreword by Lois Gibbs, New Society Publishers, Philadelphia.

Hombergh, H. van den (1999), *Guerreros del Golfo Dulce: Industria forestal y conflicto en la Peninsula de Osa, Costa Rica*, DEI, San José.

Hornborg, A. (1998), 'Toward an ecological theory of unequal exchange: articulating world system theory and ecological economics', *Ecological Economics*, **25** (1): 127–36.

Howard, A. (1940), *An Agricultural Testament*, Oxford University Press, 1940; last edition 1999.

Howard, L. (1953), *Sir Albert Howard in India*, Faber & Faber, London.

Hueting, R. (1980), *New Scarcity and Economic Growth: More Welfare Through Less Production?*, North-Holland, Amsterdam.

Human Rights Watch (1999a), 'The price of oil: corporate responsibility and human rights violations in Nigeria's oil producing communities'.

Human Rights Watch (1999b), 'Toxic justice: human rights, justice and toxic waste in Cambodia'.

Indian People's Tribunal on Environment and Human Rights (2001), 'An enquiry into the Bandra Worli Sea Link Project', Mumbai, July (www.indiarights.org).

Inglehart, R. (1977), *The Silent Revolution: Changing Values and Political Styles Among Western Publics*, Princeton University Press, Princeton.

Inglehart, R. (1999), *Culture Shift in Advanced Industrial Societies*, Princeton University Press, Princeton.

Inglehart, R. (1995), 'Public support for environmental protection: objective problems and subjective values in 43 societies', *Political Science and Politics*, **28** (1).

Jackson, T. and N. Marks (1999), 'Consumption, sustainable welfare, and human needs – with reference to UK expenditure patterns between 1954 and 1994', *Ecological Economics*, **28**: 421–41.

Jaenicke, M. (1993), 'Ueber oekologische und politische Modernisierung', *Zeitschrift fur Umweltpolitik und Umweltrecht*, **2**: 159–75.

Jansson, A.M. (ed.) (1984), *Integration of economy and ecology: an outlook for the eighties*, Wallenberg Symposium, Department of Systems Ecology, University of Stockholm.

Jodha, N.S. (1986), 'Common property resources and the rural poor', *Economic and Political Weekly*, **21** (27): 1169–81.

Jodha, N.S. (2001), *Life on the Edge: Sustaining Agriculture and Community Resources in Fragile Environments*, Oxford University Press, Delhi.

Jongh, P.E. de and S. Captain (1999), *Our Common Journey: A Pioneering Approach to Cooperative Environmental Management*, Zed, London and New York.

Kalland, A. and G. Persoon (eds) (1998), *Environmental Movements in Asia*, Curzon Press, Richmond (Surrey).

Keil, R. *et al.* (eds) (1998), *Political Ecology: Global and Local*, Routledge, London.

Kellert, S.R. (1997), *Kinship to Mastery: Biophilia in Human Evolution and Development*, Island Press, Washington, DC.

Kellert, S.R. and E.O. Wilson (eds) (1993), *The Biophilia Hypothesis*, Island Press, Washington, DC.

King, S.R. and T.J. Carlson (1995), 'Biocultural diversity, biomedicine and ethnobotany: the experience of Shaman Pharmaceuticals', *Intersciencia*, **20** (3): 134–9.

King, S.R., T.J. Carlson and K. Moran (1996), 'Biological diversity, indigenous knowledge, drug discovery and intellectual property rights', in S. Brush and D. Stabinsky (eds), *Valuing Local Knowledge: Indigenous People and Intellectual Property Rights*, Island Press, Washington, DC.

Kloppenburg, J. (ed.) (1988a), *Seeds and Sovereignty: The Use and Control of Plant Genetic Resources*, Duke University Press, Durham and London.

Kloppenburg, J. (1988b), *First the Seed: The Political Economy of Plant Biotechnology*, Cambridge University Press, New York.

Kothari, A. (1997), *Understanding Biodiversity, Life, Sustainability and Equity*, Orient Longman, Hyderabad.

Kox, H.L.M. (1991), 'Integration of environmental externalities in international commodity agreements', *World Development*, **19** (8): 933–43.

Kox, H.L.M. (1997), 'Developing countries' primary exports and the internalization of environmental externalities', in J. van den Bergh and J. van der Straaten (eds), *Economy and Ecosystems in Change*, Edward Elgar, Cheltenham, UK and Lyme, US.

Krishnaraj, M. *et al.* (1998), *Gender, Population and Development*, Oxford University Press, Delhi.

Krutilla, J. (1967), 'Conservation reconsidered', *American Economic Review*, **57** (4).

Kuletz, V. (1998), *The Tainted Desert: Environmental and Social Ruin in the American West*, Routledge, New York.

Kurien, J. (1992), 'Ruining the commons and responses of the commoners: coastal overfishing and fishworkers' actions in Kerala State, India', in Ghai and Vivian (eds).

Kurien, J. (1997), 'Industrial fisheries and aquaculture', Proceedings of the South Asia workshop and symposium on fisheries and coastal area management, ICSF, Chennai.

Larsson, J., C. Folke and N. Kautsky (1994), 'Ecological limitations and appropriation of ecosystem support by shrimp farming in Colombia', *Environmental Management*, **18** (5): 663–76.

Latouche, S. (1991), *Le Planète des Naufrages*, La Découverte, Paris.

Lavalle y García, J.A. de (1913), *El Guano y la Agricultura Nacional*, Lima.

Leach, M. and R. Mearns (eds) (1996), *The Lie of the Land: Challenging Received Wisdom on the African Environment*, The International African Institute, in association with James Currey, Oxford and Heinemann, Portsmouth, NH.

Leff, E. (1995), *Green Production: Toward an Environmental Rationality*, Guildford, New York.

Leff, E. and J. Carabias (eds) (1992), *Cultura y manejo sustentable de los recursos naturales*, CIIH-UNAM, Mexico DF.

Leipert, C. (1989), *Die heimlichen Kosten des Fortschritts*, Fischer, Frankfurt.

Leopold, A. (1970), *A Sand County Almanac with Essays on Conservation from Round River*, Ballantine Books, New York.

Levin, J.V. (1960), *The Export Economies*, Harvard University Press, Cambridge, MA.

Lipman, Z. (1998), 'Trade in hazardous waste: environmental justice versus economic growth', Conference on Environmental Justice, Melbourne (http://spartan.unimelb.edu.au/envjust/papers).

Lohman, L. (1991), 'Peasants, plantations and pulp: the politics of eucalyptus in Thailand', *Bulletin of Concerned Asian Scholars*, **23** (4).

Lohman, L. (1996), 'Freedom to plant: Indonesia and Thailand in a globalizing pulp and paper industry', in M.J.G. Parnwell and R.L. Bryant (eds), *Environmental Change in South-East Asia: People, Politics and Sustainable Development*, Routledge, London and New York.

Lovins, A. and E.U. von Weizsaecker (1997), *Factor Four: Doubling Wealth, Halving Resource Use (the New Report to the Club of Rome)*, Earthscan, London.

Low, N. and B. Gleeson (1998), *Justice, Society and Nature: An Exploration of Political Ecology*, Routledge, London and New York.

Madsen, S.T. (ed.) (1999), *State, Society and the Environment in South Asia*, Nordic Institute of Asian Studies, Curzon, Richmond, Surrey.

Maiguashca, J. (1967), 'A reinterpretation of the Guano Age 1840–80', DPhil thesis, Oxford University.

Mallarach, J.M. (1995), 'Parques nacionales versus reservas indigenas en los Estados Unidos de America: un modelo en cuestión', *Ecología Política*, **10**.

Mallon, F. (1983), *The Defense of Community in Peru's Central Highlands*, Princeton University Press, Princeton.

Martine, G., M. DasGupta and L.C. Chen (1998), *Reproductive Change in India and Brazil*, Oxford University Press, Delhi.

Martinez-Alier, J. (1977), *Haciendas, Plantations and Collective Farms (Cuba and Peru)*, Frank Cass, London.

Martinez-Alier, J. (1991), 'Ecology and the poor: a neglected issue in Latin American history', *Journal of Latin American Studies*, **23** (3): 621–40.

Martinez-Alier, J. (1993), 'Distributional obstacles to international environmental policy. The failures at Rio and prospects after Rio', *Environmental Values*, **2**: 97–124.

Martinez-Alier, J. (1995a), *De la Economía Ecológica al Ecologismo Popular*, 3rd edition, Icaria-Nordan, Barcelona and Montevideo.

Martinez-Alier, J. (1995b), 'Political ecology, distributional conflicts and economic incommensurability', *New Left Review*, **211**: 70–88.

Martinez-Alier, J. (1996), 'In praise of smallholders. a review essay', *Journal of Peasant Studies*, **23** (1).

Martinez-Alier, J. (1997), 'The merchandising of biodiversity', *Etno-ecologica*, **3**, Mexico, 1994; reprinted in R. Guha and J. Martinez-Alier.

Martinez-Alier, J. and E. Hershberg (1992), 'Environmentalism and the poor', *Items*, Social Sciences Research Council, New York, **46** (1), March.

Martinez-Alier, J. and M. O'Connor (1996), 'Ecological and economic distribution conflicts', in R. Costanza, O. Segura and J. Martinez-Alier (eds), *Getting Down to Earth: Practical Applications of Ecological Economics*, ISEE, Island Press, Washington, DC.

Martinez-Alier, J. and M. O'Connor (1999), 'Distributional issues: an overview', in J. van den Bergh (ed.), *Handbook of Environmental and Resource Economics*, Edward Elgar, Cheltenham, UK and Northampton, MA, USA.

Martinez-Alier, J. with K. Schlüpmann (1987), *Ecological Economics: Energy, Environment and Society*, Blackwell, Oxford, 1987, paperback edition with new introduction, 1991.

Martinez-Alier, J., G. Munda and J. O'Neill (1998), 'Weak comparability of values as a foundation for ecological economics', *Ecological Economics*, **26**: 277–86.

Martinez-Alier, J., G. Munda and J. O'Neill (1999), 'Commensurability and compensability in ecological economics', in M. O'Connor and C. Spash (eds), *Valuation and the Environment*, Edward Elgar, Cheltenham, UK and Northampton, MA, USA.

Masjuan, E. (2000), *La ecología humana y el anarquismo ibérico. El urbanismo 'orgánico' o ecológico, el neomalthusianismo y el naturismo social*, Icaria, Barcelona.

Mathew, W.M. (1981), *The House of Gibbs and the Peruvian Guano Monopoly*, Royal Historical Society, London.

Matthew, R.A. (1999), 'Introduction: mapping contested grounds', in D.H. Deudney and R.A. Matthew (eds), *Contested Grounds: Security and Conflict in the New Environmental Politics*, SUNY Press, Albany.

Matthews, E. *et al.* (2000), *The Weight of Nations: Material Outflows from Industrial Economies*, World Resources Institute, Washington, DC.

McCay, B.J. and J.M. Acheson (eds) (1987), *The Question of the Commons: The Culture and Ecology of Communal Resources*, University of Arizona Press, Tucson.

McCully, P. (1996), *Silenced Rivers: The Ecology and Politics of Large Dams*, Zed, London.

McDaniel, C.N. and J. Gowdy (2000), *Paradise for Sale: A Parable of Nature*, University of California Press, Berkeley.

McDonald, D. (ed.) (2001), *Environmental Justice in South Africa*, Ohio University Press, Athens.

McGrath, D. *et al.* (1993), 'Fisheries and the evolution of resource management in the lower Amazon floodplain', *Human Ecology*, **21** (2).

McNeill, J.R. (2000), *Something New Under the Sun: An Environmental History of the Twentieth-Century World*, Norton, New York.

Mellor, M. (1997), 'Women, nature, and the social construction of "economic man"', *Ecological Economics*, **20** (2): 129–40.

Melone, M.A. (1993), 'The struggle of the Seringueiros: environmental action in the Amazon', in J. Friedman and H. Rangan (eds).

Melville, E. (1994), *A Plague of Sheep: Environmental Consequences of the Conquest of Mexico*, Cambridge University Press, Cambridge, UK.

Menon, M. (2001), 'Kashipur: bullets for bauxite', *The Hindu Survey of the Environment 2001*, Chennai, 2001.

Meyer, E. (1998), 'Forests, Chena cultivation, and the colonial state in Ceylon 1840–1940', in R. Grove, V. Damodaran, S. Sangwan (eds).

Mezger, D. (1980), *Copper in the World Economy*, Heineman, London.

Mikesell, R.F. (1988), *The Global Copper Industry*, Croom Helm, London.

Mises, L. von (1951), *Socialism: An Economic and Sociological Analysis*, Jonathan Cape, London.

Moguel, P. and V. Toledo (1999), 'Café, luchas indígenas y sostenibilidad. El caso de México', *Ecología Política*, **18**.

Mol, A. (1995), *The Refinement of Production: Ecological Modernization Theory and the Chemical Industry*, Van Arkel, Utrecht.

Mol, A. (1998), 'Ecological modernization: industrial transformation and environmental reform', in M. Redclift and G. Woodgate (eds), *The International Handbook of Environmental Sociology*, Edward Elgar, Cheltenham, UK and Lyme, US.

Mol, A. and D. Sonnenfeld (2000), *Ecological Modernisation Around the World*, Frank Cass, London.

Mol, A. and G. Spaargaren (2000), 'Ecological modernization theory in debate: a review', *Environmental Politics*, **9** (1): 17–49.

Moody, R. (1992), *The Gulliver File: Mines, people, and land: a global battleground*, Minewatch-WISE-Pluto Press, London.

Morehouse, W. and M. Arun Subramanian (1986), 'The Bhopal tragedy: What really happened and what it means for American workers and communities at risk', A preliminary report for the Citizens Commission on Bhopal, Council on International and Public Affairs, New York, 1986.

Morton, M.J. (1992), *Emma Goldman and the American Left*, Twayne, New York.

Mosse, D. (1997), 'The symbolic making of a common property resource: history, ecology and locality in a tank-irrigated landscape in South India', *Development and Change*, **28** (3).

Mukta, P. and D. Hardiman (2000), 'The political ecology of nostalgia', *Capitalism, Nature, Socialism*, **11** (1): 113–33.

Mumford, L. (1956), 'The natural history of urbanization', in William L. Thomas *et al.* (eds).

Mumford, L. and P. Geddes (1995), *The Correspondence*, edited and introduced by Frank G. Novack Jr., Routledge, London and New York.

Munda, G. (1995), *Multicriteria Evaluation in a Fuzzy Environment: Theory and Applications in Ecological Economics*, Physika Verlag, Heidelberg.

Muradian, R. and J. Martinez-Alier (2001a), 'Trade and the environment: from a "Southern" perspective', *Ecological Economics*, **36**: 281–97.

Muradian, R. and J. Martinez-Alier (2001b), 'South–north materials flow: history and environmental repercusions', *Innovation*, **14** (2).

Mydans, S. (1996), 'Thai shrimp farmers facing ecologists' fury', *New York Times*, 28 April.

Naredo, J.M. and A. Valero (1999), *Desarrollo Económico y Deterioro Ecológico*, Argentaria-Visor, Madrid.

Nash, R. (1982), *Wilderness and the American Mind*, 3rd edition, Yale University Press, New Haven and London.

Netting, R. McC. (1993), *Smallholders, Householders: Farm Families and the Ecology of Intensive, Sustainable Agriculture*, Stanford University Press, Stanford.

Neurath, O. (1973), *Empiricism and Sociology*, M. Neurath and R. Cohen (eds), Reidel, Dordrecht and Boston.

Nijar, G. Singh (1996), *TRIPS and Biodiversity, the Threat and Responses: A Third World View*, Third World Network, Penang.

Nimura, K. (1997), *The Ashio Riot of 1907: A Social History of Mining in Japan*, Duke University Press, Durham and London.

Norgaard, R.B. (1989), 'The case for methodological pluralism', *Ecological Economics*, **1**: 37–57.

Norgaard, R.B. (1990), 'Economic indicators of resource scarcity. A critical essay', *Journal of Environmental Economics and Management*, **19**: 19–25.

Norgaard, R.B. (1994), *Development Betrayed: The End of Progress and a Coevolutionary Revisioning of the Future*, Routledge, London.

Novotny, P. (1998), 'Popular epidemiology and the struggle for community health in the environmental justice movement', in D. Faber (ed).

O'Connor, J. (1988), 'Introduction', *Capitalism, Nature, Socialism*, **1**.

O'Connor, M. (1993a), 'On the misadventures of capitalist nature', *Capitalism, Nature, Socialism*, **4** (3): 7–40.

O'Connor, M. (1993b), 'Value system contests and the appropriation of ecological capital', *The Manchester School*, **61** (4): 398–424.

O'Connor, M. (ed) (1996), 'Ecological Distribution', special issue of the *Journal of Income Distribution*, **6** (2).

O'Connor, M. and C. Spash (eds) (1999), *Valuation and the Environment: Theory, Methods and Practice*, Edward Elgar, Cheltenham, UK and Northampton, MA, USA.

O'Neill, J. (1993), *Ecology, Policy and Politics*, Routledge, London.

Odum, H.T and J.E. Arding (1991), 'Emergy analysis of shrimp maricul-ture in Ecuador', working paper, Coastal Resources Center, University of Rhode Island.

Opschoor, J.B. (1995), 'Ecospace and the fall and rise of throughput inten-sity, *Ecological Economics*, **15** (2): 137–40.

Ostrom, E. (1990), *Governing the Commons: The Evolution of Institutions for Collective Action*, Cambridge University Press, Cambridge.

Paarlberg, R. (2000), 'Genetically modified crops in developing countries: promise or peril?', *Environment*, **42** (1), January–February.

Padua, J.A. (1996), '25 años de ecologismo en el Brasil', *Ecología Política*, **11**: 7–20.

Padua, J.A. (2000), '"Annihilating natural productions": nature's economy, colonial crisis, and the origins of Brazilian political environmentalism', *Environment and History*, **6**: 255–87.

Painter, M. and W. Durham (eds) (1995), *The Social Causes of Environmental Destruction in Latin America*, University of Michigan Press, Ann Arbor.

Parijs, Ph. van (1995), *Real Freedom for All: What (if Anything) can Justify Capitalism?*, Clarendon Press, Oxford.

Parikh, J.K. (1995), 'Joint implementation and the north and south cooperation for climate change', *International Environmental Affairs*, **7** (1), 22–41.

Passet, R. (1979), *L'economique et le vivant*, Economica, Paris, 2nd edition 1996.

Pearce, D. and K. Turner (1990), *Economics of Natural Resources and the Environment*, Harvester Wheatsheaf, New York.

Pearce, F. (1991), *Green Warriors: The People and the Politics behind the Environmental Revolution*, The Bodley Head, London.

Peet, J. (1992), *Energy and the Ecological Economics of Sustainability*, Island Press, Washington, DC.

Peet, R. and M. Watts (eds) (1996), *Liberation Ecologies*, Routledge, London.

Peluso, N. (1993), *Rich Forests, Poor People: Resource Control and Resistance in Central Java*, University of California Press, Berkeley.

Peña, D. (ed.) (1998), *Chicano Culture, Ecology, Politics: Subversive Kin*, University of Arizona Press, Tucson.

Pengue, W.A. (2000), *Cultivos transgénicos. ¿Hacia dónde vamos?*, Lugar editorial/UNESCO, Buenos Aires.

Pérez Cebada, J.D. (ed.) (2001), *Minería y Medio Ambiente en Perspectiva Histórica*, Universidad de Huelva Publicaciones, Huelva.

Perrings, C. (1987), *Economy and Environment: A Theoretical Essay on the Interdependence of Economic and Environmental Systems*, Cambridge University Press, Cambridge.

Pfaundler, L. (1902), 'Die Weltwirtschaft im Lichte der Physik', *Deutsche Revue*, **22**.

Pietila, H. (1997), 'The triangle of the human economy: household–cultivation–industrial production. An attempt at making visible the human economy in toto', *Ecological Economics*, **20**: 113–27.

Poffenberg, M. (1996), 'The resurgence of community forest management in the jungle Mahals of West Bengal', in D. Arnold and R. Guha (eds).

Pollack, A. (1999), 'Biological products raise genetic ownership issues', *New York Times*, 26 November.

Popper-Lynkeus, J. (1912), *Die allgemeine Naehrpflicht als Loesung der sozialen Frage. Eingehend bearbeitet und statistisch durchgerechnet. Mit einem Nachweis der theoretischen und praktischen Wertlosigkeit der Wirtschaftslehre*, Carl Reissner, Dresden.

Primavera, J.H. (1991), 'Intensive prawn farming in the Philippines: ecological, social and economic implications', *Ambio*, **20** (1): 28–33.

Princen, T. (1999), 'Consumption and environment: some conceptual issues', *Ecological Economics*, **31**: 347–363.

Pulido, L. (1991), 'Latino environmental struggles in the Southwest', PhD thesis, University of California, Los Angeles.

Pulido, L. (1996), *Environmentalism and Economic Justice: Two Chicano Struggles in the Southwest*, University of Arizona Press, Tucson.

Purdy, J., 'Shades of Green', *The American Prospect*, 3 January 2000.

Quiroga, R. and S. van Hauwermeiren (1994), *El tigre sin selva: consecuencias ambientales de la transformación económica de Chile*, IEP, Santiago.

Raumoulin, J. (1984), 'L'homme et la destruction des ressources naturelles: la Raubwirtschaft au tournant du siècle', *Annales*, **39** (4).

Rees, W. and M. Wackernagel (1994), 'Ecological footprints and appropriated carrying capacity', in A.-M. Jansson *et al.* (eds), *Investing in Natural Capital: The Ecological Economics Approach to Sustainability*, ISEE, Island Press, Washington, DC.

Rens, I. (1996), 'Bertrand de Jouvenel (1903–1987), pionnier méconnu de l'Ecologie Politique', in I. Rens (ed.), *Le Droit International face à l'Ethique et à la Politique de l'Environnnement*, SEBES, Georg, Geneva.

Reyes, V. (1996a), 'Sangre de drago. La comercialización de una obra maestra de la naturaleza', *Ecologia Politica*, **11**: 79–88.

Reyes, V. (1996b), 'The Value of Sangre de Drago', *Seedling* (GRAIN), **13** (1).

Robleto, M.L. and W. Marcelo (1992), *Deuda ecológica*, Instituto de Ecologia Politica, Santiago, Chile.

Rocheleau, D. *et al.* (eds) (1996), *Feminist Political Ecology*, Routledge, London.

Ronsin, F. (1980), *La Grève des Ventres. Propagande Néo-Malthusienne et Baisse de la Natalité en France, 19–20 Siècles*, Aubier-Montaigne, Paris.

Sachs, A. (1995), *Eco-Justice: Linking Human Rights and the Environment*, Worldwatch Institute, Washington DC.

Sachs, W. (ed.) (1992), *The Development Dictionary: A Guide to Knowledge as Power*, 2 ed, London.

Sagoff, M. (1988), *The Economy of the Earth*, Cambridge University Press, Cambridge.

Salleh, A. (1997), *Ecofeminism as Politics*, Zed, London.

Saro-Wiwa, K. (1995), *A Month and a Day: A Detention Diary*, Penguin, London.

Sauvy, A. (1960), *General Theory of Population*, Basic Books, New York.

Schmidt-Bleek, F. (1993), *Wieviel Umwelt braucht der Mensch – MIPS, das Mass oekologische Wirtchaften*, Birkhauser, Berlin.

Schmink, M. and Ch. Wood (1987), 'The political ecology of Amazonia', in P.D. Little and M. Horowitz (eds), *Lands at Risk in the Third World*, Westview Press, Boulder.

Schnaiberg, A. *et al.* (1986), *Distributional Conflicts in Environmental Resource Policy*, Edward Elgar, Aldershot, UK and Brookfield, US.

Schwab, J. (1994), *Deeper Shades of Green: The Rise of Blue-Collar and Minority Environmentalism in America*, Sierra Club Books, San Francisco.

Scurrah, M.J. (1998), 'Forest conservation and human rights in Peru: the conflict over the Chaupe Forest', *Journal of Iberian and Latin American Studies*, **4** (1).

Selden, T. and D. Song (1994), 'Environmental quality and development: is there a Kuznetz curve for air pollution emissions?', *Journal of Environmental Economics and Management*, **27**: 147–62.

Shabecoff, P. (2000), *Earth Rising: American Environmentalism in the 21st century*, Island Press, Washington, DC.

Shiva, V. (1988), *Staying Alive*, Zed, London.

Silliman, J. and Y. King (eds) (1999), *Dangerous Intersections: Feminist Perspectives on Population, Environment and Development*, South End Press, Cambridge, MA.

Sivaramakrishnan, K. (1999), *Modern Forests: Statemaking and Environmental Change in Colonial Eastern India*, Oxford University Press, Delhi.

Skaggs, J.K. (1994), *The Great Guano Rush: Entrepreneurs and American Overseas Expansion*, St Martin's Press, New York.

Stonich, S. (1991), 'The promotion of non-traditional exports in Honduras: issues of equity, environment and natural resource management', *Development and Change*, **22**: 725–55.

Stonich, S. (1993), *I am Destroying the Land! The Political Ecology of Poverty and Environment Destruction in Honduras*, Westview Press, Boulder.

Stonich, S. (1999), 'Comments to A. Escobar; After nature: steps to an anti-essentialist political ecology', *Current Anthropology*, **40** (1).

Strong, K. (1977), *Ox against the Storm. A Biography of Tanaka Shozo: Japan's Conservationist Pioneer*, Paul Norbury, Tenterden, Kent.

Stroup, R.L. (1997), 'Superfund: the shortcut that failed', in Anderson, T.L. (ed.), *Breaking the Environmental Policy Gridlock*, Hoover Institution Press, Stanford.

Sundar, N. (1998), 'Asian women: empowered or merely enlisted?', in A. Kalland and G. Persoon (eds).

Swyngedouw, E. (1997), 'Power, nature and the city: the conquest of water and the political ecology of urbanization in Guayaquil, Ecuador', *Environment and Planning A*, **29**: 311–32.

Szasz, A. (1994), *Ecopopulism: Toxic Waste and the Movement for Environmental Justice*, University of Minnesota Press, Minneapolis.

Tamanoi, Y., A. Tsuchida and T. Murota (1984), 'Towards an entropic theory of economy and ecology – beyond the mechanistic equilibrium approach', *Economie Appliquée*, **37**: 279–94.

Taylor, B.R. (ed.) (1995), *Ecological Resistance Movements. The Global Emergence of Radical and Popular Environmentalism*, SUNY Press, Albany.

Taylor, D. (2000), 'The rise of the environmental justice paradigm', *American Behavioral Scientist*, **43** (4), January.

Tegbaru, A. (1998), 'Local environmentalism in Northeast Thailand', in A. Kalland and G. Persoon (eds).

Thomas, W.L., C.O. Sauer, M. Bates and L. Mumford (eds) (1956), *Man's Role in Changing the Face of the Earth*, University of Chicago Press, Chicago.

Thomas-Slayer, B., D. Rocheleau *et al.* (1995), *Gender, Environment and Development: A Grassroots Perspective*, Lynne Rienner, Boulder and London.

Thurow, L. (1980), *The Zero-Sum Society*, Basic Books, New York.

Toledo, V.M. (1990), 'The ecological–economic rationality of peasant production', in M.A. Altieri and S. Hecht (eds).

Toledo, V.M. (1996), *Mexico: Diversity of Cultures*, Cemex, Mexico.

Toledo, V.M. (2000), 'Rodolfo Montiel y el ecologismo de los pobres', *Ecología Política*, **20**: 13–14.

Toledo, V.M. (2001), 'Biocultural diversity and local power in Mexico: challenging globalization', in L. Maffi (ed.), *On Biocultural Diversity*, Smithsonian Institution, Washington, DC.

Torres Galarza, R. (1997), *Entre lo propio y lo ajeno: derechos de los pueblos indigenas y propiedad intelectual*, COICA, Quito.

Varea, A. *et al.* (1998), *Ecologismo Ecuatorial*, 3 vols, Abya-Yala, Quito.

Viola, E.J. (1988), 'The ecologist movement in Brazil (1974–1986): from environmentalism to ecopolitics', *International Journal of Urban and Regional Research*, **12** (2).

Visvanathan, S. (1997), *A Carnival for Science: Essays on Science, Technology and Development*, Oxford University Press, Delhi.

Visvanathan, S. (1999), Unpublished paper on environmental pollution in Delhi, Carnegie Council Project on Environmental Values, New York.

Vitousek, P., P. Ehrlich, A. Ehrlich and P. Matson (1986), 'Human appropriation of the products of photosynthesis'. *Bioscience*, **34**: 368–73.

Vivekanandan, V. and J. Kurien (1998), 'Aquaculture. Where greed overrides need', *The Hindu Survey of the Environment*, Chennai.

Vogel, J.H. (2000), 'El cártel de la biodiversidad. Transformación de los conocimientos tradicionales en secretos comerciales', Quito (available at www.elcarteldebiodiversidad.com).

Vos, Jan de (1988), *Oro verde: la conquista de la Selva Lacandona por los madereros tabasqueños, 1822–1949*, Fondo de Cultura Económica, Mexico.

Wackernagel, M. and W. Rees (1995), *Our Ecological Footprint*, New Society Publishers, Gabriola Island and Philadelphia.

Wapner, P. (1996), *Environmental Activism and World Civic Politics*, State University of New York Press, Albany.

Wargo, J. (1996), *Our Children's Toxic Legacy: How Science and Law Fail to Protect Us from Pesticides*, Yale University Press, New Haven and London.

Waring, M. (1988), *If Women Counted: A New Feminist Economics*, Harper & Row, San Francisco.

Weber, M. (1909), 'Energetische Kulturtheorien', *Archiv für Sozialwissenschaft und Sozialpolitik*, **29**, reprinted in M. Weber (1968), *Gessamelte Aufsätze zur Wissenschaftslehre*, 3rd edition, J.C.B. Mohr (Paul Siebeck), Tübingen.

Weiner, D. (1988), *Models of Nature: Ecology, Conservation and Cultural Revolution in Soviet Russia*, Indiana University Press, Bloomington.

Weiner, D. (1999), *A Little Corner of Freedom: Russian Nature Protection from Stalin to Gorbachev*, University of California Press, Berkeley.

Wenz, P. (1988), *Environmental Justice*, State University of New York Press, Albany.

West, P. and S. Brechin (1991), *Resident Peoples and National Parks: Social Dilemmas and Strategies in International Conservation*, University of Arizona Press, Tucson.

Westra, L. and P. Wenz (1995), *Faces of Environmental Racism: Confronting Issues of Global Justice*, Rowman and Littlefield, Lanham, MD.

Wielenga, B. (1999), *Towards an eco-just society*, Centre for Social Action, Bangalore.

Wolf, E. (1972), 'Ownership and political ecology', *Anthropological Quarterly*, **45**: 201–5.

World Resources Institute, Wuppertal Institut *et al.* (1997), *Resources Flow: The Material Basis of Industrial Economies*, WRI, Washington, DC.

Wright, D.H. (1990), 'Human impacts on the energy flow through natural ecosystems, and implications for species endangerment', *Ambio*, **19** (4): 189–94.

Zimmerer, K.S. (1996), 'Discourses on soil erosion in Bolivia. Sustainability and the search for a socio-environmental "middle ground"', in R. Peet and M. Watts (eds).

Index

Names with the prefixes de, van (and variants) and von are filed under the substantive part of the name following the prefix, for example, de Bruyn, S.M. is filed as Bruyn, S.M. de.

Ballod-Atlanticus, K. 51
Bangladesh
   fair trade networks and ecological debt
      239
   farmed shrimp production 86
   shrimp farming and mangrove
      conservation conflict 87
Barco, Virgilio 213
Barham, B. 216
Barnett, H.J. 46
Basel Convention on Hazardous Waste 1989
   environmental justice in the United States
      and South Africa and 183–4
   toxic imperialism and 258
Bassey, Nnimo 103, 104–5
Batalla, G. Bonfil, *see* Bonfil Batalla, G.
Bates, M. 10, 158
Bathia, B. 195
bauxite mining
   India 261–2
Baviskar, A. 126
Beanal, Tom 65
Beaumont d'Erlanger, Emile 222
Beck, Ulrich 37
Beinart, W. 9, 182
Berkes, F.
   Cree, management of resources 254
   common property 20, 72, 74, 121
   SEN and 207
Berry, Kate 128
Berry, Wendell 177
Bertell, R. 247
Besant, Annie 51
Bhatt, Chandiprasad 124
Biodiversity Convention 1992
   prior informed consent and 243
   purposes of 133–4
biopiracy
   ayahuasca and 140
   Biodiversity Convention 133–4
   'bioprospecting' contracts 136–7
   CITES 134
   defined 132
   chinchona and 132–3
   epibatidine and 133
   genetic composition of population and
      141
   Inbio-Merck agreement 134–7
   'J'oublie' berry and 141
   naming ecological distribution conflicts
      and 259
   neem tree and 141
   rosy periwinkle and 140–41
   sangre de drago and 138–40
   Shaman Pharmaceuticals 137–41
   see also agricultural biopiracy

'bioprospecting' contracts
   biopiracy and 136–7
Blaikie, P. 48, 72, 259
Blanco, Hugo 263–4
Bleek, F. Schmidt, *see* Schmidt-Bleek, F.
Bode, Thilo 16
Boff, Leonardo 2, 206
Bolivia
   mining liabilities 219
   material interests and sacred values 254
   oil 106
Boltzmann, Ludwig 163
Bond, P. 179, 180
Bonfil Batalla, Guillermo 147
Bonifacio, José 208
Bonifaz, Cristóbal 108
Bonifaz, John 108
Bonilla, H. 221
Borrero, J.M. 259
Boserup, E. 47, 71
Bougainville
   copper and gold mining 64
Boulding, Kenneth 20
Boussingault, Jean Baptiste 221
Bové, José 241
Boyce, J.K. 239
Brazil
   biopiracy 140
   ecological debt and 226
   ecologically unequal exchange theory and
      215
   environmental movements and the state
      204–5
   forests and environmentalism of the poor
      121, 122–5
   GM soybeans and 243, 244–6
   hydroelectricity subsidies to aluminium
      smelters 127
   transgenic-free zone, as 240–42
Brechin, S. 254
Brimblecombe, Peter 165
Britain
   nuclear power 68
Broad, R. 86
Broadbent, J. 57, 63, 67, 253
Bromley, D.W. 74
Brookfield, H. 48, 72, 259
Brosius, J.P. 113, 256
Brower, David 4, 170
Bruggemeier, F.J. 67
Bruyn, S.M. de 29
Bryan, Richard H. 192
Bryant, B. 169
Bryant, Raymond 73, 257
Bulffi, Luis 53
Bullard, R. 169, 173–4, 258

Green Belt Movement (Kenya)
forests and environmentalism of the poor
121
green belts
urban unsustainability and 159
Greenpeace
Ecuador's mangrove ecosystem and 82–3
environmental movements and the state
200
Stone Container in Costa Rica and 114
toxic imperialism and 258
Grillo, Eduardo 146
Groot, Rudolf de 26–7
Grove, Richard 8
Grueso, L. 84
guano
oversupply of primary commodities and
low prices 220–22
The Guardian Weekly
MOSOP opposition to Shell 103
Guatemala
oil 107–8
Guha, Ramachandra
environmental movement and 1
environmentalism of the poor and
12–13
Ken Saro-Wiwa and Shell and 103
environmental struggles and 121
gender and environment and 210–11
naming ecological distribution conflicts
and 260
plantations are not forests and 112, 113
'post-materialism' and 4
resistance as path to sustainability and
204, 205, 206
SEN and 207, 208, 209
social conflict and environmentalism and
54, 57
two styles of political ecology and 256
wilderness and 9
Gujarat
irrigation and water policy 130–31
see also India
Gupta, Anil 11

Haberl, H. 2, 6, 40, 41, 70
Hagler, Michael 82
Hall, C. 41
Hall, Peter 157–8
Handberg, H. 95
Hanna, S. 72
HANPP
unsustainability and 39–40
Hardiman, David 130, 210
Hardin, Garrett 74–6
Harney, Corin 192

Hartmann, Hans 115
Hauwermeiren, S. van 226
Hayek, F. von 33, 41
Hays, Samuel 5, 9
hazardous waste, *see* Basel Convention on
Hazardous Waste 1989
health hazards
hormones in beef and 242
health and safety
workers' struggles for occupational,
naming ecological distribution
conflicts and 260
Hershberg, E. 4, 13
Hicks, A.H. 29, 222–3
Hildyard, N. 126, 259
Hille, J. 4–5
The Hindu
contempt of court by Patkar and Roy
126
Hirsch, F. 100
Hobsbawm, Eric 209–10
Hoechst Chemical-Quijano
court case 201
Hofrichter, R. 171, 176, 258
Hombergh, H. van den 115, 116
Honduras
shrimp farming and mangrove
conservation conflict 83–4
Hornborg, A. 217–18
Howard, A. 36
Howard, Ebenezer 158
Hueting, Roefie 21
human rights
environment and 203–4
environmental justice in United States of
America and 174–5
forests and violations of 118
oil conflicts and violations of 103–4, 108,
111, 270–71
plastics dumping and violations of 184
Human Rights Watch
Cambodia plastics dumping and human
rights abuses 184
Niger Delta human rights abuses 103,
270–71
Humboldt, Alexander von 7, 132
Hump, Governor 169
Hunt, Sterry 41
Huot, Marie 51–2
Hussain, Haji Saidin 86–7
hydroelectricity
dams and water policy ecological conflict
126–7, 129
ecological debt and 225
in Kerala 255
Hynes, Patricia 48–9